SUBMARINES AT WAR

Eternal vigilance, the margin of safety. Lookouts aboard the USS *Cero* at sea during World War II.

SUBMARINES
AT
WAR

The History of the American Silent Service

Edwin P. Hoyt

𝔰𝔡

STEIN AND DAY/*Publishers*/New York

The maps captioned "The Pacific" and "The Solomon Islands" are from Mark Arnold-Forster's *The World at War,* and are reprinted courtesy of Stein and Day/*Publishers.* The drawings captioned "Early Submarines" and "Submarines at the Turn of the Century"; the maps captioned "The Battle of Midway," "Allied Landings in N. Africa," and "The American Submarine Campaign in the Pacific"; as well as the graphs captioned "Japanese Shipping Losses" and "Japanese Shipping Available" are from Vice Admiral Sir Arthur Hezlet's *The Submarine and Sea Power* and are reprinted courtesy of Stein and Day/*Publishers.*

First published in 1983
Copyright © 1983 by Edwin P. Hoyt
All rights reserved
Designed by L. A. Ditizio
Printed in the United States of America
STEIN AND DAY/*Publishers*
Scarborough House
Briarcliff Manor, N.Y. 10510

Library of Congress Cataloging in Publication Data

Hoyt, Edwin Palmer.
  Submarines at war.

  Bibliography: p.
  Includes index.
  1. United States. Navy. Submarine Forces—History.
I. Title.
V858.H68   1982   359.8′3   81-40808
ISBN 0-8128-2833-X

CONTENTS

1. THE MEN WHO BRAVE THE SEA 1
2. THE EARLY SERVICE 19
3. MIDPASSAGE 39
4. DOLDRUMS 47
5. THE S-5 DISASTER 57
6. FROM PIGBOATS TO FLEET BOATS 67
7. THE CLOUDS OF WAR 83
8. MAKEY-LEARN 89
9. THE SUN RISES ON AND ON 101
10. CHANGING THE GUARD 117
11. ATTACK ON AMERICA 129
12. HARD TIMES 141
13. UNCERTAIN OFFENSIVE 149
14. THE BLOCKADE BEGINS 175
15. THE BLOCKADE TIGHTENS 181
16. THE ODDS CHANGE 195
17. OUT OF THE COLD 205
18. WOLF PACKS AND LIFEGUARDS 215
19. THE LOSSES RISE 227
20. SCOURING THE EMPIRE 237
21. UNSUNG VICTORY 253
22. INCREASING VIGILANCE 267
23. MASTERS OF THE PACIFIC 287
24. THE NEW DIRECTION 297

BIBLIOGRAPHICAL NOTES 309
BIBLIOGRAPHY 311
INDEX 317

ILLUSTRATIONS

Frontispiece

Lookouts aboard the USS *Cero*

Between pages 82 and 83

Four A-boats at the bottom of the Panama Canal
The *F-4* is lost
Diving for the *F-4*
A World War I German U-boat on display in America
An American submarine at Pearl Harbor in the early twenties
Torpedo being loaded through submarine hatch
Marx X torpedoes
Four R-boats at the Brooklyn Navy Yard
The USS *Squalus* salvaged from the deep
S-boats rafted alongside a tender
Forward torpedo room of a S-boat
The commissioning of the USS *Bonita*
The USS *Dolphin* without a deck gun
Submarine Squadron 5 in 1940

Between pages 194 and 195

The U.S. submarine base at Pearl Harbor
Captain John Crowell sacrificed himself to protect U.S. secrets
The USS *Growler* after a collision
The USS *Crevalle* rescues Americans from the Philippines
Periscope view of sinking Japanese destroyer
Test-fired torpedo explodes against Hawaiian cliff

Vice Admiral Charles Lockwood being decorated
Skipper of the USS *Bonefish* reports with hole in pants
Engine room of a fleet-class submarine
USS *Sealion* rescues Allied P.O.W.s from sunken Japanese
    transport
Captain Hogan playing cribbage in *Bonefish* wardroom
The "scoreboard" of the *Bonefish*
The USS *Darter* aground on Bombay Shoal
Japanese warship slips to bottom
Japanese merchant man sunk by USS *Drum*
Deck gunners attacking Japanese ships
The USS *Wahoo* at sea
The USS *Bullhead,* the last U.S. submarine sunk in the Pacific
    war
The battle flag of the USS *Barb*
The crew of the USS *Flasher*
Pogy Pete, submariner without equal

Between pages 299 and 300
More than fifty submarines before decommissioning in 1947
Control room of the USS *Nautilus*
President Kennedy at the periscope of the USS *Thomas Edison*
Control panel of the USS *Lafayette*
Launching the USS *Tunny*
The USS *George Washington*
The Trident submarine USS *Ohio*
The firing of a Polaris missile

Maps, Charts, and Drawings

Early Submarines . . . . facing page 12

Submarines at the Turn of the Century . . . . facing page 13

Allied Landings in North Africa . . . . facing page 88

The Pacific . . . . page 103

The Battle of Midway . . . . facing page 140

The Solomon Islands . . . . facing page 158

The American Submarine Campaign in the Pacific . . page 220

Japanese Shipping Losses . . . . facing page 282

Japanese Shipping Available . . . . facing page 292

SUBMARINES
AT
WAR

THE MEN WHO BRAVE THE SEA

O N the night of November 18, 1943, the submarine USS *Sculpin* was cruising east of Truk, the powerful Japanese naval base in the South Pacific. She was one of ten American submarines assigned to support the invasion of the Gilbert Islands and her task was to sink any warships or merchant ships that tried to bring reinforcements up to the Gilberts. Her skipper was Fred Connaway, on his first patrol as a commanding officer. Also aboard was Captain John P. Cromwell, commander of Submarine Division 43 at Pearl Harbor. Cromwell had been sent along because Vice Admiral Charles Lockwood, the commander of American submarines in the Pacific Fleet, wanted him to form a submarine "wolf pack" to go after Japanese shipping in the area after the invasion was launched.

Captain Cromwell knew all the details of the coming Operation Galvanic—the invasion of the Gilberts—and also a great deal about Ultra—the radio intelligence code-breaking program through which the Americans "read the mail" of the Japanese fleet throughout World War II. Through code breaking, Admiral Lockwood was often able to send submarines to specific places to await enemy ships that he *knew* would be coming along, because the Japanese had sent messages ahead to the bases or escort forces. Ultra was one of the most important secret weapons the Americans had in the war against Japan.

Late on that night of November 18, Commander Connaway sighted a Japanese convoy that was on its way from Truk to the Marshall Islands. He made a wide sweep around the convoy, to get into position

1

for a dawn attack, and then he submerged and waited for the convoy to come up. But as the convoy came toward the submarine, the convoy commander spotted the periscope of the *Sculpin* and adopted the most effective line of defense. He turned the whole convoy toward the submarine, presenting narrow bows-on targets, and the grave danger that the submarine would be rammed. Connaway took the *Sculpin* down deep, and the convoy passed over and went on its way.

If Commander Connaway was to attack the convoy, he would have to repeat the night's performance: Surface, make a high speed (17 knots) sweep around the end of the convoy, then submerge and wait again to attack. He brought the *Sculpin* to the surface to begin the chase. But the commander of the Japanese convoy was an experienced officer, and he knew what he could expect from the submarine he had just chased below the surface. Accordingly, he had left behind one of the escorts of the convoy, the destroyer *Yamagumo*, with the task of dealing with the American submarine if it surfaced. Hardly had Connaway brought the *Sculpin* to the surface when the *Yamagumo* launched a high-speed attack. Connaway took the submarine down deep again but the *Yamagumo* dropped a pattern of depth charges and did some damage to the boat as it submerged. It did not seem to be too serious. But Commander Connaway and his officers did not know that the depth charges had put the *Sculpin*'s depth gauge out of commission. And that depth gauge was to a submariner what an altimeter is to a pilot in a storm—the only way of knowing precisely where the craft is in relation to the surface.

Connaway kept the *Sculpin* down for several hours. The Japanese destroyer seemed to remain around for a while, but then the engine sounds died out and it appeared that she had left the area. At about noon, Commander Connaway decided to come up—not to the surface but to periscope depth to have a look around the area. Running on the quiet electric motors, the submarine began to rise. Ensign W. M. Fielder, who was serving temporarily as diving officer, began to order water pumped out of various compartments to lighten the boat. They began pumping at 400 feet, and went up to 300 then 200, then 150, 125. There, the depth gauge stuck, and Ensign Fielder did not know it. He kept pumping water out of the boat, and the boat kept rising, bows up, although the gauge still said 125 feet. Suddenly, with no warning, the submarine broached, her bows shot high in the air and she settled back with a splash that could be seen for miles around. The *Yamagumo*, which had stopped a mile away, lost no time in charging down on the submarine. Connaway spun the periscope, saw the rush of the destroyer, and took the *Sculpin* back down. But there was no time, and as he moved the depth charges began exploding around the boat. This time the damage was severe, the pressure hull began to leak in several places, the diving planes stopped working, and the steering mechanism failed. Connaway decided he would have to surface and fight, and he gave the orders that brought the submarine back to the surface, with the deck gun crew rushing up to man the four-inch gun.

That little gun was small defense against the five-inch guns of a destroyer, plus the machine guns and antiaircraft guns she could bring into play. With the first few shots, a salvo struck the *Sculpin*'s bridge, killing Commander Connaway, his executive officer, and the gunnery officer. The senior officer left aboard ship, except for Captain Cromwell, who was not properly part of the crew, was a reserve lieutenant, G. E. Brown, Jr. Lieutenant Brown saw the damage and did the only thing he could do: scuttle and abandon ship. He gave the orders.

But Captain Cromwell felt he dare not abandon the submarine. The Japanese were known to employ torture to get information from American captives, and Captain Cromwell knew too much. The Gilberts invasion was just under way; more important, if the Japanese could get the secret of Ultra from him then what he knew to be an enormous advantage to the American navy would be lost. The Japanese would change their naval code, and Ultra would be rendered meaningless.

Captain Cromwell did not hesitate to make the fateful decision. Knowing that the *Sculpin* would never come up again, he elected to go down with her. Ensign Fielder, distraught at the error that had brought them to this state of affairs, decided he would not go to the surface and be captured, so he too stayed below as the crew scrambled

3

out of the hatches. So did eight others: some dead, some wounded, and some perhaps fearing capture more than death. The *Sculpin* went down with them, while others struggled up.

On the surface, the *Yamagumo* approached gingerly. The Japanese were not interested in rescuing the crew, but did want some prisoners for interrogation. One crewman of the *Sculpin*, pulled out of the water, was seen to be wounded and the Japanese threw him back to die. Another struggled when the Japanese saw his wound, and broke away to hide among the uninjured who were huddled on the deck of the destroyer. Altogether, of the *Sculpin* crew of eighty-four officers and men, forty-one were saved and taken to Truk for interrogation. After the questioning, they were divided into two groups, and dispatched to Japan for imprisonment. Twenty-one of the Americans were put aboard the aircraft carrier *Chuyo*, which had just brought a deckload of planes to Truk. Twenty men were sent north aboard the *Unyo*, another carrier.

The two carriers headed back toward Japan, but only the *Unyo* made it. En route, once again the Ultra system worked perfectly; the Japanese sent a message ahead to Tokyo giving the position, course, and speed of a convoy of three carriers returning to Japan, and Pearl Harbor radio alerted the submarines in the area between Iwo Jima and Japan. Off the Japanese coast lay the submarine USS *Sailfish* (once named the *Squalus*, but recommissioned after she sank and was salvaged). In the teeth of a typhoon, the *Sailfish* attacked the convoy and sank the 20,000 ton *Chuyo*. Twenty of the twenty-one of the *Sculpin* survivors, imprisoned in the hold, went down with the Japanese carrier. (In a way it was full circle: the *Sculpin* had been on maneuvers off the coast of New England with the *Squalus* in 1939 when she sank, and the *Sculpin* had found and stood by the stricken submarine until the salvage crews could arrive. Four years later the *Sailfish-Squalus* had sent her benefactor's latest crew's survivors to their death without knowing it.)

The *Sculpin*'s survivors who had been shipped on the *Unyo* arrived safely in Japan where they were sent to work in the copper mines. A few survived the war, to return and tell the tale of the last patrol of the *Sculpin*. Her story represented all the aspects of the submarine service: daring, endurance, and bravery beyond the call of duty. Finally, when

4

the truth was known, Captain Cromwell was awarded the congressional Medal of Honor, but as so often happened with "the silent service" the award was made posthumously to a widow.

The daring, the danger, and death had been a part of the lives of submariners since the earliest of times. And as far as the Americans were concerned the earliest of times began with the war of the American Revolution. By that time there was already a considerable history of attempts by men to adapt to the environment of the sea, largely for military purposes or search for treasure. Aristotle wrote of sponge fishermen who had air sent down to them in cauldrons, so that they might remain under water for several minutes on a dive. Alexander the Great of Macedon experimented with what would be known today as a bathysphere. Leonardo da Vinci conceived of a submarine and a diving helmet. Cornelis Jocobszoon Drebbel, a Hollander, apparently invented a submarine or submersible *and* a source of oxygen to renew the air inside. This remarkable development came in the seventeenth century; it was the first recorded finding about a scientific problem that would bother submarine enthusiasts for three centuries. The problem was the development of the true submarine, which did not depend on surface means for its oxygen supply. Only in the middle of the twentieth century was that problem solved, and the true submarine became a reality. Until after World War II, all practical underwater craft were submersibles, not submarines. The submersibles had to secure an oxygen supply from the air, whether by a pump, a snorkel, or by rising to the surface to fill the boat with fresh air and compress more fresh air into its tanks. The atomic submarines, which produce their own oxygen, were the first true submarines.

During the seventeenth century a number of inventors, or publicists, provided plans and descriptions of submarine devices. The trouble with almost all of them was their impracticality. The Spanish and the English made some use of diving bells, but these were so dangerous that they were used only for the recovery of sunken treasure. Sir Edmund Halley, the English astronomer, developed a practical diving bell and left submariners with an additional legacy: a diver's suit that worked. The British used these devices to locate and recover cannon from sunken warships.

But it remained for an American to make the great breakthrough that made the submarine* possible. David Bushnell, an American from Maine, then a part of the Massachusetts Bay Colony, invented a practical propelling device for an underwater craft. It consisted of an oar made like a screw that could be turned by hand or foot. Turned one way it moved the craft forward; turned the other, it reversed the movement.

The Bushnell submarine was a one-man vessel. It was shaped like an egg, with the small end at the bottom, which gave it stability. The craft could bob like a cork in a heavy sea. The operator sat on a seat much like the one used by bicyclists. He operated the craft by admitting water in to submerge it. He closed the hatch, which gave him thirty minutes of air supply inside, and then let in more water to submerge completely. The water, plus a lead keel, kept the device even more stable. To propel it, the operator used a foot-operated rudder, and two levers that turned the screws. When he wanted to surface, he worked a pair of pumps which forced the water out the bottom of the submarine. The instruments consisted of a depth gauge and a compass with a luminous dial (because once under water he was in the dark).

As the American colonists began to fret under King George III's rule and talk of rebellion moved through Massachusetts, David Bushnell began to think of his submarine device as a possible weapon. In 1775 when fighting broke out, he offered the idea to General George Washington, and when the British declared a blockade of American ports, the general began to believe that Bushnell's vessel might offer one way to help break the blockade. But Bushnell still would have to design a weapon that his submarine could employ against British ships. Bushnell did. It consisted of a bit or augur that passed up through the bow of the submarine. The operator could bring his craft up against the bottom of a ship, and then bore into its hull. The augur could be disconnected from the handle, and the submarine cast off, leaving the bit fixed in the hull. Behind the submarine was a sort of

---

*Having described the true submarine as opposed to the submersible, I shall from this point on use the popular term for both.

6

shelf above the rudder, which could carry a powder magazine with one hundred and fifty pounds of gunpowder, quite enough to blow a sufficiently large hole in the bottom of an eighteenth century warship. A rope from the magazine to the screw-augur in the hull of the warship would then drag the magazine against the bottom of the ship and hold it snug, through buoyancy. A clockwork device fixed to the magazine then was actuated and after the submarine had time to get away, the clock triggered the detonating device, the magazine exploded, whereupon a large hole was made and, hopefully, the ship sank. That was the theory.

The soldier who took this ingenious submarine into action was a young American sergeant named Ezra Lee. When the British occupied New York harbor, General Washington decided the time had come to use the submarine. She was named the *Turtle,* an apt title in view of her method of operation.

Sir William Howe, the British commander, arrived in New York on July 2, 1776 and with about ten thousand men landed on Staten Island. Ten days later his brother, Admiral Lord Richard Howe, arrived in New York harbor with a fleet of warships and one hundred and fifty transports bearing more troops and supplies for the war against the colonists. The flagship, HMS *Eagle,* was anchored off Governor's Island. Lord William Howe's ship, HMS *Asia,* was not far away. During July and August the British forces on Staten Island were augmented until they numbered about thirty-two thousand men, as opposed to Washington's five thousand men on Manhattan and in the Bronx.

One day in late summer Washington gave the word to try the attack against the flagships. Sergeant Lee got into the *Turtle,* closed down the hatch, and admitted enough water to lower the craft so that only his tiny observation window was exposed. Rowboats towed him down the river until he was near the British fleet.

The rowboats then cast off, so they would not arouse the attention of the British picketboats that patrolled the perimeter of the fleet, and Sergeant Lee turned his screw and moved the *Turtle* close to the *Eagle.* He let more water into the boat, submerged, and brought the *Turtle* up against the flagship. He began to screw the augur, to attach it to the warship. But as bad luck would have it, his augur came up against one of the iron straps that supported the *Eagle*'s rudder and could not penetrate. By the time Sergeant Lee realized that he was getting nowhere, his air supply was running low, and a strong tide had come in, which tended to pull him away from the *Eagle* and kept him turning the screw to stay in place. The exertion increased his oxygen consumption, and finally he had to come up for air. As he did, the odd bump arising from the water drew the attention of the officer of a picketboat nearby, and the crew gave the alarm. Lee heard the noise through his open hatch, shut it and submerged, as the commotion in the fleet began. As a safety precaution he jettisoned the magazine with its one-hundred and fifty-pound charge and the clockwork detonating mechanism. Sergeant Lee escaped on the incoming tide back up to Manhattan waters, as the clock ticked on. Finally it exploded in mid-harbor with explosive noise and an enormous splash, but not close enough to any warship to do damage.

So the first American attempt to use a submarine in war failed. The *Turtle* was never used again. The British said she was sunk a little later in the war while moving with a small boat. The American story has it that she was dismantled and moved inland to keep her out of British hands. But the *Turtle* then disappeared, and Bushnell turned his inventive genius to the construction of torpedoes that could be launched from shore or from a small boat; he also worked on a system of military mines which involved the use of kegs of powder strung together and set afloat. This latter device gave rise to a song, "The Battle of the Kegs," but the torpedoes and the kegs were no more decisive in the naval battles of the Revolution than the *Turtle* episode had been. In fact, there was a sort of animus even among Americans against such "unholy" instruments of warfare as the submarine and torpedo, and after the Revolution, Bushnell moved south to Georgia and adopted the name of Bush, so that he would not be connected with the submarine. He really was no longer interested in taking credit for three major developments in naval warfare: the propeller, the conning tower, and the torpedo.

Ten years after the American Revolution, the newly formed French republic declared war on Great Britain, and in the search for new and better weapons, experimentation on submersible boats was renewed. Several French inventors developed submarines, but none of them was very impressive. Robert Fulton, an American from Pennsylvania, tried to make his fortune with a submarine he called the *Nautilus*. The French were interested. So Fulton developed a second *Nautilus* and the French commissioned him to run "tests" against the British. But the whole concept of submarine warfare was repugnant to French morality, and in the end Emperor Napoleon Bonaparte called Fulton a fraud and a man without morals; Fulton then left France to try to sell his submarine to England. The English were interested and Fulton staged at least one attack on his former friends across the English Channel. The attack failed and the war between Britain and France ended, started again, and ended again. Thereupon Fulton came home to America where the submarine was so unpopular that he turned his attention to the propulsion of surface craft by steam power.

The submarine and the spar torpedo came into use again during the War of 1812 and the blockade of Long Island Sound by the British but there was no real development of modern submarine methods for many years. Overcoming their previous scrupples, the French planned submarines and built some of them. In 1825 a French naval officer prepared plans for an eighty-six foot submarine, *L'Invincible*, but it was never built. Another Frenchman named Catera built a submarine that worked, but it was driven by oars like a galley—most unsatisfactory. Dr. Payerne, another Frenchman built a submarine that really worked in salvage operations, but it was not useful as a warship. In 1851 an American named Lodner D. Phillips built a submarine on Lake Michigan and proved its viability by taking his wife and two children for a day-long dive. Unfortunately, later on, he went out once too often, and did not come back. The real development in this period was in individual diving gear. In 1825 William James invented the first effective self-contained diving dress, with a copper helmet and air tanks that would sustain a diver for an hour. Late in the 1830s the British worked on diving helmets and used them to salvage the *Royal George,* a 108-gun warship that had sunk in Portsmouth harbor.

A French-American named Alexandre Lambert built a diving bell with an air lock. In America, England, France, Italy, and Russia the interest in submarines continued. The Germans had a try at it, too. But none of the craft involved seemed to come to grips with the problems of propulsion and weaponry—until the American Civil War began in 1860.

The Confederacy felt the greatest impetus toward submarine development because early in the war the Union navy undertook various blockades of Confederate ports. From the promotional description of a German submarine, the Confederate press seized upon the name *David* to apply to various submarine craft. The allusion was to David's victory over Goliath in the Old Testament. A number of these craft were built, to various specifications, most of them out of boiler iron.

One such was brought up to attack the Union blockaders at Charleston harbor on October 5, 1863. This boat was about fifty feet long, nine feet in diameter and powered by a steam engine that pushed her along the surface at seven knots. Her armament was a single spar torpedo which poked out in front of the boat. Her commander was Lieutenant Glassell of the Confederate navy, and her engineer was a civilian named Tombs. The crew consisted of volunteer seamen. On October 5 she came out to attack the Union ship *New Ironsides,* a vessel with sloping sides (so cannonballs would bounce off), twenty Dahlgren cannon, and several Parrott rifled-cannon. The *David* came out at dusk and made her attack in the failing light at nine o'clock that evening.

She approached quite close to the *New Ironsides* before the night lookouts saw something. They thought they saw a raft of logs drifting rapidly on the tide toward the ship and gave the alarm. Then someone insisted that this was an enemy weapon of some sort, and the alarm became general. The ship's guns were lowered as much as possible, but they could not depress them far enough to aim at the low-lying vessel coming toward them. Someone shouted that the "thing" was going to ram them.

In the *David*, Lieutenant Glassell aimed the spar torpedo at the beam of the enemy ship and came closer. The riflemen of the Union

10

vessel began firing with carbines. The Confederate crewmen took shelter behind various protuberances and returned the small arms fire. The *David* plunged ahead until the spar torpedo rammed into the side of the *New Ironsides* and exploded. The *New Ironsides* rolled back in recoil, the *David* smashed backwards, went under, and came up again. Lieutenant Glassell thought his craft was sinking and abandoned ship, followed by all of the crew but two. Those in the water were picked up by the enemy.

Mr. Tombs, the civilian engineer, and one other man stayed aboard their vessel, restarted the engine, drove her off into the night and escaped, while Glassell and the others were captured. The attack was not very successful. The *New Ironsides* did not sink. She did not even need a major dockyard repair job.

But this attack was successful in a sense, and it encouraged others, including two Confederate naval captains, one of whom was Horace Hunley. He had begun building a submarine in New Orleans. When that city was captured he had moved to Mobile and built a submarine which was towed to Fort Morgan, near Charleston port, for another attack on the Yankee blockaders of that harbor. But on the way the little convoy ran into a storm and the *David* foundered. Hunley went back to Mobile to try again. His new machine was sixty feet long, and propelled by manpower—eight men working a long crank that turned a propeller. Another man piloted the vessel with a spar torpedo on its nose. The idea was to run the boat up against the enemy, as had been done with the *New Ironsides*.

This *David* was put into the hands of a young Confederate naval lieutenant named Paine. On his first voyage, trying out the boat off Charleston, a paddle-wheel steamer came by too close, the wake flooded the two hatches of the *David*, and the eight crank turners below were drowned, while Lieutenant Paine leaped out of the hatch and was saved. The *David* went to the bottom.

A few weeks later she was salvaged and a new crew of volunteers was assembled. She went out again, but this time ran into rough weather, which flooded the hatches and sank her again. Six of the eight crank turners were caught below and drowned. Lieutenant Paine and two other men got out and survived.

11

Once again the *David* was brought up from the mud. She was cleaned up and made ready a second time, but once more as she was getting ready for a trial, heavy weather came up, and she did not even get away from her anchorage this time, but sank at anchor. Lieutenant Paine and three crewmen survived.

By this time the volunteer section at Charleston had the windup and Lieutenant Paine was declared to be a Jonah, with whom no man would go to sea in a *David*. So he was relieved of his command, and another officer took his place as the engineers brought the *David* up once again, pumped her out, and got her ready for action. But as she went out to sea, once again she sank, and this time the whole crew was lost, including the new officer in charge.

She was pulled out once more, fixed up, given a new crew and promptly ran afoul of a ship's cable and sank. Only the officer and one other man survived.

By this time the *David* had so bad a reputation as a man-killer that no volunteers could be found in the various naval organizations to try her again. But the high command wanted that *David* to sink something other than herself, so an army infantry officer named Lieutenant Dixon was put in command, and somehow he managed to find six volunteers (probably riflemen, not sailors). On February 17, 1864, the *David* went to sea again, this time with a specific target selected for her, the new Union corvette *Housatonic*.

All the commotion attendant to the previous failures had alerted the Union forces. Also, several smaller submersibles had been employed, and a visiting naval officer from abroad had seen a small Union ship careened over in shallow water with a hole in its side and had talked to the officer who said he had done the damage. So the men of the *Housatonic* were at least emotionally prepared for attack by a submarine.

The date selected for the attack was February 17, 1864. Lieutenant Dixon was a determined man and he had more faith in the *David* than many before him. He chose to take the frail vessel across the bar and out of the harbor, then turn around and attack the *Housatonic* from the seaward side, where he would hardly be expected. They set out in the afternoon to catch the tide and by dark had turned about to begin

12

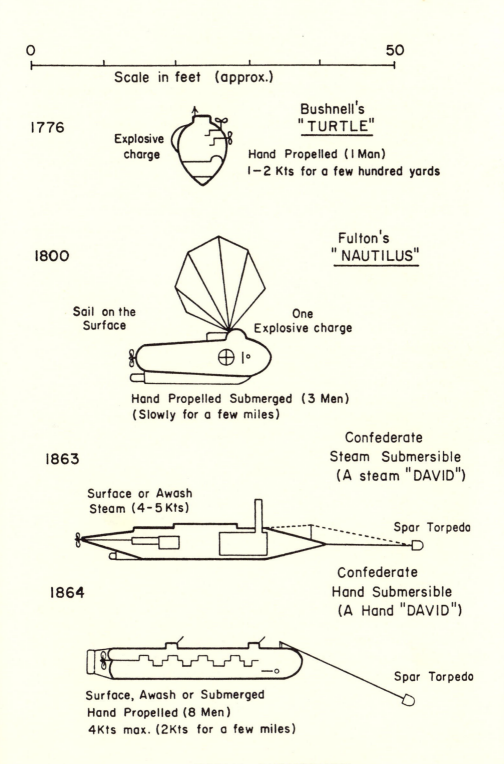

0   50

Scale in feet (approx.)

1776

Explosive charge

Bushnell's "TURTLE"

Hand Propelled (1 Man)
1−2 Kts for a few hundred yards

1800

Fulton's "NAUTILUS"

Sail on the Surface

One Explosive charge

Hand Propelled Submerged (3 Men)
(Slowly for a few miles)

1863

Confederate
Steam Submersible
(A steam "DAVID")

Surface or Awash
Steam (4−5 Kts)

Spar Torpedo

1864

Confederate
Hand Submersible
(A Hand "DAVID")

Surface, Awash or Submerged
Hand Propelled (8 Men)
4 Kts max. (2 Kts for a few miles)

Spar Torpedo

EARLY SUBMARINES

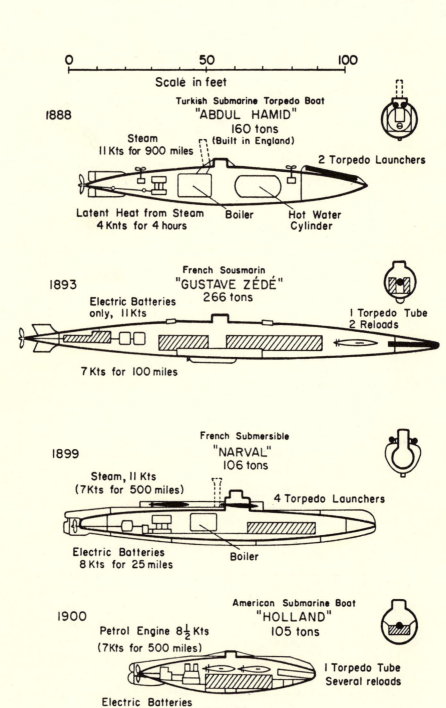

Scale in feet

0   50   100

1888

Turkish Submarine Torpedo Boat
"ABDUL HAMID"
160 tons
(Built in England)

Steam
11 Kts for 900 miles

2 Torpedo Launchers

Latent Heat from Steam
4 Knts for 4 hours

Boiler

Hot Water
Cylinder

1893

French Sousmarin
"GUSTAVE ZÉDÉ"
266 tons

Electric Batteries
only, 11 Kts

1 Torpedo Tube
2 Reloads

7 Kts for 100 miles

1899

French Submersible
"NARVAL"
106 tons

Steam, 11 Kts
(7 Kts for 500 miles)

4 Torpedo Launchers

Electric Batteries
8 Kts for 25 miles

Boiler

1900

American Submarine Boat
"HOLLAND"
105 tons

Petrol Engine 8½ Kts
(7 Kts for 500 miles)

1 Torpedo Tube
Several reloads

Electric Batteries
7 Kts for 24 miles

SUBMARINES AT THE TURN OF THE CENTURY

their attack. Just before nine o'clock the officer of the watch of the *Housatonic*, Lieutenant M. J. K. Crosby, saw something moving seaward that caused him to give the alarm. The drums began to sound to call the men to action stations, and the engine room crew tried to start up the stopped engines while the seamen went to slip the anchor.

But they were too late. Lieutenant Dixon's ruse had been completely successful. The *David* came down inexorably on the *Housatonic*, the torpedo on the end of the spar exploded just forward of the mainmast on the starboard side, where the magazine was located below. The explosion of the torpedo triggered the magazine ammunition, the ship ripped open from end to end, and the topmasts came tumbling down. Ensign Hazeltine, Captain's Clerk Muzzy and three seamen were drowned or blown up, and the rest of the officers and crew took to the rigging to save themselves. The *Housatonic* sank but luckily the water was shallow and the rigging stood up above the harbor—festooned with seamen.

Lieutenant Dixon and his men tried to escape. The crank turners labored mightily, but at best they could give the boat only a few knots, and now they were faced with a new problem. The explosion had created a vacuum inside the sinking *Housatonic* and the water rushed in to fill it. The suction pulled the *David* into the hole her men had created, and the submarine stuck. All aboard were drowned.

That effort of February 17 was the last attempt the Confederates made to use submarines. The risk and the cost, even if successful, were so great that the Confederate navy turned to other methods to try to outwit and defeat the superior Union forces.

The Union experimented with "semisubmersibles" as well, but with no greater success than the Confederates. Their one tried weapon of this sort was the *Keokuk*, a cigar-shaped double-turreted monitor which could be submerged to a position just on the surface, like a board awash, by use of ballast tanks.

The *Keokuk* was one hundred and sixty feet long—longer than many surface vessels—and thirty-six feet wide. She had twin engines and two screws. Her hull was made of iron plating two inches thick with an inner hull almost an inch thick. She carried eleven-inch guns and a crew of one hundred. She was obviously overweight and unwieldy, yet the Union navy expected much of her, as she was sent in by Admiral DuPont to attack Charleston harbor and retake Fort Sumter. But the Confederates spotted the strange low-lying craft and peppered it with shells from the shore guns. A seam must have opened, and the enormous weight of the plating took her to the bottom of the harbor. So ended the efforts of both sides to use submersible craft in the Civil War.

In the years that followed somewhere there was always someone trying to build a submarine—in France, Russia, Germany. But the successful boats were not made for war, and the warships almost invariably sank. In 1872, O. S. Halstead designed a submarine he called *Intelligent Whale*. The U.S. Army put up the money for the boat, but when it was completed and began trials, the troubles began. A certain General Sweeney put on one spectacular demonstration. He took a crew out in this twenty-six foot boat, then donned an underwater suit and attached an explosive to the bottom of a sacrificial ship. The explosive went off, and the ship sank most satisfactorily. But later, after the government accepted the *Intelligent Whale*, it began to drown crews. Thirty-nine men were drowned (three whole crews) before the craft was abandoned, brought to shore and set up on the lawn of the Brooklyn Navy Yard—whether as an ornament or a warning was not stipulated.

In the last quarter of the nineteenth century submarines were developed and built by the score, and a number of them succeeded in making dives to the bottom, remaining underwater for various lengths of time, and returning unharmed to the surface. A number of them sank, carrying inventors and backers to a watery grave. None made a satisfactory war submarine. In every country the submarine fever seemed to have taken hold, and the sensational press that was common in the period seized upon the experiments and made preposterous claims for the future of the submarine. Thorsten Nordenfeldt, a Swedish armament maker, designed a submarine that attracted much military attention. Its major new feature was a torpedo tube, capable of launching one of the steam-driven torpedoes that were just then being developed as weapons. But she was balky and so were the next two boats that Nordenfeldt built. They sometimes refused to

14

submerge. Yet the sultan of Turkey bought one, then discovered that nobody in Turkey knew how to operate it or repair it. The *Nordenfeldt II* ended her life rusting alongside a Constantinople (now Istanbul) dock.

In 1888 Nordenfeldt built a third boat that looked more like a modern submarine than most of the others. It was one hundred and twenty-five feet long, steam driven, and had two small conning towers. The Russians bought her, but she sank off Jutland in 1888.

At the time that Nordenfeldt's experiments were grabbing world headlines, an Irish-American named John Holland was experimenting with undersea craft, first in Ireland and then in New Jersey, after he emigrated to America. He had enough success and encouragement to build four different boats and form the Holland Torpedo Boat Company, and on his fifth attempt the army began to take notice. At the same time another New Jersey man, Simon Lake, was building submarines, not to be used as weapons, but for salvage operations. His boats took the fancy of the sensationalist press. Simon Lake's name almost became a household word, but the American military was not interested in his vessels. Salvage was all very well in its place, but what was wanted was a submarine for war. Lake was in direct competition with John Holland, and Holland devoted his efforts to the creation of a warship. Holland finally got a small grant from the U.S. government to build a submarine but that project bogged down in red tape. But Holland's efforts were successful enough so that he was able to form a company and secure backing; in 1900 his Electric Boat Company sold the U.S. Navy a submarine for $150,000. She was called the *Holland*, and the navy liked her well enough to order five more of the same. The Vickers arms company in England was licensed by the Electric Boat Company and built five more Holland-type boats. Meanwhile Simon Lake was more successful in dealing with foreign governments than with his own. He sold two submarines to the Austro-Hungarian monarchy, the *U-1* and the *U-2*. He sold eleven boats to Russia. Then he went to Germany, where Admiral von Tirpitz was just embarking, with Kaiser Wilhelm's backing, on an attempt to overshadow the British Royal Navy. Tirpitz was enthusiastic about Lake's designs, and gave the word in Berlin that they were to be adopted. The Krupp armaments company dealt with Lake, and finally managed to take over all his patents and push him out of his own business. From these events the German U-boat program was developed, for Admiral Tirpitz was the first to see the submarine as an offensive weapon rather than as a blockade breaker and coastal patrol vessel. Lake returned to America, where he went into business in competition with Holland's Electric Boat Company.

By this time, early in the twentieth century, the nations of Europe and the Americas were engaged in armaments competition and the submarine had an important place with many of the navies. No longer were inventors the key to the success of the submarine, but espionage, and industrial efficiency came forward. In half a dozen countries there were competent submarine builders, all vying to build the fastest, the most durable and the best armed. Many of these submarines sank in trials or on duty, and scores of submariners were drowned. The British developed the A-class submarine, but many of those boats were plagued. The *A-1* was sunk by an ocean liner in a collision. The *A-5* blew up when she was loading gasoline for her new internal combustion engines. The *A-8* sank during maneuvers, and the *A-9* collided with the steamer *Coath*. All these boats were built under the license from Holland's company.

The Germans, doggedly improving on Simon Lake's work, were quietly building superior submarines, which they called *Unterseebote* (U-boats). The *U-1* was completed in 1907. She was 128 feet long, made twelve knots on the surface and nine knots submerged. She, too, was powered by gasoline engines. She had a cruising range of two thousand miles. The *U-2*, launched in 1908, could cruise for three thousand miles. By 1910, constantly improving, the Germans had produced eighteen U-boats. The nineteenth boat showed a vitally important change in submarine design. It carried two six-cylinder engines produced by Dr. Rudolph Diesel of Nuremberg. She could move at fifteen knots on the surface, and was a far safer craft to operate than those previously built. From that point on the U-boats were diesel-powered, and soon other navies adopted the diesel engines.

In 1909 Holland's Electric Boat Company decided to expand and build its own engines. Frank T. Cable, Holland's engineer in charge of operations, was given the job of finding a new site for a plant. He settled on the old port of New London, Connecticut on the Thames River, and the Electric Boat Company moved there. A new era had begun.

2

THE EARLY
SERVICE

I T took a brave man to go beneath the surface in one of those early submersibles, and even then had the first submariners understood their chances of survival in those craft they would have had reason to pause. The problem—reduced to essentials—was design: the earliest boats were designed to go down well, but not nearly as well designed to come back up.

Simon Lake and John Holland were the first Americans to address themselves to the problems of practicality in a useful way. Almost simultaneously, following different roads, they created submersibles that did come back up—most of the time.

Propulsion was a major problem. The *Hunley* and other submersibles of the *David* class of the Confederacy were hand propelled, which was safe enough unless they got in trouble. Then they did not have the power to get out of their difficulties. The steam engine was tried several times, but it required an enormous amount of oxygen and overheated the boat. The internal combustion gasoline engine was next, but after a few explosions the submariners learned that gasoline engines in underwater vessels were not safe. The method of propulsion that eventually became standard for nearly half a century was the diesel engine combined with electric motors. That system was evolving early in the twentieth century.

Early in the 1900s Simon Lake addressed himself to the problem of buoyancy. His *Argonaut II* looked more like a pilot boat than a submarine, with a high foredeck and stern overhang. This boat could carry a crew of eight on a cruise of three thousand miles, but the engines were cranky. John Holland addressed himself to that problem: He'd use steam power on the surface and electric power underwater; his *Holland IX* followed that design. But Holland was still thinking of his submersibles as surface ships at least as much as "submarines" and not paying very much attention to the problem of reducing their profile. The *Holland IX* carried a pair of collapsible masts that were fine in theory but not particularly effective in operation.

Back from his unhappy business with the Germans, Simon Lake set up as Holland's principal competitor for the business of the U.S. Navy. Until 1900 the navy had not been particularly keen on submarines but as Britain, Germany, France, and Austria plunged into the arms race, the American admirals had some second thoughts. The United States, they told Congress, had to develop a submarine fleet to defend itself against all the other submarine fleets in the world. If that reasoning was a little murky, still it was the sort of talk that American congresses liked to hear. The word "defense" has often masked the attraction of the naked sword.

When the Germans took over the Simon Lake designs and began to improve on them, they also brought enhanced secrecy to submarine development. With all those navies competing for power, half of them hoping thus to rule the seven seas, it was inevitable that naval authorities would give an important place to submersibles and to the closeness with which their plans were held. Not only did each designer have to keep his secrets as before, but when he once involved himself with the government of his choice he was bound to it and its system for keeping official confidences. The old way, in which designers hawked their latest submarines to various governments, came to a sudden end. Holland and Lake had only one customer, the United States government, and the same was true of German, French, and other designers. John Holland was at least partly responsible for this change: In 1904 when Holland had an order from the U.S. government to build a number of submarines, he also worked on an experimental boat called the *Fulton*. He was really much more the inventor than the practical man. When the American government took a look at the *Fulton* and rejected the design, Holland went abroad and sold the submarine to the Russian government. The year was 1904, the Russians were at war with Japan, and the United States had declared its neutrality; as a consequence, the Holland maneuver was an enormous embarrassment to President Theodore Roosevelt. It could not have been managed ten years later but that year Holland had the submarine crated, shipped to the port of Kronstadt, then disassembled and shipped in pieces on the Trans-Siberian Railroad to Vladivostok, where it was reassembled to fight the Japanese.

The next year, Holland again embarrassed the American government by selling five submarines to the Japanese navy. Frank Cable, known as Captain Cable because he was "Trial Captain" for his submarines, took the five boats in crates to Yokosuka Naval Yard, assembled them, tried them out, and then taught the Japanese how to use them. So an American was responsible for one aspect of developing the Japanese navy, even though at the time American relations with Japan were extremely uneasy, and did not get any better as the years passed.

The American government began its serious submarine development in 1907 with competitive trials taking place between Holland's *Octopus* and Simon Lake's *Lake*. But as far as contracts were concerned, Holland held the clear leadership for a number of years. After the 1907 trials the navy decided to encourage both designers to keep their products at home, and subsidized both firms—by contract. Even as this was occurring in other countries, notably Germany, the foreign governments were taking over the responsibility for the design and construction of submarines, rather than leaving it in the hands of private entrepreneurs. In the United States this submarine procurement concept was still ten years away.

SS-1, the *Holland,* was the first U.S. Navy submarine. She was 53 feet long, powered by a gasoline engine that moved her at eight knots on the surface and five knots underwater, and carried a crew of seven. Her armament consisted of a single eighteen-inch torpedo tube and an eight-inch "dynamite" gun.

The next seven U.S. Navy submarines were also A-class Holland boats. The navy wavered between using the old naval system of calling naval vessels by names, and the new German fashion of designating submarines by number. The seven A-boats were the

Plunger, Adder, Grampus, Moccasin, Pike, Porpoise, and *Shark.*
They were soon known as the *SS-2* through *SS-8,* but to the men who
served in them they were uniformly known as "pigboats," which was
scarcely a term of endearment. In 1914 when a young U.S. Naval
Academy graduate named Charles A. Lockwood was assigned to
submarine service in the Philippines, he felt that his career was
already in a shambles. The "pigboats" were almost universally
detested by white-water navy men, who regarded the battleship as the
acme of naval perfection. The very name "pigboat" indicated contempt; the comparison was with the "sea pig," the unkind name
uniformed mariners used to describe the porpoise. The sea pigs, said
the naval types, were a bunch of clowns—and the inference was
unmistakable. Of what possible use was a submarine in an era of fast
battleships (15-20 knots), fast cruisers, and destroyers? The pigboats
could carry torpedoes. So what? So could a destroyer or a torpedo boat
(the destroyer or torpedo-boat destroyer, was an evolution of the
torpedo boat), and they could deliver torpedoes faster and more accu-
rately than the pigboats. Submarines were useful perhaps to battle
other submarines, and sometimes as "eyes of the fleet," but those were
the only concessions the battleship sailors would make. Service in
submarines, except for a very few men regarded as more than a little
strange, was seen as a hindrance in a naval officer's career.

The A-boats were fat little teardrops and in the beginning they were
cluttered with all sorts of John Holland's inventions. Holland
believed in automation; it was his dream to build a submarine in
which the operator would sit on a seat and push buttons—which
would make everything work. He would have been very much at
home in a modern nuclear-powered submarine. But in the A-boats the
trouble was that the automated systems continually broke down. As
the Electric Boat Company was building these vessels, the workmen
became convinced that although the U.S. Navy had accepted the
design, there would be hell to pay when the boats went into service.

When this conclusion became gossip, Lawrence Y. Spear stepped
in. Spear was an 1890 graduate of the U.S. Naval Academy who had
served his stint on warships, then gone into the U.S. Navy Construction Corps and finally resigned from the navy to become vice-

president of the Electric Boat Company and chief of the subsidiary that was building the new diesel engines that were under development in 1911.

When *SS-3*, the *Adder,* was under construction the mechanical difficulties inherent in Holland's inventions appeared one after another. The rudders, buoyancy tanks, diving planes, were all supposed to be operated by push buttons. But sometimes these did not work—and such situations could be disastrous.

In 1904 the *Porpoise (SS-7)* was undergoing trials off Newport, Rhode Island, when suddenly the diving planes went out of control and the submarine went to the bottom in 125 feet of water. The crew managed to use the hand pumps to pump the water out and bring the boat to the surface. When she was taken into drydock the difficulty became apparent. Holland's system for closing the sea valves did not always work properly. So Lawrence Spear, the new vice-president, consulted with Captain Cable, who had Holland's confidence, and while the inventor was busy elsewhere, they ripped out all the "gadgets" and replaced them with hand-operated pumps and cables. Holland came down to the dock, saw all his special equipment lying in a heap, and exploded in rage. He found Cable and demanded to know who had ordered the equipment changed. Larry Spear had done it, Cable said.

"You might expect it from a young whippersnapper from the navy. He's ruined my life work." Holland broke into tears and stamped out of the room. Later Cable was able to reason with him, and the mechanical steering and pumps remained. But forever after, when anything went wrong between design and construction of the Holland boats, the old man blamed Larry Spear for the trouble.

The A-boats were not quite 64 feet long, again with gasoline engines. The "dynamite gun" had been abandoned, probably saving many submariners' lives. Deck guns were not regarded as useful or necessary until the Americans learned how they were employed by the German U-boats in World War I.

The B-boats were also Holland boats, considerably larger than the previous class. Only three of these were built, the *Viper (SS-10),* the *Cuttlefish (SS-11),* and the *Tarantula (SS-12).* They were slightly

23

faster than the A-boats, carried a crew of ten, and had two torpedo tubes.

Next was the C-class—nearly three times as large as the A-boats, and another Holland design. They could make ten and a half knots on the surface. They incorporated two torpedo tubes and carried a crew of fifteen men. On the surface the boat looked like a small fishing craft, planing along low on the water with the officer of the deck and his lookouts jammed together around the conning tower. The forward deck extended only halfway to the bow, and the periscopes were only slightly retractable; they stood a good fifteen feet above the hull when the boat was on the surface. Five of these boats were built: *Octopus, Stingray, Tarpon, Bonita,* and *Snapper—the SS-9* to *SS-16.* Then came the D-class, more Holland boats—*Narwhal, Grayling,* and *Salmon,* which brought the hull numbers to *SS-19.* These boats were still larger and each had four torpedo tubes.

All these were gasoline powered and they suffered from the drawbacks of the gasoline engine, particularly explosive vapor, which caused a number of accidents. Also, the early storage batteries had problems. One day aboard the *Octopus (SS-9)* when the storage batteries were being recharged, someone forgot to open the battery compartment ventilating system, and hydrogen collected above the cells. A spark set it off and the battery compartment erupted in explosion and fire. No one was hurt and the boat was fortunate to remain afloat, but she spent much of 1907 in drydock under repair. The *Stingray (SS-10)* suffered a similar explosion a little more than a year later, and the result of that second accident was a major alteration of the storage battery system to improve ventilation.

Holland's Electric Boat Company continued to dominate the U.S. Navy submarine force for several years. The D-class was followed by the E-class: *Skipjack (SS-24)* and *Sturgeon (SS-25).* The E-class was notable because these two boats were the first to be powered by diesel engines. They carried crews of twenty; they also had bow planes to help them submerge and surface, as well as radios to communicate with the fleet.

The F-class were again Holland boats: the *Carp (SS-20), Barracuda (SS-21), Pickerel (SS-22),* and *Skate (SS-23).* They were bigger vessels, up to 400 tons, longer (142 feet), and carried twenty-two men.

Simon Lake got into the field then with the G-class submarines which reverted to the gasoline engines. The *Seal,* which was *G-1* could make fourteen knots on the surface. She also made a record dive of 256 feet below the surface. The next two G-boats, *Tuna* and *Turbot,* were also built by Lake and were very satisfactory (aside from the gasoline engine). But the fourth G-boat, *Thrasher (SS-26),* was designed by an Italian and built by the American Laurenti Company. It was most unstable and regarded as a potential disaster by all who sailed in her. There would be no others of that particular model in the U.S. submarine fleet.

The nine boats of the H-class were still very much like the older ones. Again they were Holland boats. The K-boats got up to more than five hundred tons and the number of crew rose to twenty-eight. The same was true of the eight L-boats. By this time the submarine was beginning to look much like the ultimate in American submersibles, which would be the fleet-class vessels. The L-boats were nearly 170 feet long, and they had the sleek lines that indicated streamlining. The conning towers were low and the periscopes fully retractable. Diesel propulsion had definitely replaced gasoline. The L-boats were also new in the sense that they had modern deck guns—three-inch guns on the earliest models.

Even before the United States entered the war in 1917, American fleet units were dispersed widely around the world to protect U.S. interests. By that time submarines had already been sent as far abroad as the Philippine Islands. In 1909 the A-boats had been shipped to the Pacific, followed by the B-boats in 1912. Actually, they had come in 1908, but the decision to keep them there indefinitely was made later. The *Porpoise (A-6)* was the first American submarine to make a dive in Pacific waters of the Far East, at Manila Bay. But the problem of those early boats was range. In 1911 the submarine fleet decided on a daring excursion, from Manila to Zamboanga on the tip of Mindanao, a distance of one thousand miles. This was an enormous undertaking, and the fleet was accompanied by the submarine tender *Rainbow* on a cruise that lasted three months!

Those early boats had their troubles. In 1910 while cruising off Cape Cod, the *C-4 (Bonita)* stopped off at Provincetown. The next morning she went out on a dive, running out submerged. She made

25

the training dive and then returned to port, again submerged. The commissioning skipper of the *Bonita*, Lt. F. V. McNair, Jr., had made her a tight ship, and she so remained. As they came back, toward Provincetown, the skipper looked through the periscope and saw the gunboat *Castine* lying at anchor and decided to run in toward her to the submarine's anchorage. He turned the periscope over to a quartermaster.

"Split the *Castine* in two," he said. The quartermaster took over, and came right straight at the gunboat's broadside, as ordered. This particular quartermaster was actually a gunner's mate whose experience was limited. The captain walked away, expecting to be notified when they came close to the harbor. But currents, or the tide carried them inshore faster than the captain expected, and the next thing he knew about his position came with a shock, as the *C-4* struck the *Castine*. The submarine was down far enough to pass under the gunboat, but the periscope struck the warship amidships, pierced a hole in her bottom, and she began to take water. The crew turned to and managed to beach the *Castine*, otherwise she would have sunk in deep water. The acting quartermaster could certainly not be faulted. He had carried out his orders to the letter. What was needed, obviously, was a better watch-keeping system.

That became even more obvious one day in 1911 when the *Salmon (D-3)* was in the course of a training dive in Long Island Sound off New London, Connecticut. As she was moving along in her assigned area, underwater, the boat was suddenly shaken as if it had run into some submerged object. When the *D-3* surfaced, the skipper discovered that the big bell that was located in a superstructure on the bow, had been carried away, the supports cut right out of the boat. Something had certainly snipped it off, clean as a whistle. No one could explain until someone at submarine headquarters began comparing the track charts of various submarines that day, and discovered that another submarine had wandered out of its assigned area and crossed the path of the *Salmon*. So it was a collision, but one of the luckiest in naval history.

The assignment of the A- and B-boats to the Philippines was more than a move to bolster American naval power abroad. Ever since the Russo-Japanese War the Japanese were regarded in military circles as the potential enemy of the United States. One reason for this was a recognition of Japanese expansionism early in the century. (Teddy Roosevelt sent The Great White fleet around the world largely to show the Japanese our naval power and thus persuade them with his big stick to refrain from belligerent activity against American interests.) Japanese expansionism was no secret. Before the turn of the century the Japanese had swallowed Formosa and ten years after the century began they took over control of Korea. But the specific Japanese quarrel with the United States came out of the Russo-Japanese War, mediated by Teddy Roosevelt, in which he had deprived the Japanese of the fruits of victory, the jingoists claimed. The war had very nearly bankrupted Japan and her officials believed the old adage that to the victors belong the spoils. But Teddy Roosevelt refused to countenance Japanese demands for spoils in the form of money or goods, particularly in view of the fact that Japan had begun the war by a surprise attack in Manchuria. So by 1909, although there was much cross-talk, Japan was fixed as the nation most to be feared in the Pacific.

As the Panama Canal neared completion, American relations with Japan continued to be difficult. The canal would present the United States with a new defensive problem; it would not take much effort for an aggressor to destroy the locks and render the canal unusable. So even as the locks were being built and tried out in 1913, the U.S. Navy worried about protecting the canal. This problem became one of the most important on the agenda of the Navy Department. Someone decided that the submarine force was ideally suited for the defensive task.

On May 2, 1913, the *Castine*, now in use as a submarine tender although never designed for the task, and a fleet of five submarines set sail under sealed orders for the wide open sea, with no idea of their destination. They knew they were going somewhere far away, because they were provisioned for six months and had been assigned the collier *Mars* to supply the *Castine*. But where?

When the ships were at sea, Lieutenant (jg.) Richard S. Edwards opened his sealed orders as commander of the expedition, and read what he was to do:

> To proceed to Colon, Panama, without stopping at any port en route, there to remove the engines and batteries from the submarines, the hulls hauled up on the beach, the engines, batteries and hulls to be placed on flat cars, transported across the isthmus by rail to Balboa, there to be reassembled for services in the Pacific in waters adjacent to the Panama Canal—for the purpose of repelling possible attacks by the Japanese.

Someone in the Navy Department obviously had the wind up, but the militant tone of the orders was contradicted a few days later and a wireless message reached the force at sea. The message ordered Lieutenant Edwards to put in at Guantanamo Bay, Cuba (the base wrested from Spain and retained after the Spanish-American War) to await developments.

No one believed that those little submarines (the five C-class boats with 10 knot speed and 275 tons displacement) could travel very far under their own power. They were towed, two by the *Castine* and three by the *Mars*. But since the sea was calm during much of the voyage the submarines did chance it and made a part of the trip under their own power.

At Guantanamo there were new orders. There wasn't such a big hurry as had seemed the case a few days earlier. The submarine commanders were told to keep their boats at Guantanamo and to train the crews. The officers lived aboard the *Castine* and the enlisted men aboard the coal ship. Later the *Castine* was detached from the group and replaced by the old monitor *Ozark*. The men trained some more. Finally on December 7, 1913, the force got under way again for the Canal Zone. This time they would travel the six hundred miles south under their own power. It was the longest voyage yet made by a submarine force.

On arrival at Colon, Lieutenant Edwards looked for orders, but there were none. In fact, General Goethals, the builder of the Panama

Canal, wanted to know what they were doing down there and who had sent them. But the orders finally came along, detailing the little fleet to stand guard on the Atlantic side of the canal.

Life was pleasant, if unconventional, for the navy men at Panama. The married officers soon brought down their wives and lived in an abandoned nurses' home on the Colon hospital grounds. The bachelor officers lived aboard the tender *Severn* (the old sailing ship *Chesapeake*) which had replaced the ships that brought them down; so did the enlisted men. But in the tropical waters, the bottoms of the submarines soon became fouled and it was necessary to clean them. There was no dry dock in Panama, but the submariners managed to get the use of one of the Colon locks, and put the boats inside on cradles. All was well—until one of the canal dredgers sprang a leak and had to be brought into the lock for repairs. What to do? The answer: "nothing." The submarines remained in their cradles, sealed, with sea valves and main ballast tanks opened. The lock was flooded, the dredger brought in and shored up, and the lock drained. It was, as the pigboat men said, "a stationary dive."

The submarines were also active on the Asiatic Station; there the A- and B-boats operated under the grandiloquent title: First Asiatic Submarine Division. The commanders of most of these boats were midshipmen once removed—brand new ensigns. In fact Ensign Charles A. Lockwood, an ensign of the class of 1912 at the U.S. Naval Academy, was in 1914 made skipper of the A-2, the *Adder*. The major task of the submarine force in the Philippines was to fly the flag, and thus help keep down Filipino nationalism; the force was also to patrol the coastal waters enforcing American neutrality in the early days of World War I.

Back in America meanwhile the navy was enjoying one of its relatively rare periods of opulence. The German submarine war of 1915 gave Congress something to think about, and when the Navy Department had the temerity to ask for sixteen new submarines of the new O-class, Congress obliged without a whimper, although the boats would cost half a million dollars each. Meanwhile, the navy was also building three boats of the T-class, the forerunners of the later fleet class submarines. They would carry six torpedo tubes and two three-inch guns, as well as a crew of four officers and thirty-four enlisted men.

Over the years of development of the American submarine fleet there had been many accidents. Indeed, with the A- and B-boats, navigation was so unreliable that they ran aground relatively frequently, and although grounding a naval vessel was usually a matter for a court of inquiry or possible court-martial, a number of submarines went on the beach and nobody was charged with violation of regulations.

For example, when Ensign Lockwood ran his *A-2* aground one day, he calmly sent back to Cavite for a tug and for materials to scrape and paint the boat's waterline. They might as well improve her while she was canted over on the beach, he had decided. The result of that accident was an unofficial commendation from his divisional commander for good thinking.

Several boats narrowly escaped destruction from battery explosions; hydrogen and gasoline fumes posed equal hazards. In 1915 the *E-2* was drydocked in the Brooklyn Navy Yard when the alkali batteries she was testing suddenly exploded. The result was the death of five men, and injury to several others. That was the end of the alkali batteries. Thereafter submarines used lead-acid batteries.

But the first serious submarine disaster since the days of the *Hunley* and the other Confederate *Davids* occurred in 1915 at Honolulu.

On March 25, the *F-4 (Skate)* was moored at the municipal pier in Honolulu Harbor. That morning she set out on a training dive. She moved through the harbor to the mouth, out past the reef and then along the coast past Pearl Harbor and Barber's Point. Lieutenant (jg.) Alfred L. Ede was in command of the submarine, and Ensign Timothy A. Parker was executive officer. There were nineteen men in the crew. Their diving area was located off Barber's Point and when they reached it, Skipper Ede gave the order to dive. The *F-4* went down. She was seen by the keeper of the Barber's Point lighthouse, who did not pay too much attention, since submarines were forever coming and going in the area. But shortly after the *F-4* dived, the keeper heard an explosion and saw smoke.

The submarine was due to return to her mooring that afternoon, but she did not appear. When she had not appeared by nightfall, her absence was reported and the next morning a search began. When the news broke, the lighthouse keeper volunteered his information, but since the place he had seen the explosion was not quite where the *F-4* should have been no one paid much attention. The searchers found the submarine later that day in 305 feet of water, she was sending up an oil slick and air bubbles. Attempts were made with underwater sounding devices to get some sign of life from the men below, but the signals went unanswered. It was apparent that the men down below were all dead. There was no way that they could survive that sort of immersion with the air supply in their four-hundred-ton boat.

There was no hope for the men, but the navy wanted to recover that submarine, to discover what had gone wrong. No one in Hawaii was capable of making the effort required to raise the vessel. Five deep-sea divers from the Brooklyn Navy Yard were rushed to Honolulu. Rushed, of course, is a relative term. In 1915 rushing meant taking a train to San Francisco and then a warship to Honolulu, a week's voyage. The divers were Chief Gunner George D. Stillson, and chief gunner's mates, Frank Crilley, W. F. Loughman, F. C. L. Neilson, and S. J. Drellishak. Along with them came Assistant Surgeon George R. W. French. This was the finest salvage crew the navy could muster: Stillson was a salvage expert who had invented many of the devices then in use. Drellishak held the world's deep-sea diving record: 274 feet.

In 1915 deep-sea diving was far more art than science and the equipment that had evolved was cumbersome and difficult to handle. The diver got into a rubberized canvas suit that fit tightly at wrists and ankles. The neckhole of the suit was fitted with a circular brass plate and the heavy metal diving helmet fitted tightly onto that plate. The diving helmet had large glass screens at front and sides; from the top extended the air hose and venting hose; and the air hose, attached to a rope lifeline ended in a pump at the other end, which was manned by the diving tenders. Compressed air was pumped down to the diver through the air hose.

To get to the bottom the diver used weights. The helmet probably would have taken him down by itself, it was that heavy, but he would have landed upside down on the ocean floor, and that is not generally a useful position. He wore heavy boots with lead weights on the soles, and a heavy weighted belt, so that his center of gravity was more or less normal.

When the diving crew reached Honolulu it was agreed that no one could possibly be alive inside the submarine after all those days of immersion. So the mission was salvage and not rescue.

Before any dive could be attempted, the divers had to get into condition. They tried to do this by simulating the pressures under which they would have to work off Barber's Point. A large steel tank was fabricated and riveted together stoutly and set up so that compressed air could be forced inside. This was the early "recompression chamber" and the purpose initially was to determine whether or not the divers could withstand the pressure at three hundred feet. No one knew, because no one had ever dived that deep before and lived to tell the tale.

The four divers all passed the first test. Then Crilley was the first to go down. The navy assembled the vessels and matériel: three tugboats, one dredge, two scows, and half a dozen barges to carry air flasks, diving equipment, and salvage gear. Crilley, on that first dive, attached guide lines to the submarine. The other divers followed and secured hawser to the lines and then got them fixed to the boat. With the donkey engines on the dredge and the tugs, the four-hundred-ton *F-4* was lifted about twelve feet off the bottom, enough to allow the salvage crew to tow her inshore and reduce the depth at which they'd have to work. This became the procedure: Lift as high as possible, tow until the submarine grounded, then send divers down to shorten up the lines, lift again, and tow.

When the *F-4* grounded in 275 feet of water, Loughman was the first diver down to begin the usual process. He had worked for an hour or so, as long as he ought to stay down, and had gotten some of the lines tightened up. When it came time to surface Loughman followed the standard procedure: he came up part way, and then stopped. The purpose of that maneuver was to equalize the pressure inside his suit. If the divers did not follow that procedure they were likely to get into trouble. A diver breathes air under pressure. Air is 80 percent nitrogen and under pressure, the nitrogen moves more rapidly and in greater bulk into the bloodstream and the body tissues. The greater the pressure, the more nitrogen builds up. The trouble arises because nitrogen does not dissipate from the body tissues as rapidly or easily as oxygen and other gases. Thus a diver had to stop at forty or fifty foot intervals on his way up and wait until the nitrogen moved out of the body tissues. That way, when he reached the top the body had almost neutralized the effects of the pressure. If the diver did not do this, or if he remained under pressure for a long period of time, the nitrogen buildup then caused serious changes in his body. Sudden release of the pressure would create pockets of nitrogen in the tissues, which gave him "caisson disease" (discovered by tunnel builders) which was commonly called "the bends" because the victim was bent and knotted in pain. Or, even worse than the bends, which could be treated by immersion in a tank with pressure turned up and then gradually reduced, was air embolism. In this illness an air pocket in the bloodstream disrupted the movements of the heart and arteries and the victim often died.

Loughman came up from 270 feet to 220 feet and stopped, to remain twenty minutes or so and equalize the pressure in his suit before going on. But somehow, while waiting, he became entangled in the lines and cables that extended down to the *F-4*, and try as he might, with his knife and by pulling, he could not extricate himself. He could move neither up nor down.

After this situation became apparent to the men on the surface, Chief Gunner's Mate Frank Crilley went down to try to help. He found Loughman only half conscious after his enormous exertions to free himself, and he found the diver's air hose and lifeline tangled dreadfully around one of the steel cables that led from the salvage vessels to the *F-4*. Crilley began to work to move Loughman around and around the cable, and thus free him. By this time Loughman was unconscious and gave no help at all. The work went slowly and the time passed. Actually it was four hours before Crilley managed to free Loughman and get him to the surface, and when the divers came up it seemed doubtful if Loughman could survive. His head and shoulders were badly bruised, and he was unconscious from the effects of the pressure. After many months of hospitalization he did survive, although he was crippled as a result of the accident. Crilley continued in the salvage program and ultimately was awarded the Congressional Medal of Honor—one of the few people to receive that medal in peacetime—for his unusual bravery in rescuing his companion.

As for the *F-4*, it seemed that the salvage crews inched along, hauling the submarine up as far as possible, just a few feet above the bottom, and then dragging her toward land along the slope of the shore. The whole plan nearly failed when they got the boat into sixty feet of water. The divers discovered that the hull had cracked, and threatened to break up after all that pulling and hauling. So the effort was suspended while eight big pontoon floats were built at the Mare Island Navy Yard in California and shipped halfway across the Pacific Ocean by the four-stacker armored cruiser USS *Maryland*. The pontoons made the lifting relatively easy; soon the *F-4* was brought to the surface and towed into Pearl Harbor's dry dock.

The submarine command then proceeded to inspect the hull, after the dead were brought out and decently buried. What had caused the disaster? Had there been an explosion, as the Barber's Point lighthouse keeper insisted?

The indications were that there probably had been such an explosion, involving the storage batteries. Sulphuric acid had leaked through the lead lining of the forward battery tank and had eaten its way through the tank. This action weakened the submarine's single hull. It seemed likely that when the *F-4* began its last dive, the hull had given way, the water had rushed into the batteries and caused an explosion, and as the submarine plunged downward, chlorine gas had killed all those crew members who were not drowned. It was not an immediate process; that much was clear from the positions in which the dead were found. Some of the crew were alive when the boat hit the bottom. They tried to bring her up, but there was no hope with all that weight in the boat. Fifteen crew members managed to get into the engine room and shut themselves in, but the gas and water followed and they all died. The *F-4* tragedy did have one salutary effect: the navy immediately began plans to change submarine design to avoid such accidents, and later that year when the *E-2 (Sturgeon)* nearly suffered the same sort of accident off Brenton Reef lightship, the indications were almost certainly proved. The *E-2* had dived, and gotten down to fifty feet, when someone smelled chlorine gas. It may have been the white mice that the submarines carried after some of the early disasters. They were extremely sensitive to gas, and passed out long before humans could sense its presence. If the captain of the submarine had blown the ballast tanks to get to the surface quickly, he might have created a new disaster; the result would have been increased pressure on the single-hull plates, and if there was a weak plate (which there was) the boat might have gone down. But the skipper pumped out the ballast tanks, which did not increase pressure, and brought the submarine to the surface. After she was examined, in light of the *F-4* incident, the changes that would bring about the double-hull system were put into effect.

The Electric Boat Company also built the first double-hulled submarine, the *SS-47*, the single boat built in the M-class. Even as she was being built in 1917, the concept of submarine use was changing. What the navy decided it wanted (and all navies were the same in this regard) was a fleet-class submarine. Fleet class meant a boat that was capable of long voyages—to travel with the fleet. The old idea of the "defense" flotilla of submarines had given way to the idea of the submarine as an offensive naval weapon and as a commerce destroyer. The Germans proved both points. When World War I broke out in 1914, eleven German U-boats set forth into the North Sea and the English Channel to harry their enemies. This first attempt was a failure; they sank no ships and the British battleship HMS *Birmingham* sank the *U-15*. Actually British submarines drew the first blood of that sort in the war; the *E-9* torpedoed the German cruiser *Hela* at anchor in the Helgoland Bight, and sank her a few days after war was declared.

The Germans retaliated quickly enough; Lieutenant Commander Otto Hersing in the *U-21* attacked the British cruiser HMS *Pathfinder* in the North Sea and sank her. If the navies of the world needed further proof of the value of the submarine as an offensive, rather than defensive, weapon then the Germans gave it to them on September 22, 1914, when Lieutenant Commander Otto Weddigen in the *U-9* torpedoed and sank the British cruisers *Hogue, Aboukir,* and *Cressy* in about an hour.

The Germans had long since decided that commerce raiding would be a major part of their effort on the high seas when they went to war with England. When the war broke out, cruisers in various parts of the German Empire were detached from regular duties to raid enemy shipping. Most infamous of these was the *Emden* which terrorized the Indian Ocean for months before she was sunk by a British warship. The Germans also armed their fast passenger liners and turned them into "auxiliary cruisers" and so did the British. But as the war moved along, one by one the German surface raiders were hunted down (with a few exceptions such as SMS *Wolf*) and the German naval command decided to use submarines to raid commerce.

Early in 1915, Admiral von Tirpitz decided to begin a submarine blockade of Great Britain. The vestiges of "civilized" warfare still existed; the rule had always called for protection of noncombatants; that meant that if a German ship chased and stopped a British freighter, the passengers and crew were taken off and usually sent to some neutral port, either in their own boats or in another merchant ship. If a ship was sunk in flight, the warship would stop and render assistance to the survivors. But if submarine warfare were to be instituted all that had to end. The essence of submarine warfare was stealth, and stealth could not be achieved by surfacing, firing a shot across the bows of a merchant vessel, and then standing by while the ship was boarded and then sunk. A submarine captain who did that was liable to be fired upon by a deck gun, and his boat sunk under him. Or a radio message could easily bring swift retaliation from hunting destroyers. It was obvious from the beginning, when the Germans decided to use the submarine as a commerce raider, that the whole nature of sea war would change.

On February 4, 1915, the Imperial German government announced that on February 15 a blockade of the British Isles would begin. The first passenger ship, the SS *Falaba,* was sunk on March 28. The world was furious with the Germans, but it made no difference. On May 1 a U-boat sank the American ship *Gulflight,* and then the fat *was* in the fire, because the U.S. vessel had been sunk without warning, and

America was officially still neutral in the war, although many American ships were already carrying contraband to England.

Six days later the fire blazed up when the *U-20* sank the British liner *Lusitania* without warning, and 1,198 people died, including 139 Americans. Other nations expressed shock and alarm at the German policy, and it was one of the major goads which eventually brought the United States into the war on the side of the western Allies. The Germans had few surface ships at sea, so the submarine war was all one-sided except in such places as the Dardanelles, where the British employed submarines as elements of the fleet and sank some vessels. But commerce raiding in World War I belonged to the Germans exclusively.

After 1916 the Imperial German government turned all its shipyards to building submarines; that year they built 188 of them. The next year the Germans built 291 U-boats, and in 1918 they built 372 such boats. But this progression of building did not mean the Germans had so many submarines. As the submarine grew more dangerous to shipping, antisubmarine warfare techniques also grew more effective. In 1914 the Germans lost only five U-boats. But as the sinking of warships and merchantmen grew evermore serious, the British devised methods to counteract the U-boats. The convoy system, first devised by Winston Churchill in 1915, (to counteract the *Emden* in the Indian Ocean) was finally accepted by the Royal Navy long after Churchill had been forced to resign as first lord of the Admiralty in 1915. The convoy cut losses of merchant ships sharply, because to attack, the U-boats had to run the gauntlet of escorting warships. The warships developed new weapons: The listening device, or hydrophone, was one of them. The hydrophone was much like a doctor's stethescope, because it could pick up sound waves made by enemy ships; they sent back a telltale signal. The surface warships also began to use depth charges, which could be set to explode at certain levels below the water's surface. As aircraft came into more use in the war, they began to fly over submarine-infested waters; equipped with depth bombs they were often effective against the U-boats. The British also made good use of fake merchantmen for a time. These were actually merchant ships, rebuilt to hide heavy guns, and carrying depth charges. Many of these ships were much faster than they looked. They were manned by Royal Navy crews and their purpose was to entice submarines. When a submarine attacked them, preferably on the surface, the British would try to sink it by gunfire, or if the U-boat submerged, they attempted to sink it with depth charges. The most effective of these vessels was the *Q-19*, which trapped three U-boats in the course of a few hours one night off Gibraltar. She lay in deep water in the Mediterranean that night, apparently damaged and looking as if she could not get away. Three U-boats converged on her. The first appeared at a few moments before midnight. The Germans surfaced, opened fire, and the *Q-19* crew apparently made efforts to get the ship underway and escape. The Germans continued to shell, carrying away the foremast and wounding eleven members of the crew. Two more U-boats joined the party, and soon they were all firing shells at the hapless vessel. The crew then sent a "panic party" into lifeboats and these men rowed away from the ship. The Germans were jubilant and they moved in closer. Suddenly the bulkheads of the *Q-19*'s deckhouse fell away, and a 47 mm gun appeared. The gun crew began firing and with the first shot knocked the senior German officer off the bridge of his submarine. In an hour they had sunk all three U-boats.

The submarine had become the greatest danger on the sea to Britain, and the British took evermore heroic measures to stop the depredations. The undersea boats had changed the nature of naval warfare in less than twenty years.

3  MIDPASSAGE

IN the middle of the summer of 1916 the United States government came to the conclusion that the American defense effort had to be strengthened enormously. On August 29 Congress passed the Naval Appropriations Act which authorized a grand shipbuilding program; submarines were not left out. More submarines were ordered, and early the next year the secretary of the navy turned the coaling station at New London, Connecticut, into the United States Navy's submarine school. For the first time, submarine operation was accepted as a naval specialty.

In the early months of the war, the Germans had the advantage with their growing submarine fleet as the British experimented to learn how to combat the menace. The Germans even sent submarines across the Atlantic to attack British supply ships, and several operated off the American coast, notably near Nantucket. On July 9, 1916, the submarine *Deutschland* arrived off Cape Henry, Virginia. But she was not a warship, her flag proclaimed, but a ship of the North German Lloyd Lines, and her mission was to trade the dyes that she carried for six hundred tons of nickel, tin, and rubber, all vital elements for the German war machine. The *Deutschland* was an enormous submarine for her time: 315 feet long, and drawing 17 feet. She was an anomaly, however, and the experiment in using submarines of that day to carry cargo was not pursued.

After Congress declared war on Germany, the U.S. Navy submarine service prepared in earnest to get into the fight. Actually by that time there was not too much use for American submarines in the Atlantic;

the British had begun to be effective with their antisubmarine tactics, particularly the convoy system, and since the Germans had virtually no surface ships at sea there was not much for U.S. submarines to accomplish. Nevertheless the decision was made to send American submarines across the Atlantic.

The voyage alone was a dangerous enterprise for these small craft, which were still so unstable. To take over the first contingent the navy chose Lieutenant Commander Thomas K. Hart, who had distinguished himself in Hawaii as commander of submarines. In fact Hart had established the submarine base at Pearl Harbor, and his K-boats there had set a new submarine torpedo performance record. The American flotilla was to sail from the Philadelphia Navy Yard to Halifax, Nova Scotia, and then to the Azores. Some of the skippers and crews of the K-boats that would make the voyage were skittish about the long trip. They had reason to be. The K-boats were still of the single-hulled variety which meant that they were extremely vulnerable to external pressure and rough seas. In midsummer, when the assignment was made, the Atlantic seemed calm enough, but as fall approached they knew they could expect rough weather. *K-1*, *K-2*, *K-5*, and *K-6* were ordered to make the trip, and Lieutenant Commander Hart told the skippers where they were going. When? That depended on how soon they could get ready.

The submarine commanders were polled as to how long it would take each of them to get ready for the voyage. About two weeks they said, so Lieutenant Commander Hart set the sailing date for September 15. But on September 14, when he asked the skippers if they were ready, they said were not. So, how long would it take them, said a patient Commodore Hart. Another two weeks, they said, and he shifted the sailing date to September 30, 1917.

On the day before the sailing date, Commodore Hart again called his captains together. Were they ready? No. This time he did not ask them, but he told them: They were sailing in one week's time and any submarine not ready to move under her own power would start ignominiously at the end of a tow.

On October 7 the flotilla sailed for Halifax. Only one boat was on the end of a towline, and its crew, shamed, were working furiously to move under their own power and cast off that line from the tender *Bushnell*. Before the voyage was over, all four K-boats were self-propelled.

Commodore Hart dropped his K-boats at their new base at Ponta Delgada in the Azores and then went back to America to bring another force of submarines across the Atlantic. These were *L-1*, *L-2*, *L-3*, *L-4*, *L-9*, *L-10*, *L-11*, and the *E-1*. The last of these was dropped off at the Azores to join the K-boats, and the L-boats went on to Bantry Bay, on Berehaven Island in Ireland, which would be their base.

So American submarines were in the war. Some, the O-boats, patrolled off the American coast from Cape Cod to Key West. Their mission was to prevent attack by German U-boats on American and British shipping, but they never saw action of that sort. Rather, they ran the danger that was to become so well-known later: a British convoy captain sighted the *O-6* on patrol one day in 1918 and without further ado the convoy's escorts opened fire on the "U-boat." Lieutenant C. Q. Wright, Jr., the skipper, could not get her down before she had been hit by six shells, which damaged the conning tower and forward ventilator so badly that when the *O-6* finally did submerge she leaked dangerously and Lt. Wright was afraid to stay down more than a few minutes. He surfaced, and this time an American destroyer placed the *O-6* under fire and she was hit again and again before she was able to identify herself.

Off the Irish coast the L-boats had their troubles, too, most of them with friendly forces. One day the *L-10* was patrolling between Ireland and England, and in the course of the patrol made a dive. Somewhere inside the submarine there was an oil leak, and that day the crew of the *L-10* learned how potentially fatal an oil leak can be. The U.S. destroyer *Sterett* was on patrol that day, too. In the course of her patrol, she came across a patch of ocean that showed a trail of oil. Aha, a U-boat, said the officer of the deck, and in best antisubmarine warfare fashion, laid a pattern of depth charges up front where the submarine ought to be. The American destroyer skipper had the location right on the nose, and Lieutenant James C. Van de Carr was aroused there in the deep by the shock of numerous explosions all around the *L-10*. The skipper ordered the ballast tanks blown, and the submarine shot to the surface, the deck crews came rushing out of the conning tower and gave the recognition signal, in time to keep the *Sterett* from sinking her with her guns.

The British had been in the war for four years, and their experience made them salty old hands, while the Americans were all new at the war game, and not overly competent. How many chances to attack enemy U-boats were missed will never be known, but a few encounters suffice to tell the tale. One day Lieutenant Commander Lewis Hancock, Jr., took the *L-4* out on patrol from the Irish base at Bantry Bay. While patrolling submerged, the officer at the periscope spotted a German U-boat basking motionlessly on the surface; it was undoubtedly charging its batteries. Skipper Hancock lined up the U-boat for a shot and fired a torpedo. Someone aboard the U-boat spotted the torpedo coming, and the U-boat came to life, moved ahead, dived, and the torpedo missed astern. The *L-4* missed a U-boat in another such setup, too. And what was the reason? It could have been a miscalculation of distance or current by the skipper. It could have been a bad run by the torpedo, which in turn could have been caused by mechanical or human error. Human error was an enormous problem in torpedo firing, because the "fish" of 1918 were very touchy and the gyroscopes, which controlled their course, were quite liable to malfunction if jostled too hard. So the *L-4* had the distinction of missing two setups against the U-boats, which was a sort of record.

Lieutenant A. C. Bennett in the *L-11* also missed a chance for glory one day when he was on patrol in Irish waters and, while submerged, sighted a U-boat on the surface. Determined not to make the error of the *L-4*, Bennett fired two torpedoes at the U-boat, the second one fired five seconds after the first. But the second torpedo overtook the first and blew it up with an enormous explosion, thus telling one careless U-boat captain that somebody was out there after him. The U-boat dived, and Lieutenant Bennett never saw it again.

But one American submarine did have a part in the destruction of a U-boat, even if the event would not win any medals for anyone. This was the *L-2*, that was under the command of Lieutenant Edgar A. Logan. Early in July 1918, the *L-2* went off on a war patrol south of the Irish coast, and after several uneventful days, she began her return to the base at Bantry Bay. On the evening of July 10, after dark, the *L-2* surfaced and continued to move ahead, clearing the air in the boat and charging its batteries. Suddenly the boat was shaken by a violent explosion and Lieutenant Scott Umstead, the officer of the deck, saw a column of water rise about 25 feet off the starboard quarter. When it dropped back, he also saw six feet of periscope sticking up out of the water. He sounded the diving signal and the lookouts scurried into the conning tower as the submarine started down.

As the *L-2* submerged, Lieutenant Logan decided to try to ram the enemy boat and he circled the area. The *L-2* came close enough so that the crew could hear the sounds of the U-boat's propellers, but Logan could not bring the bow to bear on them. He ordered the hydrophone operators to work, and tried to track and follow the U-boat with their help. But the U-boat's underwater speed was superior to the L-boat's 10.5 knots underwater, and the enemy submarine moved steadily away until the sounds were lost. Skipper Logan ordered the *L-2* to the surface. When they came up there was nothing around them. There was no hope of finding the enemy in the darkness, so Logan resumed his course for Bantry Bay.

No one ever determined precisely what caused the explosion on the U-boat, although the radio intelligence section finally determined that the boat was the *U-65*, which never made it back to her home port. Perhaps the *U-65*, trying to fire a torpedo at close range at the *L-2*, suffered a premature explosion, either in or just outside the torpedo tube. But that would probably have caused the U-boat to sink immediately and she did not. Another explanation was that there were two U-boats in the area, one of which fired on the *L-2*, but whose torpedo hit the *U-65* instead, damaging her so badly that she soon sank. The *L-2* came off almost unscathed, but later when she was dry-docked, the workmen discovered a hull plate in the starboard quarter that had been dented, undoubtedly from the force of the nearby explosion.

Until the November armistice, the American submarines continued their patrols, always unrewarded. Those L-boats were constructed to withstand a dive of two hundred feet. Below that depth the single hulls were in danger of being crushed by the pressure of the sea water. But how much could a modern (1918) submarine really take?

43

The crew of one American boat unwittingly discovered an answer one day in the English Channel.

Once again, the participant in the unwilling experiment was the hapless *L-4*. Lieutenant Hancock had submerged the craft, but it was not moving properly, and he diagnosed the trouble as too much weight. The officer of the watch gave the order to blow a thousand pounds out of the adjusting tank, which controlled final dive trim. But a new man, a manifold operator, opened the sea valve to the larger auxiliary tank by mistake, and instead of ejecting water, the submarine took on several thousand pounds of extra weight. The *L-4* began to drop very fast. The captain called for full speed on the electric motors, and the diving planes set in the surface position, but before the propellers could grab, the *L-4* settled into the deep mud at the bottom and, of course, stopped. The depth gauge said they were in 294 feet of water, almost half again more than the safe depth for the boat.

They tried to pump out the water, but the pumps would not work against the high pressure: they had not been designed to so operate. There was only one way to save the boat. The skipper ordered the water moved from the auxiliary tank to the adjusting tank, and then a thousand pounds was blown out by compressed air. The valves were closed, the auxiliary tank was opened again and another thousand pounds of water was drained off and blown out. Finally after several rounds of this, positive buoyancy began to show, and the skipper ordered all but essential hands aft, and the motors, which had been shut down, started up again. At the same time, he blew the bow ballast tank, and the submarine's bow began to rise. It reached an angle of six degrees, which broke the suction holding the submarine down, and in a few minutes the boat was rising at an angle of fifty degrees. They had been on the bottom for an hour and ten minutes, and both submarine and crew had shown no ill effects.

Such operational incidents offered almost the only excitement on the Irish station for the remainder of the war. In the Azores, the little flotilla of older boats did a big job in just staying afloat, without ever coming to grips with the enemy. Very late in the war, eight of the boats were dispatched for European duty, with the tender *Savannah*. But they did not leave Newport until November 2, 1918, and by the time they reached the Azores, the armistice between Germany and the Allies had been signed. So the First World War ended without any really effective action by American submarines.

4  DOLDRUMS

WHILE the K-boats and the L-boats had been at war, the rest of the submarine service trained and watched. Sometimes the training was as dangerous as a combat operation, as in the case of the *A-7*. She had just undergone an overhaul at Cavite Navy Yard in Manila Bay in the summer of 1917, and had come back to her finger pier at the submarine base. On the morning of July 24, 1917, she was scheduled to go out into the South China Sea on a routine operation. The skipper, Lieutenant (jg.) Arnold Marcus, used the electric motors to get her out into deep water and then gave the order to shift over to gasoline engine drive. But when the gasoline engine was cranked up, instead of starting, it exploded, and killed Lieutenant Marcus and seven enlisted men. It was the old story: gasoline fumes from a leaky valve. The submarine force in the Philippines also suffered another accident much like it. One day the *A-2* was fueling at the gasoline dock. Everyone who served in the gasoline-fuel submarines was aware of the dangers of the fuel, and the gasoline dock was isolated from all the others, standing furthest out toward the bay. The *A-2* finished fueling, and the skipper, Ensign Edmund W. Burrough, gave the orders to take her back to her finger pier, next to Machina Wharf in the submarine basin. She was moving astern, with Skipper Burrough on the bridge supervising the activity of the helmsman and the seamen hauling in the lines. Again without warning, an explosion reverberated through the base. It blew the wooden grating on the steering platform (inside the conning tower) fifty feet in the air, and as the grating went up it took the bridge awning along with it. Skipper

Burrough and the helmsman were blown off the bridge and struggled in the water alongside. Black smoke began to pour out of the conning tower and the vents. Out of the smoke of the main hatch came a black, burned figure, face charred, shirt ripped off so that the horrible burns that had seared the flesh were clearly visible from the shore. The seamen on deck rushed to help the man, but he screamed, "Don't touch me, don't touch me," and then fell to the deck. The men came up and identified the man, it was Chief Electrician J. C. Schaefer. He died in the hospital a few hours later.

Schaefer was the only fatality of that accident, but two others in short order brought a sudden stop to submarine operations in Manila Bay. The Asiatic Fleet command ordered a complete review of procedures and for two weeks every submarine was inspected and cleaned; new regulations for submarine operations were issued. The new rules insisted that fuel lines must not leak, carburetors must not grow sludgy or spit, gasoline must not spill, and fumes must not develop. Had those orders been obeyed by nature, machines, and men, the accidents would never have occurred. From that point on there were no further explosions in American gasoline-fueled submarines, but the submariners spent most of their time making sure that was so. Fortunately they were not in combat.

There was still a great deal to be learned about submarine operation and navigation at sea, too. One day in 1916 the *H-3* had gone aground on the California coast, making a marvelous picture for the newspaper photographers. She was a beached mechanical whale, lying helpless on the sand. One night in 1917 the *D-2* sank alongside the dock at the submarine base in New London. An engine room sea valve had leaked and no one was there to see it happening.

Often the errors were human. That same year the *F-1*, *F-2*, and *F-3* were on maneuvers off Point Loma, California, when the area suddenly fogged up. The boats were close together, and when the skipper of the *F-1* changed course suddenly, the boat crossed the path of the *F-3*. In the fog the officer of the watch of the *F-3* did not see the other submarine and the *F-3* ran squarely into the *F-1*, striking just behind the conning tower. The hole was so large that only five of the crew of the *F-1* had a chance to escape before the submarine went down in six hundred feet of water with nineteen men.

The raising of the *F-4* had proved that the salvage experts could work in three hundred feet of water, but no one saw how anything could be done at twice that depth. Besides, what would there be to salvage? The F-boats were designed to withstand no more than two hundred feet of pressure, and although the *F-4* was still hanging together at 304 feet when found, it could not be expected that the boat would have withstood the pressure at six hundred feet. What was down there was undoubtedly a flattened mass of metal. The *F-1* was left to rest in her watery grave.

The problem in 1918—or one of them—was that submarines did not have navigational equipment equal to the strains that had to be imposed on it. One day early in 1919, Lieutenant Commander Charles A. Lockwood was ordered to take the *N-5*, which had been commissioned in 1918, from the New London base to the Philadelphia Navy Yard. One of the submarine's electric motors had burned out and had to be rewound. It was February and the nor'easter season was on. The submarine rounded Montauk Point on the northeast tip of Long Island and headed southwest, for Cape May, which marked the entrance to Delaware Bay and then the Delaware River that would take them upstream to Philadelphia.

Almost as soon as they got into the Atlantic they were hit by a nor'easter, and the winds came howling down at Force 5, and Force 6, and higher. They were in the middle of a gale, and the seas began running fifteen feet above the submarine, which gave her a terrible beating.

The boat rolled and pitched like an amusement park thrill ride. It was not long before the gyrocompass, which had been designed for the relatively stable decks of a surface warship, broke down completely. The boat had a magnetic compass aboard but the magnetic compasses are highly responsive to electric currents and the boat was crisscrossed with them. At midnight Skipper Lockwood was on the bridge when the quartermaster sighted a light off the starboard bow. No light should be there, by rights, since they were supposed to arrive off Cape May at around four o'clock in the morning.

Skipper Lockwood's J-factor (Jesus-factor) was working overtime that night. He had a hunch that something was very much wrong and he ordered the boat stopped. A seaman came up with a lead line and began throwing it. Eight fathoms, he reported—48 feet of water. They had obviously been blown toward the lee shore by the gale, and while they were not in danger at the moment, the better course of action was to move out to sea, which Lockwood did until he had a more comfortable cushion of water underneath the hull. Then he ordered the anchor dropped and they waited for morning, hoping they would have a better view of the coast. When morning came they found that they were off Barnegat light, and about fifty miles off course.

With that sort of navigating equipment a submarine skipper had plenty of use for the J-factor, and the difficulties were certainly known to the men who operated the "pigboats." For that reason, the Americans, the British, the Japanese, and the French all wanted to have a good look at the German U-boats and, when the war ended in 1918, they got it. The Treaty of Versailles stipulated that the Germans give up their U-boat fleet and not build anymore submarines. Many of the German submarines were destroyed, but 176 were surrendered to the Allies more or less intact. The German sailors who delivered the vessels to Harwich and Plymouth were none too happy with the task, and they did their best to sabotage the U-boats in ways that would not be readily apparent. The *U-111*, for example, was run for the last hour or so, as it came in, with the oil valves of the starboard engine closed off—so the bearings burned out. But the U-boats were invaluable nonetheless to show how the enemy (the major submarine maker of the world) built an undersea craft. For the Americans there was another reason, which brought a reluctant Congress to support the navy's interest in the warships. The American effort in World War I had been expensive and had been financed with money that the Treasury had to raise through the sale of Liberty Bonds. At the end of the war, more money was needed to pay the debts, but patriotism had suddenly become a less salable commodity, and in the new Victory Bonds the government was offering, every stop had to be pulled out. The U-boats, the Treasury Department hoped, would be used for exhibition to promote the sale of the new bonds.

The U.S. got six of the captured U-boats: the *U-117*, *U-140*, *U-111*, *UB-88*, and *UC-97*. Six experienced submarine commanders, six executive officers, and 120 seamen were sent to England to bring the boats back. Included were Lieutenant Commander Freeman A. Daubin and Lieutenant Commander Charles Lockwood. Lieutenant Commander Vincent Astor, the executive officer of the tender *Bushnell,* was more or less in charge of the operation. After a great deal of difficulty, because the Americans knew nothing about U-boat construction, and only a handful of them could read German, they got the submarines back to America and began the triumphal tours around the country.

Once the tour was over, the U-boats were put into the hands of the designers and engineers, and their various parts were photographed, diagrammed, and studied until no more could be learned from them. Then they were disposed of, usually as targets for naval gunners.

The other countries involved were doing the same. The British studied their U-boats and learned from them, and so did the Japanese, who in some ways made the best use of all of the German boats and their torpedoes. Mostly what they had already learned was that the submarine was the most devastating weapon ever produced for the total war effort of an island kingdom. Britain and Japan were quickest to learn the lesson.

Although the western Allies had fought "the war to end all wars" there was no hiatus in the building of submarines after it was over. During the war the Americans had begun building the R-class, which would comprise twenty-seven boats. The R-boats went to 680 tons, had an overall length of more than 186 feet, a speed of 13.5 knots on the surface, and 10.5 knots underwater. They were, as were all modern boats, powered by diesel engines, had four torpedo tubes, and a three-inch gun for armament. They carried crews of about twenty-nine men. The word "modern" has meaning here: the R-boats were the vessels that spanned the two wars. Some of the O-boats were not scrapped until 1946, but they had been virtually moribund for a long time. When war broke out, they were "in mothballs," laid up and decommissioned. Some were put into commission and served as training boats. Some of the R-boats actually served in combat.

The First World War also saw the beginning of formalized submarine education for the men of the U.S. Fleet. When Ensign Lockwood joined the submarine force in 1914 it was simply the luck of the draw.

51

A submarine was a vessel and treated as no more by the brass. Officers and men were assigned to the "pigboats" as needed, not by preference. To some the duty was onerous; to others it was exciting. But they learned by experience, and from practitioners on the job.

By 1917 it was apparent that the submarine had become too complex for an officer or noncommissioned officer to be effective on a short tour of duty, particularly if he came from a battleship. Consequently, on January 17, 1917, the U.S. Navy submarine school was organized at the submarine base at New London, Connecticut. Lieutenant Felix Y. Gygax was the officer in charge. Actually the formal training preceded that by a few months; the men selected to run the school had to be at least a step ahead of their students, so the instructors were brought to New London in the autumn of 1916 and given a course supervised by Rear Admiral A. W. Grant, commander of the submarine flotilla of the Atlantic Fleet. The course was conducted ashore; on his flagship, the *Columbia*, and aboard submarines of the flotilla which were anchored in New London harbor.

The organization of the school came just in time to meet the need: The U.S. declared war on Germany in April, and the submarine building program was speeded enormously. During the summer of 1917 the first class of sound-listeners was organized for enlisted men. In the autumn regular classes began. Officers were taught how to dive, how to fire torpedoes, and the secrets of the complicated electrical systems in the boats. To most of them, except those who had specialized in engineering at the Naval Academy, it was an uncharted world. This special training helped, but it did not prevent accidents. In 1919 the *G-2* sank in 80 feet of water off New London when she was serving as a guinea pig for depth-charging tests. The depth charges were built better than the submarine was to withstand them; the shock opened seams, and the boat went down. Three men were drowned.

In 1920 a human error brought about a most embarrassing disaster. The *C-5* was sitting at a pier at the submarine base at Coco Solo in Panama; the electricians' mates were adding water to the batteries, using a hose that ran from a main on the dock. At the end of the day, when the crew went ashore, no one remembered to turn off the valve on the hose. The next morning, when the crew arrived at the pier, the *C-5* was sitting on the bottom.

Officers made as many mistakes as did the men. One day in 1920 the *H-1* was operating off the coast of Lower California, and the skipper gave orders to take her into Magdalena Bay. He did not check his charts closely enough. He saw that there were two entrances to Magdalena Bay—or so it seemed. Actually one was a false entrance. The *H-1* fetched up at the false entrance and was grounded. In trying to get ashore, four of the crew, including the skipper, were drowned. The fact that they were among dozens of ship's crews that had gone astray at this particular spot was of little solace to the navy; such careless accidents had to stop. There was a general tightening up of requirements and training in matters such as navigation.

But the accidents did not stop. In 1921 the *R-6* sank in thirty-two feet of water in San Pedro Harbor, while moored alongside the tender *Camden*. Someone had left the outer doors of one torpedo tube open. The R-class submarines were designed to prevent accidents and that oversight should not have caused trouble: each torpedo tube was fitted with a glass tube and trycock which indicated when there was water in the torpedo tube. Further, each torpedo tube had an interlocking mechanism designed so that when one door was open, the other had to be closed. But both mechanisms failed that day, and when the torpedoman opened the tube, a stream of water twenty-one inches in diameter began to flood into the torpedo room. There was no way in the world that the torpedoman could close that brass door, and he fled, giving the alarm, as the *R-6* settled comfortably down onto the bottom.

In 1921 the builders began delivering the new S-boats, the first American submarines to displace more than 1,000 tons. They were 211 feet long, could make 14.5 knots on the surface, and 11 knots submerged; they carried a crew of thirty-eight officers and men. They were armed with four twenty-one inch torpedo tubes and a four-inch deck gun. Some of these boats were built at navy yards and some by private builders. Simon Lake's company built several of them; one proved that errors could be made not only by mechanics and submariners, but by naval architects as well.

In Lake's design he had planned that the submerging valves of the *S-48* should be constructed to open *against* the force of the water. He reasoned that the inflowing water current would close the valves automatically if something went wrong. One of Lake's draftsmen decided this was an error and reversed the process to make the intake valves open with the current.

As the *S-48* was completed and made ready for sea, workmen swarmed around her morning and afternoon, but not at lunch. When the noon whistle blew, everyone left for his meal. One January day as they were completing the job a workman who was screwing on one of the covers dropped his tools at the sound of the whistle and went ashore to his lunchbox, as he always did. When he came back to the submarine, the foreman told him to do something else, and without thinking about it, he left the little screwing task unfinished and went on to the next one.

The *S-48* was scheduled for sea trials. Thirty-six employees of the Lake company and five representatives of the navy went aboard for the occasion. It was a festive day, and a launch accompanied the submarine to sea, off Bridgeport, Connecticut. But the launch had engine trouble and limped back to Bridgeport before they reached the test area. When they arrived, the test captain gave the order to "take her down" and the *S-48* dived. My, how she did dive! The water began to rush in from the ballast tanks to the cover left open by the careless workman, through the manhole, and into the engine room. She sank immediately, and the crew barely had time to escape into the control room and dog down the watertight door. She hit bittom at 75 feet, and hung there, with her bow inclined slightly upward. There were no witnesses. If she did not reappear in the afternoon and search parties were sent to sea, no one would know where to find her.

Fortunately the test crew included a number of old hands with Simon Lake's company. They saw that the problem was to raise the bow: the stern would never come up since that manhole was open to the sea. If the valves had been properly designed they would have closed automatically, and the stern could have been pumped out with compressed air, but not now. The crew began lightening the bow. They moved all portable equipment aft. They blew the forward ballast tanks. The bow came up, but not to the surface.

Then someone remembered a sounding device, invented by Lake, that had been built into the boat. He had designed a double-ended valve, six inches in diameter so that the upper end could be opened, the bottom one closed, and a lead dropped into the pipe. The upper valve was then closed, leaving only passage for the lead line, and the lower valve opened. Thus a sounding could be taken from the bottom of the submarine while she was underwater. The *S-48* had loaded a number of small pigs of lead for this trial, so that they would simulate the weight of a submarine prepared for duty. The crew began dropping pigs of lead through the sounding valve system, and finally dropped enough weight to bring the bow of the *S-48* above the surface. Then, one by one, the men inside the boat went out through the torpedo tubes. When the *S-48* did not reappear at the proper time search vessels did indeed come out, and they found the submarine with her bow sticking out. All hands were saved. As for the *S-48*, Simon Lake came hurrying up from New York City and supervised the salvage operation. A seagoing derrick was brought up on a barge, and it pulled the stern of the submarine out of the mud. The torpedo tubes were closed up tight to prevent her from reversing. With the stern up, the diving valves were shut, and the boat was then pumped out and taken back to her berth. She survived until 1946 when she was finally sold.

In the summer of 1921 President Warren Harding called for a conference on armaments and foreign policy to resolve a number of differences that either remained from World War I or had developed since. Four of the world powers (Great Britain, France, Italy, and Japan) were invited to Washington. Russia (whose Bolshevik government was still not accepted by the United States) and Germany, which was still regarded as a defeated enemy, were not invited. The British began to argue for a ban on military submarines. Peace groups in the United States and Britain assembled at docksides and manned launches that chased after submarines. One energetic bunch tried to scramble aboard a submarine and sabotage her conning tower so she could not dive. But such excesses got as far as they usually did, which was to land the protesters in jail and let the course of events proceed. Officially the British might have been making headway in the fight, for after World War I, there remained a residue of resentment against submarine war, even among the big powers. But the British government went too far, tried to prove that the submarine was not an effective weapon, and the argument bogged down in technicalities. The moral question was lost in the confusion.

Out of the Washington Conference came several international agreements including one to control the arms race by formal limitations on warship tonnage. But the major emphasis was on big ships—battleships and cruisers. In the end, the French refused to ratify a clause in the naval treaty that prohibited commerce raiding, so submarine control ended as only a pacifist's dream.

In the postwar years all the major powers rushed to further develop the submarine. The British, who had a real fear of German resurgence, developed an acoustic submarine detection system. It was the result of a joint Allied effort begun during the war by a group called the Allied Submarine Detection Investigation Committee, and when perfected the British called the device ASDIC. This system was far superior to the old hydrophone listening. A supersonic "ping" was emitted by the ASDIC, and this was reflected by any metal hull at ranges up to a mile (It also reacted at times to whales, wrecks, and other bits of scrap, but that was an incidental difficulty.)

One aspect of the Washington Conference brought about the U.S. Navy's decision to build much larger submarines. The powers had agreed not to build new naval bases or extend old ones in the Pacific, outside Japan. The result, as the admirals saw immediately after the conference, was to put the Pacific in Japanese hands. American fleets were constrained to use either Pearl Harbor or the Philippines bases, and none other. British fleets could not go closer to Japan than Singapore. So the answer for both powers had to be the development of long-range submarines.

5  THE S-5 DISASTER

IMMEDIATELY after the Washington Conference (1921-22), the United States Navy began looking toward a future in which large submarines would play a major role; large meant boats capable of traveling across the Pacific and waging war there. The first of these craft to be designed were the V-boats, which displaced two thousand tons, and made 21 knots on the surface. They were to be 341 feet long. The Electric Boat Company continued to build S-boats and finally delivered fifty-one of them, the last in 1925. But the navy's focus was on the fleet boats.

Submarines still had their difficulty in adjusting to the underwater environment, but not nearly as much as in the past. Of the major accidents in the 1920s, most were caused by human error, not mechanical failure. In 1926 the mishap aboard the *S-49* was mechanical; while she was warming up her diesel engines and getting ready to depart from her berth at the New London base, a bank of batteries exploded, triggered by a mechanical fault in the ventilating system, which had allowed the buildup of hydrogen. Three men died as the result of that accident and seven others were injured.

But most of the accidents were caused by foolish errors. In 1923 the *S-38* visited Alaska and while moored along the tender *Ortolan* in Anchorage Bay, she suddenly sank by the stern. The investigation showed that an eager beaver of a new hand had set about cleaning the equipment in the electric motor room. In his enthusiasm he scrubbed up everything in sight and finally came to one valve cover that was green with verdigris around the edges. He removed it to shine it up, and the water came rushing in; the cover protected a sea valve that was located well below the waterline. The *S-38* was towed in toward the beach to the shoals, the water pumped out, and the craft refloated without any damage. No one was hurt.

That same year the *O-5* was rammed by the United Fruit steamer *Abangares* in Limon Bay off the Atlantic side of the Panama Canal. She sank in less than a minute and three men were lost. But two others, trapped in the torpedo room forward were rescued after thirty-one hours, using techniques developed in a far more serious disaster, the sinking of the *S-5* in 1920.

On September 1, 1920, the new submarine *S-5* was cruising fifty miles off the Delaware Capes. Her skipper, Lieutenant Commander Charles M. Cooke, Jr., had commissioned her, seen her through the first six months of her life in the U.S. Navy. Now he was taking her down the Atlantic coast on a recruiting tour which had begun at Boston and which was to include the port cities to the south. She had been running on the surface all the way down from Boston until that morning. The first port of call was Baltimore, so Cooke had a way to go. But a submarine must train all the time, and on the morning of September 1 Skipper Cooke took her down and ran submerged for five hours. After that he had to surface to charge the batteries. Shortly after noon the batteries were up, and just before 1 P.M. the skipper ordered a crash dive, part of his training program.

When the skipper gave the word "rig for diving" every man hurried to his diving station. They knew what was coming because "Savvy" Cooke had warned them that he was going to carry out a trial required by the navy's rules for engineering performance: a four-hour, full-power run followed by a crash dive, and then a one-hour submerged test at full power on the batteries.

When a submarine submerged, it was the general practice to leave the main air induction valve open until the diesel engines had stopped turning. The diesels sucked so much air that if the supply was shut off before they stopped, they would use up the air in the boat that was meant for the men. The trick was to close that air induction valve at precisely the right moment, and it was deemed so important that the job was in the hands of the chief noncom of the boat, Chief Gunner's Mate Fox.

The air induction system of the S-5 was simple but extensive. It consisted of a sixteen-inch pipe that ran vertically down through the boat to the inside top of the inner hull, and then along the hull to the various compartments. This was how the inside of the boat "breathed"; each compartment was hooked to the system by a five-inch pipe, and all these including the main induction pipe were controlled by hand valves. Generally, there was no cause to close the five-inch valves that led into the torpedo room, battery room, control room, engine room, and motor room because closing off the main valve closed all.

But as the S-5 went down on her crash dive, Chief Fox was not at his post—he got there just as the boat slipped under water. The main induction valve had a history of sticking, and the chief carried a wrench with him when he approached it. This time he was in a hurry. He grabbed the valve with the wrench, gave a mighty twist, and the valve stuck. Sixteen inches of water began pouring into that main system, and in the five attached compartments five-inch mains began spouting water.

Chief Fox wrenched and pulled, but there was no way he could free the stuck valve, particularly against that enormous pressure. In every compartment of the boat men scrambled for the air intake valves and tried to twist them shut. But in the forward torpedo room, the valve could be reached only by standing on a torpedo, and the torpedo was covered with grease for protection. No one could get that valve closed, so the captain ordered the torpedo room abandoned, and the water-tight door to the battery room dogged down to keep the water contained.

By the time all valves were secure, the torpedo room was totally flooded; the engine room, the control room, the battery room, and the motor room had all taken tons of water. More than seventy tons had flooded the bilges in the motor room. One main electric motor was grounded out. The skipper ordered all ballast tanks blown and full power back on the remaining motor. But in spite of all that had been done, the *S-5* nosed down and stopped with a crash, her depth gauge registering 170 feet. She was on the bottom, with her stern high in the water. Then it settled down and the submarine was flat in the mud.

The predicament was clear: they had gone down so suddenly that they did not even know their precise position. Even so, at 170 feet there was no way they could communicate with the surface. They could not expect anyone to even begin searching for them for at least two days, and then finding them was a virtual impossibility. If they were to survive, the men of the *S-5* must save themselves.

The internal communication systems still worked, so Cooke had reports about conditions in the various compartments. One more attempt was made to close the main induction valve, but it was stuck tight. Cooke ordered the torpedo room blown to drive the water out, but nothing happened. He ordered the men in the motor room to try to lighten the boat by pumping the water out of the bilges. But the pumps were not designed to move water at a pressure of one hundred and fifty pounds per square inch, which they faced on the bottom. The gaskets blew and the pumps were inoperable.

Lieutenant Commander Cooke surveyed his options, and there was one. The boat rested in 183 feet of water, allowing 13 feet from keel to the deck of the control room where the depth gauge stood. The S-boat was 231 feet long. Skipper Cooke still had the after main ballast tank to work with. It was flooded, but if it was emptied of water then the stern should rise almost vertically, and stick out of the water. That way at least they might be found before they died from asphyxiation. Also, if they could once get the stern into the air, they might just be able to work their way up, and drill through the hull to get fresh air. The alternative was seventy-two hours of life before the air gave out. But they did not have that much time. The air used to try to blow out the torpedo room had cut their margin. They might have enough to last two days, no more.

Lieutenant Commander Cooke explained the problem and his solution to the men in the boat, and all agreed that it was the only way. Fortunately the battery room was intact, they still had reserve power and the lights and other equipment operated. The problem was to lighten the boat, get every bit of weight out that could be ejected, and then to try to break the suction and move the stern up. Cooke proposed to do that by reversing the one good motor, as he blew the ballast tanks. First the fuel oil was ejected, taking out some weight. Then all tanks were blown, and at the same time the motors went into full power in reverse. The depth gauge still read 170. The boat shivered, the gauge inched up, until it stood at 163. The stern came up. The suction was broken, but the boat was still heavy amidships and hung in the water. Now came the test: Cooke ordered the men to open the motor room and engine room doors, and let the water flood forward. It did, and spilled into the control room. The stern moved up a little more. Then the motor started again and this time it gained; the stern began to rise, shot up out of the water and broke the surface. Tools, equipment—everything that was not fastened down—came tumbling down, followed by the slipping, sliding men. One man fell all the way to the forward end of the battery room and was totally immersed in the water. He almost drowned before he could be fished out.

The battery room had to be evacuated immediately, because the onrush of water had hit the batteries and they were beginning to generate chlorine gas. The men were gotten out, the door secured and shut, but debris had collected in the fittings and the door could not be secured against seepage of gas. Safety now lay upward in the engine and motor rooms, and the other compartments had to be evacuated. Getting up was a mountain climber's job. The angle was seventy-five degrees; to climb up the men had to grasp anything that would hold them and haul themselves upward.

By the time the men began to move the chlorine had infiltrated the control room. Cooke ordered it evacuated, and as he passed through, the last of thirty-three men and four officers, he dogged down the door behind him. For the moment they were safe.

But they still had the major problem: How to get out of the trap that their submarine had become. They had two gallons of water for all of them and a few cases of rations that had been stored aft. But—most important—they had perhaps forty hours of air left. The hull of their submarine was three-quarters of an inch of tempered steel. Now came the ordeal.

Skipper Cooke ordered the men to find places that were as comfortable as possible and to lie quietly so they would use a minimum amount of air. The air had to be retained for those who were going to try to get them out.

The skipper then made his way up into the very tail of the boat, the tiller room, which was 18 feet long. By tapping, he estimated that about seventeen feet of the S-5 stuck out of the water. The next step was to get a hole for fresh air drilled into the tail of the boat—in the part sticking out of the water. He assembled the tools, and soon enough discovered that the only one that could possibly open the hull for them was an electric drill. But power was the problem. To get adequate power, they would have to bring a battery up from the battery room, on the other side of the control room, both of them full of chlorine gas. To do the job the man who went down would have to shut the control room door, dog it down, go into the battery room, get the battery, return, open the control room door, get out with the battery, close the door, and dog it down so that the chlorine would not kill them all. If something happened to that man enroute he was as good as dead.

The executive officer, Lieutenant Gresham, insisted on making the trip; he rigged up a makeshift mask, went in, found a battery, and reappeared safe and more or less sound. But the battery he had brought was dead. Seaman Stephen Gavin volunteered to go for another and brought a live battery back. With this they were able to drill and slowly they began to make progress against that three-quarters of an inch of steel. No man could hold the drill for long. The compartment was set and the drill shorted out. The 12-volt current went right through the drill operator, giving him muscle spasms and mild shock. But by spelling one another they kept going, and eventually (no one knew exactly how long) they made a hole through the plate into fresh air. When they struck it. Cooke was at the drill, and when he announced that now they had a chance the weary men gave a cheer.

But the tiny hole did not help the ventilation in the boat much. They continued to drill, until they had made a hole three or four inches wide, shaped like a triangle. By this time many of the men were exhausted. Through the hole, after dawn, Captain Cooke spotted a ship, but the vessel went straight on by, paying no attention to the strange object sticking up from the sea. They continued to enlarge the hole in the stern, but oh, so slowly. The electric drill broke down. The hacksaw blades they had begun to use when the hole was large enough had given out. The work went slower and slower.

By noon on September 2 the hole was five inches by six inches and it did not seem that it would get much larger because the men were exhausted.

Suddenly the man working at the hole looked out and saw a ship. He shouted. Skipper Cooke came up and looked. What they had to do was attract attention. He called for a piece of pipe and some oil rags. He would wrap the rags around the pipe, set fire to them just outside the hole and wave the pipe to make a smoke signal. But no one had a match that was dry enough to light. Seaman Joseph Youker tore off his undershirt, which was still more or less white and handed it to the skipper. Cooke tied it to the end of the pipe and thrust his distress signal through the hole and began waving. The ship was about two miles off, but she passed out of sight. They continued to work on the hole, slower and slower. There seemed very little hope if a ship that close had not paid any attention.

But at 2 P.M. the same ship was sighted again, this time only about a quarter of a mile away. Cooke thrust the pipe out again and began waving furiously. The ship was obviously looking over the strange wreck that stuck out of the water. The waving caught the attention of the men on the bridge, and the vessel came alongside. She was the *Alanthus,* an ancient cargo ship, and the only reason she had stopped was that the skipper saw this strange object, thought it was a buoy, then figured he was off course and came up to try to identify the buoy. Cooke's frantic waving of his pipe had done the rest.

The *Alanthus* was not able to offer immediate release. She had no cutting equipment aboard. Her radioman had missed the ship in the last port and no one else could run the radio. But they could be of use nonetheless. Skipper Cooke asked them to rig lines to support the stern of the S-5 so a blow could not shift her. He asked for an air hose, but the air hose leaked and did not provide any fresh air for the trapped men. He asked for fresh water, and that they got.

There was another way the *Alanthus* could help and she did. She ran up distress flags and late that afternoon she began making smoke to call attention to herself. Late in the day a ship passing by in the distance altered course, and came up. She was the steamship *George W. Goethals* of the Panama Line. She put over a boat and the chief officer, the radio operator, two doctors, and the chief engineer came alongside the sunken submarine for consultation.

The *George W. Goethals* did not have any cutting equipment, either, but she did have an operating radio, and she sent out a message to the navy to come and help. The message was picked up by a ham operator in Connecticut, and the navy began to act. They had the position and instructions to bring cutting materials. The battleship *Ohio*, which was at sea, was ordered to the scene. Two destroyers were sent up from the Norfolk Navy Base, one from New York, and another from Philadelphia. A torpedo ship came from the Brooklyn Navy Yard.

Would they arrive in time? That was the question. The men of the S-5 had been in their prison for 36 hours. Three of them had inhaled enough chlorine gas to knock them out and one had not recovered consciousness. All were short of breath and weak from the bad air. The chief engineer of the *George W. Goethals*, decided he could not wait for the navy if the men were to be saved. He began work with the tools he had: drills, ratchets, hacksaws, and a crowbar. His men were fresh, they could keep going for hours. By 10 P.M. they had enlarged the hole to a foot wide in one direction and ten inches in the other. By midnight the hole was twenty inches in diameter. By 1:45 A.M. they had made the hole large enough so that a man could come through; the survivors began to be moved out, the unconscious first, the injured next. The men were so weak it took a full hour to get them all out of the wreck. The last man out was Skipper Cooke, who secured the watertight door into the motor room before he left.

When the *Ohio* arrived, her men secured a towline to the stern of the S-5 and towed her in toward shallow water. But the weather began to kick up. The destroyer *Biddle* took the survivors off the *George W. Goethals* and headed for Philadelphia and medical help. Skipper Cooke remained with the *Ohio* to work on the salvage job. All went well, in spite of the weather and the tow began. But the wind grew stronger and the seas higher, and at a crucial point in deep water the towline parted. The *S-5* went down to the bottom. She would never rise again. Later, when salvage experts came to try to raise the boat, they found that the water was too deep for the then-current state of the art of salvage. Somewhere, about forty miles off the Delaware capes, she lies there still, the first of the S-boats to go down.

6

FROM PIGBOATS
TO FLEET BOATS

IN the middle 1920s the submarine service was changing. The U.S. Navy had begun concentrating on larger submarines, and the V-class were being built. The Portsmouth Navy Yard was taking a more active role in the building of submarines; the navy was assuming the leadership from the designer-engineers. An inventor named Herbert Grove Dorsey was developing a system of sound-ranging called sonar, which was at least as effective as the British asdic. Sonar worked by transmitting supersonic waves directed like a beam of light. The periscopes were improved enormously, and the new submarines were equipped with two of them. The first was just like the old ones, a low power 'scope that gave normal vision, for use in the old way. The other periscope was binocular and bifocal; it had range finders and could be directed to scan the sky for aircraft.

In the development of periscopes, the Americans learned from the Germans. Those six U-boats had excellent periscopes, much better than anything the Allies had developed. Their tops narrowed down to less than an inch in diameter, which made them extremely difficult to see on the surface of the sea. In the 1920s and 1930s the Americans worked on their 'scopes, trying to match the effectiveness of the German designs. The effort was to upgrade the American optical industry to the level of German optics, which then were the best in the world. It took time; the American periscopes even in the 1930s were still inferior to the German designs of 1918. But late in the 1930s, the U.S. Navy's General Board, the major policymaking body—which determined such questions as the size of submarines that should be built—agreed that submarine periscopes needed their attention, and so the long overdue changes began to come. The next problem, as happened so often, was that many of the people involved in building the old American periscopes were still active in the Bureau of Construction and Repair, and they fought change every step of the way. That change came at all was through the pushing tactics of the young submarine commanders—who had to live with the product.

The same could not be said of torpedoes. The American torpedo of the pre-World War I days was a four-cylinder machine powered by compressed air, which was produced by a flask of oxygen gas. The flask was heavy and although the torpedo made about eighteen knots, it could travel only about a thousand yards before the oxygen was exhausted. Before the United States entered World War I the need for improvement was obvious, and the Bureau of Ordnance expanded the navy's only torpedo factory at Newport, Rhode Island, and built another in Alexandria, Virginia. A new design was adopted, the Mark X, based on the British steam-driven Whitehead torpedo. It carried a warhead of 500 pounds of explosive at thirty-six knots for thirty-five hundred yards. The Virginia facility did not last long; once the war ended the politicians began complaining about defense expenditures, and the Alexandria arsenal was closed.

The problem of the torpedo was both military and political. In the years after World War I the major naval powers adopted hull armor as standard. In 1922 one battleship expert stated flatly that battleship armor was so strong that no torpedo in the world could penetrate it. Politically, all the nations but France had agreed that the submarine was to be used primarily as a warship to fight warships, and not as a commerce destroyer; even the French insisted that their refusal to sign that clause of the Washington Naval Treaty concerned wording and not the concept. So (except for the Germans, who were not a party to the treaty) the naval powers made their plans with the idea that the submarine was a fleet unit. The torpedoes designed to be carried by submarines, other warships, and aircraft were constructed with that in mind.

In 1921 a young submarine officer named Ralph Waldo Christie was assigned to take a postgraduate course in mechanical engineering at Massachusetts Institute of Technology. That year Christie went down to the Naval Gun Factory in the Washington Navy Yard for a demonstration of the Mark III torpedo. It attained ninety horsepower and was the talk of the navy yard. Christie and his fellow officer, Lt. Carlson, were instructed to explore the possibilities of increasing the oxygen content of the air flask to create long runs and more speed. They managed to increase the oxygen content to 40 percent of the whole, and later with the help of MIT and the navy research laboratory they found a way to carry oxygen in liquid form with a catalyst to evolve it into gas, which eliminated the air flask entirely. Out of this came a weapon called the "naval torpedo." It was never put into production because of technical difficulties.

The concentration instead was on something much more akin to the past. In 1928, as research officer at Newport's torpedo factory, Lieutenant Christie also witnessed the test of the Mark XI torpedo, which achieved a shaft horsepower of three hundred and fifty. For the next thirteen years the researchers concentrated on evolutionary designs—the Mark XIII for use by aircraft; the Mark XIV for submarines; and the Mark XV for surface ships. These would be the torpedoes with which the United States would enter World War II. The Mark XIV still carried a 500-pound warhead. That was a result of a controversy within the navy over submarine size and capability. Captain and later Admiral Thomas C. Hart was the most influential submarine officer in the fleet, and he favored a small boat. When others suggested that the United States should build big boats with ten torpedo tubes, he snorted in disgust: Big warships, small submarines, said Captain Hart. He lost the argument finally in the meetings of the General Board, but not before the submarine torpedo design had been finally influenced. The working torpedo would be lightweight, which meant no increase in the size of the warhead.

The designers and engineers, Ralph Christie among them, worked on other torpedoes. The electric torpedo was designed and built in 1927, but laid aside pending development of a better battery. The Newport technicians developed a patterning device, which would enable a torpedo to run in a straight path or an angular pattern—but it was put aside. A radio-controlled torpedo was built, but it was not

69

effective at less than twenty-five thousand yards so it was put aside. And as for the Mark XIV torpedo, the General Board, and not the torpedo designers, was responsible for many of its coming difficulties; the Navy's moneybags department was responsible for most of the rest of them.

In 1938 when the General Board met, the torpedo experts were almost unanimously of the opinion that the Model 1 Mark XIV torpedo should go into general manufacture. But the board decided that this torpedo, which traveled at 48 knots for six thousand yards, was not adequate for the jobs that might be faced. They insisted that the torpedo be redesigned to employ a longer range at slower speed as well. It was done. The range of the high speed was cut to forty-six hundred yards, the high speed was cut to 46 knots, and a low speed range of 31.5 knots for nine thousand yards was built in.

To go with the Mark XIV torpedo, the navy had a Mark VI exploder, the result of the long preoccupation with sinking battleships. Since the battleships were highly protected on their sides against a torpedo explosion the trick was to get beneath the battleship and hit it up where there was no armor. The germ of this idea had been found in a German device of World War I, a magnetic mine, which traded on the presence of a magnetic field surrounding any metal ship. The principle was simple: a magnetic compass was attached to a mine, and hooked to the detonator. The compass pointed north, but when a ship passed over it or very near, the needle of the compass would swing toward the ship, the movement of the needle would set off the detonator, and the mine would explode. In 1922, while still at MIT, Lieutenant Christie began working on the concept. The whole idea was shrouded in secrecy, and only a handful of people knew anything about it.

By 1924 the Newport torpedo station people were confident that they had successfully adapted the magnetic principle to a torpedo warhead. They wanted to make live tests. They suggested that some of the many big warships the United States was scrapping under the terms of the Washington Five-Power Treaty be turned over them for tests. The Bureau of Ordnance refused on grounds that live tests were not necessary. Finally in 1926 they did get an old submarine, the *L-8*, and blew it up very nicely with a magnetic warhead. But this was not a battleship. The exploder was far from perfect; one of its major defects was a mechanical and electrical relay that worked erratically. But one day, early in the 1930s, Christie went to the General Electric laboratories in Schenectady and visited Dr. Hull who was working on electromagnetism and who had built the world's only magnetometer. Christie arranged to borrow it and used it to measure the magnetic lines of the force under a large vessel in dry dock. Out of that experiment came the development of a new vacuum tube to replace the old relay system.

So heavily surrounded by secrecy was the Mark VI "influence" exploder that virtually no operating submarine officers understood it. The Mark XIV torpedoes actually had two exploders, the magnetic and the contact. In fact, the designers had anticipated that the contact exploder would be in general use, that the magnetic would be activated only when attacking a heavy warship such as a battleship or cruiser.

After months of argument, the navy finally acceded to Christie's repeated requests that large ships be made available for testing so that much better data on magnetic fields could be secured. In 1930 the navy agreed and the cruiser *Indianapolis,* and two destroyers went off on a secret mission to the Pacific off South America, where a hundred torpedo shots were fired beneath the *Indianapolis.* The torpedoes had dummy warheads, but these were hooked up with electronic devices that were supposed to register "hits." The technicians came back pleased with the results. But dummy warheads did not tell the story, and Christie at Newport kept agitating for target ships to explode. The navy would not give him one; it was a question involving the navy's budget, so no live tests of the Mark VI exploder were ever conducted before World War II. The secrecy was still complete, the fleet was issued a dummy contact exploder, the Mark V, and the Mark VIs were stored away in secret places. Furthermore, Captain Markland, the assistant chief of the Bureau of Ordnance, blocked the printing of a descriptive pamphlet that would explain to submarine captains how the new exploder worked. When the Mark VI exploders were delivered to the submarine bases late in the 1930s they were locked away in warehouses and even their existence was a secret from all but the absolutely top echelon of command. "The result of this regard for secrecy was that those who needed to know were ignorant of this new and intricate device and how to use it."*

Early in the 1920s the Americans experimented with the large submarines, based on the German "cruiser" class. These were 342 feet long and displaced two thousand tons. Three keels were laid in 1921 and construction began. Then came the Washington Conference, and the cutback in the U.S. Navy which reflected a national antipathy to war and congressional demand for cuts in military spending. Soon the navy shrank to seven thousand officers and one hundred thousand men, and the V-boats were outmoded before they were launched.

Submarines were still having their troubles. The British, who ended the war with a raft of E-boats, found that they were too small for the fleet and planned an M-boat which at three thousand tons was the largest submarine in the world. It did not last long in service. Every country's submarine service continued to suffer accidents, largely because the state of the art was still ragged.

On September 25, 1925, the U.S. submarine *S-51* left the New London base for sea exercises. She carried her regular crew and four student officers from the New London base who came along as part of their training. The skipper was Lieutenant Rodney H. Dobson. That first night, while moving on the surface off Block Island, the *S-51* was struck by the steamer *City of Rome*. It was a mighty blow, a hole thirty inches wide was ripped in her hull on the port side, just behind the conning tower. The steamer than ran over the submarine, forcing her underwater, and the *S-51* sank in less than a minute. The accident happened so quickly the crewmen were unable to close the watertight doors, so the water rushed through the whole boat. Three men who were asleep in the battery room managed to get up through the conning tower hatch and were rescued. Seven other men were seen in the water by these three, but the *City of Rome* did not pick up any of the others. When the captain of the *City of Rome* reported the position of the accident, he was several miles in error (which probably

---

*Admiral Christie to author, 1982

accounted for the collision). But when the navy sent help, the oil slick and a stream of bubbles showed the location. She was in the open sea, in 152 feet of water, fourteen miles east of Block Island. Divers went down, but there were no signs of life. Six officers and twenty-seven enlisted men had been killed in moments.

The *S-51* was salvaged, although the effort took many months and turned out to be little more than an exercise for the salvage crews. She was towed to the Brooklyn Navy Yard, but it was not long before she was scrapped. But Captain Ernest J. King, the officer in charge of the salvage effort, learned a good deal in the operation. Unfortunately, two years later, King had the opportunity to put his knowledge to use again, in the salvage of another submarine—the *S-4*.

On December 17, 1927, the *S-4* was conducting training exercises off the tip of Cape Cod. Just as she emerged from a run between two buoys that marked a measured mile, the U.S. Coast Guard cutter *Paulding* came running down from a patrol off Cape Cod. She was particularly busy this Christmas season trying to intercept rum-runners who brought their cargoes up from Cuba or down from Canada and met bootleggers who came out in small boats to pick up the precious but illegal cargo.

The skipper of the *Paulding* seemed to know precisely where he was and he was keeping clear of the measured-mile course that the submarines used. A coast guardsman at the Provincetown station sighted the cutter rounding Race Point Light and heading southeast at high speed. She was going somewhere in a hurry, making eighteen knots. As two coast guardsmen watched, the cutter suddenly changed course near a fishing vessel and turned sharply to the east. The pair watched and saw the feather wake of a periscope ahead of the *Paulding* and then saw the *Paulding* bear down on it. It was just after 3:30 in the afternoon that the *Paulding* ran over the *S-4* plowing into her starboard beam. The submarine went down like an enormous stone. The *Paulding* stopped and lowered lifeboats. But all that came up was an oil trickle and air bubbles.

Most of the officers and crew were amidships or aft in the submarine, but Lieutenant (jg.) Graham Fitch and five torpedomen were forward in the torpedo room. When the crash occurred and the boat started going down, water came pouring into the battery room. The water rushed in, and soon lapped over the coaming of the bulkhead between the battery room and the torpedo room. It was coming so fast that Lieutenant Fitch did the only thing possible. He slammed the watertight door and dogged it down. Aft, Lieutenant Commander Roy K. Jones, the skipper, and thirty-three men managed to escape the flooding control room and find protection behind the watertight doors that protected the engine room and motor room from the two flooded compartments amidships.

The *Paulding* sent a radio message to the navy immediately but it was late that night before divers arrived at Provincetown and then they had to wait for the salvage vessel *Falcon*, the only salvage ship on the Atlantic seaboard at that time. Seamen in a surfboat went out to the area and began grappling in an attempt to locate the hull of the *S-4*. At 10:45 A.M. on December 18 they found it. It was nearly 2 P.M. on that second day before a diver went down to the hull of the submarine. He moved around the vessel and found six men alive in the torpedo room—ascertained by tapping out Morse code. He moved aft where most of the men should have been. He tapped; there was no response. The diver returned to the surface with this information for Captain Ernest King and Admiral Brumby who were responsible for the operation. They decided to blow the ballast tanks and try to raise the submarine. But they soon discovered that the main ballast tanks had been ruptured by the collision and would not hold air. Another diver went down with an air hose, but he fouled it on the wreckage and then blacked out in his efforts to free it. More precious time had been lost.

By the time another diver freed the first one and got him back to the salvage ship it was nearly morning. The weather roughed up and the *Falcon* had to cast loose from the submarine. She took that opportunity to run the sixty miles to Boston to deliver the stricken diver to a hospital. She was back on the submarine position that afternoon. The men in the torpedo compartment of the *S-4* were still alive, but growing weaker; but they were still alive forty-eight hours after the sinking. The question was: Would the storm lift in time so that they could be rescued?

The men aboard the *Falcon* used listening devices to catch the pounding on the hull by Fitch and his men. They responded by sending pinging signals by, and Fitch was able to catch those. There was still hope. Then the high pressure forced a leak in the glass of the observation port in the top of the torpedo compartment; as a result, in a few hours, Fitch reported eighteen inches of water in the torpedo room. The storm renewed itself and work on the surface became impossible. Then the air ran out and it was all over for the forty officers and men of the *S-4*. After remarkable performances of skill and perseverance by many men, and especially by Commander Edward Ellsberg, the salvage expert and diver, the *S-4* was finally raised on March 17, 1928. So much national attention had been focused on the tragedy, because press and public knew that some of the men down there had lived for days after the sinking, that the normal inertia of the military mind to new ideas was swept aside. A full investigation of the sinking proved something the submarine department should have known long before—that the safety devices in submarines were totally inadequate: For example it was not enough to have oxygen; a soda lime solution had to be used, too, to filter out the carbon dioxide. The problem was understood, but had never been addressed by the authorities. Lieutenant Commander Jones and his control room crew had been forced to abandon the control room because a green baize curtain had been sucked into the ventilation duct for that compartment, jamming the valve so it could not be closed and letting the water flood the control room. Once that compartment was abandoned, Skipper Jones had no control of the boat. These and other deficiencies came to light in a series of tests on the repaired *S-4* during the next few months. Why were the tests not made earlier? For the same reason that torpedoes were not tested by exploding them against proper targets: expense. Congress had cut the navy's budget to the bone in the postwar years and the admirals "made do." Actually they did not make do at all, but convinced themselves that they had, and therein lay the worst of the difficulties: the inertia factor.

Out of the wreckage of the *S-4* came a new appreciation of safety and a new understanding of what must be done to make it possible to save men who were trapped in submarines beneath the sea. One of the

75

prime movers in all this was Lieutenant C. B. (Swede) Momsen of the Bureau of Construction and Repair. He and Chief Gunner C. L. Tibbals and diver Frank Hobson developed an escape compartment that would make it possible for submariners to get out of a sunken submarine and survive the pressures of doing so. Momsen and diver Edward Kalienewski proved that it was possible to come up, using the lung, from a depth of two hundred feet. So much attention had been brought to bear on the S-4 tragedy that high honors were awarded. Momsen and Chief Gunner Tibbals were each awarded the Distinguished Service Cross for developing the lung. Chief Gunner's Mate Thomas Eadie was awarded the congressional Medal of Honor for first going down and finding the S-4; and then for saving diver Fred Michels when he became entangled in the wreckage while trying to get air to the still-living men of the S-4.

As far as the public was concerned, submarines came to their attention only when they got into trouble in those years after World War I. There were plenty of tragedies worldwide: The Japanese lost the big I-63 in deep water just off the home islands and there was no hope of saving the men or the boat; the British lost the Thetis in the Irish Sea; the French lost the Phénix off Indochina; and on May 23, 1939, the Americans suffered still another submarine disaster.

The new fleet submarine Squalus was cruising off Portsmouth, New Hampshire, undergoing some of the testing she needed as the newest boat in the American fleet. Lieutenant Oliver F. Naquin was in command and he had a crew of fifty-eight officers and men. Fifteen miles off the Portsmouth Navy Yard, Lieutenant Naquin gave the order to dive, and the boat began to submerge as the men carried out their special duties. Civilian engineers were along, checking the timing on various maneuvers. In the control room Machinist's Mate Second Class Alfred G. Prien was watching the "Christmas tree," a board that was so named because it consisted of red and green lights. When all systems were working properly the red and green lights showed which valves were open and which closed. The red lights meant *open*, and of course in diving they meant danger. But as Prien shut the valves that kept the water out he saw the lights changing to green and all was well; he reported all valves closed. The boat continued down. The bridge began to go under and then at thirty-five feet the tops of the main induction valves touched water. Five feet more and the bridge was under water. All this happened in seconds. The submarine hit fifty feet, and then from the engine room came the cry that water was flooding in.

In the control room Skipper Naquin heard and responded.

"Blow all ballast," he ordered. From the engine room came another call over the squawk box, or internal communications system. The main induction valves were still open, no matter what was indicated on the "Christmas tree." The air came hissing into the compartments, and the *Squalus* responded drunkenly: She lost her horizontal trim, the bow went up 20 degrees with a snap, and the weights within the boat teetered. In the forward torpedo room (these new fleet-class boats had torpedo rooms fore and aft) a new safety device, the forward bulkhead guard, automatically closed off the room from the rest of the boat. The torpedomen here immediately felt the change; the boat sprang upward until the bow was pointing up at forty degrees. Wrenches and other tools jumped out of their places and went skidding along the deck. Crewmen slid and fell down toward the transverse bulkhead that separated the torpedo room from the next compartment.

In the control room, Electrician's Mate Lloyd Maness started to shut the watertight door that separated the control room from the engine room. But the men in the engine room, where the water was streaming in through the open valve, cried out for him to leave it open, and they began clawing their way to get through that door. Four men made it, as the submarine's bow inclined ever upward. The door, which weighed two hundred pounds, swung back into the engine room. As the angle increased, so did the difficulty of closing that door. After those four men had come through, Maness tried to close the door but it was too heavy for him. The angle was all wrong; it would not close.

Maness could see the water pouring into the engine room and lapping upward toward the control room. One last man, Pharmacist's Mate First Class Raymond O'Hara managed to get through the door, half swimming to make it. And then, as the *Squalus* lost forward momentum and began to slide back down toward the bottom, Maness was able to slam the recalcitrant door shut and dog it down—cutting off the engine room compartment and the back of the boat—thereby preserving the integrity of the control room.

The boat slipped downward. At 242 feet the stern plunged into the marl of the bottom. The bow settled and finally stopped at an upward angle of twelve degrees.

Almost immediately a new complication developed. In the forward battery room, just ahead of the control room, two cables had come loose from the batteries and struck each other. A puff of smoke went up and sparks flew. Chief Electrician's Mate Lawrence Gainor rushed to the emergency switch and pulled it. The short circuiting stopped, but in a moment the lights flickered and went out. The emergency system was still intact, giving an eerie yellow-green glow. But as more sea water reached the batteries, the emergency lights flickered, then went out. The boat was in darkness.

It was not quite nine o'clock in the morning. Since the *S-4* disaster, a new system of communications had been put into effect in the submarine service. When a boat dived for tests, the skipper sent a message giving position and a prospective time for further communication. At 8:40 A.M. the *Squalus* had radioed that it was diving for an hour. That was the last message received at the Portsmouth Navy Yard Operations Office.

When the hour went by, the radiomen began to listen for a new message. When it had not come by the end of two hours they became concerned, and the operations officer was notified. These tests had been planned carefully and something seemed to be going wrong.

By 11:20 A.M. the base radio station was transmitting an almost-constant signal to the *Squalus.* There was no answer.

Rear Admiral C. W. Cole, the commandant of the Portsmouth Navy Yard, ordered the *Squalus*'s sister ship *Sculpin* into action. She set out for the last known position of the other submarine. What worried Admiral Cole was a half-forgotten report made a few days earlier that the air intake valve on the main induction had failed to open. It had been rebuilt but that fact still nagged the admiral when he thought about it.

Aboard the sunken submarine, the power failure had severely limited the courses of action open to Skipper Naquin and his men. The one source of light was a battery-operated hand lamp. Naquin checked the intercom; it was as dead as the lights. He rapped on the forward battery room door and heard an answer. He opened the door, and found that the battery room and the forward torpedo room were relatively sound, although the acrid smell of smoke from the short circuits still hung in the former. He ordered the release of one of the new safety devices developed after the sinking of the *S-4* —a rescue phone buoy. These buoys were located in deck compartments fore and aft, and could be released from inside the boat. The buoy went up, released a red dye which colored the surface for some distance, and then floated high enough so that the bright yellow of the buoy was easily visible to rescuers. Once the rescuers arrived on the scene, they could use the self-powered telephone to talk to the men in the submarine. They would even know which part of the submarine had sent up the buoy; the two were marked "*Squalus*-bow buoy" and "*Squalus*-stern buoy."

Having done that, Skipper Naquin brought all the men out of the forward battery compartment and secured the door, because he feared that the battery room might begin producing chlorine gas. He tried the engine room door, but there was no response to his tapping. The men who had escaped suggested that at the rate the water was entering it would be full from top to bottom. He asked O'Hara, the last man out, if he knew whether or not the men aft had managed to dog down the door in the after torpedo room. O'Hara said he did not know.

Usually the interior of a submarine was warm, even hot, no matter what the temperature of the water was. The moving machinery, the lights, the galley stove all tended to create excess heat, to say nothing of the body heat of the men. But now, with all lights out, and all power gone, the submarine grew cold, even though on the surface it was a warm May day. In the submarine the temperature was 34 degrees Fahrenheit. The cold was a problem but at least they had plenty of air, another gift from the ghost of the *S-4*. The *Squalus* carried a supply of the soda-lime compound that neutralized the carbon dioxide in their atmosphere. They had enough oxygen to

79

provide air for four days. They also had a Momsen lung for each man, and the boat's compartments were equipped with emergency air connections—which meant rescuers would be able to pump air into the boat without difficulty.

They settled down to wait. Skipper Naquin counted noses. There were thirty-three officers and men in the forward compartments. That left twenty-six people aft, about whose fate they were uncertain.

On the surface the *Sculpin* reached the area and adopted a spiral approach, making a wide general sweep and circling in. Finally a lookout spotted the red smudge of dye and then the yellow buoy with its telephone. The *Sculpin* came alongside and snagged the buoy. In a moment Captain Warren D. Wilkin was talking to Lieutenant John Nichols in the forward torpedo room of the sunken vessel. Skipper Naquin came forward and took the telephone.

Naquin gave Captain Wilkin what information he could about the sinking, the condition of the engine room, and the problem in the battery room. He could not say much about the situation aft, except that the engine room had been the source of flooding. As for the condition of the men, he did not know. It was ominous, too, that only one telephone had come up to the surface.

As they were talking, a rolling sea caught the *Sculpin* and moved her abeam. The telephone line was three hundred and fifty feet long, but it may have been snagged on the sunken submarine. The connection went dead without notice. The line had snapped. That rescue device needed to go back to the drawing board.

Captain Wilkin was able to send a sensible message back to base, however. He gave the exact position, and the depth and heading of the sunken submarine. He described the cause of the accident and said that Skipper Naquin suggested the rescuers close the induction line and then hook up air lines to the flooded compartments and blow them, moving the water out, Wilkin also radioed that he was anchoring over the *Squalus* position and would await instructions from the base.

Again the salvage vessel *Falcon* came out to the site of the wreck but this time she had a new weapon against the sea, another result of the

S-4 sinking: A rescue chamber invented by Allen R. McCann, who had participated in the effort to save the men of the *S-4*. But the parting of the telephone cable had cost the *Sculpin* her link with the *Squalus* and Captain Wilkin had to find her again. Contact was regained at 10 o'clock that night when Signalman Ted Jacobs's tapping on the *Squalus*'s hull was picked up by the *Sculpin* and she returned a Morse message with pinging. By six o'clock in the morning the *Falcon* had dropped four anchors over the *Squalus* and was holding her position.

Four hours later, diver Martin Sibitsky was on his way down. By good luck, the grappling line on which he went down had snagged on the foredeck of the *Squalus* within six feet of the forward hatch. He could hear the survivors below him tapping on the hull. Sibitsky then attached a cable by shackle to the center ring of the hatch cover. Before 11:30 A.M. he was back on the surface and the nine-ton rescue chamber was on its way down, carrying Chief Machinist's Mate William Badders and Torpedoman First Class John Mihalowski. At 12:10 the rescue chamber landed over the hatch.

After that the lower chamber of the rescue device was fitted tightly around the hatch, water kept out by bolts and a gasket. The time went by. It was one o'clock that afternoon when the men in the submarine saw the forward hatch cover begin to turn slowly. With a hiss the hatch opened and the men below could see up into the rescue chamber. Six men and one officer were sent up. Blankets, sandwiches, and soup were lowered to the men below. The hatch closed and the twenty-six men in the forward compartments waited. It was 1:20 in the afternoon.

Two more times that afternoon the chamber went down, and brought back nine men each time. Down below, Lieutenant Naquin, Lieutenant Doyle, the diving officer, and six enlisted men remained, waiting. No one knew how many men might be waiting aft.

At 8:30 that night the chamber came down and picked up the last men from the forward compartments. The chamber frustrated everyone this time: it became stuck at one hundred and fifty feet, hanging between surface and bottom, and was immobile for four hours before divers freed the chamber and it was hauled up.

It took most of the next day to repair the chamber and its cable. At 6 P.M. on May 25 the operators, Badders and Mihalowski, went down again. They attached the chamber to the after hatch, and opened it. There was nothing in the darkness below but water, sloshing over the hatch top. Every man aft had perished.

As for the *Squalus,* she was salvaged, repaired, given the new name *Sailfish,* and sent off to join the Asiatic Fleet at Manila in October 1941. She arrived just in time to bolster Admiral Thomas Hart's slender force against a growing threat from Japan.

our of the A-boats in the locks at the anama Canal. One night someone left a alve open and the next day all four boats ere sitting on the bottom in thirty feet f water.

LOST SUBMARINE AT LAST LOCATED

F-4 Lies at Bottom of Mouth of Honolulu Harbor; No Hope for Crew

WASHINGTON, March 29.—Searchers for the lost submarine, F-4, reported late today that they had determined the location of the vessel within a radius of fifty yards, and that she lay at the bottom of the mouth of Honolulu harbor in water ranging from forty-three to sixty fathoms in depth.

Rear-Admiral Moore, at Honolulu, cabled to Secretary Daniels the following received by wireless from Lieutenant Smith, commanding the searching fleet:

"We know location within radius of fifty yards; depth varies from forty-three to sixty fathoms. Honolulu harbor light bearing 24 degrees, true distance 2800 yards."

HOPE FOR CREW ABANDONED.

The last remote hope that any of the submarine F-4's crew might be alive has been abandoned by the Navy Department, and today Acting Secretary Blue ordered Rear-Admiral Moore, commanding the Honolulu naval station, to report the exact location of the sunken boat and the depth at which she lies, that the Navy Department may estimate the probability of salvaging the hull and recovering the bodies of her commander and crew.

CLOSE TO HARBOR ENTRANCE.

HONOLULU, March 29.—Vessels searching for the missing United States submarine F-4 again have recommenced sweeping the ocean floor with cables.

Naval officials declare their confidence in their theory that the F-4 is submerged close to the harbor entrance. They base their opinion largely on the reports of fuel oil seen on the surface of the sea, on the stream of air bubbles rising to the surface, and also on the recovery of a piece of brasswork brought up by the line from the tug Navajo. This piece of brass has been identified by the naval authorities as from the F-4.

Naval officials say they have abandoned hope of rescuing the twenty-one men aboard the submarine. They say their work is one of recovering the bodies and getting what salvage there may be in the vessel, which they apparently believe is wrecked.

DIVING-BELL TO AID.

The diving-bell being built under the supervision of W. C. Parks, a civil engineer, is expected to aid in the finding of the F-4. The bell is a fifty-four-inch iron pipe, seven feet in length, fitted with glass portholes. It is planned to lower this diving bell with an observer inside connected by telephone with the vessel above. The bell will be moved as directed by the man below until the submarine is found. The observer will then direct the placing of the hoisting cables.

AGRAZ A DARING DIVER.

SAN JOSE, March 29.—Jack Agraz, who set a new world's record for deep-sea diving of 215 feet, off Honolulu harbor, in searching for the F-4, is a San Jose man and brother of Emil Agraz, chief of the Santa Clara county motor police squad.

Since boyhood Agraz has had a reputation as a swimmer and diver. He is a gunner's mate on the U. S. submarine F-1.

Agraz went down unprotected from the weight of the water, except for a girdle and a helmet. This system of diving was developed by himself. Other divers have failed to adopt the plan.

When the huge dry dock Dewey sunk at Manila, Agraz worked eight hours a day seventy feet under water, in the task of raising it. On one occasion he was in a compartment from which the water was being pumped, when the suction drew him up into the mouth of the pipe. He spread out his arms and was able to resist the current, but his helmet was drawn off. Another diver managed to seize it and thrust it on over Agraz's head, and he continued to work. Coming up after the day's work was done, he seemed to think the experience was nothing remarkable, and only said, "I had a sort of close call, didn't I?"

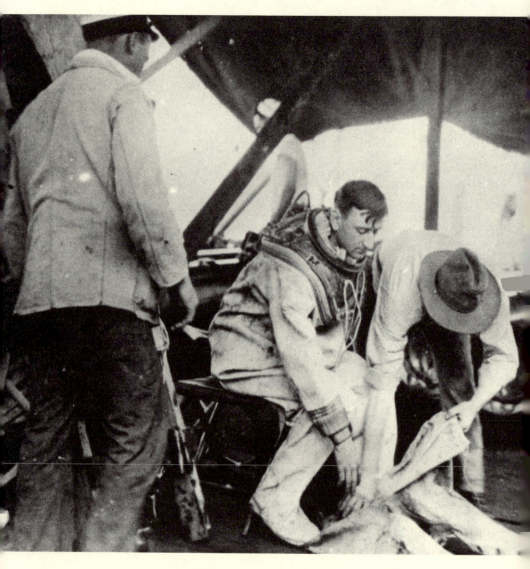

In diving for the *F-4*, William Loughman was stuck at 250 feet.

At the end of World War I, Lieutenant Commander Charles A. Lockwood, Jr., was assigned as executive officer of the *UC-97*, to bring the German submarine back to America for tests and for exhibition in the bond drive of 1919.

One of the early flying boats comes up alongside this World War I submarine at Pearl Harbor (Ford Island is in the background), and Navy Secretary Denby boards the boat. The year is 1922.

The old Far Eastern Fleet. Note the Mark X torpedo being loaded through deck hatch of submarine.

Four R-boats in the Brooklyn Navy Yard.

After many days of work, the pontoons did the job, and the USS *Squalus* came up from the sea.

S-boats rafted alongside a tender.

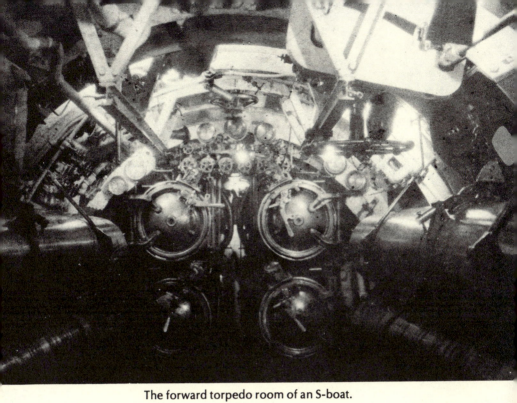

The forward torpedo room of an S-boat.

The USS *Bonita* (SS-165) during new commissioning ceremony at New London, Connecticut.

One of the V-boats, the USS *Dolphin* (SS-169). This photo was taken during one of the periods before World War II when a deck gun was regarded as unnecessary.

SUBMARINE SQ. 5
U.S. ASIATIC FLEET 1940
U.S.S. CANOPUS

U.S.S. S-36
U.S.S. S-37
U.S.S. S-38
U.S.S. S-39
U.S.S. S-40
U.S.S. S-41

U.S.S. PORPOISE
U.S.S. PIKE
U.S.S. TARPON
U.S.S. PERCH
U.S.S. PICKEREL
U.S.S. PERMIT

7

THE CLOUDS
OF WAR

DURING World War II, the Allies and the Rome-Berlin-Tokyo Axis fought the war beneath the sea in three theaters and the U.S. Navy was active in two of them: The Pacific and the Atlantic. Only in the Mediterranean was the American naval—and submarine— presence no more than incidental. The invasion of North Africa brought American surface ships into the battle around that continent, but the American submarines were not needed; the British boats won that phase of the war hands down.

Adolf Hitler had foreseen his war with England, but he had not wanted it to turn out like the First World War of 1914-18. His attention to the German navy had been less than thorough since his ideas of strategy were entirely different from those of the leaders of Imperial Germany. He never came to share the kaiser's preoccupation with the British fleet and the seven seas. His directives in preparing for war ordered the submarine fleet to concentrate its efforts against British warships and to refrain from attacks on merchant shipping. He remembered that a major reason for the American entrance into World War I had been the U-boat sinking of the liner *Lusitania,* and he wanted to avoid annoying the Americans. But on the first day of the war that began in September 1939, one of Hitler's U-boat captains sank the liner *Athenia* with the loss of one hundred and twelve lives, including those of twenty-eight Americans. Hitler was furious and ordered an end to attacks on merchant ships. For the next few weeks the German U-boat fleet concentrated on British warships and sank a number of them.

83

In the fall of 1939 and the early months of 1940 Hitler had another end in view. He fully expected to march through the continent of Europe, and then, once France fell, to negotiate a peace with England that would guarantee him the fruits of his victory. But when France fell, Winston Churchill had just assumed power as prime minister of England, and he announced that Britain would fight to the last man to destroy Hitler and nazism.

Hitler's velvet glove came off. With the fall of France the Atlantic ports from the North Cape to the Bay of Biscay were opened to the U-boats, which put them two days closer to the mid-Atlantic than the old German bases. Focke-Wulf Condor-200 reconnaissance bombers, earning their title of the "Scourge of the Atlantic," began operating from French bases. They could find British convoys in mid-sea and direct German naval units to them. The U-boats began the war of attrition that was intended to bring Britain to its knees—and which very nearly succeeded.

Shortly after Germany invaded Poland and World War II began, the United States declared its neutrality, and the U.S. Navy was given the task of maintaining a "neutrality patrol." Less than a year later American involvement began on the side of the British. A Caribbean Naval District was established under Rear Admiral Raymond A. Spruance, and American submarines began patrolling the Virgin Passage from a base at St. Thomas in the Virgin Islands. In September 1940, after the American merchant ship *Steel Seafarer* was sunk by the Germans in the Red Sea, President Roosevelt ordered the navy to "shoot on sight" when confronting German warships or planes and to ask questions later. The American submarine service was really at war from that point on. Early in 1941 Rear Admiral Richard S. Edwards was made commander of submarines, Atlantic Fleet, and in February he organized for war. His command consisted of the two new coastal submarines *Mackerel* and *Marlin* and a flock of old boats, going back to the C-class which had gone into operation in World War I. The only really operational boats were those of the S-class. A good share of Edwards's boats had to be reserved for the protection of the Panama Canal.

Many plans were laid for American submarine participation in the

Battle of the Atlantic, but the first action came in the fall of 1941 when five submarines of Squadron Five plus the experimental *Mackerel* were assigned to Argentia, Newfoundland to establish an antisubmarine patrol. This dispatch of submarines to a foreign port for military purposes was a warlike act; but it was one of many warlike acts taken after the torpedoing of the U.S. destroyer *Kearny* which cost eleven American lives and the sinking of the USS *Reuben James.* Most Americans did not know it but after September 1940, the United States was a belligerent in the war against Germany.

Admiral Edwards accompanied the ships to Argentia, which gave an indication of the degree of official sanction of the move, but neither the navy nor President Roosevelt could quite bring themselves to send American submarines out to sink German submarines. It was one thing to protect cargo ships in waters off the American shores and even halfway out into the Atlantic Ocean. It was another matter to set out to deliberately sink warships with warships. No patrols were actually made.

In the spring of 1941 the navy acquired Ordnance Island in St. George's Harbor, Bermuda, for use as a submarine base; it was done under the terms of the Lend-Lease Act of 1941 in which fifty overage American destroyers were traded to Britain. In June, U.S. submarines began regular patrols in the Atlantic and Caribbean close to the American shores. But the first American contact with a U-boat came after the Japanese had attacked Pearl Harbor. A submarine patrol line was established from Nantucket Light to Bermuda and submarines were detailed to sections of this line. On February 10, Lieutenant Dudley W. Morton sighted a submarine on the surface in his patrol area. His crew fired four torpedoes at the U-boat, but all of them missed. While he was reloading (his *R-4* was equipped only with four torpedo tubes) the enemy boat submerged and moved out of range.

Lieutenant James D. Grant's *R-1* had the next meeting with a U-boat one day in April. He ordered one torpedo fired, saw an explosion, and heard what he said were breaking-up noises; the U-boat disappeared. But there is no evidence from German sources that it was sunk.

The *R-5* saw a U-boat but was not close enough to attack. The *R-7* fired four torpedoes at another, but missed each time. Again the U-boat escaped during the reload, proof if anyone needed it that Mark X torpedoes and four torpedo tubes were not enough.

The reason for the misses was probably not only mechanical. These were the first torpedoes fired by the young skippers with the intention of sinking ships. The Germans had been at the war business for almost two years, and on the other side of the world the Japanese had been fighting more or less steadily since 1931. The Americans were very new at warfare, and in the peacetime years the level of training had been geared to a minimal budget and an enormous dependence on the two oceans as the United States line of defense. American sailors were not well-geared to combat and it would be nearly a year before matters improved a great deal. As Vice Admiral Ralph Christie, the torpedo expert, put it: "The torpedo fired is a flown bird. It is no longer available for inspection, unlike, say, the engines of the Torpedo Data Computer. But it is always blamed for failures, overlooking other probable causes . . ." (which were human error).

The experimental submarine *Mackerel*, which had both bow and stern torpedo tubes, encountered a U-boat on the night of April 14 that fired first—but missed. The next morning the *Mackerel* fired two torpedoes from her stern tubes—and missed! The following day Lt. Commander J. F. Davidson sighted a U-boat, probably the same one, and he fired, and missed. The *S-17* encountered two U-boats while patrolling off Panama, and played underwater tag with one of them. At one point the U-boat apparently fired a torpedo, because the men of the *S-17* swore it came alongside, but if it was fired it missed.

But in all, there were few American submarines operating in the Atlantic during World War II. The problem was not German merchant shipping, or even German surface warships, but German U-boats; American destroyers, destroyer escorts, and aircraft were far more adaptable to combatting this menace than were U.S. submarines. Besides, the American submarines were all badly needed in the Pacific, where Japanese merchant shipping and Japanese warships were the problem.

That American emphasis on the Pacific had not been the desire of the British. At the time that Admiral Edwards assumed overall command of submarines in the Atlantic Fleet and escorted that force up to Newfoundland, grand plans were afoot for American participation in the Atlantic war. Captain Ralph Christie had just been appointed tactical commander of submarines, Atlantic Fleet. Captain Charles Lockwood was serving as naval attaché in London and agitating for more submarines to get into the European fight (even before the war began for the United States). But Admiral Thomas C. Hart, who had taken over as commander of the Asiatic Fleet had to have reinforcements in Manila, and all the navy had to send him was submarines. This deprived the Atlantic Fleet of the use of the boats, much to Churchill's displeasure. Roosevelt tried to make it up to him by giving the British the use of half a dozen S-boats for the duration. Those S-boats were early models and not very useful for antisubmarine patrol, but by having them the British were able to free several of their more modern submarines for work more important than coastal patrol.

In the summer of 1942 Admiral Christie had been sent to the Southwest Pacific with the best of the S-boats to begin an effort there to counter the Japanese expansion southward. That move deprived the Atlantic Fleet even further. Churchill insisted that the U.S. submarines must participate in the Atlantic war, and although Admiral King was opposed to the decision, President Roosevelt overruled him and sent six new fleet-class submarines to operate from a base at Roseneath, Scotland. In fact, those particular boats were not a great loss to the Pacific war effort, as it turned out, because they were equipped with Hooven-Owens-Rentschler (H.O.R.) engines, which the submariners soon came to call "whores," which, from examination of the record, seems to be a libel on the ladies of the evening. The H.O.R. engines were unreliable, unwilling, and constantly broke down in service. In the planning for the invasion of North Africa in 1942, a squadron of six U.S. submarines was allocated to the naval effort; all of these boats were equipped with H.O.R. engines and only five of them completed the voyage. Later, the *Gunnel* broke down a thousand miles from the Roseneath base. All four main engines broke down and the *Gunnel* had to make port on a small auxiliary engine. Skipper Charles Herbert Andrews in the *Gurnard* managed to complete an Atlantic patrol with those H.O.R. engines, but only by never using more than three of them at once, and never at full power. Even so, two of the engines broke down and he had to cut short the patrol.

The H.O.R.-engined boats all had to go home for extensive repairs and eventually for replacement of the faulty engines. Their design, the result of a necessary speedup in diesel engine production for naval vessels, was quietly scrapped in favor of more reliable diesels. The American submarines in the Atlantic Fleet did not distinguish themselves although they made a number of war patrols. In the middle of 1943 all U.S. submarines were withdrawn from the Atlantic Fleet and sent to the Pacific theater where they were needed badly. They had not sunk a single Axis vessel or a U-boat.

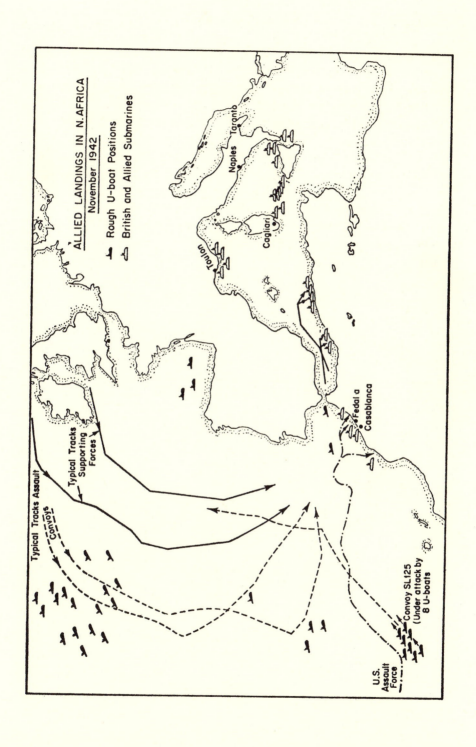

ALLIED LANDINGS IN N. AFRICA
November 1942

⊢ Rough U-boat Positions
↰ British and Allied Submarines

Taranto

Naples

Cagliari

Toulon

Fedal a
Casablanca

Typical Tracks Assault

Typical Tracks
Supporting
Forces

Convoys

Convoy SL125
(Under attack by
8 U-boats)

U.S.
Assault
Force

8  MAKEY-LEARN

THE Japanese began their conquest of Southeast Asia in 1941 with some strange ideas, based on misinformation from their intelligence services, and on a highly developed sense of racial superiority that the militarist hierarchy in Japanese politics had fomented since the 1920s.

The intelligence errors consisted first of all of factual mistakes. The Japanese did not realize that the American fleet-class submarine developed in the 1930s was nearly as effective in terms of range and armament as their own I-boats, which could cross the Pacific Ocean from Japan, cruise along the American coast on patrol, and return to Japan without touching any base.

During the years between the wars one of the most persistent critics of American submarine design was Commander Charles A. Lockwood, who had served in all sorts of boats under all conditions. As commander of Submarine Division No. 13 in 1936, Lockwood was unrelenting in his attack on the H.O.R. engine. He wanted six forward torpedo tubes and four aft. He wanted a deck gun of at least five inches. He wanted better and longer periscopes, better radio, better sonar, better torpedo data computers (TDC), and more speed. Time after time fleet exercises proved that the American submarines were not up to the American destroyers; the destroyers hunted down and "sank" the submarines with such regularity that the commander of one destroyer division claimed his unit could find and eliminate 70 percent of all submarines that came within his range. Submarine commanders were criticized, and sometimes careers were ruined, if they were "caught" during maneuvers. The way not to get caught was to be very cautious, and never stick one's neck out. That became the standard operating method for peacetime submarine commanders.

Late in the 1930s, Commander Lockwood's pleas were heard and the U.S. Navy began building submarines more to his liking. The *Tambor*-class vessels were 310 feet long and displaced 1,500 tons. They were powered by General Motors Winton engines, carried the ten torpedo tubes that Lockwood wanted, as well as twenty-four torpedoes. They had the new TDC; the five-inch gun; the longer, thinner periscope; and some other improvements. They could make around twenty knots under some circumstances on the surface, although usually their effective speed was several knots less. In 1938 Admiral Thomas Hart, who had been through the whole submarine command, was named chairman of the navy's General Board, and he did all he could to scuttle the fleet-class submarine concept (which would have prolonged the war for years, had he been successful). Lockwood and several other young submarine officers who were abreast of the times (Hart was then sixty years old and no longer used to listening), managed to save the fleet-class building program, although they lost the five-inch gun, which would not return until well into the war.

The infighting caused the navy to go slow on the submarine building program, so that by mid-November 1941 there were not nearly enough submarines to go around; and, as of 1938, there was still only one source of torpedoes for the submarines, the navy factory at Newport, where they were virtually handcrafted. In 1938 Commander Christie managed to secure the reopening of the old Alexandria (Virginia) factory and authorization for a third factory at Keyport, Washington. But he estimated that at the rate they were being built, the Navy would be short twenty-five hundred torpedoes in 1942. And that was not all. The "security" bug had so overpowered the navy brass that the Mark VI exploder was still supersecret, which meant that nine out of ten submariners did not know anything about it and most of the others did not know its limitations and advantages.

In December 1941, the submarines of the U.S. Navy's Pacific Fleet were under the command of Rear Admiral Thomas Withers, Jr. He was experienced in submarines, but not in modern ones. His chief of staff was Captain Charles Wilkes Styer, who had commanded a division of the *Salmon* class, which were among the first fleet-class submarines. They were ideal leaders for the submarine force because they understood how inexperienced nearly all the crews really were. The American submariner understood what he was about, but what he was about in peacetime and what he would be doing in war were two entirely different matters. The crews knew how to run a submarine but not yet how to fight with it.

Withers sent his people on patrols they considered unnecessarily demanding and stringent. At home they were considered proficient if they could take a boat down to one hundred feet underwater. Withers took some of them up in aircraft and showed them submarines in Hawaiian waters, clearly discernible beneath the surface, in *more than* one hundred feet of water. Some of the skippers were convinced and slowly the message spread throughout the force. Withers also insisted that on each patrol the crews take their submarine down to the test depth of the boat. This depth varied on the different submarines, depending on modernity, but Withers knew very well that it would not be long before these men would be wishing they could get to the very bottom, when the depth charges started falling all around them.

Withers was able to issue the explosive warheads in exchange for the peacetime dummies, and the Mark VI exploders, but since the navy had never authorized the publication of the operating manual for the latter device, the Pearl Harbor skippers did not understand that the magnetic exploder was for use against armored warships, and that it would be ineffective against small vessels. At the moment, U.S. submarine doctrine indicated that the submarines would be shooting at nothing but warships anyhow; the Washington Five-Power Treaty provision against commerce raiding was still a part of navy policy. Even early in December 1941 on most submarines only the skipper had the slightest knowledge of the Mark VI exploder, and that only through an oral briefing by Admiral Withers and his staff.

When the Japanese bombed Pearl Harbor on December 7, there were only three boats sitting in the submarine base, the *Narwhal,*

Dolphin, and *Tautog.* The *Cachalot* was in the navy yard for repairs. Elsewhere in Hawaiian waters there were five other submarines; a few of these were attacked by "friendly" warships. The *Thresher,* returning from a patrol to Midway, had her first battle experience—with an American four-stack destroyer that tried to ram her. Waiting outside Pearl Harbor for the antisubmarine net to open, she was bombed by U.S. Army planes.

The first American submarine actually to face an enemy ship at sea was the *Argonaut,* which with the *Trout* was on patrol off Midway Island. The *Argonaut* was an anachronism, an old V-class boat used as a minelayer, and not really expected to perform as an attack submarine. She was commanded by Lieutenant Commander Stephen George Barchet, an old football star from the Naval Academy class of 1924. Discovering naval gunfire at Midway shortly after learning that the Japanese had attacked Pearl Harbor and that the wraps were off on submarine warfare against all enemy craft, Barchet suddenly got cautious. He took the *Argonaut* down deep and approached Midway slowly. Up above somewhere there seemed to be an invasion force. That would mean a number of cruisers and destroyers, all dangerous to a submarine. As they approached they heard the sound of destroyer propellers. Barchet went to 125 feet and stayed there, making a "sonar approach" as was advocated by Withers for general purposes. He never did get close enough to make an attack, and the Japanese force, which consisted of two destroyers, bombarded the installations at Midway to their hearts' content and then withdrew.

A week later, Barchet had another chance. He was deep in the water and his sonar suggested that there were three or four destroyers overhead. He stayed deep, tracked the ships, and made no move to attack. His executive officer, William Schuyler Post, Jr., came up: "Don't you think we ought to at least put up the periscope and take a look?"

The remark made the captain furious, and when they returned to Pearl Harbor he sent an angry letter to Admiral Withers recommending that Post be dismissed from the submarine fleet. Post was transferred forthwith to the staff of Commander Allan McCann, the commanding officer of Squadron Six. But finally, it was Barchet, not Post who was transferred out as unsuitable. When his patrol report came in, senior officers were extremely critical of the timidity shown. Admiral Withers suggested Barchet should have made a night periscope attack, or a surface attack. And Barchet, like many a peacetime submarine commander, quickly disappeared from the service. Post eventually became one of the most distinguished of the Pacific theater's submarine commanders. He went out first as executive officer of the *Thresher*, and on the basis of his performance was assigned as skipper of the *Gudgeon*.

What happened to Barchet was happening elsewhere. The seniority system served well enough in peacetime, but the best spit-and-polish officers were not usually the best fighting men, and the greatest difficulty the submarine service would face in the first few months of World War II was the lack of aggressiveness shown by many skippers. Coupled with the real problems of the Mark XIV torpedo and the real problems and lack of understanding of the Mark VI exploder, the U.S. submarines were getting off to a shaky start.

On the night of December 10, Lieutenant Commander Willis Ashford Lent, in the *Triton*, encountered a Japanese ship on the horizon. He, too, went deep, made a sonar approach, fired four torpedoes from his depth of 120 feet, then went further down and away. The crew heard explosions and assumed they had sunk a Japanese ship. But they had not, and when Lent returned to Pearl Harbor he faced an unpleasant time. Throughout training, the doctrine had been to use the sonar attack and stay safe. But just recently the German U-boats in the Atlantic had been wreaking a new degree of havoc by employing the night surface attack—at which Commander Otto Krestschmer was unsurpassed. The American high command reversed its thinking, and the commanders who obeyed the old rules felt the bite of official disapproval. But Lent, unlike some of the others, learned fast, and from that time on showed a new degree of aggressiveness that finally led him to command of a squadron.

After the Japanese attack, the American submarines began to venture out of Pearl Harbor to seek the enemy. Seven boats were ready to go. They went under some restrictions, the most compelling of which was "don't waste torpedoes." Admiral Withers said that with good reason: there were only a hundred torpedoes left at Pearl Harbor after these submarines sailed. Withers was told by Washington that he could only expect to receive twenty-four torpedoes each month—that would equip one submarine to go on patrol. So when the first boats went out they had one hand tied behind their backs, figuratively speaking.

Those early boats from Pearl Harbor accomplished something—but not a great deal. Skipper Joseph Grenfell in the *Gudgeon* encountered a Japanese submarine and sank it. This was the *I-173,* and the sinking was confirmed. He fired three torpedoes to do it, but was not criticized for the expenditure of armament. He also laid claim to a freighter sunk in the waters off Japan, but that was apparently illusory. He, too, was criticized back at Pearl Harbor for lack of aggressiveness; he should have spent more time on the surface the fleet command said. Lieutenant Commander Stanley Moseley took the *Pollack* to Tokyo Bay and stood off that water. He fired a lot of torpedoes and claimed three ships. (Two were allowed.) When he came home, nobody criticized him.

Lieutenant Commander David White's *Plunger* was the first Pearl Harbor boat to take a tremendous depth charging. A Japanese destroyer saw the submarine, found it, passed over and dropped twenty-four depth charges, nearly all of them uncomfortably close. When he got home, Admiral Withers complained that he had used up too many torpedoes, including one affair where he used two shots to sink a freighter.

The Pearl Harbor submarines did not produce much in the first days of the war because the skippers and crews were not yet trained in the art of war. But they were not alone; the Japanese had sent a number of submarines to Hawaii, then moved them off to the West Coast of the United States, and although they sank a few ships, they did not really concentrate on merchant shipping. Had they done so they might have created far more difficult conditions for the Americans than they did.

But as the American submarines came back into Pearl Harbor most of the skippers got bad marks from Admiral Withers and his staff. The bad marks really should have belonged to the submarine command and to Washington, because nearly all the captains were doing what they had been taught to do. The proof was that although Withers criticized, all but one of the seven captains were awarded the Navy Cross, the highest medal given except for the Congressional Medal of Honor. The only captain who failed to win the coveted award was one who had funked in the middle of his patrol and turned command of the submarine over to his executive officer. Meanwhile, in the Philippines, the submarines of the Asiatic Fleet were also having their difficulties, more so because on the second day of the attack, December 9, the Japanese bombed the submarine base in Manila Bay, and the *Sealion* was damaged so badly that she had to be scrapped for parts. Admiral Hart had earlier ordered most of the boats in the Philippines on patrol so the damage was not as great as it might have been.

The rest of the submarines were sent out as soon as it became apparent that the Japanese had control of the air and could attack more or less as they wished.

Of the twenty-two submarines that had been at sea when the war began, their accomplishments were little more than those of the seven Pearl Harbor boats. The *Tarpon* ran into heavy seas off Luzon and was very nearly sunk when an enormous wave washed over her deck and sent tons of water cascading down the conning tower hatch. Her crew had hardly recovered from the shock when a Japanese ship appeared in the periscope. Lieutenant Commander Lewis Wallace made a try at her with the sonar approach he had been taught, but in the middle of it a torpedoman accidentally fired a torpedo, and the effort was lost. Lieutenant Commander Frederick Burdette Warder, in the *Seawolf*, was assigned to patrol off the east coast of Luzon, and when he reached Aparri he discovered a number of Japanese ships in the harbor. The major vessel was a seaplane tender and Warder moved in around a destroyer to attack. He fired four bow torpedoes, set to run under the ship and blow it up—the magnetic exploder in play. But the four torpedoes passed under the ship and did not explode. Warder turned the submarine around and fired four torpedoes from the stern tubes. He saw one of them hit against the plating and make a large splash of water but none exploded. When he returned to Manila, Warder complained about the torpedoes, but higher authorities were disinclined to believe him. They had too much experience with human error in those early days of the war. The prime case, in the first days in the Philippines, was that of Lieutenant Commander Charles Lawrence Freeman's *Skipjack*; moving east toward the Palau Islands, Freeman encountered a Japanese aircraft carrier escorted by a single destroyer. His sonar operator reported a range of twenty-two hundred yards and he set his torpedoes accordingly, fired and got no hits. Afterward, the sonar operator realized that he had misread the range; it was three thousand yards instead. That was a sterling illustration of the reason that the sonar approach was not much good: There was no way the skipper could check on the figures he was given.

The captains, too, were sometimes rattled. The skipper of the *Pickerel* sighted a patrol boat, and began an attack, and then saw a destroyer and decided to shift his approach. The crew became so confused that both ships got away. Later this same captain fired five torpedoes at a patrol boat and missed with all of them.

Actually, the first enemy ship to be destroyed by a submarine (and the first ever by an American submarine) was the *Atsutasan Maru*, which Lieutenant Commander Chester Carl Smith attacked in the *Swordfish* on December 15, 1942. He also claimed three other ships but not all of them were credited in the postwar analysis of sinkings. All the inadequacies of skippers, crews, and torpedoes showed in these first few days and it was a hard job for anyone to sort them out. Lieutenant Commander Tyrrell Dwight Jacob was the first skipper to decide that the root of most of his troubles was the magnetic exploder on the torpedoes and he ordered the torpedomen to deactivate the exploder on this first patrol. He also decided that the torpedoes ran too deep.

The *Sailfish* (the old *Squalus*) came in for more than her share of bad luck in these early days. On the morning of December 10 the boat was off the northeast tip of Luzon when her skipper sighted a Japanese cruiser traveling with several destroyers. Unfortunately the destroyers sighted the *Sailfish* at about the same time. The skipper went down to one hundred feet to attack, got off one torpedo which apparently exploded just outside the tube and nearly shattered the eardrums of all aboard; and then the destroyers went after the *Sailfish* with a vigorous depth-charge attack. The skipper of the *Sailfish* was Lieutenant Commander Morton Claire Mumma, Jr. He had been chosen for the job because he was a strict disciplinarian and the *Sailfish* had come to sea bearing that sad reputation as a death boat. Mumma had announced that any seamen who referred to the past history of this submarine would be in trouble and he threatened several with court-martial. Again, as was to be shown many times above the sea and below it in the early days of World War II, the true disciplinarians, the obvious choices for command jobs, were not always fighting men. In this Japanese attack, Skipper Mumma went to pieces. He had the presence of mind to tell his executive officer to lock him in his stateroom and take over. The exec did so, sent a radio message to Captain Wilkes in Manila and got permission to bring the boat back to port. On arrival, Mumma was relieved of his command, but Wilkes got him a medal nonetheless, on the theory that the service could not stand too many public failures just at this point. Undoubtedly the "club" attitude of the Naval Academy graduates also had something to do with it. It would take many months to sort out the fighters from the timid souls, and a number of careers would be destroyed in the process.

In the next few weeks the submarine force would suffer every sort of failure—radio, torpedo, and command. The most ardent supporter of the Mark XIV torpedo had his convictions tested when he learned of such difficulties as the one the *Perch* faced, when a torpedo she had fired at a merchant ship circled and very nearly sank the submarine!

The commander of the *Stingray* missed a chance at the main Japanese invasion fleet that was heading for Lingayen Gulf when timidity forced him to stay down instead of attacking. Of course, how much good a single submarine would have done was debatable; it certainly would not have stopped the invasion, or even have slowed it down. When Captain Wilkes learned of what had happened he dispatched six other submarines to the scene. The *S-38* sank a transport, the *Hayo Maru*. The other five tried vainly to penetrate the destroyer screen that stood off the harbor, doing an excellent job of anti-submarine patrol. Several of these boats received battering depth-charge attacks. No other submarines would succeed in what they had been assigned to do, which was to serve as coastal defense ships to stop the Japanese invasion.

The submarine captains and crews did their best to defend the Philippines but the odds were against them all the way. The lack of readiness for war showed in nearly every patrol, and the Japanese were not waiting for the Americans to learn. By Christmas the American military situation was desperate. On Christmas day even General MacArthur announced that the U.S. forces were withdrawing from Manila and he declared the Philippine capital an open city to avoid further destruction. The submarine command was shifted to Corregidor Island at the end of the Bataan Peninsula. Captain Wilkes moved into one of the tunnels of the old Spanish fortress. The submarine command's equipment consisted of a camp cot, a typewriter, and a radio receiver. Admiral Hart decided to move down to Surabaya, the Dutch base on Java to carry on the fight. He expected to go by plane, but on the eve of his departure the Japanese bombers destroyed all the American flying boats, so he went south by submarine, in the *Shark*.

The American military supplies in the Philippines were destroyed by General MacArthur's orders as the troops and naval forces moved out. The effort was thoroughly confused and the submarine command was neither consulted nor notified that all fuel oil stocks were to be burned or dumped to keep them out of Japanese hands. When Captain Wilkes learned of the loss of his Cavite fuel dump he was dismayed to say the least. There was nothing on Corregidor. He did manage to save 300,000 gallons of fuel oil for the submarine command and that was all. Since a fleet-class submarine needed at least 50,000 gallons of fuel oil for a patrol, it was certain that the submarine fleet would very soon have to find a new base. The Philippines defense force could not possibly do more than hold a position—a fingernail hold—on Bataan and Corregidor for a short time.

On the eve of the Japanese attack most of the ships had been sent south to the Dutch East Indies. The old *Langley* was the only U.S. carrier in the Asiatic area and it was virtually useless. The navy privately blamed General MacArthur and the Army Air Corps for failing to act when they had a few hours notification that Pearl

Harbor had been bombed. It would have been possible, theoretically, for the B-17 bombers at Clark Field to stage a raid on Japanese air fields in Formosa before the Japanese sent off their air strike on Manila. That presupposed a degree of organization and intelligence flow that the navy certainly did not have, and could hardly be expected of the army.

Nowhere was the navy failure more apparent than in the conduct of submarine operations. Clay Blair, Jr., noted that it would have been easy to establish a new base in the southern Philippines—a base which could have survived for at least many more weeks. And had the surprise element been blunted by stopping that first air attack, the navy could have brought up a carrier or two from Pearl Harbor and aided in the defense of the Philippines. But the Pearl Harbor operations were in the same state of shock as the Philippines at that moment. Admiral Husband Kimmel had just been relieved (for political reasons) as commander of the Pacific Fleet and Admiral Pye, who was holding the fort until the new commander could arrive was in no position or condition to take that sort of action. The entire U.S. Navy was in flux; Admiral Stark, chief of naval operations, was just then being superseded by a whole new system of command with Admiral Ernest J. King at the top.

There was really no hope that any carrier could come; naval doctrine had already written off the Philippines. If by some miracle a carrier had been dispatched by Pye, two of the four carrier admirals would (on their records) have failed to meet the enemy. Only Vice Admiral William F. Halsey and Rear Admiral Aubrey Fitch were showing the sort of aggressiveness that was needed to make carrier operation effective. The entire American defense effort had to swing into gear before the war could be prosecuted aggressively. The submarine record in the Philippines is as good an illustration as any of the problem: people failure. In 1941 the Asiatic Fleet submarines made 45 attacks on Japanese shipping, military and merchant. The result was many claims but actually only two large merchant ships and one small one were sunk. To be perfectly fair the submarine force should be credited with some ships damaged, but the Japanese kept no records of ship damage and repair that survived the war so there is no accurate way to assess the damage except by guessing. Any damage, of course, was valuable to the American cause since a damaged ship tied up escorts and port and dry dock facilities that could otherwise be used by warships. Throughout the war the results of the U.S. submarine effort would be obscured by the failure to assess damage to enemy shipping as well as sinkings.

On December 31, Captain Wilkes decided that he could no longer operate from the Corregidor base. The Japanese had complete mastery of the air, and the old tender *Canopus* had been hit by bombs so that it was doubtful if she could outrun a gunboat if she tried to escape from Manila Bay. The submarines were harried constantly by Japanese aircraft. All work had to be done at night and the submarines in port for resupply had to remain submerged in Manila Bay during the daylight hours. Captain Wilkes could see no way to continue. The problem, however, was what to do with the Asiatic Fleet submarine establishment. It consisted of several hundred officers and men, electricians, boilermakers, optics experts, welders, divers, machinists, and torpedo specialists—all of whom were in short supply in a navy that had to expand greatly. But there were only ten submarines left in the area, and Captain Wilkes estimated that each could carry twenty-five extra passengers, so only two hundred and fifty of the shore crew and the survivors of the *Sealion* could be taken off "the rock." The rest would remain with the army forces to surrender and become prisoners of war if they survived that long. Wilkes divided his staff: Captain James Fife and half of the staff of the Asiatic Fleet submarine force set off in the *Seawolf* for Darwin to establish a new submarine base which could be responsive to the demands of General MacArthur, who had moved down to Australia to prosecute the war; Captain Wilkes and the other half of the staff boarded the *Swordfish* and left for Surabaya to join Admiral Hart. That evacuation ended the first phase of the naval war in the western Pacific. The next phase was to be the holding action in the Dutch East Indies.

9

THE SUN RISES
ON AND ON

AS of January 1, 1942, the Asiatic Fleet submarine force consisted of twenty-eight boats. With this force and the handful of cruisers and destroyers (there were no battleships in the Asiatic Fleet) Admiral Hart was supposed to cooperate with British, Dutch, and Australian forces to save the Dutch East Indies from Japanese occupation. The Japanese were determined to take the Indies, above all other territory in the Pacific, for the Dutch East Indies oil fields were the key to their entire war effort, and the real reason for their attacks on Pearl Harbor and the Philippines. The Japanese either would secure the oil resources of Southeast Asia or their war machine would come to a grinding halt. It was as simple as that, and so any effort the Allies might make to save Java and Sumatra was bound to bring about immediate response by the greatest force the Japanese could muster.

The Japanese assault on the Dutch East Indies was launched from the southern Philippines, and Admiral Hart decided that the best use of his submarines would be to stop the drive at the beginning, so a number of them were concentrated around Mindanao. Others were sent on patrol off the coast of the Asian mainland and Formosa. They arrived too late to stop the Japanese who had already sailed for the East Indies, one force moving west through Makassar Strait and the other along the eastern shore through the Molucca Passage. The Japanese army had already occupied large segments of the Malay Peninsula and several units were moving against Singapore. The British troops who tried to stop them were as woefully unprepared as were the Americans in the Philippines.

To herald the new year and the new campaign, Admiral Hart divided his Asiatic Fleet into four sections and Submarines Asiatic was called Task Force Three. But as an old submariner, Hart wanted to run that force himself. This complication, plus the impossible situation in which four navies were trying to fight a war with four commands, made it almost certain that the Allies would fail. There had been little chance anyhow, given their antiquated weapons and shortage of capital ships and carriers. The first Japanese force to hit the East Indies arrived off Tarakan on January 10, 1942. Three U.S. submarines were sent to the area but they arrived too late to stop the landings. The *Stingray* sank the *Harbin Maru* off Hainan and the *Pickerel* sank the *Kanko Maru* off the Philippines, but most of the submarines did not attack targets, or if they did, they missed with their torpedoes.

When Lieutenant Commander Jacobs had become convinced that the magnetic exploder on his torpedoes was faulty he and his torpedo officer deactivated the Mark VI exploders, but his torpedoes still failed. Jacobs knew a lot more about torpedoes than most of the skippers because he had served two years as a postgraduate student in naval ordnance and had taken a course in torpedo maintenance and operation. After several more failures in which every element was isolated as far as possible (periscope observations checked by two people, angles checked by two people, and all observations checked against the torpedo data computer), Jacobs concluded that the Mark XIV torpedoes ran ten feet deeper than they should and told this to Captain Wilkes. But all Jacobs's complaint did was to start an argument in the submarine force that would continue for months. The Bureau of Ordnance did announce at this time that the old Mark X torpedoes, which were used by the S-boats, did run four feet deeper than claimed, but as for the new torpedoes the experts insisted that there was nothing wrong that minor adjustments could not cure. At this point they suggested that loose gaskets could make the warheads fail.

The first submarine lost from the Asiatic fleet was the *Shark*. She disappeared in the vicinity of the Molucca Passage and was believed to have been sunk by a Japanese destroyer depth-charge attack.

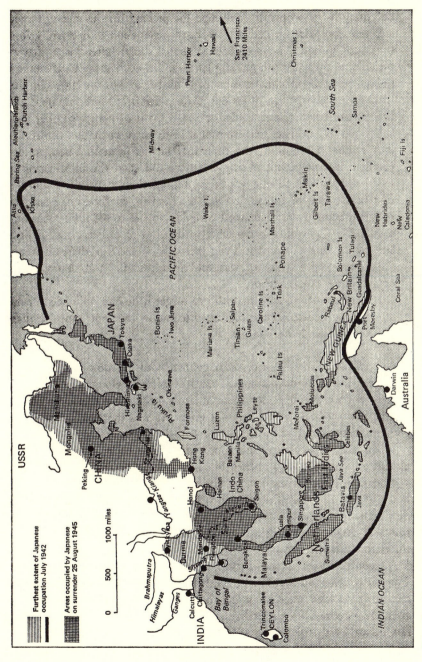

The Pacific

The Americans made many claims during those days of sinkings of Japanese warships and merchant vessels, but virtually none of them were factual. Largely it was a question of improper assumptions; once a torpedo or spread of torpedoes left the submarine and exploded, many skippers assumed that they had hit the target and destroyed it or at least damaged it. But the fact was that most of the torpedoes did not hit anything. Because of timidity or incompetence, several skippers were relieved of command. But there could be accidents and difficulties over which a submarine commander had no control, and such was the case with Lieutenant Commander John McKnight in the *S-36*. He was moving through the Makassar Strait when he got into trouble. Even to go into the strait was a dangerous job, because the U.S. charts were totally inadequate—which means inaccurate in this case. The weather was foul and McKnight was navigating by dead reckoning. Since he knew nothing about the currents and obstacles in the area he was, in effect, depending on blind luck, and on January 20 his luck deserted him. The *S-36* ran hard aground on Taka Bakang reef at the southern end of the strait. The coral rammed a hole in the hull and the forward battery room flooded. There was no way the boat could be gotten off and saved under wartime conditions and McKnight sent a message in the clear that he was sinking. He also gave the position, by name.

Jacobs's *Sargo* intercepted the message to Captain Wilkes and rebroadcast it. Jacobs then took the submarine toward the *S-36* and that night he saw her searchlight. A Dutch plane flew over and a small Dutch boat came out and took off about half the crew. McKnight decided he would try to save the submarine, but while he was working to that end the weather worsened and it seemed unlikely that he could succeed. Since his message was in the clear he had to expect that the Japanese had intercepted it and that a Japanese warship might appear at any moment. When the Dutch ship *Siberote* showed up, McKnight decided to abandon ship and scuttle it and he did so in short order. All hands were saved and McKnight escaped with his record unscathed. He had lost his boat through unavoidable circumstances.

Every day the submarines of the Asiatic Fleet reported action, and there was action, but it was almost never successful for the American submarines. In this second month of the war they sank only three more freighters among them, although altogether they saw literally hundreds of enemy ships. Not one Japanese warship was sunk by a boat of the fleet. Since several of the skippers were complaining about the torpedoes, Washington flew an "expert" out to see what was wrong. He found nothing wrong, but tried to turn the torpedo gyroscopes around—which would have caused the torpedoes to curve and possibly sink the submarine that fired them. So much for the experts. The skippers of the Asiatic Fleet were less than convinced, but the admirals still saw too much evidence of human error to allow them to pay much attention to the complaints, particularly since all who had been involved in the design and building of these torpedoes and warheads continued to swear by them as loudly as the angry captains swore at them. Admiral Hart's staff officers were not sympathetic to the submariners' complaints but Captain Wilkes, who listened when his commander spoke up, became convinced that there was something drastically wrong with the torpedoes or the warheads, and he supported them in their complaints. Without the concurrence of the command of the fleet, and with the Bureau of Ordnance in Washington adopting a highly defensive attitude there was not too much that could be done at the moment. But the pressure was already building.

The Pearl Harbor submarines were not a great deal more successful in the month of January 1942. Three of them had set out in December for Japanese home waters. The *Gudgeon* patrolled off one entrance to the Inland Sea and the *Plunger* off the other. The *Pollack* stood off Tokyo Bay. The *Pollack* sank two merchant ships but wasted most of her torpedoes when they apparently ran true but did not sink the targeted ships. The *Gudgeon* did not sink any ships. The *Plunger* sank another merchant ship and spent a good deal of time underwater dodging Japanese depth charges. Except for whatever shock value the sinking of three merchantmen so close to Japan might have had, these patrols were less valuable than others from Pearl Harbor which returned to one of the oldest concepts of submarine employment as the "eyes of the fleet."

One of the serious problems of the Pacific command in the early days of the war, and it lasted for nearly three years until air and submarine reconnaissance cleared up most of the questions, was the paucity of accurate information about the area in which much of the warfare in the Pacific would take place. Before World War I the Marshall, Caroline, and Marianas islands had been German colonies. The Germans, preparing to contest with Britain for power on the sea, had never been openhanded about dispensing their charts. When Germany's colonies were split up by the victorious Allies in 1919, the British and their dominions took some of them, and the Japanese took the three mentioned above. Under the rules established by the Versailles treaty and the League of Nations these colonies were a trust, a mandate; the idea was that eventually the islanders would become self-governing. But the Japanese had no such concept. The Marianas became a major source of sugar and other agricultural products for the Japanese home islands. The Carolines became a major naval region, with the big base at Truk. The Marshalls became lesser naval bases and air bases.

The Japanese trusted no Europeans, and after the militarists came into power there in the 1920s the buildup was carefully screened from the other powers. Charts of these waters were either unavailable or wildly inaccurate. The British, with a foothold in the Gilberts, were able to secure some information, but generally speaking the Western knowledge of the central Pacific region went back to the days of sailing ships. Plan Orange—the U.S. Navy's war plan in case of hostilities with Japan, called for operations through the Central Pacific, so more accurate navigational information was vital. In recognizing this need and acting on it the caretaker command at Pearl Harbor in December had provided a useful service for which Admiral Nimitz could be grateful when he arrived at the end of the month to assume command.

Four fleet submarines left the Pearl Harbor base late in December to undertake reconnaissance of the mandated islands. They were not well-equipped for the task; their periscopes were not fitted to accommodate cameras but they moved in close to shore and got pictures through the periscopes with ordinary cameras of the beaches of the

106

various atolls. They also observed the character and amount of traffic going in and out of the lagoons around the islets, and it was thus that Admiral Nimitz was informed that Kwajalein was a major Japanese base. That information was passed along to Admiral Halsey who was preparing to go out on a strike against the Japanese, and so the first effective aircraft carrier action of the war was a direct result of information obtained by these submarines. As time went on the art of periscope photography would improve and submarine intelligence reports would become far more valuable than they had been in the past.

By the end of January a new submarine doctrine was shaping up at Pearl Harbor. Everything had changed from the peacetime method of operation. Admiral Nimitz, who had served a stint in submarines himself, was quick to see how extended were the Japanese supply lines, which ran from the home islands down to the Dutch East Indies and soon would reach Rabaul. Japan had to supply these new bases, and that meant merchant shipping. If the Americans could sink enough ships, they could starve these bases and make them easy prey for invasion when the United States had managed to build up its strength in the Pacific. At the moment Nimitz had only two usable weapons, the carrier force, which was extremely limited (four carrier task forces were available) and the submarines. Nimitz had more than twenty and new ones were expected very soon. Pending a buildup which would enable the Pacific Fleet to launch an invasion of one or more of the Japanese-held islands, these two forces had to carry the war.

From Pearl Harbor the results achieved by the submarines tended to be disappointing. The *Tuna* sank one freighter off Japan, but only after Skipper John Leslie DeTar had deactivated the troublesome Mark VI exploder. When he returned to Pearl Harbor Admiral Withers was furious that he had done so.

But the fact was that many of the submarine captains in the Pacific and Asiatic fleets had reached the same conclusion and without saying much they were deactivating the exploder when they got on station. Admiral Withers, who was firmly sold on the magnetic exploder, did not like it. Nor did he like many other developments

107

that he noted among his submarine crews. The *Triton* sank two ships, firing twelve torpedoes at fourteen ships in all. For that period it was an excellent performance, but Admiral Withers was not happy. He complained that the skipper, Lieutenant Commander Willis A. Lent, spent too much time worrying about Japanese patrols, particularly aircraft. The admiral also believed that Lent had used too many torpedoes. The poor skipper of the *Grayling* was given an extremely bad report when he returned to Pearl Harbor because he had missed several Japanese carriers.

Missed was the problem word; Skipper Eliot Olsen was patrolling off Truk in the Carolines when Admiral NImitz' radio intelligence section intercepted and translated a secret message from the Japanese fleet regarding its Carrier Division Two, which was about to sail for the Palau Islands. This intelligence system was to be responsible for many tips to the submarine force throughout the war, but knowing that ships were coming and even having coordinates did not always help a great deal. Ships were known to change course in the middle of a voyage for any number of reasons. They were known to give one plan of voyage and take another route, for reasons best known to the captains. It was one thing for Pearl Harbor to announce that the *Akagi* and *Kaga* were sailing; it was another to intercept them. Olsen had received the message and he missed the two carriers. He did have an encounter with the smaller carrier *Hosho*, but it was of the sort that was all too common among the American submarine captains in those early days of the war. He was traveling at sonar depth, down deep, and when the operator announced the sounds of heavy screws Olsen brought the submarine up to periscope depth and took a look. It was the carrier, accompanied by a single destroyer. At this point Olsen ordered the torpedo tubes to be made ready, and prepared to attack; but he was much too late and never did get into position to fire.

Back at Pearl Harbor Admiral Withers was more than a little annoyed; gone were all the prewar warnings to take caution. The *Grayling* was scathed by the command for timidity. Eliot Olsen had never taken her in closer than ten miles from Truk and the implication was that he should have sat at the mouth of the harbor. But where Admiral Withers really faulted his captain was for spending so much time so deep. That was no way to catch enemy ships, he said, and of course it was true, but it was not what he and the others had been teaching the younger men for years.

With the exception of the few sinkings by Asiatic and Pacific fleet boats during these first two months after the attack on Pearl Harbor, the most successful enterprises of the submarines involved "special missions." These voyages were cordially (and sometimes not so cordially) detested by the submarine captains and crews, because they involved going out of patrol service to undertake some special activity. But the fact was that the U.S. Navy was in a desperate situation and there were all too few warships to do the work. Furthermore, only by stealth could some of these tasks be accomplished at all.

One of the first military problems to require special submarine missions was the development of a guerilla movement in the Philippines. When the Americans moved into Bataan Peninsula and Corregidor, not all the soldiers and Philippines Constabulary officers and men went along. Some escaped into the hills and ran before the Japanese until they came to remote areas. South of Manila the troops were on their own from the beginning and their survival outside of a prison camp depended on their wits. Within a few weeks after the surrender of General Wainwright to the Japanese, word reached MacArthur's headquarters by radio that several guerrilla bands were operating in the Philippines, and that they wanted ammunition and supplies. The demand was not answered immediately. General MacArthur had some thinking to do about the guerrillas before he could make any decisions.

Nonetheless the first special mission of submarines did go to the Philippines, but to the regular forces still at that time holding out on Corregidor. Lieutenant Commander Frederick B. Warder in the *Seawolf* left Darwin with thirty-seven tons of .50 caliber ammunition and delivered it on January 27. He also brought out 25 army and navy airplane pilots. Next came the *Trout* on February 3, carrying in 3,500 rounds of three-inch ammunition; she came out with two tons of gold bars, eighteen tons of silver pesos, and the mail. She returned to Pearl Harbor—but not directly. Lieutenant Commander Frank Wesley Fenno, commonly known as Mike, had other ideas. If he had been given a choice he would never have accepted the special mission in the first place. Having performed most of his mission already, he felt it only proper to go out and try to sink some ships, too. Accordingly, he started patrolling through the Formosa Strait, which was in the heart of Japanese territory. There he sank the freighter *Chuwa Maru*. He fired some more torpedoes at a small patrol boat and missed. Then he went back to Pearl Harbor. He was greeted by Admiral Withers as a hero, although his exploit had not been any more remarkable than several others of the period. But there was a reason: Mike Fenno had not pulled the wires out of his magnetic exploders, and his sinking of an enemy vessel was the sort of evidence that Admiral Withers wanted in the face of a growing unbelieving corps of submarine captains. A cynic might say Fenno was hailed for another reason as well—all that gold and silver that belonged to the Manila banks. By the order of President Roosevelt, Fenno was awarded the Army Distinguished Service Cross and all his crewmen got Silver Star medals. For a little while Mike Fenno was not sure whether he was going to get a medal or a court-martial, for he had signed a receipt for all this treasure and when he delivered it at Pearl Harbor, instead of the five hundred and eighty-three gold bars that were supposed to be aboard the *Trout*, the crew could find only five hundred and eighty-two. Each of the bars was worth $14,500, so it was a matter of some importance. Fenno figuratively "battened all the hatches" and began tearing the *Trout* apart. Much to his relief the missing bar turned up; one of the cooks had been using it as a paperweight.

Another boat that came out in January was the *Seadragon*. She was off Lingayen Gulf and after missing torpedo shots at one convoy, Skipper William E. Ferrall encountered a five-ship troop convoy, fired torpedoes at two ships and sank one of them, the *Tamagawa Maru*, that was carrying Japanese troops and equipment. It was a first for the submarine.

After that success Ferrall was ordered to put in at Corregidor and rescue members of the naval radio intelligence unit in the Philippines. Admiral King had decided these people were too valuable to the war effort to be allowed to go into Japanese prison camps for the duration of the war—even if they could survive there. Ferrall also brought out several other officers, whose names had been listed for him; also brought out was radio equipment, spare parts for submarines, and twenty-three torpedoes which were in such short supply at Surabaya.

Since there was a hopeless situation on Corregidor those leaders who were to be brought out had to come out by submarine. On February 19, the *Swordfish* was back again and this time Lieutenant Commander Smith brought out Manuel Quezon, the president of the Philippine Commonwealth and his party. He landed them at Panay, and from there they made their way to Australia. Smith went back into Corregidor and picked up U.S. High Commissioner Francis B. Sayre and his party and took them to Australia.

The *Sargo* also participated in these salvation missions, carrying a million rounds of ammunition to U.S. Army troops who were still fighting on Mindanao at the end of February. The Manila submarines were scattered around the Dutch East Indies, off the Philippines, and moving in and out of Australia. A few of them were achieving very good results. There were still twenty-six of them in February, although at any given time a number were off on special missions or in port for whatever sort of repairs could be made without much equipment or many parts. Lieutenant Commander James Dempsey in the *S-37* made an impact on the Japanese when he sank the destroyer *Natushio* off Makassar City in the Flores Sea. The submarines had their problems: the *S-37* and the *Tarpon* both ran aground, but both managed to get off and back to Java bases.

There were many more opportunities to sink warships and transports, for the Japanese were moving rapidly to take control of the Dutch East Indies and no one was able to stop them. Too many chances were missed, whatever the reasons; but Captain Wilkes was much more understanding with his men than was Admiral Withers at Pearl Harbor with his. Wilkes's attitude is amazing when one recalls that in the last-ditch efforts to defend Java all available American submarines were patrolling in waters literally alive with Japanese ships—and they did not manage to sink one. Certainly there was a lot of human error, but too many torpedoes struck too many ships with no result other than dull thuds; the Torpex warheads often failed to

111

explode. It was a most frustrating time for the submarine captains and their crews.

By the end of February 1942 the battle was virtually over and the Allies had lost. Captain Wilkes had moved the tender *Holland* down to Tjilatjap on the south coast of Java. Admiral Hart had gone back to Washington, having asked for recall because the battle was being fought largely by the Dutch and he felt the Dutch should be in charge. For all practical purposes, the submarines were the only elements of the Asiatic Fleet that remained to fight on. When the Battle of the Java Sea was lost and the cruiser *Houston* was sunk, Captain Wilkes and his staff left Java for Australia to fight again. There was very little to crow about. The *S-39* sank a big Japanese tanker. Lieutenant Commander Voge in the *Sailfish* sank the Japanese aircraft ferry *Kamogawa Maru,* thinking she was an aircraft carrier. There was a lot of difference, but the Japanese still lost an important ship.

But the Americans lost the submarine *Perch,* as the Java campaign came to an end, and that constituted another unhappy "first" for the submarine service.

There had already been several "firsts." The *Plunger,* patrolling out of Pearl Harbor, had been the first U.S. submarine to be equipped with radar. The *Plunger* was also the first U.S. undersea boat to undergo a really arduous depth charging and survive. In the waters off Japan she was attacked by a Japanese destroyer whose crew showed that they knew a lot more about antisubmarine warfare than the Americans did at that stage of the war. The destroyer dropped twenty-four depth charges on the *Plunger,* one so close that it broke open the alcohol tank in the after torpedo room. The Japanese did not have American sonar but they did have their own echo-ranging system, which was accurate to 3,000 meters. The old-fashioned hydrophones were able to obtain a bearing at five thousand meters. The depth charges were the then-standard Japanese three hundred and fifty pounders (about one hundred and sixty kilograms). The *Plunger* survived the depth charging and when she returned to Pearl Harbor the skipper wrote about the experience in his patrol report, which served as guidance for the command and for the next boats to go out, since copies of information from the logs were usually distributed.

The *Perch,* operating in the Dutch East Indies, did not have the advantage of these reports. At the end of February, patrolling not far from Surabaya, she was even more alone than Lieutenant Commander David Hurt, her skipper, imagined. Her radio transmitter was not sending out her signals after February 25.

On the night of February 25, Hurt spied a large freighter which was escorted by a destroyer. He attacked on the surface in a fashion that would have been approved heartily by Admiral Withers. The destroyer lookouts saw the submarine as it fired torpedoes and the destroyer began shooting back. The Japanese were good gunners and they put a shell into the radio antenna trunk before Hurt could take the boat down. Hurt made a report of the attack several hours later after he surfaced and repaired the damage. The torpedoes had missed, but the Japanese had set their depth charges for too-shallow explosion (a pattern they followed for a number of months early in the war) and so the battle was a draw, except for the damage to the radio trunk. The radio worked only sporadically. The *Perch* could still receive messages if she could not always send them, and on the last day of February she received the general message sent out by Captain Wilkes for his submarines to assemble off Java to try to stop the stream of Japanese transports that were landing troops to occupy the island. On the night of March 1, Lieutenant Commander Hurt sighted a pair of Japanese destroyers through his periscope and got ready to attack. The destroyers were apparently unaware of the submarine's presence so Hurt let them approach to about a thousand yards, and then prepared to fire torpedoes from his four stern tubes. But as he prepared the destroyers suddenly got the scent, and came charging down on the submarine. Hurt was not unduly alarmed. He knew from experience that the Japanese tended to set their depth charges for shallow explosion. The chart showed deep water under him, so he went down as one destroyer passed directly overhead. Sure enough the destroyer's depth charges exploded harmlessly above the submarine. But almost immediately thereafter, the crew felt an enormous bump, and the *Perch* buried her nose in the mud. The chart was inaccurate, to put it mildly. Hurt and his crew were stuck and they would have to remain down until they could somehow extricate the submarine from the seabed.

113

But they had no chance. The destroyer returned on another run. This time the charges were set to explode at one hundred feet and they did. Four of them dropped in a neat pattern next to the hull of the *Perch*. One destroyed most of the electrical circuits in the motor room; the port shaft quit operating; the engine room gauges broke; the pressure hull began to leak from the concussion; and a ceramic toilet bowl burst into pieces.

The destroyer came back for a third run and did more damage: One periscope was jammed; the boat's leaks grew worse; the boat was also leaking air and oil, which actually turned out to be a blessing. The destroyer above was the *Amatsukaze,* and her captain was convinced that the submarine below had been sunk forever. The *Amatsukaze* went away.

When the noise of the enemy screws could no longer be heard, Skipper Hurt decided it was time to try to get out of the mud, and after considerable effort, managed to break the boat out of the suction of the bottom and bring it to the surface. The damage was severe. The number one engine would not start at first, and when it finally did start it ran away because the governor was damaged beyond the ability of the crew to repair it at sea. The number four engine would not start at all. So Hurt had two engines to operate and patrol in a leaky boat with defective periscopes and faulty radio.

The boat was on the surface, traveling as well as possible two hours later when the lookouts sighted a pair of destroyers again. And again the destroyer lookouts sighted the submarine. Hurt took the *Perch* down, fast. The destroyers charged in. The second group of depth charges came close enough to do more damage to the submarine. One more run—this time the Japanese destroyer captain put his string of depth charges right on the deck of the *Perch*. The whole boat was shaken. Two torpedoes were shocked into starting "hot runs" in their tubes. When the runs ended no one knew the state of the warheads and exploders—they might go off at any moment as far as the torpedomen knew, blowing the bow out of the submarine. Another depth-charge run—more damage. It was remarkable that the *Perch* was holding together at all with the number of shocks she had taken. This run smashed the toilet in the officers' head.

114

By this time it was nearly 8:30 in the morning. The *Perch* seemed to have been under attack all night long. The destroyer captain made one more run. The depth charges caused the pressure hull forward to bulge inward two inches. The battery rooms were flooding with sulphuric acid that spilled from cracked batteries. Two air tanks leaked out their compressed air. The internal communications system went out. The Japanese destroyer captain, seeing bubbles as the other had done earlier, and oil leaking, decided he had sunk a submarine and steamed off to other duty.

The *Perch* was in desperate condition, but she was still manageable —perhaps. Hurt decided to try to save her. All day long they sat on the bottom making whatever repairs they could. They repaired both electric motors and the shafts. They pumped the water out of the boat. They pumped out all the ballast they could get out. At 9 P.M. on March 2 Lieutenant Commander Hurt and his crew managed to bring the *Perch* to the surface. Most of the equipment that wasn't broken had to be operated by hand. The barometer was broken so they had no accurate measure of the air pressure in the submarine. After an enormous effort they managed to start one of the four engines and get it going at enough speed to make five knots. The boat leaked so badly, even on the surface, that the pumps had to be run continuously. Because his deck gun would not train, and the single engine working was vibrating as though it would shake the boat apart, Lieutenant Commander Hurt decided that he had best give up his patrol and head for a friendly port. He headed south at five knots. After she began to move, Hurt decided to make a trim dive to see if the *Perch* could be controlled under water. The answer was that she could not, and by trying they put so much water into the boat, with no way of getting it out, that when they surfaced again they could come up only enough to barely expose the bow deck.

Certainly no one could fault the crew of the *Perch* for their effort. A repair party came into the conning tower. They found a three-eighths of an inch opening in the conning tower hatch between the gasket and the steel rim. As they worked to repair the sprung hatch, without which they could never dive, along came three Japanese destroyers. The nearest one opened fire as soon as she was within range, and the second shell was so close that it was just a question of time. The *Perch* could not dive. She could not speed away. Skipper Hurt could not even fight because the torpedoes could not be fired, and the deck gun was out of commission. It was about then that they noticed that the three destroyers were accompanied by two cruisers. Lieutenant Commander Hurt gave the order to abandon and scuttle the boat. First Lieutenant Kenneth Schacht and one seaman went into the engine room and opened several vents, then ran for the conning tower. All the others were on the deck, which was jutting upward with only the bow sticking out of the water. Schacht and his partner barely made it up the conning tower ladder, out the hatch, and onto the deck as the water poured into the submarine. Every man escaped safely as the *Perch* sank, and they floated in their lifebelts and swam and waited for the Japanese to come. All were rescued to become prisoners of war. They were the first of the submarine force to be captured.

10 Changing The Guard

DURING the first three months of the Pacific war the Japanese had shown much more skill than the American submariners. The Fourth Squadron, operating out of Camranh Bay, Indo-China, claimed to have sunk several ships in the Dutch East Indies area during January and February. The Fifth Squadron operating in the Indian Ocean, claimed more. The Sixth Squadron, working in Philippines waters, did not have much luck. After the Pearl Harbor attack several of the I-boats moved to the U.S. West Coast. They did not make much of a dent in coastal shipping, but they did scare Americans with some shelling along the coast, and one or two American vessels were sunk. On the way home to Japan, the *I-9* launched the seaplane she carried and it made a reconnaissance flight of Pearl Harbor. Then, on January 11, the *I-6* put a torpedo into the U.S. carrier *Saratoga,* and damaged her so severely that she had to be sent back to the U.S. for repairs. That cut the American carrier force down to three. Other Japanese submarines bombarded Samoa, and their planes made reconnaissance flights over Australia and Tasmania. Their performance exceeded that of the Americans in every way; but the same could be said of the Japanese military—in all ways. As the attackers, they had the advantage of knowing where they were going to strike and, of course, they had prepared for many months. The Allies, woefully undermanned and without much modern military equipment, were reduced to response—except in the case of the submarines. There it was a matter of unfamiliarity with the strictures and chances of wartime operations, and an almost complete unfamiliarity with their

117

principal weapon, the torpedo. That condition had to be laid at the door of a pinch-penny Congress and a naval administration that did not try hard enough in peacetime to put across the message that defense was a serious matter that could not come cheap. The Japanese submarines missed opportunities just as did the American. They exaggerated their claims, telling Tokyo that they had sunk the *Saratoga* and the *Lexington* (which was unhurt). When Admiral Halsey raided Kwajalein after the patrol report of the *Dolphin*, several Japanese submarines were in the area and they came out to try to find him, but Halsey moved in and out so quickly that the I-boats did not even get a glimpse of the carrier task force.

After that point, with the Japanese conquests already exceeding the fondest hopes of their military planners, the Japanese navy tended to grow cocky (with the exception of Admiral Yamamoto). Although the Japanese naval plan called for employment of submarines first as auxiliaries to the fleet and second as commerce destroyers, that second role was almost immediately ignored. The Japanese had started out strong, and for months they caused enormous pain to the Americans by sinking vital warships. Yet their failure to follow their own policy restricted the effectiveness of their submarines, even as the American submarine effort expanded almost immediately. In Washington, Admiral King felt the pressure of the German U-boat campaign in the Atlantic every day and he had no difficulty in seeing what could be done to an enemy by striking at his lines of communication and supply. In the Pacific, Admiral Nimitz was of a similar mind, moved also by the hard fact that those three carriers represented a very slender force with which to strike the enemy; his only other real weapon was the submarine. So changes began to come quickly.

Late in February came indications that the Japanese were planning to move further south. Captain Wilkes had scarcely arrived in Australia and established a temporary submarine base at Fremantle on the west coast when Japanese navy messages, intercepted by the Pearl Harbor code breakers, indicated that the invasion of Australia was very near. Half a dozen of the Manila submarines had arrived in Australia and could be sent out again. But first a few of them needed some changes—particularly in command. The captain of the *Skip-*

jack was relieved, largely because he had refused to accept the new tactics, which called for attack by periscope, day or night, or on the surface. Lieutenant Commander Freeman had continued to use the sonar attack from the deep, and that was not acceptable. The submarine was taken over by Lieutenant Commander James Coe, who had made a satisfactory record in the *S-39*; he'd sunk a tanker, and carried out with distinction a special attempt to rescue a British admiral. (The admiral was supposed to have fled to a small island off Singapore, but when Coe arrived after a narrow escape the Admiral was gone.) Another change was made on the *Searaven,* but for an entirely different reason; Lieutenant Commander Theodore Aylward was relieved because he had developed high blood pressure and complained of pains in the chest.

The submarines were moved around to face the "threat" but again they had the old problems. Lieutenant Commander Warder and his *Seawolf* were sent to Christmas Island. There he saw four Japanese light cruisers lined up. He fired torpedoes and then fired them again from a range as short as a thousand yards. He and the crew heard explosions and "breaking up noises." The *Seawolf* was attacked, depth charged, rose again and fired more torpedoes and heard more sounds of success. The Japanese came out to sink him, his sonar man heard his torpedoes hit, and he remained in the area for another few hours. He saw the cruisers come out of port, heading somewhere, and he attacked them again. All indications were that he had more hits. The Japanese destroyers then went after him and depth charged the submarine for nine hours but the *Seawolf* managed to escape and get to Australia. Warder was not very happy with his results. Nor was Lieutenant Commander Lucius Chappell in the *Sculpin* happy with his own. He had fired nine torpedoes at three freighters and failed to get a hit. He was so disgusted he asked for permission to leave the area and then returned to Fremantle to find out what was wrong.

It seemed that problems involving the old peacetime way of doing things were forever cropping up. The threat to Australia proved illusory. The carriers and other ships that had been seen apparently heading south were actually going into the Indian Ocean for an attack, and when this was certain the ring of submarines that had been drawn around Australia was sent elsewhere. The crews wanted to go back to what they considered to be their legitimate occupation—which was sinking ships. But the nagging problem of the men and women on Corregidor remained and for the United States there was only one way to give any assistance at all. Whatever had been said earlier about a powerful relief force coming to help was only the illusion of the damned. There was no force to send—the battleship fleet had been immobilized by enemy bombs and torpedoes; only a few of these vessels were seaworthy at the moment; there were only three carriers in the Pacific, and (happily this was something the survivors on Corregidor knew nothing about), the American Joint Chiefs of Staff had made a firm commitment to the British to expend every effort on the Atlantic war at the expense of the Pacific.

The submarines in the Pacific were called upon to do jobs the crews found onerous. Lieutenant Commander Chapple's *Permit* was assigned to go to Corregidor and take off General Douglas MacArthur and his family and staff. After some grumbling, Chapple went on his special mission early in March. Enroute he got the word by radio that MacArthur had grown nervous and decided to escape via PT boat, and that he was to pick up the party on a small island near Panay where the Japanese would be unlikely to search. When the *Permit* arrived at the island Chapple found only the crew of one of the four PT boats involved, the boat having broken down. He picked up the fifteen-man crew. With MacArthur gone, Chapple had new orders to go on to Corregidor and pick up some others who were regarded as too valuable to leave in captivity. A senior naval officer who came aboard was in charge. Chapple was ordered to load more survivors including some more code breakers. He left Corregidor with one hundred and eleven people aboard the boat, which meant stuffing into his vessel nearly twice as many people as it was meant to hold.

Outside Manila Bay the senior naval officer was overcome by a sense of duty and he ordered Chapple to carry out a war patrol instead of heading directly to Australia. In the peacetime navy, a senior officer's word could make or break a junior officer's career and like all other young professionals Chapple was in the habit of obeying direct orders. Knowing it was stupid, and even foolhardy, Skipper Chapple went on a dangerous patrol with a boat overloaded with personnel deemed so valuable they had to be rescued.

Off Marinduque Island he found three destroyers steaming together, fired three torpedoes, missed, and for his efforts got a depth-charging attack that kept the boat submerged for nearly twenty-four hours. Just to keep the overloaded boat full of breathing air, he had to use up much of the oxygen in the sub's storage tanks that was meant to blow ballast. He made another attack on a merchant ship and again missed with the torpedoes. Then he went on to Australia, where when Captain Wilkes heard what risks he had taken, gave poor Chapple a verbal scourging for endangering the code breakers, the lives of his crew, all the others he'd taken off Corregidor—as well as the submarine itself. What was said to the senior officer who had forced the issue was never recorded in the annals of the submarine service.

By the end of March 1942, the situation of the Americans on Corregidor was growing desperate and there was no real hope that it could be resolved by anything but surrender to the Japanese. But as long as they remained on "the rock" they had to be the responsibility of Wilkes's command. Day after day came plaintive radio messages, calling for help. *Seadragon* and *Snapper* were sent to deliver more supplies and to take off more people. Lieutenant Commander Hamilton Stone took on twenty-seven passengers and headed back to Australia. He, too, ran into three destroyers, but instead of attacking, because he had the load of passengers aboard, Stone avoided the enemy and dived deep. When he returned to Australia, he was chewed out by Wilkes for precisely the opposite reason that had brought about the roasting of Lieutenant Commander Chapple. The underlying factor at this point was the unsatisfactory performance of American submarines in the Pacific. If Captain Wilkes was unhappy, Admiral Nimitz was more so, and Admiral King, who was known for his low boiling point, was the unhappiest of all. King had served his time in submarines in his younger days and he expected a lot, particularly when he could see how it should be done—as he did every day when he read the worrisome reports of German U-boat ship sinkings in the Atlantic.

As April drew to its end, Captain Wilkes prepared to send three

121

more submarines to Corregidor to carry food in and to take out people. None of them completed the voyage; Bataan surrendered and Corregidor could not be far behind. But the skippers of these submarines were not very sympathetic; instead they were resentful of having been called to "special missions" and pleased when the missions were called off. Americans at home would not have appreciated this attitude but it was an indication of the ruthlessness that had to be engendered in the submarine force if it was to become successful. No one had ever said that submarine warfare was a pretty business.

In this particular situation the high command was right and the submarine captains were wrong. Lieutenant Hiram Cassedy's *Searaven* was sent to Timor to rescue some thirty Australian air force men who were hiding in the jungle from the Japanese who'd occupied the island. Skipper Cassedy didn't like it, but he did more than his duty: the *Searaven* lay off shore for more than two days while submariners went ashore in rubber boats, searching for the Australians, and hoping to find them before the Japanese came upon either party. Lieutenant Cassedy's shore party found and rescued the thirty men. This sort of gesture, as the navy command recognized, was more important than a dozen Japanese ships, for the effect on the morale of coast watchers, aviators, and sailors was electric. It was hard enough on service morale to know that thousands of Americans had to be abandoned on Corregidor. Had the navy failed to supply the beleaguered garrison there and to rescue as many as possible the result could have been disastrous.

The last physical contact with Corregidor was made by Lieutenant Commander James Dempsey in the *Spearfish,* who was patrolling in Lingayen Gulf at the end of April 1942. The patrol had already been successful: He had sunk two merchant ships. Since the fall of Corregidor was expected momentarily and he was in the area, he was told to go into Manila Bay and bring out some more "special" passengers. The group consisted of twelve officers, twelve army nurses, and one officer's wife. The baggage consisted of military records, and a complete roster of the thousands who had been left behind—to surrender to the Japanese a few hours later. Once again this rescue made the headlines in America, a pathetic reminder that at least an effort had been made by somebody to help those abandoned in the Philippines.

Perhaps, too, the submariners of the Pacific would have had a different outlook on the value of their rescue missions if they had known more of the story of the results. An outstanding example was the rescue of one code breaker, Thomas Mackie, who had correctly assessed a Japanese message as presaging war early in December; he was brought out on one of the last trips. Later, after the unsuccessful Japanese attempt to land troops at Port Moresby, which brought on the Battle of the Coral Sea, Mackie picked up, decoded, and translated a Japanese message which outlined the new army plan to take New Guinea by moving across the Owen Stanley mountain range. General MacArthur had plenty of warning and was thus able to mount a successful defense. That message was so important that had Lieutenant Commander Chapple done nothing else during the war, he would have served better than most men simply by saving this code breaker to work again.

At the submarine base in Fremantle on the west coast of Australia and also at the Albany base to the south (where Captain James Fife was in command of the submarines and the tender *Holland*), there was much talk and not much argument about the deficiencies of the American torpedoes. In the officers' clubs there was an equal amount of talk about the deficiencies of a number of the submarine captains who showed alarming timidity in what was supposed to be a profession of tigers. The latter situation prevailed at Pearl Harbor as well, but the former did not at this time. Admiral Withers was a firm believer in the Mark VI exploder and the Mark XIV torpedo. His opinion was reinforced by the reported experience of Lieutenant Commander Fenno, who went out to the shores of Japan in March, and came back after staying on station for almost a month; he claimed to have sunk five ships for a total of more than thirty thousand tons of shipping and to have damaged a number of others. He had carried out twelve attacks and fired twenty-one torpedoes.

Some changes in command of the submarines in the Pacific area began to occur. The first change was the relief of Captain Freeman

Daubin who was sent to the Atlantic to command the submarine force in response to the continued British demands for U.S. submarine activity. Also, the invasion of North Africa would be coming up, and a highly competent and experienced submarine officer was needed to manage the small U.S. submarine force that would be engaged in that operation. Daubin's replacement in command of the Pearl Harbor submarine base under Admiral Withers was Captain Robert H. English, another highly experienced submarine command officer, who had served as chief of staff to the Pacific Fleet submarine command earlier. English was another believer in the Mark VI exploder, and he would listen to no criticism of the device. He had "been there" when it was first tested. Withers threatened that anyone heard complaining about the exploder would be kicked out of the submarine force.

This attitude, all too common among the "experts" who had devised various weapons was hardly conducive to the improvement of the scores of American submarines. One squadron commander happened to know from experience in the Atlantic that the Germans (on whose early inventions the American magnetic exploder was based) had decided the magnetic feature was unreliable and abandoned it. Withers refused to listen to that sort of negative and divisive talk.

Pearl Harbor captains came and went as did those in the Southwest Pacific force. It was going to take some more time to shake out the timid and replace them with fighting men. It was not the sort of problem to make commanders happy, but as the admirals soon discovered there was no better way to discover who would fight and who would not, than to throw them into combat. The same difficulty dogged the high command in the first year of the war, not excluding the submarine service, and just then at Pearl Harbor, the submarine force was a remarkable example. Virtually all the officers who had been involved in patrols were in agreement that there was something drastically wrong with the torpedoes, and most of them settled on the Mark VI exploder as the responsible factor. But Admiral Withers and his staff were operating in the same way in wartime that they had in peacetime—taking for granted the claims of the Newport torpedo factory and the Bureau of Ordnance that the torpedoes were excellent and that all error was human error. Whenever the experts were asked to test the torpedoes in live firings, they retreated to the position that torpedoes were in too-short supply to "waste" them by finding out if they worked. The result was that while the Pearl Harbor command dispatched seventeen war patrols in the first three months of the Pacific war, the submarines sank only fifteen ships, although they fired scores of torpedoes. If that was not waste the skippers (privately, not within the hearing of their immediate superiors) would have liked to have been shown what waste was.

In retrospect, many negative decisions were made during these first few months of the war. Admiral Hart, who had returned to Washington to become chairman of the U.S. Navy's General Board, had always felt that the fleet submarines were too big and had too many "gadgets" to be successful. This prejudice was aired once more, and the result was that Admiral King decided to send a number of S-boats to the Pacific to help with defenses. And that's how Captain Ralph Christie left the Atlantic and came to the Pacific. He brought his boats to Brisbane and that became a new base for an S-boat fleet.

The early months of 1942 brought other major changes. Captain Wilkes was unhappy with the performance of the Australia submarines. In April the only decent patrol record was that of the *Skipjack,* which sank three ships off the Indo-China coast. Most of the submarines sank nothing at all. One result was the replacement of Captain Wilkes. It was true that he was "overdue" for rotation in peacetime terms. But his post as commander of submarines for the Southwest Pacific was an important one, and should have carried flag rank. Wilkes was highly regarded as an aggressive fighter, and so when he was sent home he got command of the new cruiser *Birmingham*. But that was not the same as running a submarine fleet; Admiral King had decided he wanted to make a change. The new Southwest Pacific submarine commander was to be Captain Charles A. Lockwood, who was, as much as anyone, responsible for the development of the fleet-class submarines. Almost like ships in the night, captains Lockwood and Wilkes met and passed. There was virtually no time for exchange of anything but courtesies, and so Lockwood did not have the benefit of Wilkes's thoughts about the

American torpedoes' performance. That was the navy way, and it was conceived and had been followed just so that a new commander would not be prejudiced by the ideas of his predecessor. Fortunately for the Australia submarine command, Lockwood was a good listener. When Lieutenant Commander James Coe came back from his relatively successful patrol in the *Skipjack* and presented a bill of particulars against the Mark XIV torpedo in his patrol report, Lockwood listened. On a trip south to Albany to check in with Fife, he had already heard from "Fearless Freddie" Warder, who was called that by his crew because of his Christmas Island ferocity in attacking those cruisers time and again. Lockwood had also heard from Ferrall, Stone, Hurd, and Chappel about their troubles. The story was almost always the same: premature explosions, or no explosions at all. The skippers voiced a general distrust of the Mark VI exploder and of the Mark XIV torpedo. Several of them were so frustrated that they were considering requesting return to general duty rather than remain in submarines.

Captain Lockwood understood immediately that morale was a major concern; he arranged for two rest camps that would let the crews get away from the naval life for a while. One was in Perth nearby, and the other at the beach. He was constrained to write a report on what he found (before he began operating), for his old friend and commander, Admiral Richard Edwards, who had fleeted up (been promoted temporarily) to become Admiral King's chief assistant. As another old submariner, Edwards wanted to know what was wrong in the Southwest Pacific. Lockwood told him what he thought: That part of the problem was bad command decisions—the boats were not sent to the right places at the right times—but that much of it was inside the submarines. There the causes he mentioned were three: inexperience, timidity, and bad torpedo performance. In some cases of timidity the problem was simply one of misunderstanding. The old doctrine of the deep approach persisted in the submarine service even after several months of war. The way Lockwood put it to Edwards indicated that he thought that many of those who had not been aggressive could be straightened out by the application of a little psychology and education. Lockwood was always an optimist and a strong believer in his people.

Settling in at the new job demanded that Lockwood read all the patrol reports of the submarines that had come from the old Asiatic Fleet, and he did. What he found prompted him to begin serious consideration of the possible faults of the American torpedoes, and in this he was the first high-ranking officer to raise official questions about the torpedoes. Captain Wilkes had shared his skippers' feelings about the torpedoes, but he had never enjoyed the break that it would have taken to come to grips with the problem. For at the root of it all was the Bureau of Ordnance, which had accepted and certified, and thus gained a vested interest in the magnetic exploder and the Mark XIV torpedo. Lockwood began at the beginning. One of his early actions was to write a letter to the Bureau of Ordnance asking if there were any tests to indicate that there might be credibility in the submariners' complaint that the torpedoes ran too deep or that the Mark VI exploder was less than perfect. He got a rocket back, one that the protective society of the Bureau of Ordnance was to live to regret. The poor performance, said the message, could only be the fault of the captains and crews of the submarines. It was impossible that anything could be wrong with the torpedoes or the warheads.

When Lockwood saw that message, he saw, too, that no help could be expected from higher authority in Washington, and he started his own investigation of the torpedo failures. He could never have accomplished the job had there not been one other change: A few days after taking command, Captain Lockwood was promoted to rear admiral. That gave him the flag rank that the Bureau of Ordnance had to respect.

11

ATTACK ON
AMERICA

FROM the start of the war Admiral Isoroku Yamamoto had been dubious about the prospects. In the inner council meetings of the navy he had opposed war from the beginning of the discussions in the 1930s, when the Japanese army and political leaders had decided that no parity for Japan would be allowed in a world dominated by Europeans. Yamamoto warned particularly against war with the United States. He had served a hitch as Japanese naval attaché in Washington, and had been mightily impressed with the potential industrial capacity of the United States. If a war began, he had predicted in the councils, Japan might easily win the first few rounds, but in the end, American industrial might would overpower the island kingdom. There was no way, Yamamoto told his associates, that Japan could win such a struggle. Those views nearly got Yamamoto assassinated, and in fact accounted for his having the job as commander in chief of the Combined Fleet. His friends in the Navy Ministry were so fearful for his safety that they shanghaied him off to the fleet to save his life. It was no joke; several ministers and important government figures were assassinated by the ardent nationalists who insisted that Japan must claw her way to a position of dominance over all the Pacific. They have been called fanatics, a term usually reserved for small groups of violent dissidents. In Japan the group was not small.

When war did come, Yamamoto did his best for Japan. The raid on Pearl Harbor, the raid on the Trincomalee base that wiped out British sea power in the Indian Ocean, the move south to build up Truk and

Rabaul as major Japanese bases, and the general conduct of the war at sea were all the responsibility of Admiral Yamamoto.

After the success of the Pearl Harbor raid, which was not a success in Admiral Yamamoto's judgment, he planned another operation. His great disappointment at Pearl Harbor was to find the American aircraft carriers absent. Had he been able to knock out the four carriers as well as the battleships, Japan would have been able to negotiate a peace then and there, Yamamoto believed. He was wrong, of course, on two counts. First, with their noses bloodied and the memory of a "dastardly" attack stinking in their nostrils, the Americans were in no mood to talk peace, no matter how badly the navy was hurt. Second, the ease with which the Japanese forces conquered Hongkong, Singapore, the Malay Peninsula, the Dutch East Indies, Burma, and moved to the borders of India and within sight of the shores of Australia excited the Japanese jingoists and they began to believe that conquest of the world was not beyond their grasp. Yamamoto could never have stopped the war as long as Japan was winning easy victories.

Yamamoto's plans, then, had to be two-edged, aimed at imposing another defeat on America in the hope that peace could be negotiated to consolidate the new gains together; but if the Americans refused to quit, then to be in a position to take further action to punish them and strengthen the Japanese position. After Trincomalee, the plan for the next major naval operation called for attack deep within the American sphere of influence in the eastern Pacific. To be sure, the army wanted to move against New Guinea, and Yamamoto had to provide fleet support, including the two heavy carriers *Shokaku* and *Zuikaku*, light carriers, seaplane carriers and all the other elements of an invasion fleet. But those units, sent south in support of the landings to be made at Tulagi and Port Moresby, were supposed to be returned to the Combined Fleet's main force in time for an entirely new operation, much more important than anything since the Pearl Harbor foray.

As matters turned out, the push south to Port Moresby was contested by the Americans at the Battle of the Coral Sea. In that first struggle of carrier against carrier the American *Lexington* was sunk, but so was the Japanese light carrier *Shoho,* and worse, from the Japanese point of view, the big carrier *Shokaku* was damaged so badly she could not participate in the next operation, although her services were required. At the Coral Sea the Americans and Australians had put the first crimp in the Japanese military plans since the beginning of the war. The damage might have been much greater, had the American submarine force been better organized.

At Pearl Harbor the code breakers learned immediately from intercepted Japanese messages that the *Shokaku* was damaged and that she and the *Zuikaku* were heading back to Japanese waters. They also knew the way they would come—via Truk. The Pearl Harbor command took the intelligence, added to it, and then informed the submarines on station. There, the first egregious error was made: Pearl Harbor overestimated the damage the *Shokaku* had suffered and underestimated the speed she could attain on the voyage. Admiral Withers believed the ship had been hit by several torpedoes, and she may have been; but in the attack the torpedoes did *not* explode and the carrier had not suffered any underwater damage as Withers believed.

Withers looked at the big situation chart of the Pacific Ocean in his office; it showed the disposition of the Pacific Fleet submarines on patrol. Commander Joseph Willingham's *Tautog* was on its way from Pearl Harbor to Fremantle to join the Southwest Pacific submarine force. Admiral Withers sent a radiogram to Willingham, telling him the details and ordering him to head for the south end of the Truk atoll to guard Otta Pass. On May 10, having traveled for two days mostly on the surface although he was in Japanese waters, Willingham arrived on station. He waited but no wounded carrier came by.

Lieutenant Commander Donald McGregor in the *Gar* was patrolling amid the atolls of the Marshall Islands when the Battle of the Coral Sea developed. Admiral Withers ordered him to Truk as well, to patrol Piaanu Pass, on the western side of the atoll. McGregor did not travel on the surface, but at periscope depth, and he did not arrive until May 13. He saw nothing moving in the area except a single ship whose behavior was so peculiar he believed it was a "Q-ship" put out to entice and sink American submarines.

131

Lieutenant Commander Chester Bruton in the *Greenling* had already been assigned to patrol the North Pass of the Truk area and had sunk a Japanese merchant ship, the *Kinjosan Maru*. Bruton was ordered to move from the North Pass area to cover the Northeast Pass into the Truk naval base. There, from the *Greenling*'s patrol pattern, along the outside of the reef that protected the inner lagoon, Bruton could see ships moving out from Truk base, but he could not attack across the reef. He reported these movements and was told to remain where he was and continue to report on ships he saw.

The *Shokaku* arrived at Truk on May 11, but she did not use Willingham's route. Instead she came in the South Pass, which was not guarded and went out the North Pass. Piaanu Pass and Otta Pass were both heavily mined and big ships were warned against them. Admiral Withers's intelligence did not indicate this condition, so he had made a wrong guess.

At least Bruton had a look at one of the carriers, the *Zuikaku*, when she showed up a few days after the *Shokaku*. He saw her coming out the North Pass, escorted by four destroyers. But there was no way he could get at her unless she changed course, and she did not. He had been so close, and he was so far away.

Both carriers had been missed at Truk through the errors of the submarine command in Pearl Harbor, but that was not the end of it. Admiral Withers began to move the submarines in the north around to try to intercept the carriers before they could get back to Japan. The *Cuttlefish* was patrolling in the Marianas, but that island group covers millions of square miles of ocean and although Withers ordered alertness, the two carriers did not pass anywhere near the submarine's patrol area.

Admiral Withers continued to try. He ordered the *Grenadier* to patrol the Bungo Suido, the southern entrance to the Inland Sea and the bases of Kure, Kobe, and Osaka. He ordered the *Drum* to guard the Kii Suido, the northern entrance to the sea. The *Pollack* was moving out from Pearl Harbor on patrol to eastern Kyushu waters when she was diverted by Withers to try to stop the carriers. But once again the miscalculation about the extent of damage to the *Shokaku* threw all Withers's plans awry. The *Pollack* arrived in the area a day after the carrier had gone inside the Inland Sea and neither of the two guards at the entrance saw hide nor hair of it either—for the same reason.

Lieutenant Commander Charles Kirkpatrick in the *Triton* was not called into the affair but he was patrolling off Okinawa, listened in to the messages, and charted the *Shokaku*'s probable course. He came closer than anyone to getting a shot at her when on May 16 he spotted the carrier and a destroyer four miles away. He tried to catch up but the carrier was too fast for him. He surfaced and ran at nineteen and a half knots, but the *Shokaku* got away.

The *Zuikaku* was coming along behind. But the submarines had no better luck with her. Very early on the morning of May 21 she passed by the *Pollack* so close that Skipper Moseley could see her, but he realized too late that this shape was that of an aircraft carrier. He fired four torpedoes from two thousand yards. This time it was human error; the skipper underestimated the speed of the carrier and all four torpedoes missed. So the effort expended to trace and attack the two big carriers failed dismally. There were, however, some positive results of the changes in patrol pattern. Willingham's *Tautog*, sitting off the south end of Truk, came upon a hospital ship and he nearly fired on it, at first believing it to be one of the carriers. Then along came a freighter, the *Goyo Maru*, which had been a part of the aborted Port Moresby assault force. Willingham put a torpedo into the merchant ship and the captain ran her up on the beach to save her. Next, Willingham ran across a Japanese submarine and then another. He took two shots at the second, but missed. A third submarine came along, and he took another two shots. At least one torpedo hit and hurt the *I-28* but did not sink her. The *Tautog* came closer to fire again; the Japanese submarine fired two torpedoes, while Willingham fired one and sent the boat down to the bottom. The Japanese torpedoes missed but Willingham's did not and he came home to base to tell the tale of his three submarines in one day.

The *Triton* also had its taste of victory after losing the carrier. On May 17 she encountered a Japanese submarine, that was on its way from Japan to Kwajalein atoll, and fired one torpedo. The *I-64* stuck her bow up in the air and then slid down stern first to the bottom.

The torpedo failures continued—whether they were failures of the weapons or of the operators. The *Gato* fired five torpedoes at a Japanese carrier off Roi-Namur Islands in the Marshalls and the crew claimed two hits. But the next day they saw the undamaged carrier safely inside the reef. The *Drum* sank the seaplane tender *Mizuho* and won another first: she had destroyed the largest ship yet sunk by the Americans in the Pacific war. But the *Grenadier* got into position to attack a Japanese convoy of seven ships. She chose the largest, a transport, and fired four torpedoes spaced to hit in a pattern from bow to stern. The first and the last hit as expected, but the middle two did not explode. Lieutenant Commander Lent, who had taken over this submarine for her second patrol, decided then and there to join the antiexploder club. But he did sink the ship, the *Taiyo Maru*, and he possibly did more damage to the Japanese war effort than anyone else did all month. The ship was carrying a group of Japanese scientists and technicians to the Dutch East Indies to organize that area's industry and natural resources for the Japanese war effort. Not all the scientists were lost but their equipment was.

In May 1942 the tide was turning for the American submarines. The nonperforming captains who had been in command of many boats simply because they had the seniority under the old peacetime system had been transferred out and younger men had come in filled with determination to sink ships, and warned by their elders to be aggressive at all costs. They had the same experience that the other captains shared: difficulty with torpedoes. Lieutenant Commander Charles Kirkpatrick in the *Triton* went into the East China Sea on his first patrol. He attacked a Japanese convoy and fired four torpedoes, two at each of two freighters. Two of the torpedoes hit, sinking the *Taei Maru*. Two missed the other ship. Kirkpatrick, concluding that the torpedoes ran deeper than he had been told, set one for a shallow explosion and fired it at the *Calcutta Maru*. It hit and exploded, the ship broke its back and sank. On this patrol Kirkpatrick also sank the *Taigen Maru*.

The torpedo shortage was still critical. Lieutenant Commander DeTar in the *Tuna* was criticized for wasting torpedoes—seventeen shots to sink one ship was the result, although he had fired at six. No wonder. When Lieutenant Commander Lewis Parks in the *Pompano* went out he had to use the old Mark X torpedoes that were built for the S-boats because of the shortage. But Parks did well enough, with those slow torpedoes he sank the eight-thousand-ton freighter *Atsuta Maru* and under the nose of an escorting destroyer at that. Yes, matters were improving. The submariners were learning some of the Japanese tricks too, as well as some of the deficiencies of the Japanese antisubmarine system. The most glaring of the latter was the limited size and depth of the standard Japanese depth charge. It was built to explode at not over two hundred and fifty feet and at three hundred and fifty pounds (some were smaller) it was not powerful enough to do great damage unless the attacking vessel achieved very nearly a direct hit.

The internal affairs of the submarines were improving then, but the organization was still not what it should have been at this stage of the war. In mid-May, Admiral Withers was also replaced and sent to take command of the Portsmouth Navy Yard. Captain English was promoted to rear admiral and given command of the Pacific Fleet submarines. New blood and new ideas were coming into the force.

Almost immediately Admiral English was faced with the problem of a new Japanese threat against an American base, but like everyone else at Pearl Harbor he suffered from lack of information. What base? Shortly after the brief encounter at the Coral Sea the volume of naval radio traffic from the Combined Fleet flagship, the battleship *Yamato*, began to increase heavily.

The new Japanese plan called for the capture of Midway Island, the advanced American submarine and air patrol base 1,200 miles northwest of Hawaii, and of strategic islands in the Aleutian chain off the tip of Alaska. The purpose was four-fold: To deprive the Americans of their forward base and secure an advance base for Japan within striking distance of Hawaii; to draw out the American fleet and destroy it so that Japanese movement to Australia and possibly to Hawaii could not be stopped; to establish a foothold on the edge of the North American continent which would give the Japanese navy bases for attack on the West Coast; and to threaten the United States with invasion so that Washington would be eager to come to the peace table.

That was Yamamoto's reasoning. How far it was shared by the

Imperial General Staff is another matter; the easy victories of the past six months had been heady stuff to the militarists in Tokyo. Plans were drawn for the occupation of Hawaii and boasts were made about the day when Japanese troops would parade in the streets of Sydney. Were Yamamoto successful it seems doubtful that his hope for a settlement would have been realized.

The Midway plan operations began early in May with submarine activity. Six I-class boats were assigned to the Aleutian Islands and conducted reconnaissance of those rocky bits of land. Then they moved into a line along the 50th parallel and waited for their attack force to come up. Sixteen submarines were assigned to the Midway attack, six of them were supposed to go to French Frigate Shoals, north of Hawaii, and meet Japanese flying boats there and refuel them. They were to conduct reconnaissance of Pearl Harbor and report on the movements of the American fleet. But Admiral Nimitz outguessed the Japanese. He was informed of the heavy radio traffic and was sure of a coming offensive somewhere. Covering his bases, he sent two seaplane carriers up to French Frigate Shoals and when the plane—carrying Japanese I-boats arrived they were faced with the choice of announcing their presence by an attack or backing off. They backed off to preserve the Midway plan. Thus the Japanese were deprived of that all-important knowledge about the American fleet.

The submarines then formed two scouting lines to watch for the U.S. fleet when it came out, as it was supposed to do, too late to stop the invasion of Midway but just in time to be destroyed by the main elements of the Japanese fleet. If the surprise factor had worked, the Japanese plan might have succeeded. Yamamoto's force was more than three times that of the Americans', and Japanese morale after an astounding string of victories marred only by the Coral Sea setback, was higher than ever. But America was saved by an aspect of its technical proficiency: the Radio Intelligence code breakers isolated one point as the focus of attack but they could not identify it because of the Japanese code name. Now Nimitz pulled a trick out of the hat. He had his radio people send a message that announced that this point—Midway—called AF in the Japanese code, was short of water. The Japanese took the bait and announced that AF was short of water.

Nimitz then had warning and a chance to deploy his slender forces for one all-out battle. Yamamoto might have had a clue when the *I-168*, delayed in Japan, arrived late on station and looked over Midway. Her captain reported numerous aircraft on long-range search patterns; Nimitz had beefed up the defenses at Midway. No one called that matter to Admiral Yamamoto's attention.

Although several American submarines were posted around Japanese waters none of them caught sight of major elements of the Japanese fleet, so no alarm was given. The U.S. submarine force could not really be faulted; Yamamoto was being very careful. Part of the fleet left from Japan. Part of it came from Saipan and Guam. The *Cuttlefish* was in the area, but the Japanese kept her down most of the time with repeated depth-charging attacks. Tokyo's radio intelligence reported half a dozen U.S. submarines off the Inland Sea and sent out extra antisubmarine units to patrol off the two entrances. Thus the *Pollack*, which was offshore, was chased around for two days by destroyers. The skipper, Stanley Moseley, figured that something was up, but he never got a look at any of the fleet units and so had nothing specific to report. Moving across the Pacific the Japanese carefully stayed off the usual routes and so no American caught sight of them until they were in the Midway area.

The *Cuttlefish*, however, did sight a tanker seven hundred miles west of Midway and reported the information to headquarters. That report could hardly be regarded as definitive, but to Nimitz it all added up. He was getting ready. At the end of the third week of May he detached Rear Admiral Robert Theobald with five cruisers and thirteen destroyers to form the Northern Pacific Force and protect Alaska. That left him three carriers, eight cruisers, and seventeen destroyers to meet the four Japanese carriers, two battleships, three cruisers, and fourteen destroyers of the striking force; plus five more battleships, several cruisers, another carrier, seaplane tenders, and many destroyers that the Japanese could divert from the Aleutians operation if need be.

In the Midway operation, Nimitz did not have to depend on his submarines for information or for action, which was fortunate, because the submarine management for this battle was thoroughly inept. Perhaps it was because Admiral English was brand-new in his job. Whatever the reason, as W. J. Holmes of the radio intelligence group (and an old submariner) said, the command created a submarine plan, and it was a bad plan. It was not a matter of forgetting what the submarines were supposed to be able to do. Nimitz ordered English to make every boat in the Pacific Fleet available for the operation. English had thirty boats at the moment but only twenty-six of them could be used for one reason or another. Nine were ordered to take up position along an arc extending from a point southwest of Midway to another point one hundred and fifty miles to the north of the islands. Two were placed inside that arc. Three more were stationed two hundred miles west of Midway, three were stationed six hundred miles between Midway and Hawaii, and the patrol boats still out were ordered back toward the eastern Pacific to add to the defense line. Four were posted north of Pearl Harbor to guard against the possibility, raised by Admiral King, that Nimitz was wrong and the attack was really going to be against Hawaii. Since King's assumption was faulty, those boats were completely wasted.

The battle began on June 3 when a patrol plane from Midway spotted the invasion force seven hundred miles west of the islands. Nimitz had asked the army to move its B-17 Hawaii Defense Force to Midway and this had been done. That day the B-17s attacked the Japanese invasion force but not one of their bombs hit. Later in the day Marine Corps torpedo bombers made another attempt. It, too, failed. That day the *Cuttlefish* sighted the tanker, and Admiral English ordered the skipper to keep track of the vessel, which might lead him to the fleet. But the skipper was nervous, he figured he had done his job by reporting and he took the boat down and lost contact. It hardly seems to have made much difference.

On June 4 the Japanese were in position for their attack. The carrier force began the softening up of the defenses. Afterwards the bigger ships would bombard, and then the invasion troops would land to mop up what remained of the U.S. marine, U.S. air corps, and U.S. navy defenders. Meanwhile American planes from Midway attacked the striking force too, but without result. Another strike was already poised on the decks of the Japanese carriers, waiting to take off. These aircraft were loaded with torpedoes, because Admiral Chuichi Nagumo was a careful man, and he was prepared for a contest with the American carriers. But no carriers were sighted by the search planes of the fleet and the submarines reported that no ships had passed through their cordon. (It was true; the American carriers had come through before the line was assembled.)

With the first air strike launched from Midway, the word was sent to Pearl Harbor that the Japanese had arrived. Admiral English ordered his submarines to attack, but they were all out of position. The Japanese were coming down from the northwest, and were two hundred miles from Midway. Only two of the U.S. submarines had the slightest chance of getting near enough Midway to join the battle. The *Grouper* surfaced and ran at her nineteen-knot speed toward the Japanese, but she never got there. She was sighted by Japanese search planes which came down strafing; she submerged, and stayed down, safely out of the battle, of no use to the American force. The *Nautilus* moved slowly toward the area, at periscope depth, and just after 7:00 A.M. sighted the Japanese carrier force. Unfortunately the guardian destroyers also found her through the efforts of a low-flying plane and sound gear, and she was subjected to a depth-charge attack. But she came back up when the water quieted down and continued to track the Japanese. At 8:30 that same morning she surfaced in the middle of the Japanese fleet whereupon a battleship started firing its big guns at her. Skipper William Brockman fired two torpedoes, only one of which ran properly (the other misfired), and then the destroyers went after the *Nautilus*. Brockman took her down to one hundred and fifty feet and listened as the destroyers raced back and forth dropping depth charges in the wrong places.

Half an hour later the *Nautilus* raised her periscope and saw a Japanese aircraft carrier in front of her, but ten miles away. Brockman also saw another ship and fired a torpedo. It was a destroyer and it turned and came rushing at him. He went down to two hundred feet and evaded, still moving in the direction that he thought the carrier was going.

The air battle of the carriers began, and the *Nautilus* kept trying to come closer to the Japanese carriers, but the enemy warships were so much faster that it was a hard task. Patience was finally rewarded in the afternoon, when she came up and sighted a big carrier that was burning. Brockman fired three torpedoes from a range of not quite two miles and then dived. Several Japanese destroyers came up, and one charged in dropping depth bombs. The carrier was the *Kaga*, and she was already bound for the bottom of the sea. Two torpedoes missed but one struck solidly—and did not explode. There could be no question about that; Japanese survivors later told how several survivors swam to the floating air flask, which had broken off from the warhead, and clung to it to save themselves.

So, three American submarines had made some sort of contact with the Japanese fleet, and for the reasons described, had accomplished nothing as warships. Much of the fault was that of the Pacific Fleet command, and since Nimitz's staff was issuing the orders to Admiral English, that command had to be blamed for the poor performance of most of the boats.

As for the Japanese, they did only slightly better. Their submarines had failed in their intelligence mission and the American fleet had sneaked through to strike the first carrier blows. The Japanese carriers retaliated, and bombed the carrier *Yorktown* so successfully that she went dead in the water and was given up; then salvage efforts were begun after Admiral Frank Jack Fletcher had moved his flag to a cruiser. The *Yorktown* was rescued and it looked as though she would go back to Pearl Harbor and be repaired to fight again, but then along came the *I-168*, commanded by Lieutenant Commander Yahachi Tanabe. He saw the *Yorktown* with a destroyer alongside and fired four torpedoes. One sank the destroyer *Hammann*, and two put the finishing touches to the *Yorktown*. She lingered until the next day but finally sank. So the Battle of Midway ended with the submarines of the United States and Japan having contributed relatively little; but as was the story generally up to this time, the Japanese submarines had done better as part of the battle fleet than the Americans. But to look at it a bit less critically, at least the submarines had attacked, while the big surface ships, the American cruisers and the Japanese cruisers and battleships, had done nothing whatsoever to contribute to the struggle.

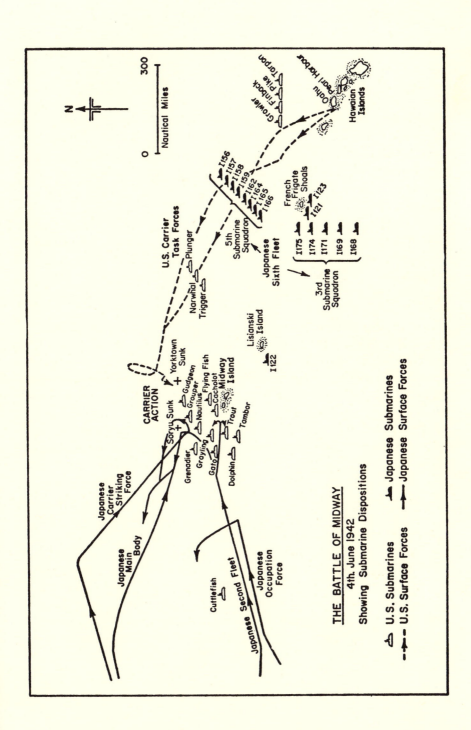

THE BATTLE OF MIDWAY
4th June 1942
Showing Submarine Dispositions

◁ U.S. Submarines
◣ Japanese Submarines
--▶ U.S. Surface Forces
──▶ Japanese Surface Forces

12 HARD TIMES

THE Japanese Combined Fleet staggered home minus four carriers, a heavy cruiser, and some of the best airplane pilots in the world. They lost nearly three hundred and fifty planes in the disaster. And disaster it was; when the *I-168* came home she was greeted at the dock by thousands of people, for her performance was all that Japan had to crow about. As for the Combined Fleet: its situation was dismal and Admiral Noguma's career was blighted by the error on his bridge that had kept the carrier decks filled with planes and allowed the Americans to make the first strike.

The submarines of the Pacific Fleet went back about their business of sinking enemy merchant shipping. Some, however, were engaged in a less exciting and far more dangerous and wearing job. These were the submarines of the Northern Pacific Force. When the war began, the navy was building up submarine bases at Kodiak and Dutch Harbor, Alaska. The first submarines, a pair of S-boats, arrived at the end of January 1942; they were the *S-18* and the *S-23*. Their officers and men soon discovered that submarine duty in these waters was unlike anything they had ever experienced before. On patrol the crew slept in their clothes to keep warm. When they were submerged the boat dripped with cold sweat; on the surface ice covered the bridge and they were very frequently in fog that limited visibility to a boat length or two. When they were not shrouded in fog they were being whipped by the fierce cold winds of the frozen north. Most of the time they were operating in darkness. When the wind blew hard it snapped the icy spindrift across the bridge to sting the faces of the lookouts. The bridge watch slipped on the deck and careened into the instruments, and many a cut and broken bone was the result. Submarining in Alaskan waters in the winter was hard, hard duty.

Although there was no indication of Japanese activity along the Alaskan coast, by April 1942 the two bases were equipped to manage anything but a major refit and more S-boats came to Alaska. Their war patrols were unexciting; they sank a few Japanese fishing boats but that was all. Their battle that spring was still with the elements, not the human enemy. But then came the electrifying news that the Japanese were planning a major assault in the eastern Pacific area, and Nimitz's decision to create the Northern Pacific Force under Admiral Theobald. There were six submarines in Alaskan waters to join that force; then it was augmented to ten under Captain Oswald S. Colclough. That was the American force when the Japanese began their twin moves against Midway and the Aleutians.

The first word of the advance came from the code breakers, but the actual sighting took place on June 2. The Japanese force consisted of the carriers *Junyo* and *Ryujo*, two heavy cruisers, three destroyers, and two auxiliary ships. Besides these there were also two separate invasion groups, more cruisers, more destroyers, and the transports bearing the troops. On June 6 and 7 the Aleutian Islands of Kiska and Attu were invaded by the Japanese with the greatest of ease. All that existed there that was of any importance were weather stations. The Japanese had it easy because Admiral Theobold had not been let in on the secret of Ultra, the code breaking system, and he did not believe the reports that came from Pearl Harbor so he paid no attention to them. Pearl Harbor had all the information he needed to defend the islands, but he chose not to do so. The Japanese moved into the Aleutians standing up.

Very little happened at sea in the next two weeks. The Japanese carriers sent planes to attack Dutch Harbor and Fort Mears which was not far away. American and Canadian pilots attacked the carriers, but without success. Then things settled down and the submariners went back to fighting the war at sea. The patrols were routine, and the American submarines did not encounter any Japanese boats, although at that point two squadrons of I-boats were in Aleutian waters. But about the middle of June the First Squadron was called back to Japan, leaving only the Second Squadron with seven boats. The Japanese boats carried out nuisance raids on cities down the coast in Washington and Oregon. The new I-boats were replaced with older RO-boats, which were the equivalent of the American S-boats.

The Japanese occupation of the Aleutian Islands meant that Japan had a long supply line to bring food and ammunition to the troops. The U.S. submarine force had a new opportunity in this, and in mid-June the *S-27* was sent to Amchitka Island, about 60 miles from Kiska, on a reconnaissance mission, to ascertain if there were any targets there. Lieutenant Commander Herbert L. Jukes, commanding officer of the *S-27*, planned to make a circle around Amchitka, and then take a look at what was going on over on Kiska. As darkness fell, he brought the submarine to the surface for a battery charge.

It was very hazy there in the half-light of the Arctic day, and the lookouts did not see the strong current that began pulling the boat and finally swept her onto the rocks just off Amchitka Island. She went up strong and stout and wedged herself in the rock. Nothing the crew tried budged her an inch. After a day of this, with high seas breaking over the bridge, Jukes decided to abandon the ship. Before they left, the radio operator managed to send off messages about their plight. Then they got to shore, four hundred yards away, by using their three-man rubber boat in relays. They were on tundra, spongy and wet, nearly freezing in the wind. But they managed to find a village that had been deserted by its Indian-Eskimo inhabitants after the Japanese bombing of the island, and they huddled in the battered buildings. After six days a searching patrol bomber found them and they were rescued.

Even as the Japanese weakened their Aleutian submarine force by sending away the I-boats, the Americans brought eight fleet-class submarines into Aleutian waters, plus another four S-boats. That meant a total of seventeen submarines. The force then began to show some results.

The *Triton*, which already had a good record in the warmer waters of the Pacific, tracked a Japanese destroyer through the murk on July 3, and on the Fourth of July she provided pyrotechnics of her own by putting a single torpedo into the destroyer *Nenohi.* (One torpedo missed.) The Japanese destroyer took an immediate list and in a few minutes she sank. The Japanese sailors and officers in their white uniforms walked off the ship into the icy waters—with no chance of survival.

June was a busy month in the Aleutians. Back at Pearl Harbor, Admiral Nimitz learned from his code breakers that the Japanese were sending many ships to these northern waters. The carrier *Zuiho* sailed for the Aleutians. So did the carrier *Zuikaku,* and that was why those fleet boats had suddenly shown up, to take advantage of the new situation.

Not long after the *Triton* had scored her impressive victory, the *Growler* encountered three destroyers at anchor off Kiska. Lieutenant Commander Howard Gilmore fired at all three of them. Japanese destroyer men were adept themselves with torpedoes and one of the destroyers fired back. As Gilmore took his boat down he could hear two torpedoes passing overhead. Then he heard explosions and he claimed to have sunk the three destroyers. Actually two of them, the *Kasumi* and the *Shiranuhi* were only damaged, but so badly damaged they had to be towed back to Japan for repairs. Gilmore did sink the *Arare* that day.

The *Finback* arrived next in the Aleutians from Pearl Harbor. She went out southeast of Aggatu and encountered a Japanese destroyer. She fired three torpedoes and reported one hit.

These successes of the American submarines caused Admiral Yamamoto to send heavy warships to the Aleutians to protect the supply line. The *Zuikaku* came, and so did the *Zuiho,* but the submarines never got a shot at them. The war in the north was fought at this point between submarines on one side and patrol vessels and destroyers on the other.

The Japanese realized quickly enough that they were overextended in the north if they wished to pursue other avenues, and they did. The Imperial General Staff puzzled over the next step in the war for a time. Whatever the next move was going to be, it was not going to be reinforcement of the Aleutian Islands or an attempt to attack the United States mainland. Admiral Yamamoto quietly laid plans to build up an airfield on Guadalcanal Island. The Japanese held a seaplane base on Tulagi Island across a narrow strait from Guadalcanal; once the airfield was built, the Japanese could stage planes down from Rabaul, the main air base in the southwest Pacific, and attack Australia and the supply lines that led to the United States. Thus they could cripple General MacArthur's attempt to build up forces and start the long road back to Manila.

So the Japanese in the Aleutians languished, beset by their enemies, the most potent of which was the weather.

Despite the setback at Midway, at this point in the war, the Japanese still had the initiative, and the Americans were responding to Japanese moves. In the submarine war, the Japanese were well out in front, having disabled the carrier *Saratoga* and sunk the carrier *Yorktown*, while the largest ship sunk by the Americans was an aircraft ferry. What solace the people at home got was from exaggerated reports issued by the commands. It was not a case of deliberate falsification as it was with the Imperial General Staff in Tokyo, which virtually never reported on losses and concealed from the Japanese people what the Americans knew about the sinking of those four carriers at Midway. Rather, the misinformation put out by the Americans was the result of overoptimistic reporting by the submarine captains, who were led to believe by the sound of torpedo explosions that they were sinking or damaging ships when too often they were not. And occasionally there was a clearcut naval victory, as with the *Nautilus* which was on patrol off Tokyo Bay late in June 1942 when she encountered a Japanese destroyer and sank her. The skipper took a picture through the periscope of the destroyer going down; the photo became a classic. It showed the destroyer *Yamakaze* sinking, stern first, with her bow high in the air, a rising sun flag painted on her forward turret. The symbolism was precisely what America wanted to see and to this point of the war in the Pacific they had seen very little of it.

The Japanese were still doing better than the Americans in the war and for the same old reason: superior experience. In their submarine command there was another major factor, and that was the excellence of the Japanese torpedoes and the inferiority of the American. If the

145

American torpedoes had responded as well as the enemy's the story of sinkings in the first six months of the war would have been quite different. But at Pearl Harbor, Admiral English was following the navy line, which was not to question the past. The Bureau of Ordnance said there was nothing wrong with the Mark XIV torpedo and the Mark VI exploder, so it must be so. One skipper after another came back to Pearl Harbor to report lugubriously on torpedo failures. No one in authority believed them; that much was obvious from the reports.

Every warship commander had to make a report of every action in which he was engaged against the enemy. In the case of the submarines these were war patrol reports, really diaries of the voyage, with special sections dealing with torpedo expenditure, mechanical difficulties, charts and land features, and even weather. Once the skipper had made his report, it went up the command ladder: to division, squadron, submarine command, fleet command, and then to Washington where various offices got copies, from Admiral King's command to the Bureau of Ordnance. The latter received only informational copies, but every command made comments on the patrol reports. In the spring and summer of 1942 the comments showed that the higher authorities were totally out of sympathy with the complaints of the submarine crews, and believed that the skippers were masking incompetence and error by blaming the torpedoes.

The torpedo problem was as serious in the Aleutian Islands as anywhere else. In all, the fleet-class boats that went to the Aleutians were credited by the U.S. submarine command with sinking six destroyers and damaging one. But the fact was that they sank only two destroyers, damaged two others, and also sank two patrol craft.

Those patrol craft fell to the *Grunion*, a brand-new fleet-class submarine that had come to the Aleutians by way of Pearl Harbor, with the paint scarcely dry. She had set out in June from New London, Connecticut for Pearl Harbor. On the way she rescued sixteen merchant seamen during the height of an Atlantic gale. They were survivors of a ship sunk by a German U-boat. Arriving in Hawaii, the *Grunion* spent ten days training, and then was ordered to the Aleutians. On July 10 *Grunion* was sent to patrol north of Kiska.

On July 15 her skipper radioed that she had attacked a Japanese destroyer, by firing three torpedoes that missed, and then had been depth charged by the destroyer. Later that day she engaged three Japanese patrol boats, sank two of them and damaged the third. For the next few days she guarded the exits to Kiska Harbor, but when she reported that the Japanese were maintaining a very tight antisubmarine screen, she was ordered back to Dutch Harbor.

She never arrived. Whether she attacked another destroyer, fell afoul of a Japanese submarine, was somehow wrecked by weather or an accident is not known. The Japanese records available after the war gave no clues. In the *Grunion*'s brief life she had been successful, but she had also suffered from torpedo failure like so many other boats.

There was one place where something was being done about the torpedo failures. Admiral Charles Lockwood, having read all the patrol reports of his new command prior to his arrival, got a dose of claims of torpedo failure all at once. Like all other submariners in the U.S. Navy he had been brainwashed over the years about the Mark XIV torpedo and the Mark VI exploder. Since he had achieved the exalted rank of captain before the war, he had never fired a Mark XIV torpedo in battle, which meant he had not fired the Mark VI exploder. What he knew about the weapons was what he learned from his skippers.

Their stories had many points of agreement. Lockwood did not believe all of them could be wrong and he decided to investigate. First he made it a point to appear on the dock every time a boat came back from patrol, and to board and go down into the wardroom immediately. He spent many hundreds of hours in the cramped wardrooms, drinking many more hundreds of cups of coffee. Nearly every skipper had the same sort of tale to tell. Lockwood began to notice some common factors. One was the presence of air-bubble trails that passed under the target ships or behind them. To Lockwood the bubbles indicated that the torpedo had actually passed beneath the vessel without exploding. That meant torpedo failure.

Captain James Fife, his chief of staff, suggested a simple experiment that had first been offered during the Java days in the Dutch East

Indies when no one had the time to carry it out. They bought a large gill net and moored it vertically outside the harbor. A submarine then came up to firing range and shot the net full of torpedoes with dummy warheads. They then measured the depth of the holes in the net and discovered that the torpedoes were running eleven feet deeper than set. Lockwood wrote another letter to the Bureau of Ordnance and got back a scornful letter which took issue with Lockwood's techniques and results. The test was most unscientific, said the bureau. But did the bureau make a scientific test? Absolutely not. The officers went back to improving their golf scores and cultivating congressmen. Lockwood's findings also made their way to Pearl Harbor, but Admiral English and his staff were not ready to either accept reality or to run their own tests. So Admiral Lockwood and his men in the Southwest Pacific submarine command had to do the best they could by themselves. The skippers began changing the depth settings to make allowances for the too-deep run. The problem was not solved, but at least someone was working on it.

Meanwhile, up in the wintry north, the war dragged on slowly, with very little happening.

13 UNCERTAIN OFFENSIVE

IN the middle of July 1942 the Pacific Fleet submarine command suddenly began to see the light. When Admiral Lockwood in Australia sent his letter about the Mark XIV torpedoes to the Bureau of Ordnance a copy went to Pearl Harbor. Admiral English's staff, heretofore so cocksure about the torpedoes and so insufferable about the skipper's complaints, suddenly learned that there were mechanical reasons for the torpedo failures and informed the submarine commanders that they were to set the depth controls on the torpedoes accordingly.

Through the influence of Admiral Edwards, Lockwood's friend, the matter of torpedo performance was brought to the attention of Admiral King, and he told the Bureau of Ordnance to recheck all its data. The bureau had not even fired the torpedo from a submarine in its tests, but from a barge. King was a hard man and as skeptical as they come, but he was now convinced that there was something drastically wrong and he said just that. When the Bureau of Ordnance got that message, the golfers began to quake, and the scoffing at the submarine captains suddenly stopped. All the bureau had to do—all it ever had been asked to do—was to make some tests. The tests were made and they proved what the fighting men contended, that the torpedoes ran ten feet deeper than advertised.

Immediately the performance of the submarines began to improve. However, there was still something wrong with the torpedoes and nearly every skipper knew it; in fact, there were several things wrong. But at least a submarine captain who got an oblique shot at a ship and

149

did not see the torpedo explode before it reached the target now really had a chance to sink enemy ships. The trouble was that with the correction of the depth problem, the problem of premature explosions increased. Some skippers also complained that the magnetic exploders were not working properly. But once again, ingrained faith in "the system" prevented either Admiral Lockwood or Admiral English from accepting those complaints. Lockwood had isolated a major difficulty; it might be the cause of all the troubles.

More important than any technical problem were the problems of command and strategy. The first six months of the war had gone by and the United States had been totally on the defensive. Several historians of submarine warfare have said that the problem was primarily one of lack of imagination by admirals, from Lockwood right up to King. It is a harsh judgment. To be sure, up to this point the American submarine offensive had been fragmented. Most of the reason for it was the defensive nature of the war. Twenty special missions were required of the Pacific and Southwest Pacific submarine commands in the early months of the war. The invasion of the Aleutian Islands had sent up a wave of concern in Washington that occasioned the dispatch of far more submarines to Alaska than were needed; of course, the historians know that but the operating officers did not. Through July 1942 the United States was still on the defensive in the Pacific. The submarines under Lockwood's command were still short of supplies, and torpedoes were so scarce that the skippers were told not to waste them on small vessels. The boats went out on patrol but in July they accomplished very little. The *Seadragon* sank three ships and damaged a fourth. The *Sturgeon* sank one freighter. The *Thresher* sank a Japanese torpedo boat tender off Kwajalein and very nearly got caught like a fish. After she had attacked the tender, she was in turn attacked by Japanese planes, and these came close enough to shake everyone up. What the skipper of the *Thresher* did not know was that the water around the Marshall Islands was so clear that viewed from an aircraft a submarine far below the surface produced a nice clear silhouette. This became all too clear when the planes continued to track the *Thresher* and brought in surface help. Lieutenant Commander Millican had deeply submerged his boat and was sitting, waiting for the enemy to go away. But instead of going away, the Japanese brought up some vessel that must have been equipped with a crane and grapnel. The Japanese dropped the grapnel over the side and managed somehow to hook onto the hull of the *Thresher*. It looked as though the boat would be hauled to the surface like one of its fish namesakes. Millican was so concerned that he burned his secret documents, including the code books, and prepared to fight it out—and perhaps be captured. But he had to try to get away. He ordered up full-motor speed and began struggling to break the grapnel's hold. He turned sharply to the right and went into a steep dive that took the submarine fifty feet below its four hundred foot test depth and finally shook off the grapnel.

At Perth and Fremantle, Admiral Lockwood was prepared to devote his efforts to improving the submarine scores. Early in July he learned that he was going to be relieved of a duty he considered onerous: as submarine commander he had also been commander of American naval forces in Western Australia. But instead of bringing less work and more freedom, the change worked out in the opposite direction. Washington sent Rear Admiral Arthur S. Carpender, a spit-and-polish officer, down to take over the command. Since he had virtually nothing else to do, he began making life miserable for Lockwood and his submariners. At Pearl Harbor the great contribution of Admiral Withers to the war was the leasing of the Royal Hawaiian Hotel in the heart of Waikiki, so that the submariners between patrols could wallow in the fleshpots of Honolulu if they wished—which most of them did. At Perth one of Lockwood's first acts had been to take two hotels, one on the beach and one in Perth, in the heart of things. Carpender came in and immediately began to complain about everything the submariners were doing. He insisted that "rest camps" be far from civilization and made Lockwood move his to godforsaken ranches in the countryside where there was not a girl within miles—and the only amusement was to go fishing. After a few days of that the submariners were ready to go back to duty without any rest. He criticized the command for ordering American beef instead of using Australian mutton and forced them to take mutton—

and rabbit—aboard the submarines heading out for patrol. This last nearly created several mutinies. He insisted that the patrol reports be written in the King's English rather than in "submarinese." The word "fish" for torpedo particularly annoyed him. Carpender made himself so obnoxious to the submarine command that Admiral Lockwood would not meet with him and their relations had to be carried on through Lockwood's chief of staff. If an officer ever set out to destroy the morale of an organization this one did, and before many weeks were out a number of submariners would very cheerfully have drowned that man, whom they considered a red tape artist, particularly after he complained that the skippers of the Southwest Pacific submarine command were not aggressive enough. That complaint was true enough; Lockwood was relieving skippers right and left. The *Snapper*'s commander was relieved after his second patrol; and that officer's relief was relieved after *his* second patrol. The reason: Lack of that aggressive spirit that is more necessary in a submarine skipper than in any other part of the naval service. Throughout the first days of the war there were timidity problems in every branch of the navy, but the submarine service suffered most. It took a special sort of mentality for a man to risk his own life and those of some eighty crewmen in order to get a shot at a Japanese ship. Many fine men failed that test, yet went on to distinguished careers in other branches of the service. Again, there was no way to tell; and youth and personality had nothing to do with it. One of the skippers Lockwood relieved was only thirty-three years old. He had stood at the top of his class at the Naval Academy and was one of its most popular members. But when it came to submarines, he didn't have "the stuff." Lockwood and his staff were well aware of the problem, yet to have a kibitzer like Carpender leaning on them was not pleasant. But the war went on in spite of Admiral Carpender. Lockwood kept away from him and immersed himself in details of his command. He reorganized the Southwest Pacific submarine force and made Captain Fife commander of Squadron Two, which comprised the boats of the original Asiatic Fleet.

One problem that nagged the Southwest Pacific submarine force was the enormous distance from Perth to the waters where the Japanese lurked. The area of responsibility of the command included all of the Dutch East Indies and the waters adjacent, as well as the Philippine Islands, and the coast of Indo-China—which was nearly thirty-five hundred miles away. A boat starting out from Perth found that it used up so much fuel that its patrol time sometimes ran out before all its torpedoes were expended. If Lockwood could find a base on the northern side of Australia it would save fuel and extend the time on station by at least two days.

Lockwood considered Darwin but rejected it for the moment because the Japanese were bombing Darwin at will from bases further north. Unitl Timor fell, Darwin did not seem to be a safe bet. He settled on a desolate spot, Exmouth Gulf, which was 750 miles north of Fremantle. Lockwood wanted to keep his submarines there and bring the crews back by yacht for leave in Fremantle, but his staff didn't like that idea and created all sorts of difficulties so that in the end Exmouth Gulf became a way station for refueling. The undersea boats left from Fremantle and returned there. They stopped at Exmouth Gulf on the way out to their stations to top off their fuel tanks.

At this point, at the end of July 1942, Lockwood had twenty submarines in the Southwest Pacific. The comments of higher authority on patrol reports (endorsements) indicate he was pleased with nearly none of them. Part of the blame had to be laid on the torpedoes, but most of the American skippers still did not seem to know what was required of them—which had to be an error in training and indoctrination somewhere along the line. Whatever the U.S. Navy was ready for in 1941 it was not the sort of war they began to fight in the Pacific. Again, historians have faulted Lockwood for showing little imagination in the disposition of his submarines. But Lockwood was fighting the battle of morale and trying to teach the commanders he retained and promoted how to use a submarine to sink ships. They also had to be prepared to get killed. Until those lessons were learned there was not much point in arguing whether the high command put the right boats in the right places at the right times. Such an argument is the prerogative of historians but it never won any battles.

To keep close to his submariners, Lockwood moved aboard the tender *Holland* in Fremantle. Every time a boat came back to port he continued to greet the men and hash over the patrol with the skipper. He learned a lot about his men that way, things that never appeared in the patrol reports, such as when a man was tired and when he was just not capable of doing the job. Aboard the boat he could also sense the compatibility or lack of it between officers and crew. The crewmen of the submarines were almost invariably brave men; they had to be to place their lives in the hands of a skipper who might or might not be capable. The timid ones came in for roasting in the officers' clubs and the enlisted men's clubs, and such talk had a way of moving through the fleet, although a commander had to have a sharp ear and many hidden lines out to hear it.

Late in July Lockwood and his staff sensed that the Japanese were preparing to move again, and they had the impression that the movement was to be directed against Australia. The recent bombings were one indication. Tokyo Rose, the Japanese propaganda broadcaster, also predicted that the Imperial army would be walking the streets of Perth before the year was out.

Then came the American invasion of Guadalcanal Island.

At the beginning of August 1942 there were two submarine commands in Australia, although administratively, Lockwood was in charge. But Captain Christie with his S-boat force was operating out of Brisbane, where his activities were closely linked to those of General MacArthur's Southwest Pacific Command. The operating area of Christie's boats included Rabaul, the big Japanese army and air base, New Britain, Kavieng, New Ireland, Buin, Bougainville, Lae, and Salamaua—all names that were virtually unknown to Americans at the time but which would be written large in the newspapers in months to come. They were sinking ships—not many—but enough to keep the Japanese alert. The *S-42* sank the minelayer *Okinoshima* and landed a spy almost on the Japanese doorstep at Rabaul. The *S-43* landed an agent on New Ireland to organize an intelligence network, and another on a tiny island in the Bismarcks. The S-boats sank merchant ships off Guadalcanal and off the Bismarcks.

But the prime accomplishment of Captain Christie's little old fleet came on the day of the American invasion of Guadalcanal Island in the Solomons.

For several months intelligence sources had been warning the Allies that the Japanese were building an airstrip on that island. The word was passed by Australian pilots who looked down and watched as the Japanese burned the grass on the natural flat field above Lunga Point. They watched as the Japanese sent in construction battalions to put up buildings and revetments and all the facilities needed to operate an airfield. The word reached General MacArthur but he didn't have the wherewithal to do anything about it, so his intelligence officers didn't get overly excited. The word was picked up at Pearl Harbor by the Radio Intelligence section of the Pacific Fleet. An intercepted and translated message reported that two battalions of Pioneers (Japanese Seabees) had moved into Guadalcanal. By mid-July the airfield was virtually completed and from his flagship in Japan Admiral Yamamoto gave orders that early the next month the fighters and bombers were to begin using Guadalcanal airfield as a staging point for raids on Australia and particularly the shipping that was coming in to build up General MacArthur's forces.

The one who got the wind up was Admiral King. He saw what Yamamoto was up to more clearly than anyone else and he told the Joint Chiefs of Staff that if it was not stopped he could not guarantee the viability of MacArthur's communication lines with the United States. There was only one way to stop the buildup and prevent the bombings: aggressive action—the invasion of Guadalcanal. King was so insistent that he got his way, and so definite that he persuaded a reluctant Admiral Nimitz, whose worry was that he didn't have the ships and the men to do the job. When General MacArthur heard about the plan he said it was suicidal; and when Rear Admiral Robert Ghormley, who had been serving in London, came down to the Southwest Pacific to take command of this force, since it was in Nimitz's sphere of operations and not MacArthur's, Ghormley agreed with MacArthur. The command problem colored MacArthur's viewpoint, but it hardly accounted for Ghormley's. MacArthur was angry because the navy was invading what he considered to be his bailiwick, no matter that the lines that had been drawn by the Joint Chiefs of Staff, and indeed that was King's intention. He did not propose to have a U.S. Army general managing a war the U.S. Navy had envisioned, if not exactly well-prepared for, over the past twenty-five years. It was more difficult to understand why Ghormley agreed with MacArthur. He had stopped in Washington on his way west from London, and King had explained the problem and the imperative need to act. Ghormley had then moved on to Pearl Harbor where Admiral Nimitz had reinforced King's statements and promised Ghormley everything he could spare for him (and a lot he could not). But from the beginning Ghormley had sat back and watched. He had not participated in the quick run-through (a disaster as an operation) that the Marine Corps landing force went through in the Fiji Islands area just before the real thing. He had not come to the preinvasion conference aboard Rear Admiral Richmond Kelly Turner's invasion flagship, but had sent an emissary instead. He commanded, but like a king of England, he reigned but he did not rule.

The invasion got off to a good start. The Japanese were completely surprised, so much so that the seaplane garrison at Tulagi was totally wiped out in a matter of hours, and there was nothing Yamamoto could do to help. On Guadalcanal the Japanese had virtually no fighting troops; there were a few guards and thousands of construction workers, many of them Koreans, whose enthusiasm for Japanese conquest was rather limited. Thus when the marines landed and moved rapidly toward the Japanese camps, the construction troops ran for the hills. In terms of morale it was a marvelous tonic for the Americans; for months Tokyo had been boasting about the natural fighting superiority of the Japanese and the weakness of the effete westerners. Suddenly, thinking the Japanese they encountered were fighting troops the Americans learned they were not ten feet tall. War correspondents communicated that news back to the United States, where there was more than a little concern that the Japanese claims might be true, in view of the conquests the Imperial Japanese army had already made. As for that army, the Americans were again fortunate in that the Imperial General Headquarters did not take the American invasion seriously. The Japanese army was the victim of its own propaganda, and the general belief in Tokyo was that the United States could not pull its weak resources together to stop the Japanese conquest of the western and southwestern Pacific regions. Only Admiral Yamamoto took the threat seriously enough to do something about it. He moved his flagship down to Truk to direct the coming battle. As for the Japanese army, the command in Rabaul was so unconcerned about the American investment of Guadalcanal that the commanding general called up only a battalion (of less than 1,000 men) to retake the island although there were more than eleven thousand Americans ashore on Guadalcanal.

On invasion day, August 7, 1942, Japanese Cruiser Division Six was at sea in the area of the Bismarck Archipelago when the word came that the Americans had landed. They headed south and Admiral Yamamoto ordered them to attack. On August 9 the augmented Japanese force fought a battle with the American invasion fleet off Savo Island and defeated the Americans smartly, sinking three American cruisers and one Australian cruiser at a cost of thirty men aboard the cruiser *Chokai*, which was hit by a stray shell. The Americans lost about fifteen hundred men killed and many more wounded; so the naval campaign of Guadalcanal opened with the worst defeat suffered by the U.S. Navy since Pearl Harbor.

But just before 8:00 on the morning of August 10 when the U.S. submarine *S-44* was patrolling off Kavieng Harbor at the northwest end of New Ireland (in the Bismarcks), her skipper, Lieutenant Commander J. R. Moore, sighted the returning ships of Cruiser Division Six. Since they were coming out of the sun and traveling in pairs, Moore decided to attack the last ship as it passed by toward the west. When it was in position to fire he could see the Japanese officers in their white uniforms on the bridge, looking around the horizon through their binoculars. Moore fired all four forward tubes of the old S-boat and then gave the order to dive. When the boat reached one hundred and thirty feet down it was suddenly hit with a shock wave. At least two of the Mark X torpedoes had run true and exploded against the hull of the last cruiser. Somehow the explosion blew up the ship's boilers and the submarine was tortured by the hideous sounds of a ship breaking up. The crew later claimed that the after-

157

math of the explosion scared them more than the depth charging that followed. The ship they had sunk was the heavy cruiser *Kako*, and she gave Captain Christie's Brisbane submarines another first: the first major warship to be sunk by an American submarine in the Pacific war.

The Americans had no reason to be cocky, however. The Japanese soon had a reprisal for the sinking of the cruiser, their revenge abetted by the Americans themselves. The *S-39* set out on her fifth war patrol early in August 1942 after a number of mishaps which included the disabling of the executive officer by pneumonia so that he had to be put ashore. On August 13 she was supposed to be offshore, east of Rossel Island in the Louisiade group. For two days she had been bucking southeast winds and a swell, and neither the skipper nor the navigator had the experience to recognize that she had been making westing all this time. They learned shortly after 2:00 A.M. on August 14, when traveling at cruising speed; with a grinding crash the submarine went up on the reef south of Rossel Island. She grounded hard, and with such forward momentum that her bow came out of the water and immediately she listed to port. The sea began breaking across her stern. The skipper, Lieutenant F. E. Brown, ordered the engines backed. It was useless. He ordered the ballast tanks blown and fuel tanks emptied to lighten the boat. It was no good; the *S-39* was high and while not dry, she was driving up on the reef and the lightening of the vessel only made her go up higher. Brown waited for high tide and tried again. The boat backed up about fifty feet but then the crew discovered that the pounding she had been taking had ruptured several tanks, and they filled with water as she backed. The boat heeled over to port and struck bottom again.

The southeast wind and sea had never stopped and they continued all day long on August 14, with seas twenty feet high breaking over the submarine and pounding her to death. Lieutenant Brown sent the word to Brisbane that he was stuck and the Australian navy sent the tug *Katoomba* which was scheduled to arrive on the morning of August 15.

As dawn came that morning the *S-39* was a wreck. She listed sixty degrees and Skipper Brown was afraid that at any moment she might

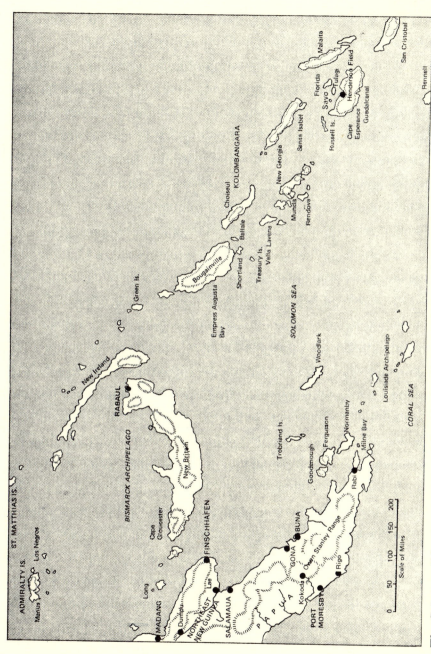

The Solomon Islands

capsize. He ordered the torpedo warheads disconnected, and fired off those in the tubes for safety. The conditions called for abandonment of the wreck, but Brown insisted on staying aboard. He did give the crewmen permission to swim ashore if they wished. Ashore meant to the relative safety of the reef that projected from the water. Lieutenant C. N. G. Hendrix swam with a line to the reef to give the men a lifeline, and Chief W. L. Schoenrock assisted him. Then most of the crew swam ashore, but a dozen of the officers and men stayed aboard until noon that day, when the *Katoomba* came in sight. She came up as close as she could in the shallow water and then began the hard job of getting the crew aboard. That task took until midmorning on August 16. Then the *Katoomba* headed back for Brisbane. There was no need to worry about destroying the *S-39* so the enemy could not use her. The boat had been delivered to the navy in 1925, so she was not filled with new military secrets, and if she had been the sea had already done a good job of erasing them. As the *Katoomba* left the scene the *S-39* was breaking up. Back at Brisbane, and not knowing the condition of the boat, Captain Christie worried and persuaded MacArthur's air force to send planes to bomb the hulk. Within a day or two the character of the wreckage could scarcely be identified. When Brown got back to Brisbane, several members of Christie's staff expected him to be court-martialed for losing his boat through navigational error. That was the old peacetime way, but it was not Christie's way in war. He had already had to relieve several skippers for what he believed was lack of aggressiveness in pursuing the enemy. Christie was impressed with the way Brown had managed the stricken boat and saved his crew. He gave Brown command of the *S-43* instead.

One reason why the Japanese did not immediately recognize the serious nature of the Guadalcanal invasion was another foray made just nine days after the marines landed near Lunga Point. This second "raid" was conducted by Lieutenant Colonel Evans Carlson with elements of his Second Raider Battalion. Carlson's Raiders were one of two such battalions; the other was already engaged at Guadalcanal. Both were the product of a long campaign Evans Carlson had been waging within the Marine Corps. Earlier he had spent several months

159

as an observer with the Chinese Communist armies in northern China and was enormously impressed with their ability to move and fight with virtually no modern resources. As he was pressing the concept of "shock troops," the idea was catching hold among the Allies. The British and the Canadians had trained commandos, who used all sorts of unorthodox methods in their warfare. The commando methods and the "gung ho" (work together) spirit he'd witnessed in the Chinese Communists were the motivating factors in Carlson's command. By the summer of 1942 his men were so well trained that in an exercise on a Hawaii beach they managed to creep up close enough to Admiral Nimitz and his staff, who were observing, that the Raiders could have silently killed them before being discovered. Nimitz was impressed and he decided to employ the unit to make a raid on Makin Island in the Gilberts, which he was looking over as the possible spot for the first major Pacific Fleet assault on the enemy. The Guadalcanal invasion was not a part of Plan Orange—the U.S. Navy's overall scheme for the war against Japan. The plan stated that the route to Tokyo was through the Central Pacific, and the Guadalcanal operation was a desperate action taken to stop the Japanese before it was too late to save Australia.

The trouble with launching an invasion against the Japanese-held islands of the Central Pacific was that so little was known about them in Pearl Harbor. Nimitz had another reason for sending Carlson and his men to Makin; it was supposed to be a fine diversion. The Japanese, Nimitz hoped, would expend many ships and aircraft on reinforcement of the Gilbert Islands at the expense of the Solomons. The raid would have to be carried out by stealth, and that meant by submarine.

On August 8, the men of Carlson's Raiders boarded Commander Brockman's *Nautilus* and Lieutenant Commander J. R. Pierce's *Argonaut*. Altogether there were 222 extra men aboard the two submarines and the voyage to the Gilberts was hardly a leisurely summer cruise. But the two boats arrived safely off Makin on August 16, and the operation began.

First the submarines made a journey around the island, just offshore, to find a suitable beach. Later skipper Haines said part of their trouble was that they did not spend enough time looking. But the boats were crowded and everyone wanted to get with it and get back to Pearl Harbor—in one piece if possible. They selected one beach, and at 2:00 A.M. on August 17 the marines began getting into the rubber boats that would take them ashore. There was some difficulty because the outboard motors did not start very well. Finally they all worked and the Raiders were ashore. All went well until one Raider accidentally discharged his rifle, which alerted the Japanese defenders on the shore not far from the beach, and then the troubles began. At 7:00 A.M. the skipper of the *Nautilus* received a message asking for fire support from the submarines' deck guns, but the communication with the beach by small radio was terrible and the submarine guns did virtually no good against the Japanese. After a while the Raiders announced that there were two ships in the harbor. The trouble was that the harbor was concealed from the submarines by a grove of palm trees, and the observer on shore was out of communication almost immediately. Brockman began firing blindly, and fired sixty-five rounds of ammunition before he decided it was a waste of time. He was wrong. He never saw the Japanese ships because the *Nautilus* had sunk them both.

The Raiders ran into trouble from the Japanese, but they managed to get back to their beach and create a defense perimeter. They were supposed to return to the submarines that night at 7:00, and after making arrangements with a local Makin Island chief to bury their dead, they prepared to go off in the boats. Evacuation was complicated because they had to go out through the surf. Several of the motors would not start. Carlson tried to get his men off the beach, but only seven boats made it to the submarines. Carlson stayed back on the beach with his Raiders and with Major James Roosevelt, the son of the President, who was his executive officer. At daylight the *Nautilus* moved in close to shore because the Raiders they had picked up told them of the troubles of getting through the surf in the rubber boats, and those ashore did not have operable motors. Two boats made it out that morning, and they were sent back manned by volunteers who took a line-throwing gun back to the beach. They were told that they probably would be attacked by aircraft and that the submarines would

161

have to submerge; but they were also told that they were not being deserted and that the sub would stay with them and reappear as soon as possible. Sure enough, at about 8:00 A.M. two Japanese fighter bombers appeared off the beach. Both submarines went down, and the Japanese planes flew around, dropping a few depth bombs. Then they turned their attention to several boats that were struggling through the water, heading for the place where the submarines had been. The planes strafed the boats and killed several marines.

Carlson moved his men around to a prearranged emergency pickup rendezvous on the leeward side of the lagoon; when the submarines surfaced that evening he signaled them to come in and pick up the men. In the darkness he counted heads and by midnight he was sure he had all the living men still on the island, whereupon they shoved off. Unfortunately he was not correct. They left nine marines on Makin who were captured by the Japanese and shipped off to Kwajalein. There they fell into the hands of Vice Admiral Koso Abe who decided he would execute them as "pirates" and had them all beheaded. When the war ended Vice Admiral Abe lived to regret his violation of the laws of war: he was tried as a war criminal and hanged.

The Carlson raid did indeed have the effect of lulling the Japanese into believing the Guadalcanal operation was not as important as it was in fact. (It had another—and opposite—effect: the fortification of the Gilberts so that when the Americans actually did attack at Tarawa the cost was very high in U.S. casualties.) So for weeks the Japanese defenders on Guadalcanal were thrown into battle against numerically superior American forces with predictable results; the Japanese were unable to recapture the airfield that the Americans had renamed Henderson Field.

Japanese naval superiority and air superiority in the Solomons were unquestionable in the beginning. The marines, navy, and army all brought planes in to combat the Zero fighters and the Betty bombers; they fought valiantly, but against heavy odds. The standard American army and navy fighter planes of that moment were not a good match for the fast, maneuverable Zeros; besides, the Japanese planes outnumbered the Americans several times. Even so, little by

162

little, the Americans began to gain equality in the air, partly because to fight at Guadalcanal the Japanese had to make a thousand-mile round trip from Rabaul bases. On the sea, the progress of the Americans was much slower. As one Japanese officer put it, the Americans were exasperating: the Japanese sank their ships, and sank more ships, and the Americans just kept bringing ships into the Solomons. The Japanese navy was already tasting the bitter future. Every error the American commanders made was canceled out in time by the enormous war production at home. The Japanese had no such leeway. With only minor augmentation, their war had to be fought with the weapons at hand in 1941.

Beneath the sea, at this point, the story was not so much different. The American submariners were still learning their trade and the Japanese submariners were practicing theirs. The U.S. aircraft carriers *Hornet* and *Wasp* came to the South Pacific. The *I-19* stalked the *Wasp*, found it easy going through the ineffective American antisubmarine screen, sank the *Wasp* with three torpedoes, then made a successful escape from the scene. The *I-15* found the *Hornet's* task force at sea, fired at the carrier, missed and hit the battleship *North Carolina* and the destroyer *O'Brien* with the torpedoes meant for the carrier. That was a new sort of luck. The *I-15* also got away as the stricken American task force limped back to Espiritu Santo, the South Pacific Force headquarters. A few days later the *I-4* torpedoed the U.S. supply ship *Althena* southeast of the Solomons.

In Australia the submarine situation became more than a little cloudy after Admiral King decided to send Rear Admiral Arthur Carpender down to Western Australia to take over as senior naval officer. Carpender had nothing else to do so he decided to command the submarines, and Admiral Lockwood objected violently. The situation was saved from total disaster when Carpender was moved over to Brisbane to take over as—in effect—admiral of MacArthur's navy. For a time that seemed to solve Lockwood's problems, but then Washington decided the old S-boats had done their duty and needed replacement, and moved Squadron Two, with Captain James Fife in command, to Brisbane. This change, cutting Lockwood's command in half, showed him the handwriting on the wall, and caused him to begin agitating to take over in Brisbane, much as he detested Carpender. But Carpender wanted no more of Lockwood than Lockwood wanted of him and would not let Lockwood make the change. It would appear that he rather hoped Lockwood might disappear into the woodwork somewhere. Matters were further complicated when General MacArthur moved over to Port Moresby and wanted Christie to come along, but Christie demurred and remained in Brisbane. Lockwood was out in left field in Fremantle-Perth, and it sometimes seems a wonder that the American submarines in Australia accomplished anything at all. Just then they were not doing very well.

The Pacific Fleet submarines were doing better, but they suffered in the second half of 1942 from the need to lend boats to Christie (who soon had twenty-four fleet-class submarines) and to cover the Truk area for Admiral Nimitz, as well as carry out what was seen easily enough as the major strategic mission of the submarines: the destruction of Japan's resources and her ability to carry on the war.

The Pacific Fleet gained a new insight into modern submarine operations when Commander Richard Voge was taken off the *Sailfish,* after four patrols, and sent to Pearl Harbor as operations officer of the Pacific Fleet submarines. He was the first high-ranking staff officer to actually have experience in World War II. He had fired torpedoes. He knew the problems of the depth settings and he suspected the unreliability of the magnetic exploders. He was well-liked when he went into the job, and soon became respected because the submarines quickly began producing better results. It was a question of giving the captains a little more room, and paying more attention to their verbal observations and reports after patrol. That autumn the problem of timidity largely vanished as younger captains came into the submarine fleet, many of them experienced on patrols as executive officers on other submarines. The patrols around Truk that summer and fall were not notably successful. The *Drum* damaged one ship; the *Grayling* damaged another. When the captains came back they were roasted for not having done better but what they were suffering from was an overabundance of Japanese patrol aircraft in the area, a matter not properly assessed by the submarine command. The Japanese had plenty of aircraft at that point in the war and they used them adeptly. Two years later the German U-boats in the Atlantic suffered from precisely the same difficulty, and their "productivity" was finally reduced to a point where it was no longer a major factor in the war.

In spite of the difficulties of patrol in the Truk area, Lieutenant Commander Henry C. Bruton, the only seagoing lawyer in the submarine force, took the *Grayling* on what started as a very poor patrol and ended up as a successful one. Early on, Bruton fired nine torpedoes at three ships and missed every time. At least some of those torpedoes must have been at fault but there was no way of telling; and complaints about the torpedoes were still received skeptically at Pearl Harbor and Brisbane. But Bruton got another chance—at a big ship he saw dimly on the night of August 4. He attacked once, thought he had lost the ship, then found it again, and attacked a second time. He sank the ship, the 12,000-ton *Brazil Maru*, which was carrying several hundred soldiers bound for Guadalcanal. That was precisely the sort of work that Nimitz wanted out of the Truk submarines at that moment. Otherwise the performance in the Truk area was lukewarm, and while the submarines were supposed to deliver information about ship movements in and out of the area, they did not get much. The best performance of all was that of Lieutenant Commander Lawson Paterson Ramage in the *Trout*. The code breakers at Pearl Harbor had word of a task group coming down, which included the light carrier *Taiyo* and several cruisers. Ramage's submarine was closest to the Japanese task group when he got the word; when he sighted it he fired five torpedoes at the *Taiyo*. At least one exploded and so the *Trout* had another first: the first damage caused to a Japanese aircraft carrier in the war.

The Japanese antisubmarine tactics were never bad; their greatest weakness was the small size and shallow depth of their depth charges, but they gave many submariners a bad time during this period. The *Flying Fish* played tag with Japanese antisubmarine forces for three days after her skipper tried to take a shot at a battleship. He sank one patrol boat but several others harried him and so did a whole succession of Japanese planes. A destroyer came up and dropped more than fifty depth charges over the *Flying Fish* and another came along to help. The pair kept the submarine down for half a day before she finally escaped with her crew thanking their stars—again, what submariners called the "J (Jesus) factor."

On balance the Truk patrols were unsatisfactory. Nearly a year had passed since the Japanese attack on Pearl Harbor but the U.S. submarine force was functioning at perhaps a third of its capacity. Too often the skippers missed opportunity by ineptitude, their own or that of their crews. The *Wahoo* was a case in point. Under Lieutenant Commander Marvin Kennedy she missed a chance at a Japanese carrier. The reason, cited by the patrol report, was that the men on watch were slow in picking up the carrier and its escorting ships; by the time they did they had to run to catch up, and then Kennedy did not run fast enough. When the *Wahoo* returned to Pearl Harbor, the skipper was in for a roasting from Admiral English, who was all too aware of the failure of his submarines to give Admiral Nimitz the support he wanted.

The *Albacore* missed a shot at the carrier *Zuikaku*. The *Amberjack* missed a cruiser and then a battleship. A few merchant ships were sunk in the area, but that was not precisely what Admiral Nimitz had in mind in these desperate days when night after night the Japanese "Tokyo Express" was running down "the Slot" between Guadalcanal and the Florida Islands, reinforcing the Japanese troops on Guadalcanal.

Because of the employment of so many submarines elsewhere (lent to Christie, sent to Truk, patrolling in the Aleutians), Admiral English did not have many boats to send to the waters near Japan. In four months he managed only twenty patrols there. They served the salutary purpose of reminding the Japanese that the "effete" westerners had some fight in them, but their results were not overly impressive either. The *Narwhal* sank two ships off Hokkaido, the northernmost island of Japan. The *Pompano*, one of the oldest of the fleet-class boats (1937) was nearly lost when attacked by a destroyer off Honshu. The *Dolphin*, which was even older (1932) was nearly sunk by another submarine; the skipper managed to steer betweeen a pair of torpedoes and escaped destruction. The *Cuttlefish* (1934) took several shots at ships and her skipper thought she sank two. The claim was accepted at Pearl Harbor but it was not a valid claim; she had sunk nothing. The *Nautilus* (1930) did sink three ships after the Makin Island raid, which proved that it was possible for the old boats to do the job with the right captains and crews. But the *Nautilus, Narwhal,* and *Argonaut* were antiques by the standards of the day. They were converted V-boats and the whole design had been abandoned as unwieldy. When the war broke out they were deemed essential to the American effort. It was a measure of the growing efficiency of the American ship production system that, by the end of 1942, Admiral English could withdraw those boats from general service and turn them over to use for the training that was so badly needed by the submarine crews—present and future.

There was no question in 1942 but that the newer submarines did make a difference. The story that received the most popular attention in this period was that of the *Guardfish,* a brand-new boat, the fifth delivered to the navy in 1942. Her captain was Lieutenant Commander Thomas B. Klakring.

Generally speaking, the submarine service had not gotten much publicity at home. The most romantic stories, as of the rescue of the dozen nurses from Corregidor, did make the papers, but Nimitz was not about to risk tipping his hand to the Japanese, and he certainly was not going to tell them about the American problems.

Yet the submarines were carrying the war against the Japanese and even though there was room for vast improvement, their victories would make good reading and shore up a battered American home front morale. For Nimitz the matter was complicated by his own genial disregard for publicity and the Navy Department's annoyance because General MacArthur's efficient promotion machine was in full gear, and many Americans believed he was carrying the war singlehandedly. A wonderful opportunity for the Pacific Fleet command arose that summer out of the patrol of the *Guardfish.*

It was Klakring's first patrol in the boat. Admiral English sent him off the northeastern coast of Honshu Island. Her first effort was dismal: Klakring fired three torpedoes at a ship escorted by a patrol boat and all missed. Surfacing after the ships had gone, Klakring found a pair of fishing trawlers and sank them with his deck gun. Such activity, he realized, was scarcely the optimum for a fleet-class submarine; but the ships he saw were carefully hugging the shore in waters that the Japanese knew but the Americans did not. Klakring decided he had to rely on his radar and his fathometer if he was going to get on with the job.

Even in daylight at this time of year the Japanese coast was usually obscured by fog. Navigation was complicated further by two currents, one outside that ran north at about two miles an hour, and one inside that ran south at about the same speed. The only way the navigator could tell the difference was by water temperature; the southern current was warm and the northern was cold.

Klakring learned all this by trial. One day he found a Japanese merchantman and started an attack. But the captain saw the periscope, turned around, and moved inshore. Klakring had the option of letting the ship go or of chasing it in waters that he knew nothing about. The radar would give him the general configuration of the land, but that was all. The rest was up to him: He did go in, he did sink the ship, and he did learn about the currents. Thereafter, at night the *Guardfish* moved outside to charge its batteries and send messages back to Pearl Harbor. Long before daylight Klakring started her back inside, "sort of groping" his way toward land. Before dawn each day the *Guardfish* submerged and sat like a spider waiting for flies—and every day the Japanese ships came to him.

One day Klakring attacked a merchantman, firing three torpedoes at her. The first porpoised repeatedly, swooping in and out of the water until it passed behind the ship. The second struck squarely and exploded. Klakring could see the column of water that shot up as high as the ship's mast. But nothing else happened. The third torpedo passed beneath the ship. Klakring decided to give chase, but abandoned the idea when he spotted four Japanese planes coming toward him. As he took the boat down, she passed one of his torpedoes in the water, the warhead broken off. Here was an indication that something was seriously wrong with some of the torpedoes, but the men of the *Guardfish* had no time to worry about that problem at the moment.

Klakring waited every day for his ships and he wasn't disappointed.

Sometimes he let a ship go by because it was too small and he wanted to save the torpedoes for bigger game. In eleven days he believed he sank six ships. They seemed to be very large ships, too, and his observations were confirmed by his executive officer and those crew members who, for a treat, were given a look through the periscope. At one point he sank two ships within a few minutes and everybody who looked agreed that they were between ten thousand and fourteen thousand tons. Overestimation of size was a common failing of submarine captains; those two ships were the *Tenryu Maru* and the *Kaimei Maru,* and the largest was only a bit over five thousand tons.

During those eleven days of playing spider, the men of the *Guardfish* had a good look at the Honshu countryside. At one point they were so close to the coast that they could see a train running along the coastal rail line and distinguish the clothing of the passengers inside. They seemed to be "all dressed up," as if they were going somewhere. A look at the chart indicated that a race track was located in the vicinity. "Maybe they're going to the races," quipped the conning tower wag.

When the *Guardfish*'s patrol time was over, Klakring turned her back toward Midway. When he arrived and submitted his verbal report, Admiral English was delighted. It was by all appearances the best patrol accomplished to date by a submarine under his command. In short order Admiral Nimitz learned about it and so did his public relations officer, Commander Waldo Drake. It seemed perfectly natural to give the U.S. Navy some good publicity for a change. So a press conference was arranged, and since there wasn't much news at Pearl Harbor, the chance to interview submariners was something out of the ordinary. The conference was a roaring success. Out of it came one of the legends of the war, "folk history" as a later generation would term it. During the conference, in response to the reporters' barrage of questions, Klakring spun a yarn. Why, he said, they had been so close to the Japanese shore that they could see the horses running at the racetrack and placed a few bets in the wardroom. That story caught the imagination of the American public, particularly after *Life* magazine gave it an enormous play in one of its famous picture-text stories. The *Guardfish* and Klakring became the heroes of the racing world.

They also became celebrated within the fleet. Klakring won the Navy Cross for that patrol, and his executive officer was awarded a Silver Star. The boat won a presidential unit citation, and even the enemy gave Klakring and his crew their own sort of accolade. The next month the Japanese navy planted a minefield along the coast where Klakring had been operating, in order to protect the outside flank of the ships running up and down the coast. This minefield was small in area at first, but eventually became much larger, and a serious problem for submarines operating off the Honshu coast. In all the hoopla little attention was paid to the torpedo problem that Klakring had experienced.

The *Guardfish* had returned from that first patrol on September 15. After a refit at Midway and the celebrated press conference, Klakring took her out again on September 30, this time toward the East China Sea. But three days later he was back; the radio, the pit log (by which they measured distance traveled), and the torpedo data computer were not operating properly. The repairs took only hours and on October 3 the *Guardfish* was going out again toward the Nansei Shoto chain of islands. The weather was foul and she did not arrive on station until October 19. Then the torpedo problem appeared again.

On the nineteenth an early morning contact put the *Guardfish* on a five-hour submerged approach toward a heavily laden freighter with plane cover. At 10:25, having reached his optimum obtainable position, Klakring fired four torpedoes from a distance of just over a mile. Nothing happened, although he was certain that at least two of the torpedoes had run straight—and then passed directly beneath the ship. Klakring rechecked all his calculations, found them accurate, and fired the last two torpedoes in the bow tubes from a distance of 2,000 yards. The last torpedo exploded at the stern of the enemy vessel. Klakring was looking through the periscope, checking for damage, when a plane dropped four depth charges close to the *Guardfish*. Klakring took the boat down to two hundred feet, remained there until he felt the danger had passed, and then came up again for periscope observation. He saw that the ship had changed course, and hoping that it was severely damaged and heading in for the beach, he chased it as the bow tubes were being reloaded. While he was pursuing the damaged ship he was attacked by two planes. At that moment the boat was just passing the one hundred and twenty-five foot mark. Suddenly the submarine leaped up by the bow to less than ninety feet before she could be brought under control. Those pilots were good. A second explosion hurt his ears, but drove the boat down instead of up. Klakring kept the *Guardfish* at two hundred and fifty feet for the rest of the afternoon while the crew pulled themselves together. He described the action in his patrol report:

> 1831 [hours]. Surfaced after a thoroughly disappointing day wherein: (a) faulty torpedo performance prevented destruction of a valuable target; (b) the damaged target had to be let go due to the severe bombing attack; (c) the radar failed so completely that the *Guardfish* would have been destroyed by the attacking planes except for the vigilance of the topside watch.

But two days later the *Guardfish* sighted a seven-ship Japanese convoy. Klakring fired four torpedoes and one ship sank immediately. The others dispersed and began firing at the *Guardfish*, which moved in on them with the periscope fully exposed. One of the ships tried to run down the submarine. Klakring swung around and fired the stern tubes. One torpedo hit the ship and blew the after gun crew forty feet in the air; the force of the explosion destroyed the stern and the ship sank in two minutes. The rest of the ships turned and ran but kept firing back at the submarine with such accuracy that Klakring decided to break off the pursuit and go deep underwater. Later he surfaced to find a Japanese patrol boat picking up the survivors; the captain of the patrol boat saw the submarine and opened fire. At that point Klakring decided that discretion was indicated and headed away on the surface in the general direction the convoy had taken when last he saw the ships. Twenty-five minutes later two aircraft appeared, forcing the submarine down, then dropped a dozen depth charges. The *Guardfish* was not hurt.

For the next ten days no action was possible; a violent storm struck the area and the *Guardfish* remained submerged as much as possible

171

to avoid the battering of wind and wave. On November 9 a ship appeared on the horizon, but Klakring couldn't manage to get close enough for an attack. On November 10 it was time to move on to another part of the patrol area east of the Nansei Shoto. On November 21 on the way back to Midway the boat was badly shaken up in an attack by a Japanese plane. When the plane was spotted coming in, Klakring made an emergency dive, but the controls to the stern planes failed and the boat went down so slowly that the Japanese pilot scored two near misses on the submarine. It was a fitting ending to a most frustrating patrol.

In the desperate battle for Guadalcanal, Japanese submarines performed far better than American. The *I-176* torpedoed the American cruiser *Chester* at a point halfway between Espiritu Santo and San Cristobal. The *Chester* did not sink but she had to be taken back to America for repairs and was out of the Guadalcanal campaign. The I-1 evacuated a number of Japanese troops from a small Pacific Island where they had been sent in anticipation of the capture of Guadalcanal, and where they then had become isolated by events.

The *I-222* was used to refuel Japanese flying boats; seaplanes that operated from the decks of surfaced Japanese submarines were used to scout American surface forces. The *I-16*, the *I-20*, and the *I-24* carried midget submarines and launched these off Guadalcanal. The U.S. transport *Majaba* was torpedoed by one of these, but managed to beach herself and was later salvaged. All but one of the midget submarines were lost in this attack and thereafter until much later in the war the midget submarines were not often employed.

In November 1942 five Japanese submarines were operating in the area Americans called Torpedo Junction, south of Guadalcanal. One of them sank the cruiser *Juneau* on November 14. Two of the Japanese submarines were sunk by American destroyers in this action.

On the American side, only one submarine had any real influence on the outcome of the Guadalcanal campaign, and she was then employed in one of the detested "special missions." She was the *Amberjack* and her skipper was Lieutenant Commander J. A. Bole, Jr. The *Amberjack* had been on patrol between Rabaul and the Shortland Islands, where she had sunk two Japanese ships, the *Shiro-*

gane Maru and the *Senkai Maru*. Bole was about to head "for the barn" at Pearl Harbor when he received orders by radio to go instead to Espiritu Santo, the headquarters of the South Pacific Force. There, Bole was informed that his boat was temporarily assigned to the commander, South Pacific Air Force. This unusual move was dictated by a desperate situation at Guadalcanal. The marine, navy, and army pilots at Guadalcanal had been fighting on a shoestring for weeks. The greatest problem was lack of aviation gasoline, and several attempts to supply fuel had been frustrated by Japanese air and sea attacks. At that moment precious little aviation gasoline was on hand at Henderson Field; mechanics were draining the tanks of crashed aircraft to keep the handful of fighter planes in the air. If the aircraft were grounded, the Japanese would most certainly be able to reinforce and resupply their troops on Guadalcanal, and the U.S. Marines would be at their mercy. All this was explained to Lieutenant Commander Bole and he was then told that his mission would be to deliver to Guadalcanal 9,000 gallons of aviation gas, fifteen army fighter pilots and ground crew members, and two hundred hundred-pound bombs.

Since the mission was so dangerous, and since it was impossible to conceal the activity that would have to take place, Bole explained to his crew the plight of the marines and the need for the action to be undertaken. For once there was no "bitching" in the boat about a special mission. Two fuel tanks had to be sealed completely (they leaked) and then steam-cleaned to accommodate the high-test aviation gasoline. The bombs were stowed in the forward torpedo room. The gasoline was pumped into the refurbished tanks and on October 22 the *Amberjack* set out with orders to proceed to Lunga Roads and report to the port officer.

Early on the morning of October 25 the *Amberjack* was on the surface, charging its batteries and proceeding slowly toward her destination when a new radioed order directed them to proceed to Tulagi, across the channel from Guadalcanal, and unload there. The reason became apparent a few hours later. The *Amberjack* had dived at dawn and reached Lunga Point. Crossing over to Tulagi would be no great problem. It meant that the aviation gasoline would have to be

173

handled twice by the people ashore, to get it up to Henderson Field. It seemed that, as happened so often, the people ashore had goofed again.

Off Lunga Point, Bole saw the fleet tug *Seminole* through the periscope and reversed his course to get away from her. Planes and surface ships in "the Slot" did not read the labels on periscopes, and if the *Amberjack*'s was spotted before she got inshore she might be bombed or suffer a depth-charge attack by American forces.

Thirty minutes later the *Amberjack* was well south of Lunga Point, when along came three Japanese destroyers which opened fire on the marine positions, particularly on Henderson Field. The destroyers sped along the shore past the Tenaru River and halfway down the island, then turned around and came back, still firing but also laying a smoke screen that concealed their activity and the fact that they had dropped off supplies for the Japanese troops on the island. The *Amberjack*, which would have had easy shots at all three half an hour earlier, was completely out of position to make an attack. Perhaps it was just as well. It would not have taken much of a shock to send that aviation gasoline and the bombs up the hill as high as Henderson Field.

Very quickly, moving at thirty knots, the Japanese destroyers were gone, leaving a trail of gray smoke hanging in the air above "the Slot." The *Amberjack* remained submerged until dusk and then headed into Tulagi Harbor. The passengers got off, the bombs were unloaded, and the aviation gasoline was pumped out of the fuel tanks into a lighter. The *Amberjack* sailed just after midnight, bound this time for Brisbane.

The use of submarines by both sides for tasks usually assigned to other vessels was an indication of the desperation of the Guadalcanal struggle. The change in balance brought about by ultimate American control of the air meant that the Americans did not again have to resort to employment of submarines for freight and passenger service—but, for the Japanese, this practice was only beginning. From Guadalcanal on, much of the Japanese submarine force would be constantly employed in resupply and rescue missions.

14 THE BLOCKADE BEGINS

T HE quarrel between the admirals—Carpender and Lockwood— had thoroughly disrupted the command of submarines in Australia. Lockwood kept asking to be moved up to Brisbane to take control of the entire force but Carpender would not have him there; he kept Lockwood languishing on the vine in Perth-Fremantle on the west coast while Captain Christie ran the submarines on the east coast of Australia. After Admiral William F. Halsey took command of the South Pacific Force in mid-October 1942, Admiral Nimitz designated Captain Christie as a task force commander directly under Halsey. This action cut the ground from under MacArthur's attempts to create his own navy and it also made Admiral Carpender's position ridiculous. He was commander of the Southwest Pacific Force but it had no submarines and virtually no other vessels. In Western Australia, Admiral Lockwood continued to operate as he had with his reduced submarine fleet, but Carpender found it virtually impossible to interfere across a whole continent. The Carpender-Lockwood quarrel, then, settled down to a stalemate.

MacArthur raised the roof in Washington about his deprivation but the best he could get out of Admiral King was the designation of six submarines to his command. Captain Christie retained operational control and all MacArthur (through Carpender) could do was tell Christie where to send them.

In Western Australia as well as at Pearl Harbor the torpedo specialists worked over the Mark XIV torpedo and the Mark VI exploder, trying to find the answers to the continued problem of torpedo failure.

By autumn 1942 even the Bureau of Ordnance recognized that something very important was amiss and a whole series of "experts" went into the combat zones to try to help. But even uncertain torpedoes became hard to come by. Lockwood was not getting the expected torpedo shipments from the United States, at least partly because the torpedo factories couldn't keep up with the demands of three Pacific commands as well as those in the Atlantic and the Caribbean. Instead of about eighty torpedoes a month, which he needed, he was getting fewer than twenty. His force had been cut back to eight boats with the transfer of Squadron Two to Brisbane but the torpedo shortage made normal operations impossible. Lockwood put his skippers on rations: twenty torpedoes per patrol instead of twenty-four. The shortage grew worse, and the moment a boat returned from a patrol, her unexpended torpedoes were removed and loaded aboard another boat just going out. Finally, out of necessity, Lockwood cut the torpedo quota to eight, and diverted some of his boats from sinking ships to minelaying.

The mines were the Mark XII magnetic mines, copied roughly from a variety the Germans had used successfully in World War I. The minelaying patrols were disliked by the submarine crews nearly as much as the special missions but there was no way out. Nearly one-third of the patrols Lockwood sent out in the last part of 1942 were minelaying missions. The areas he chose were the Gulf of Siam and the Hainan Strait off the coast of China.

The *Gar* made one of the first patrols to the Gulf of Siam and laid thirty-two mines. After minelaying she was supposed to go on patrol with her handful of torpedoes, but her skipper didn't attack any ships, and when she returned to Fremantle, Lockwood relieved him and two officers who had asked to leave the boat.

For years Admiral Lockwood had advocated the use of much heavier deck guns on submarines. His old command, the *Bonita*, had a five-inch gun but when the V-design was abandoned the big guns were also. In that 1938 quarrel with Admiral Hart over submarine design Lockwood had managed to save the fleet-class boat concept as well as the idea of submarines as an offensive force but he had to give in on the size of the deck gun so that Hart could save face; so the guns

176

had been scaled down. But three of the old V-class boat guns that had recently been removed from the boats when they were put into training service were now shipped to Admiral Lockwood, the prime advocate of big guns for submarines, to conduct experiments. He was delighted to have them and immediately two of them were mounted on submarines. The *Gar* had one, but on that unfortunate patrol into the Gulf of Siam it was never fired. The *Thresher* got the second one.

The *Gar* set out for the Gulf of Siam too to lay mines, and after this was done Lieutenant Commander W. J. Millican began looking for enemy ships. Even though he had only eight torpedoes he made four attacks; they all failed. Then he attacked a medium-sized freighter off Makassar Strait and with his five-inch deck gun, drove her into shallow water. When he returned to Fremantle there was no talk about the eight expended torpedoes that had failed to hit their targets; Lockwood was delighted that another of his theories had been proved correct: a submarine could take offensive action with a deck gun if the gun was large enough.

On Millican's next patrol he used the deck gun again against a freighter but he also had to use torpedoes to sink it. The other three minelaying missions satisfactorily completed that task but the skippers came back again to report on failed torpedoes. Millican moved in to within half a mile of a freighter before firing a torpedo; it hit, but did not explode. Lieutenant Commander Joseph Willingham in the *Tautog* failed with six torpedo attacks. He returned to Fremantle to report that with one of them he had heard the torpedo hit the side of the ship but it still did not explode. The problem continued and the patrol results were spotty because of it.

As 1942 neared its end, change was coming to the submarine commands in the Pacific. Some skippers, such as Lieutenant Commander James Coe and Lieutenant Commander Joseph Willingham, were relieved of command for excellence and sent back to the United States for leave, after which they were to take over new submarines. New submarine construction was speeding up and new crews with experienced captains were needed to man them. Some skippers, like "Fearless Freddie" Warder, were coming to the ends of their careers as submarine captains. Warder was making his seventh war patrol in the

Seawolf that October. He headed for the Philippines and on November 1 was off Davao Gulf near the island of Mindanao. The next morning he moved into the gulf and on November 2 torpedoed a Japanese freighter. On November 3 he moved into Talomo Bay and torpedoed a ship loading freight at a pier. Two of his torpedoes failed to explode and he actually sank the ship with an ancient Mark IX torpedo (an indication of the sad state of the torpedo inventory in the Fremantle arsenal).

Running out of the gulf, Warder torpedoed another merchant ship. This time one of his torpedoes began a circular run and he had to dive to escape, so he did not see the result of his shooting although he heard two explosions from the torpedoes that ran true. Five days later, still off the mouth of the Gulf of Davao, Warder torpedoed a troop carrier loaded with invasion barges.

The patrol time had run out but as Warder headed back toward Pearl Harbor he had another radio message: Run to the Palau Islands and investigate Toagel Mlungui Passage. Several submarines had reported naval traffic in the area, although the charts indicated it was not navigable by large vessels.

Warder moved the submarine cautiously into the Palaus and before he knew it was in the midst of a major element of the Japanese fleet. He counted three destroyers and an aircraft carrier and began a chase of the carrier, but his electrical system was giving trouble and he had to abandon the pursuit. After repairs were made, the *Seawolf* returned to Pearl Harbor. Warder had established the fact that the Japanese were using the Palau Islands as a major naval assembly point, and from that day onward Admiral English's submarines would hunt in the area. Warder was given leave and when he returned to the fleet it was as a division commander in the Pearl Harbor command.

Another change that came to the Southwest Pacific was far more important. Captain Christie was ordered back to the United States. The reason was the dreadful state of U.S. torpedo production. Newport and the two other factories were unable to keep up with the demand and instead of improving their record they were falling further behind every month. Captain Christie was one of the most knowledgeable men in the U.S. Navy on the subject of torpedoes, and his combat command experience was invaluable. So Admiral King decided Christie must come back and help straighten out the mess. Christie protested. Carpender, faced with the unpalatable possibility that Lockwood might be shifted to Brisbane, did what he could to stop the change. General MacArthur would have liked to see him stay; Christie was a good tightrope walker and managed to keep MacArthur fairly well satisfied while adhering to the navy's policy of giving the army no more control of any naval activity than was absolutely necessary.

But the admirals in Washington were obdurate. Christie was desperately needed; therefore Christie must come. Before the end of the year he was on his way to stateside duty and Captain James Fife was picked by Carpender to take over command of what just then was the largest American submarine force in the Pacific. Lockwood unhappily remained where he was.

The blockade of Japan had begun but it was not yet effective. In the beginning the American effort had been totally defensive and the too-deep running of the torpedoes caused a high number of failures. That problem was corrected by midyear but other torpedo problems remained, not least of all the shortage that seemed to be growing rather than diminishing; also, the need to use the submarines in rescue and intelligence missions meant that many "patrols" were not that at all but special missions. Once a submarine had to be used as a cargo carrier to carry 9,000 gallons of fuel to Lunga Roads at Guadalcanal.

This broad spread of activity disrupted the efforts to carry out an economic blockade of Japan. Every major commander in the navy knew that such a blockade was important but the imperatives did not begin to diminish until the last months of 1942. So in that first year of war the United States submarines had given little but promise. They had sunk about one-sixth as many enemy ships as the German U-boats sank in the Atlantic. They had made no dent in the Japanese shipping program; they had sunk seven hundred and twenty-five thousand tons of Japanese shipping, but the Japanese shipyards had produced nearly six hundred and twenty-five thousand tons of new ships, so the net result of the submarine activity was simply to main-

179

tain the status quo, hardly the way to win a war. Imperial General Headquarters had made allowance for the loss of eight hundred thousand tons of shipping in the first year, so the Japanese were ahead of the game.

On the positive side, the design of the boats was continually improving. The torpedoes were better than they had been at the beginning of the year, although still in short supply. The navy was learning the advantages of larger deck guns. The search radar was improved; and the aircraft radar, still troublesome, was improving. Through a strict campaign of removal of the timid souls, the quality of the submarine captains had improved enormously. Thus, by December 7, 1942, the U.S. submarine force was ready to begin the war that had begun a year before. Finally, on the last day of the year, the Imperial General Staff in Tokyo decided that too much effort had been devoted to the capture of the island of Guadalcanal and that the loss of men, planes, and ships must cease. The naval chiefs pointed out that the same results—establishment of a forward air base for attack on Australia—could be achieved at New Georgia Island and the decision to evacuate the twenty thousand troops ferried into Guadalcanal was made that day. The Imperial army generals could not understand it. They would have liked to have continued "to victory" on Guadalcanal, but Prime Minister Hideki Tojo, a general himself, vetoed the plan as too expensive. No one in Japan seemed yet able to come to grips with the reality: that the war had turned about and for the first time Japan was giving up captured territory.

15 THE BLOCKADE TIGHTENS

A S 1943 began, the Americans had a force of eighty submarines in the Pacific, nearly a 40 percent increase over that of 1942. The location of activity was changing, however. During much of 1942 U.S. submarines had concentrated in the Southwest Pacific, first because of the losing battle to save the Dutch East Indies, and then to support the U.S. invasion of Guadalcanal. But at the end of 1942 Admiral King was ready to make a change, and he ordered most of the submarines at Brisbane to move back to Pearl Harbor. Captain Fife was left with one squadron of submarines and the tender Fulton.

Most of the V-boats had been removed from active service by 1943, but the old *V-4*, rechristened *Argonaut*, was still in operation. Admiral English had sent her down to Brisbane in December to take over many of the special missions that caused so many complaints. The *Argonaut* was old and infirm but that sort of work did not demand speed so she seemed admirably suited for it. She had never been in combat; the closest to it was the special mission to Makin to land Carlson's Raiders.

Deprived of the strength Fife had expected, he decided the *Argonaut* was capable of carrying out a regular war patrol and sent her out, under Lieutenant Commander J. R. Pierce. Her patrol area was south of New Britain Island; when she arrived, the Japanese were in the process of building up the northern Solomons, so it was not long before Pierce found an enemy convoy. It was a five-ship convoy, protected by three destroyers. Pierce attacked, and the crew of a passing U.S. Army Air Corps bomber saw one of his torpedoes strike a

181

destroyer and explode; the pilot said he also saw torpedoes hit the two other destroyers. But whether it was the magnetic warhead or just bad luck, the destroyers were not damaged. They bore down on the *Argonaut*, dropping depth charges, and one of those explosives blew the boat to the surface. The Japanese destroyers then circled around like Indians attacking a wagon train, pumping shells into the stricken boat until she sank—taking down her oversized crew of a hundred and five officers and men. There was nothing the men of the bomber could do to help; they had dropped their bombs and it would have been suicidal to make a strafing attack against three bunched-up destroyers.

The sinking of the *Argonaut* started a controversy among submariners. Captain Fife had a reputation as a hard-driving commander. He didn't drink and he didn't enjoy the company of drinkers. He lived in a Quonset hut on the pier and he ran his command with an iron fist. Many officers complained that in Fife's case the quality of mercy was completely absent. Some, then, took satisfaction in blaming Fife for the loss of the *Argonaut*, but others put it down to the fortunes of war. The result was that Nimitz and his admirals did not achieve one aim: To give General MacArthur the submarines he wanted to conduct his many intelligence operations without impairing the efficiency of the patrol force. The new boats had to take over the special missions.

A big change came to the Pacific submarine force in January 1943. Admiral English was making a trip to the West Coast when his plane was lost in a storm over the mountains of northern California and crashed. Everyone aboard was killed. Admiral Lockwood was appointed to succeed English, and thus he escaped from Admiral Carpender. Captain Christie had just arrived at Newport to find out what was going on at the torpedo factory so he could start doing something about it. However he was given the Australia command and promoted to rear admiral. He turned around and went back into the heart of the South Pacific. Since he was succeeding Admiral Lockwood he went to Fremantle although the logical place for the command was Brisbane. Thus, because of the personality of one American admiral (Carpender) the U.S. submarine force in the Southwest Pacific operated in an atmosphere of unnecessary controversy for years after the fall of Java forced them down into emergency quarters.

Admiral Lockwood's command was growing every month. In 1942 the navy commissioned thirty-two new submarines, most of which would come to Lockwood. When he took over in February 1942 Lockwood also brought a message to Admiral Nimitz from General MacArthur. The general said he needed a fleet in the Southwest Pacific. Nimitz was in no position to say yea or nay but the request began its tortuous way through the military channels that would lead it to the Joint Chiefs of Staff. It would have a profound effect on all naval operations in the Southwest Pacific.

Another change, occurring gradually, was the increased effectiveness of Japanese antisubmarine patrols. The Americans were constantly improving two types of radar: The search variety which was used to determine position and locate enemy vessels; and the aircraft variety which was used to search the skies. The Japanese countered with detecting devices that could spot the radar; in other words the radar became a beam for the Japanese antisubmarine patrols. Progressively, as the Japanese patrols became more effective they were more aggressive.

One of the first submarines to encounter that new aggressiveness was Commander Howard W. Gilmore's *Growler*. She was one of Jimmy Fife's boats. She left Brisbane on New Year's Day 1943, for patrol between Rabaul and the northern Solomons. The Japanese, having decided to evacuate Guadalcanal, were already moving troops and supplies to build up the New Georgia Island base.

In mid-January the *Growler* sank two Japanese troop transports, the *Chifuku Maru* and the *Miyodono Maru*. On January 30 the *Growler* attacked another merchant ship. This time a patrol vessel intervened and Commander Gilmore was unable to complete his attack. He damaged the ship but then was driven underwater by the patrol boat, which delivered a slashing depth-charge attack producing explosions that came close enough to shake up the crew of the *Growler*. The next day, coming up to periscope depth, Commander Gilmore saw a Japanese gunboat and attacked; he fired one torpedo but instead of running true, it circled and he had to dive to evade his own shot. By that time the gunboat was thoroughly alert and there was no sense in trying again.

On the night of February 4, 1943 the *Growler* tracked a Japanese convoy headed north toward Rabaul, and when Gilmore had made the "end run" and gotten to the point where he hoped to intercept the convoy, he surfaced and charged his batteries. Two ships arrived. The visibility on the surface was so poor that the ships could barely be made out through the haze. A periscope attack might not have worked so Gilmore decided to remain on the surface, still using radar to direct his attack.

He was still tracking the two ships when suddenly the lead ship opened fire from a distance of two and a half miles. This was a new wrinkle: the Japanese were bettering their convoy system and equipping their modern merchant ships with deck guns which were called "armed guards." Those gunners of the armed guards knew what they were doing. Gilmore took the *Growler* down, but fast.

In a few minutes the two Japanese escorts were after the submarine; the sound man could tell that two sets of high-speed propellers were moving in, one on either bow. Gilmore ordered the boat rigged for the depth-charge attack that was imminent. It was not long before the explosions began. For an hour the *Growler* was battered. One depth charge exploded close to the hull, near the forward torpedo room. The explosion ruptured the gasket on the manhole that led from the torpedo room to the forward main ballast tank. Water began to pour into the torpedo room. The damage-control party stopped the leak, but the repair was only temporary. No more could be done until they got to the surface and could work on the empty ballast tank.

An hour and a half later the sound gear indicated the Japanese ships were moving away. Gilmore cautiously came toward the surface and stopped at periscope depth. He swept the horizon. He saw one ship about five miles away, and the smoke of the convoy beyond. The vessel was undoubtedly a rear guard for the convoy.

The executive officer reported that the damage in the torpedo room was under control, but that the manhole was still leaking, and the bilge pumps had to run constantly to keep the water level down.

Another depth charging before they repaired the leak would not be good.

Gilmore kept the submarine at periscope depth all day, moving westward to get out of the track of the convoy so he could surface in some remote spot and make the repairs. When night fell, and no enemies were sighted, he brought the boat to the surface and the damage was repaired very easily by the installation of a new gasket on the manhole that had been damaged. The *Growler* was ready to fight again.

Shortly after one o'clock on the morning of February 7, the watch sighted a ship about a mile and a half away, traveling away from them. Gilmore moved in to attack but so did the Japanese ship. It was a nine-hundred-ton auxiliary vessel used to carry provisions to outlying garrisons but it was more than that—it was a ship armed to defend itself.

Gilmore didn't immediately notice that the Japanese ship had changed course and swung around to intercept him. The officer of the deck did not notice either; neither did the assistant O.O.D., the quartermaster who was at the wheel, or the three lookouts. By the time the alarm was sounded the radar operator had warned that the distance between the ships was too short to allow the torpedoes time to arm. They would never explode.

Whether Gilmore had decided to ram the enemy or was trying to avoid a collision is not clear, but he ordered hard left rudder and the result was that the *Growler* struck the Japanese vessel amidships at high-speed. The submarine heeled over so sharply that the men below were thrown off their feet. Immediately the Japanese ship opened fire on the *Growler* and fifty caliber machine-gun bullets raked the deck and the bridge. Ensign William W. Williams, the assistant officer of the deck, was killed immediately. So was Fireman W. F. Kelley, a lookout. Skipper Gilmore was badly wounded and could not walk but he clung to the framework of the bridge and continued to command the boat.

"Clear the bridge," he shouted, and the officer of the deck, the quartermaster, and the two surviving lookouts hurried down the conning-tower hatch. The ship's executive officer, stood at the bottom of the ladder in the control room, waiting for Gilmore to come down. But Gilmore could not make it and the Japanese were still shooting. The submarine was in mortal danger. A fifty caliber bullet might rupture some essential watertight part or the enemy ship might ram and sink the *Growler*. Gilmore gave his next order.

"Take her down," he shouted.

It was his last order. The exec closed the hatch, the boat started down, and the bodies of the two dead sailors and the wounded captain washed off the deck as she went deeper.

When they returned to Brisbane, the story of Howard Gilmore began acquiring the patina of a legend. He was born under an unlucky star, one of his oldest friends said and the tragedy off Rabaul was the Wagnerian climax. Posthumously, Gilmore was awarded the congressional Medal of Honor, the first submariner to win the medal in World War II. The legend became a part of the submariners' tradition.

When Admiral Lockwood took over command in February 1943 at the Pearl Harbor submarine base he faced submarine skippers returning from patrol with more tales of woe about the torpedoes. One such report, which impressed Lockwood tremendously, was that of Lieutenant Commander John A. Scott in the *Tunny*.

Tunny was one of the new boats, built at the Mare Island Navy Yard in California. On her first patrol Scott took her to the waters between Formosa and the Chinese mainland to strike Japanese shipping moving in and out of Hong Kong and Indo-China. On February 8 she surfaced just after sunset and discovered a Japanese freighter about six miles away. Scott took the boat down, raced to get ahead of the ship, then submerged to forty feet. Scott moved in close, about a half mile away from the ship, and fired two torpedoes; one simply disappeared. The sound operators tracked the torpedoes in the usual fashion but this one must have sunk almost immediately. The second torpedo ran erratically and missed the target.

Scott brought the boat to the surface, checked the ship's position by radar and made another attack. The ship's gunners saw the submarine and opened fire, which for some reason Scott took as a personal affront. He decided he would get this ship, no matter what. Again he stood in close, and fired two more torpedoes. One ran straight, but still missed. That might be human error. The other circled and missed. Scott's anger had spilled over into the whole boat, and everyone agreed that they had to sink that particular ship even if it took every torpedo and every shell they had.

Scott took the *Tunny* away for a little while and reloaded the tubes. As he came in, on the surface, the Japanese ship began firing at the submarine again. Scott ignored the shells and fired three torpedoes. The first hit but nothing happened. The second missed, edging across the ship's bow. The third zigzagged and looked as though it might end up anywhere but finally turned, hit the target, and sank the ship—through sheer good luck for the *Tunny*.

Lieutenant Commander Scott told that story when he got back to Pearl Harbor. "It's a helluva thing to go all the way to the China coast to find out your damned torpedoes won't work," said one listener. And that was the way most of the skippers felt by the winter of 1942-1943.

Admiral Lockwood had heard the complaints constantly in Fremantle and had taken them with several grains of salt. But Scott's sort of story showed persistence and final success against one ship. This performance did not add up with the Bureau of Ordnance's offhand dismissal of all complaints as human errors. Such stories impressed him; the only trouble was that it had taken Scott seven torpedoes, at $10,000 each shot, to sink the freighter. Lockwood agreed with his captains that the cost was too high. As the skippers gained experience and came back to base showing that they were not trying to excuse their own errors, Lockwood's confidence in the Mark VI exploder waned. The process of erosion was speeded when the British aircraft carrier HMS *Victorious* came into Pearl Harbor and the torpedo officer told Lockwood that the British had abandoned the magnetic exploders shortly after he left London. The British officer described the new exploder they were using and Lockwood asked the Bureau of Ordnance to get a sample, through the American naval attaché in London, and study it. The suggestion was treated by the pencil

187

pushers in Washington with the contempt it did not deserve. Lockwood never saw the British exploder or heard any more about it; and the letters from the Bureau of Ordnance were as defensive as ever. The exploders *were* sinking ships, the bureau said. That was supposed to take care of the complaint. Lockwood's vigorous complaints had to be watered down, too, because just at that time the Pacific Fleet submarines were suffering from such a shortage of any sort of torpedoes and warheads that several boats had to be sent out on minelaying missions because there were not enough torpedoes to go around.

At the moment, Commander Fife in Brisbane was better off. On January 16, 1943, the *Wahoo* set off with a full load of torpedoes, sixteen forward and eight aft. Her assignment was to go as far as the Palau Islands and look into the passages there used by the Japanese fleet. She was also to stop by Wewak in New Guinea on the way north. The Japanese had landed at Wewak, and Fife and MacArthur wanted to know what was going on there. But that last order left the skipper of the *Wahoo* stumped. He was Lieutenant Commander Dudley W. Morton, and he had just taken over the boat. What or where Wewak was did not appear on any American chart. One of the crew came up with the information; he had bought a geography book in Brisbane and there on the map showing New Guinea was a speck called Wewak, in a corner of Victoria Bay. Morton had a large scale chart made from the geography book, and then he at least knew where he was bound even if he knew nothing about water depths and reefs in the area.

Eight days out, the *Wahoo* stood off Victoria Bay. Skipper Morton took the boat in submerged at 3:30 on the morning of January 24. But it was one o'clock in the afternoon when Lieutenant Richard H. O'Kane, the executive officer, announced that he was looking at the masts of a ship. O'Kane had "the conn" because Skipper Morton, also known as "Mush," had decided he could function best if he did the sums in his head and took all the factors into account before firing a torpedo. Since that was hard to do while spinning a periscope around (which meant walking it around the well) Morton turned over the periscope task to O'Kane. It was an odd system, one not used on many boats, but for Morton it was the best way.

188

As they came closer inside the harbor, O'Kane reported that the vessel was a Japanese destroyer. It was the destroyer *Harusame* and alongside its mooring were several shapes O'Kane believed to be small submarines. As Morton made the decision to attack and worked out the mathematics, O'Kane reported that the destroyer had left its mooring and was heading toward the mouth of the harbor, which meant toward the *Wahoo*. Morton decided to fire three torpedoes and did; all missed. The wakes alerted the captain of the destroyer and he sent every available man forward to look for the submarine. The destroyer came on at high speed. Morton fired two torpedoes, and missed. By this time the destroyer was rushing directly at them—less than a half mile away. Morton fired a sixth torpedo, a down-the-throat shot. The destroyer captain saw the torpedo coming and tried to avoid it. He turned sharply to starboard, and thus took the torpedo full amidships. It exploded, and the stricken destroyer stopped. Morton was sure it had sunk. In fact it had not, but perhaps worse, it had broken its back, and the captain beached it. Eventually the *Harusame* was salvaged but she was sunk later by an American bomber.

The sinking of the *Harusame* aroused the Japanese. Within half an hour planes were overhead, searching and dropping depth bombs around the harbor. Morton took the *Wahoo* down to ninety feet. Guided by the sound man he moved out through the reef.

The *Wahoo* had eighteen torpedoes left as Morton began the second part of the patrol. His orders said to patrol off Palau. The *Wahoo* moved northwest. The next day she was just above the equator on the Wewak-Palau shipping lane when two Japanese merchant ships came into sight. The *Wahoo* surfaced, ran around the end, and waited. But the ships came up too fast, and Morton had to abandon the bow shot (six tubes) in favor of the stern shot (four tubes). He fired four torpedoes, and got two hits on one ship and one on the other. He swung the boat around to use the forward tubes in case one of the ships tried to get away; then saw another ship, coming straight on in spite of the distress of the others. Morton fired again and hit the third ship, a transport, with two torpedoes.

Turning his attention to the second ship, which was damaged but still under way, Morton realized that she was trying to ram the

Wahoo. He fired two more torpedoes, down-the-throat, and got another hit but the big ship was well-compartmented, and it came on, still trying to ram. Morton had to take the submarine down and turn to escape. When the periscope broke water again, O'Kane reported that one freighter had sunk, the transport was sinking, and the captain of the ramming ship had decided to try to escape. Morton fired another torpedo from just over half a mile at the floundering transport. The torpedo passed under the ship and the magnetic exploder did not go off.

Morton shot another, and this one exploded amidships. The ramming freighter was getting away at six knots. Morton then saw the silhouette of a tanker beyond the freighter. He decided to chase them, but since his batteries were low he came to the surface. As he surfaced and the deck crew came up through the conning tower, they found themselves in a sea of Japanese survivors, troops who had abandoned the transport. "There must be ten thousand of them," said one of Morton's officers.

The "unrestricted" warfare announcements to the submarine service on December 7, 1941 was interpreted in many ways by many skippers. To Lieutenant Commander Morton, the Japanese struggling in the water were not defeated enemies, but potential killers, who were apparently bound for New Guinea; and if they arrived, they would be shooting at Allied soldiers. He decided to kill as many of them as he could. (If the U.S. had lost the war, undoubtedly this atrocity would have sent him to a war crimes trial.)

The deck guns of the *Wahoo* turned to the slaughter. For an hour they fired on the boats and life rafts; their machine guns swept the water, killing men floating in kapok life vests, hundreds, perhaps thousands of them. No one counted. Some of the men would dream of this murderous nightmare for months, but not Lieutenant Commander Morton. His government had made him a killer, and he was determined to be as effective a killer as possible. "We destroyed all the boats and most of the troops," he said.

Leaving the bloodstained waters of the sinking Morton turned the *Wahoo* in pursuit of those last two ships. He caught up with them at dusk and fired three torpedoes at the tanker. He thought he got one hit but the tanker went on. He fired two more torpedoes at her and she sank. He chased the obstinate freighter again, and her skipper fought back with his deck gun, but Morton fired his last two torpedoes; at least one of them hit and the freighter went down. End of convoy.

Morton then was ordered to head back to Pearl Harbor, not Brisbane. He sent off a victory message as he went. On the way to Hawaii he ran across the track of another convoy. With no torpedoes left, he could not be expected to attack—but he did. He waited, watched a straggling small freighter, and surfaced to attack with the deck gun. But this convoy had escorts and one destroyer came racing back to attack the American submarine. Morton took the *Wahoo* down and got away. On February 7 he brought her into Pearl Harbor with a broom lashed to the periscope, meaning that he had scored a "clean sweep" of the Japanese convoy he attacked.

As with the *Guardfish* patrol of Japan, here was an exploit made to order for the ladies and gentlemen of the press, and Admiral Nimitz turned it over to them. For the next few weeks, the men of the *Wahoo* basked in an orgy of publicity. Someone invented the sobriquet "One-boat wolf pack." Lieutenant Commander Morton was awarded the Navy Cross and the Army's Distinguished Service Cross. Every patrol endorsement glowed with praise and the submarine force was told that here was the sort of achievement they should emulate. Admiral Lockwood was delighted to learn that Morton credited his successes to the Mark VI magnetic exploder. Without that, Morton said, his down-the-throat shots would never have succeeded, and that destroyer might have put an end to the career of the *Wahoo* at Wewak.

Not one word of the publicity said anything about the shooting of the survivors of the transport as they struggled in the water or tried to hide from the American guns behind the wooden planking of their boats and life rafts. Not one word of criticism was included in the patrol endorsements. Lieutenant Commander Morton had it all down in his patrol report but not one of his superior officers—up to the commander in chief—would address the moral issue. Atrocities were committed by the enemy, only acts of war were committed by

Americans. And so the January/February 1943 patrol of the *Wahoo* stood, a memorial to the submarine service, but not the sort that most commanders and crews would like to talk about.

The *Wahoo*'s patrol certainly did nothing to increase the speed with which the Bureau of Ordnance addressed the problems of the magnetic exploders. And in fact they were not all bad: Of Morton's twenty-four torpedoes, ten had exploded; some of the others might have failed because of human error. But even if all concerned had been in agreement on the problems, there was no immediate solution. Another torpedo, the Mark XVIII electric, was coming into production, but extremely slowly because the Bureau of Ordnance worked that way.

Nor were the Japanese antisubmarine experts proceeding at any breakneck speed. The results of the first year of the war had been about what they expected in terms of sinkings. Early in 1943 antisubmarine measures were improved, but the realization that the war had turned around and Japan was on the defensive had not yet permeated the Tokyo establishment. Admiral Yamamoto knew, and the army staff in Rabaul had learned the hard way in the Guadalcanal campaign, but Tokyo was still talking about the capture of New Guinea and the march south from there.

The Japanese had radar. It was not yet installed on ships and warships, but it was coming. They were adept at the use of radio direction finders. The submarine that came to the surface and made a long transmission to Pearl Harbor might find that it had raised a nest of hornets. The Japanese had another device not duplicated in the United States, the *jikitanchiki*, a magnetic detector used by Japanese aircraft. It sensed the presence of a large metal object below the surface of the sea, so that low-flying pilots could sometimes find and then track a submarine that was submerged.

However, at this stage of the war the major Japanese antisubmarine weapon was the sonar system. The Japanese sonar was technically superior and their employment of the echo-ranging techniques was excellent. Also, as the war continued, more Japanese merchant ships were armed with deck guns that were a constant threat to any submarine trying to attack on the surface.

Most important at this stage of the war was the increase in Japanese production of antisubmarine vessels. The most effective of these were the *kaibokans*. These vessels were small, under one thousand tons. At first the Americans thought they were only coastal freighters but they carried highly trained antisubmarine personnel, and three hundred depth charges were a standard allotment.

At the time the Japanese were so short of antisubmarine vessels that escorts were unavailable for most runs; that was the case with the Palau-Wewak convoy that the *Wahoo* intercepted. The exception in the early months of 1943 was the shipping between the Dutch East Indies, Singapore, and Japan. Ships coming from that area brought rice, rubber, tin, and oil, all vital to the Japanese war effort. From the beginning, these convoys were protected by warships. Early in 1943 most other shipping had to depend almost entirely on locally supplied patrols and on air patrols. Supposedly, any alert would bring air protection to Japanese ships under attack but in fact the air force protection didn't work very well. The Japanese had also begun to sow the open waters with mines, and as the war progressed these offered more danger to the submarines than did the aircraft. In specific areas, the Japanese used all these antisubmarine devices. In the early months of 1943 the northern Solomon Islands became particularly dangerous for American vessels as Admiral Yamamoto made preparations to wrest from the Americans the initiative they had seized at Guadalcanal.

e U.S. submarine base at Pearl
rbor.

her than endanger the secrets
he Gilbert Islands invasion and
he code-breaking device used
inst the Japanese, Captain John
mwell chose to go down with
Sculpin after she was mortally
red by a Japanese destroyer.

The USS *Growler* going in to dock for repairs after a collision.

All during the war American submarines were ordered on special missions. Here is a group of survivors taken out of the Philippines in May 1944 by the USS *Crevalle*. Four of these 41 had taken part in the Bataan Death March.

This Japanese destroyer unluckily came into the periscope sight of the USS *Seawolf*. Here she starts the long trip to the bottom.

After submarine skippers reported continual torpedo failure, Admiral Lockwood finally decided to override objections from the Bureau of Ordnance in Washington and conduct his own tests. Here a Mark XIV torpedo with a Mark VI exploder blows up against a cliff at the Hawaiian island of Kahoolowe. Two of the torpedoes failed to explode, and in discovering the reason, Lockwood's technicians solved many of the problems.

Admiral Chester Nimitz pins the Legion of Merit on the uniform of Vice Admiral Charles Lockwood, commander of Pacific Fleet submarines. This award was made for Lockwood's efforts to isolate and correct torpedo difficulties that had plagued American submarines for two years.

Captain Tom Hogan of the *Bonefish* comes ashore to report back from patrol to Rear Admiral Ralph W. Christie. Hogan is wearing his only clean pair of pants. Note tear in seat.

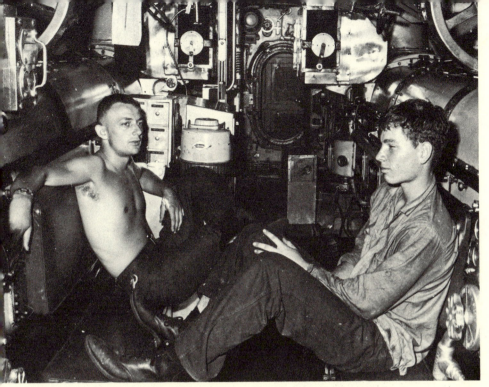

The engine room of a fleet-class submarine during World War II.

On October 15, 1944, the USS *Sealion* sank a Japanese transport that was carrying British and Australian prisoners of war from Singapore to the Japanese home islands. The Japanese abandoned ship and their prisoners, some of whom were rescued by the submarine.

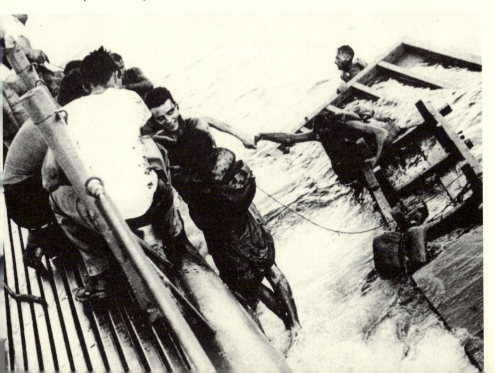

Captain Hogan, center, playing cribbage in the wardroom of the *Bonefish*.

The wardroom "scoreboard" of the *Bonefish* in 1944.

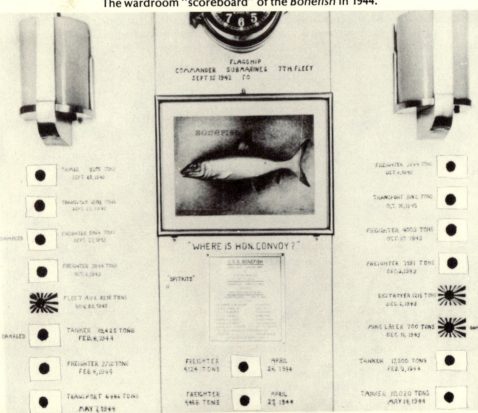

In October 1944 the USS *Darter* went aground on Bombay Shoal. She was stripped and made unusable by the enemy, but the hull remained afloat on its rock for many years.

Seen in the periscope of an American submarine, the Japanese warship slips to the bottom. *(Pacific Submarine Museum)*

The USS *Drum* sinks a Tatutake-class merchantman on April 18, 1943. *(Pacific Submarine Museum)*

American submarine gunners had to comb the surface for small Japanese ships in spring 1945. Large targets were scarce. *(Pacific Submarine Museum)*

The USS *Wahoo* at sea. Had he survived the war, the skipper, Lieutenant Commander "Mush" Morton might have been subject to court-martial for war crimes.

The battle flag of the USS *Barb*. The rayed flags represent Japanese warships; the rising suns, Japanese merchantmen. The red crosses represent aircraft, and the Nazi flag a U-boat.

The USS *Bullhead* was the last American submarine lost in the Pacific war, in the closing days of battle, in the Gulf of Siam.

The men of the USS *Flasher* march in the 1945 Navy Day parade in Mobile, Alabama, finally receiving credit for having sunk the most Japanese tonnage during World War II.

One of the famous members of the crew of the USS *Pogy* was Pogy Pete, a real submariner.

UNITED STATES NAVY
Identification Card

Pogy Pete

Name

- -

Signature

Color Hair........... Eyes..........

Weight........... Birth 10-19-43

Void after...........

- -

N. Nav. 546   Validating Officer

16 THE ODDS CHANGE

IN the autumn of 1942 the guerrillas in the Philippines began sorting themselves out. A number of the guerrilla leaders were not much more than pirates, hoping for recognition and power from General MacArthur. By January 1943, MacArthur was ready to make use of the guerrillas. Early in January, Lieutenant Commander W. S. Stovall's *Gudgeon* was dragooned into a special mission: To land Filipino Major Jesus Villamor and six guerrilla volunteers on the island of Negros with a ton of medical supplies and weapons. Villamor was the first guerrilla sent back into the Philippines, and at that moment the only one in whom MacArthur could put any real trust. The problem was that from Australia it was impossible to tell which leaders were seriously concerned with fighting the Japanese and which were attempting to build their own petty fiefdoms. There was only one way to find out: send an American emissary from Brisbane. There would be no chance that an American would embroil himself in the complex Filipino politics.

The American chosen was Charles Parsons, a longtime American resident of Manila, who had been commissioned a lieutenant commander in the U.S. Navy. Parsons and U.S. Army Captain Charles Smith prepared for their first trip into the islands. It would take them to Mindanao, where they were to deliver ten thousand dollars in cash and thousands of rounds of ammunition for .30 caliber rifles and machine guns and for .45 caliber pistols to Lieutenant Colonel Wendell Fertig, an American officer who had escaped from the Japanese and established a guerrilla band on that island. Fertig was the first

195

guerrilla leader to agree to accept MacArthur's authority without question.

Parsons had two other missions. He was to look over the other guerrilla leaders and ascertain their motives and trustworthiness. He was also to establish an espionage network in the islands.

The submarine that happened to be on hand to provide transportation was Lieutenant Commander Stephen H. Ambruster's *Tambor*. She left Brisbane late in February 1943 and arrived off Pagadian Bay on the south coast of Mindanao on March 4. Ambruster had been instructed to reconnoiter the bay and then land the party during the daylight hours. En route, however, they had learned that the landing area had been occupied by the Japanese, so Parsons asked to be landed near the village of Labangan, where one of his six men lived.

That day, just after dusk, the submarine surfaced and the crew brought up on deck a small boat which had been brought along just for the purpose of getting the Parsons party ashore. At 4:45 A.M. on March 5, Parsons and two Filipinos shoved off; they made the shore without incident. They hid the boat and went inland to find Colonel Fertig (MacArthur had just promoted him) while the *Tambor* submerged and waited. Late in the afternoon, Parsons reappeared with reinforcements and three boats to unload the rest of the men and the supplies. Within an hour the *Tambor* was on its way to sea and a war patrol.

Other submarines were carrying out MacArthur's missions throughout the South Pacific and the Southwest Pacific. At the end of December, the *Searaven* had landed seven agents on the south coast of Ceram Island. On the first day of January 1943 the old *Nautilus* evacuated half a dozen survivors of a B-24 bomber crew who had managed to hide on Rendova Island after their plane crashed. The *Greenling* had twice landed agents on the coast of New Britain Island, and the *Grouper* had picked up a flier who had managed to get ashore after a water landing near Rengi Island in the Solomons. The *Gudgeon* had evacuated twenty-eight people from the south coast of Timor. In the coming months the submarines would be called upon time and again for such dangerous but essential missions, as the Allies made their slow way back up through the island chains captured by the Japanese.

The enemy was not unaware of this activity, and as it increased, efforts were made to trap the American submarines. But the submarine skippers were always nervous on special missions and as of the spring of 1943 the safety record was unblemished.

There was more danger in normal submarine operations in the Solomons as Admiral Yamamoto's antisubmarine warfare precautions were increased. The *Amberjack*, which had delivered the aviation gasoline to Tulagi, was ordered back into the Solomons on patrol on January 24, 1943. She had made a false start and had to go back to Brisbane for the repair of several leaks in her pressure hull. The problem was that the *Amberjack*'s last refit had not been properly completed because of the demand that she get back on patrol.

She went to the Shortlands area, which was the site of a major Japanese destroyer base. As soon as she arrived off the Shortlands new reports caused Captain Fife to change his mind and she was diverted to Buka. She arrived at Buka, having encountered a Japanese submarine but without opportunity to fire, and having sunk one schooner by gunfire. She was almost immediately ordered to Vella Lavella.

On the night of February 3, Lieutenant Commander Bole was finally left alone long enough to find a freighter which he estimated at five thousand tons. He was on the surface recharging batteries when the lookouts spotted the ship. He attacked on the surface with torpedoes and the deck gun; the Japanese ship also had a gun and fought back. One man on the deck of the submarine was killed by the Japanese gun. Lieutenant Commander Bole reported that he put at least one torpedo into the freighter and it produced such a marvelous exhibition of explosive pyrotechnics that he was sure the ship sank. Apparently she did not sink, however, because the Japanese records showed no such loss.

Almost immediately Captain Fife changed the *Amberjack*'s patrol area again. She was sent to cover the traffic from Rabaul to the northern Solomons. On February 14, Skipper Bole reported on an encounter with a pair of Japanese destroyers, and radioed that he had rescued a downed flier—a Japanese. And that was the last word Skipper Bole sent to Brisbane.

On February 16, the Japanese records indicate, a submarine contact was made by a plane flying out of Rabaul and the plane attacked. It also reported the presence of the enemy submarine to the naval patrol unit and the torpedo boat *Hiyodori* and *Submarine Patrol Boat No. 18* were directed to the location to attack. After the patrol craft dropped a number of depth charges, oil, bubbles, and wreckage came to the surface. That was the end of the *Amberjack*—and the end of the Japanese pilot whose luck hadn't changed after he was shot down.

Long after the war, submarine experts wondered why no investigation was made of the strange behavior of Captain Fife's command in moving this submarine as though it were an excursion boat. The results (one schooner sunk) certainly did not justify it, and loss of the submarine might be attributed in part to constant movement into new territory, if only because of the extensive use of radio transmission and reply from the submarine that such movement made necessary. On the basis of the Japanese record for radio-fixes it seems likely that they had many indications of the position of the *Amberjack* in those few days of February and March. At Fremantle, Admiral Christie was upset but Admiral Carpender in Brisbane told Christie to mind his own business, and indicated that what happened to Brisbane submarines was not included in that category.

Carpender's statement belied the facts. In March Admiral King set up a whole new Southwest Pacific chain of command to try to placate General MacArthur without yielding control of the whole South Pacific region to him. What had been called the South Pacific Force was renamed the Third Fleet, with Admiral William F. Halsey in command. King created another new fleet, the Seventh Fleet, and Vice Admiral Carpender was its commander. This was to be "MacArthur's navy," but at the moment it still consisted largely of submarines. Christie's command was Task Force 71 and Captain Fife's was Task Force 72, but Christie was supposed to be in administrative control of all submarines in the area, an authority denied him by Carpender. This attitude was to lead to further unnecessary losses of American submarines under Fife's command.

At Fremantle the atmosphere was heating up. The captains of the Fremantle submarines had been given sympathetic hearings in their complaints about the torpedoes when Admiral Lockwood was running the show. But Admiral Christie, as a prime mover in the development of torpedoes and the magnetic exploder, would not listen to their complaints. Skipper Millican in the *Thresher* came back from a patrol to Christmas Island, complaining. His squadron commander agreed but Admiral Christie transferred Millican home "for a rest." Lieutenant Commander Ramage, the skipper of the *Trout,* complained and was barely saved from Christie's anger by his squadron commander. He went out again, fired fifteen torpedoes and sank nothing. He complained about the torpedoes, whereupon Christie relieved him and sent him home.

Who was right? There was evidence that the torpedoes were faulty. But there was also evidence that aggressive skippers who had faith in the magnetic torpedoes did well with them. Lieutenant Commander Post in the *Gudgeon* sank two big ships with his sixteen torpedoes. That was the best record made in months by any submarine skipper operating out of Fremantle. For the sad fact was that American submarines were averaging about one ship per patrol. Even that statistic is misleading because nearly half the patrols produced nothing, and only 60 percent of the patrols sank all the ships. Perhaps more than torpedoes, good performance demanded a savagery that few skippers could maintain. Certainly one indication to this effect was the next performance of Lieutenant Commander Morton in the *Wahoo.*

The *Wahoo* went out on patrol again in March. She traveled from Pearl Harbor to Midway and saw nothing. The same was true on the voyage from Midway to the Nansei Shoto off Japan. She then moved into the East China Sea and again found nothing. Morton then took the boat into the Yellow Sea, which is notable for its shallows; not precisely the sort of water a submarine skipper normally likes. Morton knew where he was going, up toward the highly industrialized area of southern Manchuria, which produced so much of Japan's iron, steel, and heavy equipment. He went clear to Dairen, the big port, and lay off that area, waiting.

On March 19 he attacked a Japanese freighter and sank it with a single torpedo. Morton brought the boat to the surface to hunt down any survivors, but there were none. He continued to patrol in this shallow water (average depth one hundred and twenty feet), and two hours later found a medium-sized transport; he chased it on the surface, then dived to periscope depth and fired a torpedo. The torpedo hit and the ship was damaged but not sunk. The transport's skipper spotted the periscope and began firing his deck gun. In this shallow water there was another consideration; a ship that had a deck gun undoubtedly had a radio as well. The greatest danger to a submarine would be to be caught by a well-manned escort vessel because there was no place to hide. Morton moved off toward the Korean coast where the port of Chinnampo was reported to be handling a large amount of sea traffic.

Two days later Morton was in position and found another freighter. He fired three torpedoes from a mile away; one of them did the job without any question. Some explosive material inside the vessel went up with a roar and a blast that shook the wash basin off the bulkhead in the forward torpedo room.

Morton moved in until he was less than twelve miles offshore. He sank another freighter. On the surface he found a large number of sampans and junks and unleashed the deck guns on them.

"Anyone who had not experienced the feel of life on the deck of a surfaced submarine with the deck gun firing and all machine guns going has not lived," Morton said. Some of his crew did not share Morton's enthusiasm for indiscriminate killing; it was too much like shooting fish in a barrel. But aboard the *Wahoo* that sentiment was best left unstated. Morton was a jolly fellow most of the time, but he had a sharp temper when aroused.

Morton was having a very easy time of it on the Yellow Sea patrol because the *Wahoo* was the first U.S. submarine to penetrate these waters, and the Japanese shared the general belief that submarines would not dare enter the Yellow Sea because of the shallows. The secret was to keep moving and the *Wahoo* did. Morton headed toward Laotigkashan Point, and off that promontory on March 23 he sank a collier. The Japanese were thoroughly alert by this time and the airwaves were popping with messages as Morton sped away toward Dairen again. Off Round Island he fired at a tanker. Three torpedoes failed; two went off prematurely and the third missed the ship. Morton fired three more, of which one struck the target and exploded. The tanker sank.

The next day another cargo ship appeared, a small one this time. Morton fired one torpedo, but it exploded halfway to the ship. He surfaced and used the deck gun and 20 mm guns to sink the Japanese vessel. Within the hour Morton was chasing another ship, and attacking again on the surface. The captain of this ship tried to ram the *Wahoo* but failed, and the submarine slipped away, leaving another cargo ship burning and sinking.

One reason for Mush Morton's phenomenal success as a submarine captain was his unusual ferocity; he had demonstrated that in the gunning down of the unarmed survivors of the transport off Wewak and the junks off Korea. He could go much further as he showed on this patrol, in an attack on a one-hundred-ton trawler. At this stage of the war with so many large Japanese ships float, most submarine skippers would have left the trawler alone. Not Lieutenant Commander Morton. He saw the vessel, surfaced, and attacked with the small deck guns; one by one, the three 20 mm guns jammed. This turn of events infuriated Morton. He had prepared for such "emergencies" back at Midway when the *Wahoo* stopped to top off the fuel tanks for the run across the Pacific. Morton had picked up a crate of "Molotov cocktails"—bottles filled with gasoline and stuffed with a rag—that exploded on impact, and spread burning gasoline across a wide area. Morton circled the little fishing boat, while his men threw the firebombs at the Japanese. The *Wahoo* left the trawler burning fiercely and the crew dead or dying.

Near the end of March, Morton moved out of the waters of the Yellow Sea, with two torpedoes still on hand. He was saving them for the run along the Formosa-Japan shipping lane, which he would pass near on his way back to Pearl Harbor. When he reached that area on March 29, Morton found a freighter and sank it with his last two torpedoes. He went back to Pearl Harbor with the greatest sinking record amassed by any submarine skipper in one patrol: nine ships, for a total of about twenty thousand tons. The only caveat that could possibly be made about the record had to do with the small size of the sunken vessels (not one was more than thirty-five hundred tons), but Admiral Lockwood and Admiral Nimitz were not going to quarrel with a record like that. Mush Morton was showing that American submarines could average a lot more than one ship per patrol.

At Pearl Harbor, Brisbane, and Fremantle, the story was still the same: The submarine captains came home complaining about the torpedoes. Some of them were almost in despair, wondering what it would take to get the "brass" to do something about the faulty weapons. What it would take would be a shock or series of shocks that could not be attributed to faulty planning, faulty calculation or any other sort of mismanagement by the skipper.

Just such an incident occurred in April 1943. Lieutenant Commander John A. Scott was out in the new boat *Tunny*. After his first patrol he distrusted the magnetic exploders so much that he changed the settings on his torpedoes, preferring to depend on direct hits rather than "influence" explosion. Off Wake Island he torpedoed a big freighter but only damaged it; his distrust of the torpedoes increased.

On April 8, the Radio Intelligence section at Pearl Harbor passed along information on the whereabouts and destination of the Japanese carriers *Hiyo* and *Junyo*, and when Commander Voge of Admiral Lockwood's staff looked at his plotting chart he saw that Scott's submarine was right in the line of their movement. He promptly sent a radio message to Scott to intercept the Japanese ships.

The message came in plenty of time, and Skipper Scott got ready to intercept. At the appointed hour, up came the Japanese convoy, including the two big carriers, accompanied by two escort carriers and several destroyers. What a haul! Not many submarine commanders ever saw so many carriers at once.

Scott was as aggressive as anyone might have wished. He kept the submarine on the surface for maneuverability. He maneuvered the *Tunny* into the middle of the formation, preparing to fire at three of the ships: three torpedoes from the forward tubes at each of the escort carriers and the four stern tubes at the largest of the two big carriers.

He set the depth of his torpedoes at ten feet, just to make sure there was no trouble with the magnetic exploders. That way, if the magnetic attraction of the ship did not blow the torpedo up as it approached, the direct impact should activate the firing pin.

As Scott prepared to attack, three small escorts also appeared and Scott had to change his shooting pattern so he would not waste torpedoes on them. He fired four torpedoes from the stern tubes at a range of less than half a mile—virtually point-blank by submarine standards. He heard the torpedoes hit and explode. He then fired the six bow tubes at other ships and heard three of them hit and explode. At this point the escorts came barreling down on the submarine and Scott had to turn all his attention to escape from the depth-charging attack that followed. Two of the depth charges were closer than anyone liked but the rest were far off and the submarine escaped without further concern for the depth bombs. When out of range of the Japanese warships, Scott surfaced and sent a radio message addressed to the *Pike* to warn that there might be some cripples coming on down toward Rabaul, the destination of the carrier force.

When the *Tunny* returned to Pearl Harbor, Scott made his report: the division, squadron, submarine command, and fleet endorsements were all a captain could ask for. Everyone thought at least one of the big carriers must have been sunk. But then came the bad news; the Radio Intelligence team brought in a report from the Japanese Combined Fleet: The *Hiyo* and *Junyo* had arrived safely at Rabaul. The auxiliary carrier *Taiyo* had been slightly damaged by one torpedo fired by a submarine. A number of torpedoes had been seen to explode not far from the major carriers.

So the evidence was there, not American evidence or excuses by American submarine commanders but in secret messages from the Japanese fleet to Tokyo. Admiral Lockwood and Admiral Nimitz were extremely disappointed. Never before (and never again in that war) had an American submarine found itself in the middle of a Japanese carrier flotilla and made an aggressive attack. Yet it had all come to nothing; no one could be blamed for the failure—it had to be the torpedoes.

Lockwood was convinced, even if Admiral Christie in Fremantle could not accept the fact, that the weapon he had helped nurture and develop was basically deficient.

The fact was that in the Southwest Pacific and the Pacific Fleet commands the performance of the submarines was less than adequate by the best standards available: the German. Making all sorts of allowances for distances and differences in targets the fact remained that the American submarines by the end of the first quarter of 1943 were not even averaging one sinking per patrol. At that rate, even though U.S. shipyards were turning out submarines at what the Germans and Japanese considered to be a phenomenal rate, the undersea boats would never whittle down the Japanese fleet or their merchant marine.

Something of consequence had to be done to rectify a deteriorating situation. But at least the failure of the *Tunny* had put the emphasis in the right place, and the concern had reached the right people. That was progress.

17 OUT OF THE COLD

F OR many months, almost since the first great shock occasioned by the Japanese landing on the edge of North America, Admiral Nimitz had maintained a powerful submarine force in the Arctic waters of Alaska with very little result.

The Japanese could not make up their minds what to do about the Aleutian Islands. Their invasion of June 1942 had been predicated on the success of the Midway operation. When that failed, instead of possessing two new bases for possible invasion of the North American mainland, the Japanese were out on a limb with a long supply line and a war that had suddenly turned around.

In the debates within the Imperial General Staff the decisions were made, and then changed. The original force had taken Attu and Kiska islands; Attu was evacuated, and then reoccupied. In this chess game, the Americans played a pawn of their own: occupying Adak, which kept the Japanese guessing. The real cost to the Americans was the necessity of maintaining the Northern Pacific Force, which consisted of several cruisers, destroyers, and the submarine flotilla as well as the support organization to supply the force. The army had to send troops to the area, prepared to invade or resist an invasion. The Army Air Corps, in the process of transition to the Army Air Force, had to divert fighters and medium bombers from Europe and the South Pacific.

The Aleutians "threat" was more illusory than real after the failure at Midway. It was most seriously felt in the editorial departments of the newspapers and in the living rooms of Seattle. But as long as the Japanese had even that toehold it could be expanded at a time when it might be most difficult for the Americans to meet a new threat. At the Casablanca Conference during January 1943 the Combined Chiefs of Staff were persuaded that a little more of the American military effort had to be diverted from Europe to reclaim the territory.

The Aleutians adventure was a drag on the Japanese military machine but the navy supported it manfully, with cruisers and land-based air forces based largely in the Kuril Islands. Early in the spring of 1943 those cruisers routed an American force in battle near the Komandorski Islands, but American air forces drove the Japanese off and prevented the destruction of the inferior American surface force. That was the end of the big convoys to reinforce the Japanese in the Aleutians. As in the South Pacific, the submarines were called in to supply the troops on the outlying islands.

Then, on May 12, 1943, the Americans invaded Attu. The Japanese had been ordered to defend the island to the last man, and that was the character of their fighting. It was the first American experience with the tenacity of the Japanese in defeat, a factor that would affect every island operation from that time onward. Four thousand Americans were landed on Attu that day, including some two hundred officers and men of an advance scouting force put ashore by the submarines *Nautilus* and *Narwhal*. They found it tough going but the outcome of the battle was decided when another seven thousand Americans came ashore.

With the fall of Attu and the virtual annihilation of their garrison, the Japanese had two options: Reinforce the five-thousand-man Kiska garrison or evacuate it. How to evacuate was the prime question. With a major American naval force poised in the North Pacific, the Imperial General Staff decided against seeking battle; instead they would take the men off by submarine. The word was sent to the Combined Fleet and to the Sixth Fleet, which was the command organization of all Japanese submarines. The secret message was intercepted by the Pacific Fleet Radio Intelligence organization and decoded. Now Admiral Nimitz knew the Japanese plans.

Thus when the Japanese submarines began to arrive in Aleutian waters, the Americans were waiting for them; the first three submarines were sunk by destroyers and patrol boats. The submarine evacuation plan was discarded and the troops were brought out by destroyers and cruisers. Late in the summer of 1943 the Americans occupied Kiska and the North Pacific threat was ended. Admiral Lockwood could have his submarines back to pursue the war of attrition against Japan. By this time most of the boats in Alaskan waters were S-boats, and the decision had already been made that they would be used for training, since they were not suitable for long-distance operations. So what Lockwood really got were the crews and they were badly needed to man the growing number of fleet-class submarines. For in that summer of 1943 the results of the American war production drive were showing as never before in the completion and dispatch of warships to the fighting forces. Lockwood's vessels now totaled more than fifty.

The growth of the submarine fleet made it possible to send more of them to Japanese home waters; and the increased experience of the submarine captains produced a slightly higher average of ship sinkings per patrol than existed before. The major difference was in numbers, however; more boats out meant more chances to sink ships even if the torpedo problem continued, as it did. Pearl Harbor, Brisbane, and Fremantle were still short of torpedoes and too many of them failed. Even so, in the middle of 1943 for the first time the sinkings went up to a rate of more than a million tons per year. The Japanese had counted on the sinking rate coming down as they won the war. The Japanese navy began to concentrate more on antisubmarine warfare and asked their shipyards to produce more antisubmarine vessels. But the Japanese production machine was already feeling the pinch of replacement. The Combined Fleet asked for carriers to replace the five lost in battle. Destroyers were needed to replace those lost in the continuing South Pacific warfare. Admiral Yamamoto was dead, the victim of an American ambush on an inspection trip to the South Pacific islands. But his dire predictions were becoming fact: skill, courage, determination notwithstanding, the Japanese were starting to fail beneath the heavy weight of American war production.

But until the torpedo problem was resolved, the American submarine war patrols would be hit-and-miss affairs, with far too many misses. More submarine skippers, including Mush Morton, came home to base from patrol with sad tales of the ships that got away. Just outside Tokyo Bay, Lieutenant Commander Roy Benson in the *Trigger* fired a spread of six torpedoes at the aircraft carrier *Hiyo* from a distance of less than a mile. He couldn't miss, and he didn't. But one torpedo exploded prematurely; two passed in front of the bow as the captain of the *Hiyo* maneuvered to try to get away. The fourth, fifth, and six torpedoes all struck the ship but the fourth let go with a thud; and the warhead dropped off the fifth. Only the sixth, which hit an oblique blow on the stern, exploded as a torpedo should. It very nearly sank the carrier, but not quite. She limped back into Tokyo Bay for repairs.

In April, Admiral Lockwood had made a trip to the mainland; after inspecting the submarine-repair and boat-building facilities at the Mare Island Navy Yard and visiting the Aleutians, he had been called to Washington for conferences about submarine performance and plans for the near future. While there, Lockwood made a speech to high naval and administration officials about U.S. submarine performance and mentioned the difficulties with the magnetic exploder. He then visited Admiral W. H. P. Blandy, chief of the Bureau of Ordnance, who had heard the speech. In the course of a heated discussion about submarine torpedoes, Lockwood discovered that there was not a single submarine officer on Blandy's staff. The bureau neither wanted nor thought it needed any advice from the men who had to use the weapons they had designed so poorly and then had so mismanaged. Blandy finally agreed to accept a few torpedo specialists from Pearl Harbor, so when Lockwood returned there he sent two men.

Not long after Lockwood returned from Washington, the *Trigger* came into Pearl Harbor and Lieutenant Commander Benson confirmed what the code breakers had already learned from the Japanese: That the *Hiyo* had been attacked by a submarine but that most of the torpedoes had failed and so she was saved.

At that time Japanese aircraft carriers were at the top of Nimitz's priority target list for submarine attack. In the previous few weeks the Pacific Fleet submarines had chances at half a dozen carriers (*Tunny*'s five and *Trigger*'s one); the results were miserable and the cause was indisputably the same: torpedo failure. Lockwood called a conference of his top submarine officers at Pearl Harbor and posed the question: Should the magnetic feature of the Mark VI exploder be deactivated? That way the exploder would work strictly on contact. There was no need for extended debate. Every one of Lockwood's staff voted for immediate deactivation. From the submarine base office, Lockwood went marching up to Nimitz's office and asked for permission to do so. Nimitz gave it without question.

When the word reached Admiral Blandy, he was furious and sent off a query to Nimitz to explain. But it was not a furious query, for Nimitz was a theater commander and a full admiral, while Blandy was just a rear admiral in Washington. He had to swallow his anger; when Nimitz responded that the magnetic feature had been discarded because no one knew when it would work and when it would not, there was nothing Blandy could do about it.

At Fremantle, Admiral Christie took the opposite view. He realized that there was something wrong with the magnetic exploder but it did work part of the time. He thought it better to have the weapon working thus, and useful for down-the-throat shots against antisubmarine vessels, than to discard it. He continued to try to find out what was wrong but the submarine commanders in the Southwest Pacific Force were ordered to stick with their magnetic exploders and not deactivate their magnetic feature. Christie still believed that much of the trouble was human, not mechanical.

Whatever the cause, a year and a half after the United States entered the war, the torpedo situation had improved only after a number of the submarine captains began making changes themselves while on patrol and then persuaded the Pearl Harbor command to change. The U.S. Navy, personified by the Bureau of Ordnance, was offering no help at all. When pressure finally forced Admiral Blandy to release some of the new Mark XVIII electric torpedoes for the war effort in the Pacific the torpedomen at Pearl Harbor found the electrics were "as full of bugs as a night in June," as Admiral Lockwood put it. The torpedo was a copy of a German design but it had been "improved" in Washington and at the Newport torpedo factory. The electric torpedoes were just not good enough to send out on submarine patrols.

With that discovery the submarine captains suffered a great letdown because they had been counting on a new torpedo to solve all their problems. Instead, they were discovering new troubles to replace the old ones.

Lieutenant Commander Lawrence R. Daspit proved that point beyond any doubt in the minds of Admiral Lockwood and his officers. Daspit was the skipper of the *Tinosa* and had been sent out on patrol with a load of the modified Mark XIV torpedoes; the magnetic feature of the Mark VI exploders was deactivated so that the torpedoes were supposed to explode on contact only.

Daspit's patrol area was off Truk, and his particular assignment was to sink tankers. He had several misadventures, including a run-in with a destroyer. Finally, with sixteen torpedoes left, he found the *Tonan Maru*, a whale factory ship that was nearly as big as an aircraft carrier. He fired fifteen torpedoes at this ship and eleven of them were duds. The others exploded with varying degrees of efficiency, but the whale ship didn't sink. He took his last torpedo home to Pearl Harbor as a horrible example of the sort of weapon the submarines were issued.

When he arrived back at the base he found the command in a swattle. Mush Morton, going out on his sixth war patrol, had refused to take Mark XIV torpedoes and elected instead to use the untried Mark XVIII electrics. Lockwood decided that if anyone was going to find out what was wrong with the Mark XIVs, it was going to have to be the Pearl Harbor submarine command. The Bureau of Ordnance had still come up with no solutions.

Lockwood organized a torpedo party at the suggestion of Captain Swede Momsen, the inventor of the Momsen lung and commander of Submarine Squadron Two. It was the sort of move that was bound to infuriate the desk admirals back in Washington. But he got the permission of Admiral Nimitz to take a load of Mark XIV torpedoes to the uninhabited island of Kahoolawe, south of Maui, and fire them against the cliffs until they got a dud. They would recover the dud torpedo by diving for it, and then take it to the torpedo shop at Pearl and dissect it to find out what went wrong. Momsen would direct the tests.

210

He chose one of the new submarines that had just arrived at Pearl Harbor, the *Muskellunge,* to fire the torpedoes. On August 31, 1943 she fired one, and it exploded properly. She fired the second, and it did the same. She fired the third Mark XIV, and it struck, raised a tiny spout of water and sank to the bottom.

Lockwood was notified and he left Pearl Harbor aboard the submarine rescue ship *Widgeon,* with the subchaser *Chalcedony* to supervise the recovery of the torpedo. Three divers went after the dud and finally discovered it in fifty-five feet of water. They got a line around the torpedo's tail fins and hauled it up aboard the *Widgeon.* No one knew whether or not the torpedo might decide to go off, like a dud bomb, but it did not; it was soon in the hands of the submarine base torpedo specialists aboard the *Widgeon.* They saw that the warhead had hit hard enough to crush the forward end. They got the crushed warhead off without incident, and found that the firing pin had traveled along its guide lines to hit the firing caps of fulminate of mercury that were supposed to explode and trigger the explosives in the warhead. But for some reason the firing pin hadn't worked. They wanted to know why.

Back at the Pearl Harbor torpedo specialty shops the experts went over the dud torpedo. No one could understand why the torpedo hadn't performed properly, but at least they had reached the first stage; now they had incontrovertible proof that the exploder didn't always work as it should.

With Admiral Nimitz's approval, the submarine men at Pearl Harbor tried another series of tests, dropping dummy warheads with exploders from a height of ninety feet onto a steel plate. These dry-land tests gave them the answer: When the warhead struck squarely against the plate—at a ninety degree angle—the impact was so great that the firing-pin mechanism was crushed. Because of the crushing the pins either did not strike the percussion caps or they struck with so little impact that the caps didn't explode. But if the angle of impact was oblique, which was regarded as a bad shot, the firing pin worked just fine.

There was the explanation for the failures of Skipper Scott in the *Tunny* against his fleet of Japanese carriers, and Skipper Benson in the *Trigger* against the *Hiyo*. Their shooting had been too good, not too bad; that last torpedo fired at the *Hiyo* had just barely caught her stern at a sharp angle and thus had done all the damage. It was a lesson to drive a submarine commander wild but it had to be publicized within the fleet. Lockwood sent radio messages to all the boats on patrol to try to make bad shots that would pay, rather than good ones that would fail.

Submarine attacks began to assume some of the aspects of billiards. But at least the submarine skippers finally knew what was wrong. At Pearl Harbor they threw away the original firing pins and replaced them with new ones made in the base machine shop. The results of the tests were sent to the Bureau of Ordnance, and finally the bureau did some testing of its own and confirmed the results. The Newport torpedo factory undertook the redesign of the exploder, eliminating the magnetic feature and the faulty firing-pin structure. Torpedo performance improved remarkably but even at the end the Mark XIV with all its modifications was never a first-class weapon, and was in no way comparable to the German or Japanese torpedoes. Admiral Lockwood would have welcomed the comments of Skipper Mush Morton on the Mark XVIII electrical torpedoes he'd taken out on his sixth war patrol but he would never get them. Morton sank several ships in Japanese waters but heading north into the strait of La Perouse the *Wahoo* was lost; attacked by a patrol vessel and apparently sunk. That brought to an end the career of one of the submarine service's most successful captains before there was time for his savagery against the enemy to become a matter of controversy. There would never be another Mush Morton in the service but there would be a more successful captain. He was Richard H. O'Kane, and he had been Mush Morton's executive officer before he got a boat of his own. With the improved torpedoes and techniques, Skipper O'Kane would pile up the most impressive record of any submarine commander in the Pacific war.

Admiral Lockwood was enormously relieved when they discovered the source of so many attack failures. The irony of the past performances was that many of the most competent skippers had been relieved of their commands for "nonperformance," when their shooting had been so good that they failed. The discovery of the bugs in the torpedoes restored the faith of higher authority in the submarine system and went a long way to repair the deteriorating morale of the American submarine service. The fighting men of the service were being brought in from the cold.

18 WOLF PACKS AND LIFEGUARDS

I N September 1943 the Japanese were more than a little worried by
the increased number of ships being sunk by American submarines
and bombers. The damage was being felt. Available shipping had
fallen to less than five and a half million tons, which was only
marginally adequate for their war economy. The rate of sinkings was
so great (with all the new American submarines coming into action)
that the Imperial General Staff had to devise some new methods of
coping with the menace. The shipping problem was the deciding
factor in the Japanese decision to make the first major pullback in the
perimeter of the new Japanese Empire. The major base at Rabaul, the
Solomons, the Marshall and Gilbert island chains, and eastern New
Guinea were left outside the new line—that was drawn from Japan
down through the Marianas Islands, the Carolines (where Truk is
located), and to the upper portion of New Guinea. These areas would
no longer be resupplied, but the troops there were expected to hold on.
It soon became apparent that without supply it would be impossible
for the garrisons to hold out at all. The Japanese Sixth Fleet, which
was the submarine service, was then given the supply mission and
reluctantly the Japanese submarine captains turned again to "special
missions" which they detested as much as the Americans did. This use
of the submarines was dictated by Tokyo and cut their efficiency as
war weapons almost to zero. For the entire year 1943 their only major
success—if one could call it that—was the sinking of the *Liscombe
Bay*, an auxiliary carrier, during the battle for the Gilbert Islands.
   In the month of September the decision to employ the submarines

as supply vessels, and other major decisions about the future of the war, were being made in Tokyo. The first of the new antisubmarine vessels were being delivered (a development of which American naval intelligence was unaware, so the U.S. submarine skippers were not warned). Brash souls in high places in Tokyo were comforting themselves with the knowledge that the American submarine torpedoes were faulty and often did not explode—just at the time that the problem had been somewhat ameliorated and the rate of sinkings was to jump.

Although Admiral Lockwood was bemused in mid-1943 by the torpedo problem, his organization was working on other methods of attacking the enemy more successfully. The most important of these was the combined submarine effort, or wolf pack, which the Germans had shown to be so effective—until the American hunter-killer groups of escorts and auxiliary carriers penetrated the middle of the Atlantic. At this stage of the Pacific war the Japanese had no hunter-killer teams, and their convoy system was rudimentary. Only a few months earlier few captains of the faster ships were willing to participate in convoys; the convoys were small, which meant they used up the services of an inordinate number of escort vessels. Until the *kaibokans* came off the ways, many of the patrol vessels were too small and slow for their job.

Scientists at the San Diego Naval Laboratory were working on many devices to assist the American submarines. One of these was a small torpedo, suitable for use against patrol boats whose draft was too shallow to make a large torpedo effective. Another was an electronic noisemaker that could jam radio circuits and prevent a ship or convoy under attack from radioing for help. Still another was a decoy device that could be expelled from a torpedo tube; it could throw an enemy sonar off the track. The most promising of all the new weapons was a frequency modulation sonar system that could be used to locate enemy minefields and antisubmarine nets stretched across the mouths of harbors and in narrow passages.

By October 1943 Admiral Lockwood had enough submarines to be able to keep approximately thirty on patrol at all times. The number of submarines in the Southwest Pacific Force was increased as well.

Finally, Admiral Christie managed to bring the majority of boats over to his side of the Australian continent. Much to the exasperation of the submarine commanders, Admiral Christie was still tinkering with the Mark VI exploder. He was well-aware of one of the major problems of the American submarines: It was their inability to sink large ships that were built with many watertight bulkheads that could be closed off between compartments. A warship could take a torpedo's direct hit on one side, and by intentional flooding of opposite compartments, even the ship's list could be corrected in a matter of minutes. The reason for the American problem was the relative ineffectuality of the U.S. torpedoes, which had only a little more than 60 percent of the explosive power of the Japanese.

Christie's theory was that only by using the magnetic exploder could effective attacks on compartmented tankers and warships be launched; he remained confident throughout the war that the Mark VI exploder could be modified to do its original job. The record of the American submarines tends both to prove and disprove his contention: Torpedoes did not do a good job against large ships like carriers, partly because the torpedo itself often failed and partly because the exploders often failed. The net result was that the Americans fought most of the war with a decidedly inferior weapon. Christie's constant effort to improve torpedo performance did not work. Had he been successful the war might have been shortened by months, and certainly the sinking records of U.S. submarines would have been much higher.

The German U-boat record in the early part of the war *was* much higher; a U-boat captain who came back from patrol having sunk only three or four ships was regarded as a virtual failure, while an American skipper who sank three ships was regarded as a success. The German rate of sinking in the early months of 1942 was so high that unless it could be reduced or stopped, Winston Churchill felt the war was going to be lost. Fortunately American production again saved the day as hundreds of corvettes and destroyer escorts came off the ways along with scores of auxiliary carriers.

By the middle of 1943 the small antisubmarine vessels were also coming into service in the Pacific as parts of the task force screens.

217

They would run up an enviable record against Japanese submarines in the next two and a half years, culminating in the exploits of the USS *England,* which would come to be known as "the submarine killer."

Altogether in 1943 the Allies in the Pacific would sink twenty-three Japanese submarines.

The wolf-pack concept had been ordered by Admiral King very early in the war but it was mid-1943 before Admiral Lockwood had the resources to employ this system. When he worked it out, he avoided copying the German organizational pattern; they had put all control into the hands of Admiral Doenitz's staff—first at Wilhelmshaven and then in Paris. That sort of control might work in the Atlantic with a relatively tight concentration of shipping shuttling east and west between North America and England but it would never do in the vast stretches of the Pacific Ocean. Instead, Lockwood developed a system wherein a senior submarine officer accompanied the wolf pack, riding in one of the submarines but not commanding it; it was the same way that a task force commander on the surface would operate. The first wolf-pack commander was Captain Momsen, the submarines were the *Shad, Grayback,* and *Cero,* with Momsen riding in the *Cero.* They left Midway for the East China Sea on October 1, 1943.

For several weeks Momsen had been devising a theory to cover their operations. One boat would attack a convoy, and the other two boats would move in on the port and starboard flanks. After the first boat had attacked, it would drop back behind the convoy to find and finish off crippled ships.

The first area of operations was off Okinawa, and the targets were ships traveling between the Japanese islands and Formosa Strait. On October 12 the *Cero* attacked a small convoy and damaged one freighter. But the two other submarines failed to make contact so they did not participate. Then on October 14, the *Shad* followed a Radio Intelligence message that a Japanese naval force was moving into this area; in the right place and at the right time Lieutenant Commander Edgar J. MacGregor discovered several cruisers and destroyers. He attacked, fired five torpedoes, and heard three hits. The destroyers

218

then came in and forced the *Shad* underwater to suffer a severe depth-charge attack. Again, the other submarines of the pack failed to get the message and did not join in. That same day the *Grayback* sank a transport, but that ship was not part of a convoy, nor was its sinking the result of any concerted wolf-pack effort.

Even when the submarines did attack together, they didn't make the sort of attack that was most effective. On October 18 the *Shad* and the *Grayback* did attack the same convoy but unfortunately their attack was not coordinated and they attacked the same ships. The ten thousand-ton transport *Fuji Maru* was hit from both sides and sank but this was not quite what Admiral Lockwood had in mind. The difficulty was not in skill or enthusiasm but in communications. In that sense there was much to be said for Admiral Doenitz's system of centralized control. The Americans were not really operating a wolf pack, nor would they in the future, although Admiral Lockwood staunchly claimed the opposite. Captain Momsen knew this but Lockwood overruled him.

The next wolf-pack effort was commanded by "Fearless Freddie" Warder but again the three boats involved operated more alone than together, and the disadvantages of their system were apparent. One of the boats was that of Commander Samuel Dealey, who achieved great fame in the service for his down-the-throat shots against destroyers and escorts. Admiral Christie gave him a nickname that was to stick, "the destroyer killer"—which ultimately may have resulted in the loss of his submarine as he tried to live up to a difficult reputation. On this wolf-pack patrol, on November 19, 1943 Dealey sank a freighter and then an escort—but without the assistance of either the *Pargo* or the *Snook*, the two other boats of the wolf pack. Dealey soon had fired all his torpedoes and left the pack for Pearl Harbor while the *Snook* and the *Pargo* continued their patrol. They attacked a convoy, but individually, not under radio direction from Warder. The *Snook* exhausted its torpedoes next and went on back to base. The three submarine commanders were agreed on one thing: The wolf pack as envisioned by Admiral Lockwood was a waste of time. Most submarine commanders felt that they could do much better if left alone than if put into a theoretical pack that had no advantages anyone could see.

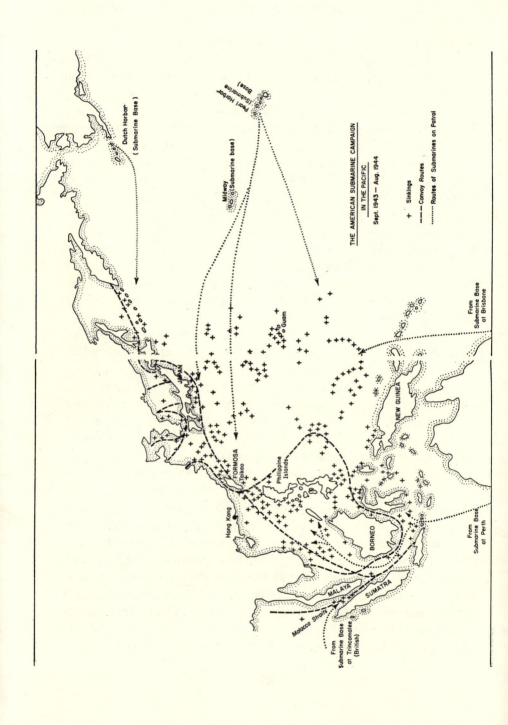

THE AMERICAN SUBMARINE CAMPAIGN
IN THE PACIFIC
Sept. 1943 — Aug. 1944

+ Sinkings
——— Convoy Routes
·········· Routes of Submarines on Patrol

Dutch Harbor
(Submarine Base)

Midway
(Submarine base)

Pearl Harbor
(Submarine Base)

JAPAN

FORMOSA
Takao

Hong Kong

Philippine
Islands

Guam

NEW GUINEA

BORNEO

From
Submarine Base
at Brisbane

From
Submarine Base
at Perth

MALAYA
SUMATRA
Molacca Straits

From
Submarine Base
at Trincomalee
(British)

In fact, the submarines tended thus to get in each other's way. At one point in a two-submarine attack on a convoy, the skipper of the *Snook* feared that one of the torpedoes he had fired might have hit the *Pargo*—it was that close and that confused during the battle. When they all returned, Warder suggested that he had been a supernumerary and that if more wolf packs were to go out, the senior submarine skipper should be in command, and not be a sort of supercargo.

The third wolf pack included the *Halibut, Haddock,* and *Tullibee,* and Admiral Lockwood, searching for a satisfactory solution to the wolf-pack problem, this time followed Warder's advice and put Commander Charles Brindupke, the skipper of the *Tullibee,* in charge of the pack. Momsen had another plan: keep the wolf-pack commander ashore, and give him authority as well as radio access to the pack. The commander would be in touch with Radio Intelligence and the fleet and would be able to concentrate on the activities of his small number of boats; whereas Operations Officer Voge, even if he slept on a cot in his office (which he usually did) had so many boats to worry about that he could not be expected to dot all the "i"s and cross all the "t"s. This time Lockwood decided against Momsen.

At this stage of the war, Japanese antisubmarine activity was growing more effective each month and they did have one superior weapon: their remarkably efficient radio-detection system. Admiral Lockwood quite rightly was concerned about the enemy ability to locate a submarine by its radio transmissions. The Germans had solved this problem in part by using high-speed, or "burp," transmission in which the actual radio message moves at a speed that is undecipherable, and is then slowed down at its destination. In that way the transmitter was on the air so briefly that the direction finders had difficulty locating the target. But the German naval radio system was more advanced than the American system in the Pacific and had different problems. Distance and atmospheric distortion were serious submarine communications problems throughout the war, and in several important engagements the failure of communications hampered American commanders. Under the circumstances the wolf-pack system simply could not be worked in Momsen's way.

This third pack was sent to the Marianas area, which was very nearly a part of Japan proper. The Japanese had settled here as they did in few of their colonies (Formosa excepted) and the native Chamorros had been pushed out of Saipan and Tinian. The two islands were important to Japan agriculturally, and they were air and naval bases as well for Japanese operations further south. As the Allies exerted more pressure on the southern bases, even Truk's days were seen to be numbered and the Palaus and the Marianas assumed a new importance in the Japanese defense scheme.

Again the submarines were unable to operate efficiently as a pack. During the first two weeks of patrol they worked independently. They then got together for a meeting at sea to plan tactics. (The skippers of the *Halibut* and *Haddock* came aboard the *Tullibee* at sea for this meeting.) But the results were not apparent. The *Haddock* did torpedo the Japanese light carrier *Unyo* after this but neither of the other boats was in a position to help, and the *Unyo* got away to return to Japan. The German use of the wolf pack against large convoys with many escorts was effective because while the escorts concentrated on one submarine the others attacked. In the confusion all of them usually got away. That was the situation until the hunter-killer teams came into action. The Americans faced small convoys with few escorts and they never got used to the pack system in this regard, either.

But if the wolf-pack technique was not a roaring success in the Pacific, the great improvement in torpedoes and "Uncle Charlie" Lockwood's heart-to-heart talks with skippers who were not showing enough aggressive spirit did pay off in 1943. Japanese shipping losses went up to more than one hundred thousand tons a month and in November hit two hundred and thirty-one thousand tons. That month the submarines averaged two ships per patrol, which was an enormous improvement over the year before. Altogether the Japanese lost 1.8 million tons of shipping that year, and were able to build only eight hundred thousand tons. They ended the year with a real decline of almost 10 percent in available shipping. So the campaign of attrition was paying off.

With the increase in the number of American submarines in the Pacific, it was no strain for them to become involved in another activity that proved enormously important to the morale of the fleet and particularly of the airmen. The year 1943 saw the rise of the "lifeguard" technique.

The Japanese had used submarines as lifeguards for airmen since the opening days of the war. The ring of submarines between the fleet that attacked Pearl Harbor and the Hawaiian Islands was there partly to pick up fliers whose planes were damaged in the attack and who had to ditch at sea. Until the Americans began launching aggressive carrier operations the problem didn't get a lot of attention at Pearl Harbor.

Preparing for the Gilbert Islands invasion, however, the carriers did make a strike on Marcus Island, and the *Snook* was sent on this mission. Her services were not needed, nor were those of the *Steelhead* in September when the fast carriers made another strike at the Gilberts to soften them up. But on October 5, the number of carriers had grown to six and these hit Wake Island. This time several planes were shot down and the submarine *Skate* was on hand to try to help. On her first attempt to pick up a downed flier she was strafed by a Japanese plane, and the *Skate*'s Lieutenant W. E. Maxson got a bullet in the back. He was treated by the pharmacist's mate and the *Skate* continued on station. All day long she was up and down, being harried by Japanese planes. She didn't manage to carry out any rescues that day. The next day the strike continued. Six miles off Wake Island, the *Skate* came to the surface. By this time Lieutenant Commander Eugene B. McKinney, the skipper, had some definite ideas for solving the problem. He trimmed the boat so that the deck was barely out of the water, stationed three seamen in life jackets on the bow, and manned the bridge alone.

Close in to Wake the Japanese shore guns tried to work over the submarine, and many splashes came close, but none hit. Skipper McKinney had a radio message from the task force that three fliers were down off Wake and he began searching for them. At noon he spotted a rubber boat in the water and went alongside; he rescued one pilot. Less than half an hour later the submarine picked up the second pilot of the day. The third pilot was still out there, about five miles off the coast, floating around in his boat. McKinney went after him.

The Japanese shore batteries at Wake were waiting and they put up

223

a concentrated fire that forced the submarine underwater. McKinney surfaced again in about half an hour and made another try. The pilot was off Peacock Point but so were three planes. McKinney hoped they were friendly but it was a bad guess; as the submarine came up the three planes peeled off in a very unfriendly way. McKinney ordered a crash dive, and as the *Skate* went down, the planes dropped depth bombs. Several of them were closer than anyone liked; at least one bomb did some superficial damage to the boat.

As the sun went down and the Japanese planes returned to their base, the *Skate* came up again to search for the flier. But despite use of an Aldis lamp to signal, there was no response from the sea.

That night life grew complicated for Skipper McKinney. Lieutenant Maxson's wound was serious and he began to run a high fever. In spite of his condition, Maxson insisted that McKinney stay on station but the skipper was inclined to try to find some help for the wounded officer, and he prepared to head for Midway Island and medical assistance. After he got going, Admiral Lockwood at Pearl Harbor received a message from the carrier task force that nine fliers were down in the sea in life rafts near Wake. Painfully, Lockwood had to issue the order to McKinney to return to station. He did so, and was back on hand on the morning of October 8. Lieutenant Maxson died that morning as the *Skate* continued her search for downed fliers.

No trace of airmen was found on that day, but on the morning of October 9 one more flier was found in his rubber raft. That night the crew of the *Skate* buried Lieutenant Maxson, the first submariner to give his life in lifeguard service. The next day, the *Skate* picked up three more aviators. McKinney remained on station until October 14, but found no more.

The first truly planned American amphibious offensive in the Pacific as part of "the road back" through the captured islands, leading eventually to Tokyo was the invasion of the Gilbert Islands; it was called Operation Galvanic. The Guadalcanal invasion was quite different, a desperation measure. The Gilberts invasion was planned from A to Z and involved what then seemed to be an overwhelming force of ships and men. Every possible precaution was taken to make the invasion a success, and in the planning stages the Pacific Fleet submarines played an important role. The *Nautilus* went on a mission to photograph Tarawa, Makin, and Abemama islands; it was necessary because the American charts were so fragmentary and so inaccurate. Then seven submarines were sent out to the Gilberts, some to report on the weather on the eve of invasion and others to serve as lifeguards for the coming air strikes. They were also to sink ships if they came across them.

The *Plunger* rescued one aviator; the *Thresher* sank a transport and the *Searaven* sank a tanker; and the *Nautilus* had the most unnerving patrol of her existence.

Commander, W. D. Irvin, taking the boat on her seventh war patrol, had been assigned to transport a detachment of seventy-eight marines on a reconnaissance mission to the island of Abemama in the Gilberts. He was also supposed to report on the weather and act as a lifeguard during air operations, and, of course, to sink ships if he found them.

The first task was to report on the weather off Bituitu Island, near Tarawa, and on enemy aircraft as well. While on the surface to carry out this mission the *Nautilus* came under enemy fire from a three-gun battery on the shore. The Japanese marksmen were excellent as they put shells so close that Skipper Irvin had to move his vessel from the area.

On the night before the invasion, the *Nautilus* was traveling in a "safety lane" established by the navy for friendly submarines. It was not the sort of place that a skipper would choose to make a dive. Suddenly his boat was attacked by an American destroyer, the *Ringgold*. The destroyer captain was aware of the presence of the U.S. submarine in the area but someone had given him the impression that the *Nautilus* had moved off on a lifeguard mission, so when a low profile appeared in the night sky, the *Ringgold* opened fire.

The *Nautilus* sent up a green recognition flare, but the destroyer crew was too busy shooting to notice. Skipper Irvin ordered a crash dive to escape; just as the submarine began to submerge, one of the *Ringgold*'s gunners hit it with a shell. Fortunately it was a dud, but the experience so unnerved the men on deck and in the conning tower

225

that the boat submerged before the bridge voice tube was closed off. The boat took in a lot of water, and then one final salvo ruptured a water line and started leaks. The next few hours were spent patching up the boat and repairing damage to the electrical system caused by the water. To maintain depth control, Skipper Irvin had to keep the boat at a steep up angle that did not make the marines feel any better. When three surface craft joined forces to try to hunt down the "enemy" the marines indicated they would prefer to be in an open boat heading toward an enemy beach instead of where they were—but there was no remedy at the moment.

Fortunately for the *Nautilus* the American antisubmarine efforts were unsuccessful, and she sneaked away and surfaced at about one o'clock in the morning. The marines were landed safely on Abemama on the night of November 20, hours behind schedule, but they were ashore. The next night the *Nautilus* landed more supplies for the marines and took aboard two wounded marines, one of whom died at sea. The next day the submarine shelled Japanese defenses on the island and that night the marines reported that all Japanese on Abemama had been killed.

After all those experiences, Admiral Spruance at last got the task force to give the *Nautilus* a friendly escort to get her back to Pearl Harbor. On balance, the submarine crew wondered if the attack on Abemama had been necessary; they knew very well that the rest of their adventures had not. As a reminder to all concerned, the *Nautilus* brought home with her a dud five-inch shell from one of the guns of the *Ringgold*. It became a war relic in the officers' club at the Pearl Harbor submarine base, a reminder that the submarine at sea had very few friends.

19 THE LOSSES RISE

T
HE third year of the Pacific war was most notable for the change in attitudes of the participants. The Americans were on the offensive and very early in the year the Japanese went totally on the defensive although the Japanese army didn't officially recognize the new situation. But the propaganda tone was the key: In 1941 and 1942 Japanese propaganda had dwelt on the changes that were coming to Asia under the Greater East Asia Co-Prosperity Sphere; the colonialist days were long gone, the Imperial Japanese forces were on the march, and the white man had no more place in Asia. (What they said ultimately turned out to be true, but not for the reasons the Japanese were giving.)

The words "ever victorious" to describe Japanese military forces passed out of the Japanese vocabulary. So did the braggadocio that Admiral Yamamoto had so lamented in the past. Every action continued to be a Japanese victory, but the victories were always won while backpedaling, a fact that did not go unnoticed on the streets of Tokyo.

Still, if the course of the war had been reversed, the Japanese in 1943 were far from defeated. American submarine losses were an indication: they rose sharply in 1943.

On January 10, the *Argonaut* was the first to be lost. The *Amberjack* was second, on February 16. Third was the *Grampus*.

Lieutenant Commander John Craig took the *Grampus* out from Brisbane on her sixth war patrol. She was last heard from on February 12, but no one worried about her until early March when she was

227

ordered to leave her station off Buka and move down the coast of Bougainville. She did not respond; she wasn't seen again or heard from and her fate is unknown. Many submariners blamed Captain Fife's policy of moving submarines around like pawns on a chessboard for this and the other early 1943 losses from the Brisbane command. But Halsey and Nimitz backed Fife, and in this particular instance there is not enough information to make any criticism. The only hint is that an oil slick was seen in Blackett Strait; that's where the *Grampus* could have been if she had followed orders after the Battle of Kula Gulf in which the Americans sank the Japanese destroyers *Murasame* and *Minegumo*. Those two Japanese destroyers had come running down through the strait to join the battle and if they encountered and sank an American submarine on the way no one would ever know, since the records were lost.

Lieutenant Commander George K. MacKenzie took the *Triton* out of Brisbane in February, bound for the Rabaul area, the main Japanese base for the buildup in the northern Solomons. She fought two convoys, fired a number of torpedoes on March 6 and 7, and reported by radio on these actions; however she made no claims because the Japanese defenses were strong and she had been forced to submerge by escorts after each attack. On March 11 the *Triton* reported on the course and speed of a convoy that she was chasing. Two days later Captain Fife warned Lieutenant Commander MacKenzie that three destroyers were heading into his patrol area. These must have been among the first of the new hunter-killer teams that the Japanese were putting together to combat the growing American submarine menace. On March 15 the Japanese reported that the team sank one submarine in the area. The submarine *Trigger*, that occupied the next patrol zone, reported making an attack at the edge of the zone at the same time that some other submarine was attacking the same convoy. The *Trigger* sank one ship; the other submarine damaged another. The hunter-killer team came up and dropped a few depth charges in *Trigger*'s area but concentrated elsewhere, and the crew of the *Trigger* heard many explosions over a long period of time. Undoubtedly they were listening to the last battle of the *Triton*.

In March, the *Pickerel* set out from Midway Island on patrol to the

228

area off northeastern Honshu, the main Japanese island. She sank two freighters in that area early in April, and then was silent. The Japanese reported submarine activity in the area, and depth-charge attacks by several of their antisubmarine craft. There was nothing definitive in the claim, but the Japanese naval authorities were as conservative in operational reports as the Imperial General Staff was reckless in public claims. On April 3 the Japanese navy reported the loss of *Submarine Chaser No. 13* to a torpedo attack in an area where only the *Pickerel* might have been. The Japanese also reported anti-submarine measures by other craft in the same area. The new anti-submarine measures included the sowing of minefields there to catch invading American submarines. These mines were sowed deep—to two hundred and fifty fathoms (fifteen hundred feet). Early in the war the Japanese had depended on old intelligence reports that gave the maximum "safe" depth of American submarines at two hundred feet or so. For months the Japanese had made the error of setting their depth charges too shallow; many a submarine and its crew took a severe bouncing with no damage whatsoever because the explosions were going off two or three hundred feet above them.

As the war progressed and submarines were sunk (and some crews captured) some information must have leaked out. But the worst security breach of all was commited by a congressman who visited Pearl Harbor on a junket and then went home to brag on the floor of Congress that the Japanese were fools who did not even know enough to set their depth charges properly. Shortly after this windbag had exploded, there was a noticeable change in Japanese antisubmarine methods. New six-hundred-pound depth charges came into use, and they were often set to explode at six hundred feet, the maximum safe depth for many of the newer American submarines. Many boats known by the Americans to have been lost were never officially claimed by the Japanese. Undoubtedly the *Pickerel* fell victim to the new Japanese vigilance.

In April the *Grenadier* was out in Malacca Strait, between the Malay Peninsula and Sumatra. The water in the strait was so shallow that Admiral Christie's staff objected to sending submarines there; but those officers were overruled because the Japanese were moving along the Indian border and the British had asked for U.S. submarine support to stop Japanese supplies from reaching Rangoon.

On April 21 the *Grenadier* moved in close to the port of Penang on the west coast of Malaya. Lieutenant Commander John Fitzgerald, the skipper, spotted a Japanese convoy within sight of the coast and attacked. But the convoy was protected by air cover; a plane forced the *Grenadier* down. Fitzgerald went to 130 feet. It wasn't enough; shortly afterward a depth bomb exploded so close to the boat that it drove her down to 270 feet. It also started leaks in the main induction (air) system and twisted the submarine's stern. Fires started in the electrical system; the hull was dented and the propeller shafts were pushed out of line. After dark, Fitzgerald brought the boat to the surface. The engineering officer got the engines to turn, but the propeller shafts were so badly bent they wouldn't rotate. If the men of the *Grenadier* were to escape captivity they would have to sail to shore and slip into the jungle. Fitzgerald put some men to work sewing a canvas sail but at dawn there was no wind. There was no recourse but to abandon the submarine. First the men destroyed the code machine, the code books, and all classified information and equipment. As they were doing this, a Japanese patrol plane came over and began an attack. The deck gunners fired and damaged the plane; it dropped its bomb on a second pass and then went away.

Fitzgerald brought the crew on deck and all the men donned life jackets. A Japanese merchant ship and escort came along and turned toward the boat. Fitzgerald ordered the submarine scuttled. The vents were opened and the *Grenadier* began to sink by the stern as the crew abandoned her. The Japanese ships first circled them; then amateur photographers came out on the deck, took pictures of the submarine going down, and the Americans struggling in the water. Finally the merchants ship put over a boat and took the Americans aboard. They were imprisoned at Penang, interrogated, and tortured. Skipper Fitzgerald was tied to a bench and subjected to the water treatment. Water was forced into his mouth and nose until he nearly drowned. Then the interrogator jumped on his belly. He was beaten repeatedly as the Japanese tried to get technical information about American submarines and codes. The interrogators inserted bamboo slivers under his fingernails. But Fitzgerald did not talk, and eventually the Japanese torturers gave up and sent the crew to a prison camp in Japan. Four men died in the POW camp but Fitzgerald and seventy others survived and were released at the end of the war.

The *Runner* went out from Pearl Harbor on her third war patrol in June and was unlucky enough to be assigned to the waters off eastern Honshu, just as the Japanese were concentrating on minelaying in the area. She must have hit a mine almost as soon as she went into her patrol area for she was never heard from again.

Lieutenant Commander Robert M. Brinker took the *Grayling* out in mid-1943. He was assigned the onerous task of delivering supplies to the guerrillas operating on Panay Island. On July 30 he left Fremantle on patrol and sank two ships, and then went to Panay to deliver the supplies. After that, Brinker moved into the Manila area where he sank one transport and attacked another. On September 10 Admiral Christie sent orders that the *Grayling* was to end her patrol and go to Pearl Harbor for a major refit; she never got there. The Japanese reported an encounter with an American submarine on the surface in Lingayen Gulf at just about this time. They did not claim to have sunk her but she never came home.

Sometimes the losses could be attributed to the problems of maintenance, as was the case with the *Cisco*. She was one of the new boats of Squadron Sixteen, which augmented Admiral Christie's force in 1943. Early in September she was assigned to patrol in the Sulu Sea area. By this time it was the practice of the Fremantle submarines to stop off at Darwin before going on patrol. The reason was the same one that had caused Admiral Lockwood to cast eyes on Darwin much earlier. After the American capture of Guadalcanal in the early weeks of 1943, the Japanese no longer bombed the area, so it was safe for the submarines to use it as a base. The *Cisco* came in to top off its fuel tanks, and then went out again. But that same evening she came back into Darwin for correction of a faulty hydraulic system. Repairs were made the same day and the next day the *Cisco* sailed again. But how well the system was repaired is another matter. She was supposed to arrive on station on September 18 in the Sulu Sea; she never reported in. The Japanese did report that on that day a hunter-killer team of antisubmarine craft and airplanes found an oil trail on the surface and carried out a long and successful attack on the submarine that had left the trace. One patrol pilot reported that two weeks later oil was still coming up from the place where the submarine had gone down.

The Japanese mining system remained unknown to Admiral Lockwood for many weeks. Since the enemy had not been known to be very active in this sort of defense it did not seem to occur to anyone that the loss of two submarines off eastern Honshu within a few weeks could be associated with a new defense. The general feeling at the time was that the boats had run afoul of planes or ships. So on August 20 the *Pompano* went out, bound for that area which had once been so profitably scoured by American submarines. A little over two weeks later it was learned from interception of Japanese coded messages that the cruiser *Nachi* had been damaged in that area and a merchant ship sunk; but the *Pompano* never confirmed these attacks, neither did it ever report back again. With this third loss, Admiral Lockwood sensed that there was something that he did not understand about the patrol area, and abandoned it entirely for the next few months.

Admiral Lockwood couldn't get the wolf-pack concept out of his mind. He did take cognizance of the reluctance of the submarine commanders to operate in this fashion; but when the invasion of the Gilbert Islands was planned, Lockwood decided he needed a senior officer on the scene to direct the movements of the submarines that would be involved. For that reason, Captain Cromwell was pulled away from his normal command of Division 43 and sent to sea as commander of the tentative wolf pack that might be formed to assault the Japanese. Thus Cromwell met his death. As described at the beginning of the book: Lockwood ordered Cromwell to form up the wolf pack but there was no reply from the *Sculpin*. When the days went by and there was no word, Lockwood knew that the boat had been lost but he didn't know any of the circumstances. Those were discovered at the end of the war and it was only then that Cromwell's heroism became known and he was awarded the congressional Medal of Honor posthumously.

For Lockwood, the worst shock of the year was the loss of the *Wahoo* and Mush Morton, his prize submarine skipper. However a new champion was developing: Lieutenant Commander Richard H. O'Kane in the *Tang*, but he didn't yet have the reputation that Commander Morton had achieved.

In fact October and November were bad months for the submarine command. The *S-44* was patrolling in the waters near the northern Kuriles in early October, 1943. Off Paramushiro, the radar man reported a contact to Lieutenant Commander Francis Brown, the skipper. Brown assumed that the vessel was a small steamer and surfaced to do battle. But instead, he found himself looking into the guns of a large destroyer which lost no time opening fire. Before Brown could dive, the enemy had put holes in the pressure hull below the waterline; the boat began to flood with no chance of plugging up the leaks. Skipper Brown ordered the crew to abandon ship. He was ready to surrender but the Japanese kept firing. A torpedoman opened the forward hatch and got up on deck to wave a white pillowcase but the shells kept coming, and the *S-44* sank. Eight men got out of the boat, into the cold water. The Japanese picked up only two, and those obviously for intelligence purposes. The others didn't have to wait long for the sea to take them.

The loss of the *S-44* was soon known because the naval authorities in the Kuriles reported proudly to Tokyo by coded message, and the Naval Intelligence team at Pearl Harbor decoded and translated the message. Skipper Brown went down with his ship and achieved a tragic first: He was the only American submarine captain to lose two submarines in battle. Nearly all the old S-boats had already been withdrawn to training commands; the sinking of the *S-44* marked the end of all their patrols. Admiral Lockwood decided they did not have the capacity for the warfare of 1943.

The next tragedy was another shocker. The new boat *Corvina* had just barely gotten into service at Pearl Harbor when the invasion of the Gilbert Islands began. Her skipper, Lieutenant Commander Roderick S. Rooney, was taking her to Australia to join Captain Fife's Southwest Pacific submarines. But, for the invasion, she was first to patrol off Truk to prevent the Japanese from sending naval reinforcements up to Tarawa or Makin. On November 16, the submarines in that area had a message from Pearl Harbor's code breakers to look out for a Japanese submarine that would be coming through their area in a matter of hours. The *Blackfish, Drum,* and *Corvina* were all in the area. The *Blackfish* kept a close watch and actually spotted the *I-176* as she moved along on the surface. But the weather was bad and the *Blackfish* skipper could not be sure the submarine was not American, so he didn't fire on her. But Lieutenant Commander Kosaburo Yamaguchi of the *I-176* had no such problem; he knew there were no Japanese submarines in the entire area except his own; so that night when he sighted a submarine silhouette on the surface he did not hesitate to fire three torpedoes. His target was the hapless *Corvina,* and she sank like a stone. Yamaguchi was the only Japanese submarine skipper to sink an American submarine during the war; the *Corvina* was the only boat lost to another submarine although the American undersea boats sank several Japanese submarines.

The boats either operating out of Australia or destined to go there were having a bad time just then. The next misadventure happened to the *Capelin,* which was commanded by Lieutenant Commander Elliott Marshall. She was another of the new boats assigned to Squadron Sixteen. At the end of October she went on patrol off Ceram in the Molucca Sea. She sank one vessel and may have damaged another but in the course of the patrol she was attacked by Japanese destroyers and sustained some damage which made the conning tower hatch leak and one bow plane operate very noisily. She went back to Darwin for repairs, and when they were made, went out again to continue the patrol in Makassar Strait. She encountered and passed messages with a pair of American boats—and then disappeared and was not heard of again.

The *Capelin* was probably a victim of the new *kaibokan* fleet that was just beginning to operate effectively in the Southwest Pacific region. The Grand Escort Force was organized on November 15, 1943 to try to stop the Americans from raising hob with the Japanese merchant navy. It included *kaibokans,* old destroyers, many small patrol boats, and four auxiliary aircraft carriers. An entire naval unit was established to deal with the escort of convoys and the patrolling of difficult areas; it was the 901st Naval Air Flotilla. The convoys were growing larger and had better protection. The Japanese surface vessels and the aircraft were getting better detection devices: radar and magnetic instruments that picked up signals from metal underwater. To combat the new Japanese equipment, American submarines were about to begin using the new frequency-modulation sonar that would prevent the sort of tragedies that had occurred off eastern Honshu earlier in the year. As Lockwood made those plans, Admiral Koshiro Oikawa, the commander of the Grand Escort Force, was also making plans of another sort. He proposed the establishment of a mine barrier along the perimeter of the new Japanese Empire; it was to run from Honshu to Borneo, specifically to protect Japan's oil resources in the Dutch East Indies. As 1943 drew to a close that plan was sent up to the Naval General Staff in Tokyo.

20

SCOURING
THE EMPIRE

THE United States entered the year 1944 with more than a hundred submarines in operation in the Pacific Ocean. There were enough boats to carry out special missions, reconnaissance of Japanese bases, give weather reports, act as lifeguards in air attacks, increase the pressure on the Japanese navy—and still carry out the mission that had to be primary: the destruction of the Japanese merchant marine.

January was a good month for the submarines and a bad month for the Japanese. More than three hundred thousand tons of Japanese ships were sunk in January. U.S. submarines were moving in close to Japan; and when one American boat left another took its place.

The result of the growing American pressure was an increase in Japanese defense efforts. The increase took various forms. The *kaibo-kan* patrol and escort vessels were on the water and Admiral Oikawa was trying to strengthen his Grand Escort Force in various ways. Some experimentation was in order.

Captain K. G. Hensel in the *Swordfish* encountered one of these experiments in January. Hensel was too old a man to be a submarine captain and in truth he was not a skipper. He had been the commandant of the navy's New London Submarine School when the war started but was so eager to get into combat that he managed to find a berth on Lockwood's staff as commander of Submarine Division 101. But he still fretted, because although he was one of the navy's experts on submarine attack problems, he had never actually taken a boat into a combat situation; he maintained that that lack decreased his effectiveness as a teacher. So he kept after Lockwood until finally a chance came to take the *Swordfish* out on a single patrol.

The boat left Midway at the end of December and encountered one storm after another on the way to Tokyo Bay, the patrol area. But she weathered them all and on January 14, 1944 she made an attack on a convoy of four merchant ships and three escorts in Tokyo Bay. She sank the *Yamakuni Maru*. The escorts came after her like sharks but she managed to get down with only a heavy buffeting. However, the next morning when Captain Hensel put her down again for her trim dive the electrical system failed; the boat went diving deep, the delicate balance system failed, and she broached, and lay floundering on the surface of the water. A patrol boat not far away turned toward them. Hensel at that point managed to get one motor working and take the boat back below where she stayed all day as repairs were made. That night she surfaced again and began to hunt.

Meanwhile the patrol boat had gone back to shore and reported that the submarine that had sunk the *Yamakuni Maru* was still lurking in Tokyo Bay. That was just what Admiral Oikawa's men wanted. They had been waiting for such an occasion.

As a part of the new plan, the Japanese had gutted the two-thousand-ton merchant ship *Delhi Maru*. They made a warship of her while retaining the merchant ship lines. She had been compartment-alized so that one or two torpedoes should not sink her; she had been equipped with sonar to find enemy submarines, plus depth charges and depth-charge throwers to sink them. She had a device that could electrically explode magnetic torpedoes before they reached her hull. She carried a fully-trained crew of Japanese navy antisubmarine sailors and a battery of deck guns concealed behind a false front that could be discarded in a matter of seconds. She was what the British had called a Q-ship when they tried this ploy in World War I against the German U-boats.

The *Delhi Maru* sailed on January 15 with a pair of PT boats as its escort and came enticingly out into Tokyo Bay. That night the *Swordfish* found her and Captain Hensel launched an attack. He fired three torpedoes at the ship—violating the rules laid down for submarine skippers: Always fire a spread so that at least one torpedo will hit.

Hensel shot all three right at the ship—all hit and all exploded. The first torpedo knocked the captain off his bridge into the sea and the other two finished the job. Hensel saw flames rising two hundred feet above the vessel after the first torpedo exploded. He did not see the others because the escorts were coming after him and he took the boat down fast. But he heard the second and third torpedoes explode, and then the ship breaking up. He thought he had hit a munitions ship and in a sense he was right; the enormous explosion was a result of all those depth charges and shells for the deck guns being on the ship. The two PT boats circled around dropping depth charges but didn't even come close to sinking the *Swordfish*. Captain Hensel sank another merchant ship a few days later, then headed back to Pearl Harbor where he later received the Navy Cross—and never again had to confess a lack of combat experience to the youngsters he was trying to teach.

As for the Japanese, the *Delhi Maru* had lasted less than twenty-four hours after she went to sea. The Q-ship experiment was officially abandoned, although some skippers claimed that they encountered Q-ships before and after the *Delhi Maru* incident. But those must have been locally manufactured by regional commanders because the Imperial Japanese navy had given up the expensive venture; Q-ships cost about three times as much to build as did a small patrol boat. Captain Hensel didn't know that he had "walked into the trap" set by the Q-ship until after the war, when the story was told.

Not all of Admiral Oikawa's new measures were so ineffectual. He had wanted to place a line of mines around the Japanese Empire, and by January 1944, the effort was well under way. Mines were laid in the mouth of the Yellow Sea, into which American submarines were moving.

The *Scorpion* went down off the Yellow Sea in January and never came back. She was undoubtedly a victim of one of Admiral Oikawa's mines.

With the minelaying continuing, Admiral Oikawa faced a new difficulty in January. The sinking of tankers had created a serious shortage of oil in Japan, and emergency measures were needed. Near the end of January two tankers escorted by one of the new *kaibokans*

239

were sent up from the oil fields of Sumatra toward Japan, through the East China Sea. They passed in front of the submarine *Tambor,* and Skipper Russell Kefauver attacked; he sank both tankers and then escaped from the *kaibokan.*

The loss of that convoy gave a special urgency to the next one, a five-tanker convoy that was escorted by several warships. The *Jack* found these ships in the South China Sea and in three separate attacks sank four of the five. The result was a really serious shortage of petroleum in Japan and the creation of even larger convoys so that more escorts could be supplied for each sailing.

Two Japanese-held areas were threatened at the moment: the New Guinea region, where General MacArthur was moving, and the Marianas, which the Japanese saw as the next target of the Central Pacific advance. Admiral Oikawa established plans for resupply of both areas, using large convoys. The convoys to the Marianas went under the code name *Matsu,* or Pine. Those bound for New Guinea were called *Take,* or Bamboo.

Matsu No. 1 was formed in Manchuria when the Japanese felt the need to bring crack troops down from the Kwantung army. That army was Japan's most experienced. It had gone into Manchuria in the 1920s and in the 1930s had begun the Manchurian war and then the war against China. The troops had been unemployed for years, standing along the Soviet border, waiting for trouble. But the trouble seemed far off because the Russians were thoroughly occupied with Adolf Hitler. The Japanese had considered launching an attack on the USSR at the time of Midway but had abandoned the idea as too costly when the Pacific war seemed so nearly won. Since that time the Japanese had been very much involved in trying to hold onto what they had captured in the early months of the war.

The entire 29th Division of the Imperial army was loaded aboard four large transports and, with a convoy escort of three destroyers, they sailed in February 1944 for the Marianas.

Near the Marianas the convoy encountered the U.S. submarine *Trout.* Skipper Albert Clark attacked the transports and sank the *Sakito Maru,* which carried four thousand troops of the 29th Division. More than half of them were drowned. He also attacked the *Aki Maru* and damaged her. Then the three Japanese destroyers began a combined attack on the *Trout* and sank her. That experience was an indication of the changing nature of the submarine war in the Pacific: the American submarines were growing more aggressive and competent at their task, but so were the Japanese antisubmarine vessels.

At about that same time came one of the unfortunate incidents of the war that could never be anticipated by anyone (and if it was, probably would not have changed matters a bit). The Japanese dispatched a convoy from Saipan to Japan and sent a message to Tokyo announcing its departure but not its nature. The American code breakers intercepted the message, and Commander Irvin in the *Nautilus* found the three-ship convoy north of the Marianas. He attacked and damaged one ship and blew the stern off another. Then he had to dive deep to escape the escort vessels that were fast and accurate in their attack. He did not know what had happened to the second vessel. She was the *America Maru*, and was carrying seventeen hundred members of the families of Japanese workers on Saipan who were being evacuated in expectation of an American attack. Many of the children, women, and old people drowned.

February, then, was another good month for the U.S. submarines and another bad one for the Japanese. They sank fifty-three cargo ships and twenty-one tankers during that month. One result was a drastic change in Japanese shipbuilding: The conversion of ships already on the ways from cargo ships to tankers. Admiral Oikawa again increased the size of the tanker convoys. It seemed to help and the sinkings went down in March.

In March the Japanese tried again to reinforce the Marianas. This time the point of origin of *Matsu No. 2* was Tokyo, the nerve center of the empire. Every precaution was taken. The convoy consisted of five big transports, large cargo ships, and several smaller ones. It was escorted by several destroyers and the light cruiser *Tatsuta*. At Pearl Harbor, Operations Officer Richard Voge learned of the sailing and sent a hot message to Lieutenant Commander Malcolm Garrison of the *Sandlance*. Skipper Garrison was low on torpedoes, having been patrolling up north near the Kuriles, but he had six left. He found the

241

convoy on the night of March 13 in bright moonlight and fired two torpedoes at the cruiser, two at one freighter, and two at another. The cruiser broke up and sank immediately; the two merchant ships were damaged. The escorts came charging down but Garrison managed to take the boat down to five hundred and fifty feet. There she sat, while for the next eighteen hours the escorts ran back and forth on the surface, dropping depth charges. Apparently these escorts had not gotten the word about the depth at which American submarines could operate, because all the charges exploded well above the *Sandlance*. The convoy had to turn back and reorganize.

That spring, as the Japanese prepared their defenses, the Americans prepared for the assault on the Marianas. The Combined Fleet had moved up to the Palaus when Truk became untenable with the shrinking of the perimeter, and a number of Japanese fleet units were identified in the anchorages, including the big battleship *Musashi*. Admiral Nimitz ordered a carrier strike on Palau and a number of submarines were sent to support it. One of these was the *Tullibee*. She was lost, apparently due to one of her own torpedoes that made a circular run in an attack on a Japanese military convoy. Only one man escaped from the submarine, to be picked up by a Japanese escort and sent to the copper mines for the rest of the war as a slave laborer.

March also marked the end of the magnetic exploder. In spite of all the discussions and the final orders to deactivate the exploder, which came from Admiral Kinkaid, Admiral Christie had made one last stab at "fixing" the Mark VI exploder in the hope that it would function correctly at last. But when the *Bowfin* went out from Fremantle under the experienced Commander Walter Griffith and reported eight bad torpedoes—and Lieutenant Commander Chester W. Nimitz, Jr. deactivated his exploders in the middle of his patrol in the *Haddo*—Admiral Christie gave up. The boats continued to have torpedo trouble, but it was never again to be quite as serious as it had been.

The changing nature of the war brought new complications for the submarine commands. By March 1944 many more boats were out and that meant the lines of demarcation of patrol areas had to be more clearly drawn than in the past. The Germans had operated on a grid system in the mid-Atlantic, but the Pacific was a much larger ocean and the system could not be adapted to it. Instead, Lockwood devised a zone system that served several purposes: To limit the areas of submarine operation, and also to prevent friendly aircraft and surface vessels from either getting in the way or into a fight with their own submarines. The patrols to the Japanese islands were increased and came to be known as "The Hit Parade" (after a popular American radio program of the day). The most productive areas were rotated among the submarines on patrol in various general areas; thus a submarine might have a week of its patrol in a "hot" area, and then have to go to one of the more obscure areas just afterwards, to more or less equalize the chances of each boat scoring successes.

Admiral King had responded to Admiral Oikawa's increased Japanese antisubmarine patrol and escort services with a new directive to the submarine fleet to concentrate on destroyers and escort craft rather than aircraft carriers and battleships. It was a reflection of the success of Oikawa's efforts. The most effective of the American submarines in meeting this challenge was the *Harder*, whose skipper, Commander Samuel Dealey, was one of the most aggressive in the service. In the second week of April, the *Harder* was operating off Woleai, where she had been stationed as a lifeguard and had rescued several aviators. While there she was beset by one of Admiral Oikawa's new hunter-killer teams. In this case a Japanese plane spotted the American submarine and then radioed his base for surface help. Along came the destroyer *Ikazuchi* ready to attack the *Harder*. Dealey waited for the destroyer to approach and soon realized that it was tracking him by sonar. He let the warship speed along until it was only nine hundred yards (barely half a mile) away from the *Harder*, and then fired four torpedoes "down the throat." That sort of shot was theoretically best made with a magnetic exploder, and again theoretically required but one torpedo, that would explode in the influence zone no matter which way the destroyer turned. But by firing a spread of four torpedoes at such close range, Dealey made sure that no matter which way the destroyer skipper turned the ship, she was going to get hit. The *Ikazuchi* was hit hard and she went down in four minutes, her depth charges exploding in the water among the survivors and adding to the havoc.

The hunter-killer patrols continued to proliferate in the Japanese defense zones. The *Scamp* ran afoul of a team in early April off Mindanao. This time the original sighting was made by escorts of a small naval force that the *Scamp* encountered on April 7. The escorts drove the *Scamp* underwater, and she stayed below for some time. She came up to periscope depth but found the Japanese force had gone over the horizon. However, they had not left the submarine's area unattended. The sub's radioman was trying to send a contact report on the sighting of the force when suddenly out of the sun came a Japanese plane whereupon the skipper took her down on a crash dive. At forty feet a depth bomb went off; it was much too close. The *Scamp* lost power. She was forced down below three hundred feet before the diving officer recovered control. The crew hustled to unjam the rudder, put out a fire in the maneuvering room, and stop up the leaks. As they were doing these tasks the plane reported back to its base, bringing forth several escort vessels that began attacking. The skipper managed to evade the Japanese and escape. The radio was out, but by the next day they managed to fix it well enough to get off a message to Captain Haines at Brisbane, who had replaced Captain Fife as commander of the submarines there. (Fife had gone back to Washington to take a desk job.) The submarine *Dace* was sent to the *Scamp*'s assistance and escorted her into Seeadler Harbor in the Admiralty Islands, which had been taken over as an advance base by the Southwest Pacific submarine force.

The Japanese antisubmarine force was increasing in skill and effectiveness every month. Early in April, the *Gudgeon* left Pearl Harbor for a patrol in the Marianas area, where she would be operating near the *Sandlance* and the *Tunny*. No more was heard from her but at first this was not regarded as ominous because Pacific Fleet submarines were taking more care to maintain radio silence than they had in times past. One day in May, the crews of the *Tunny* and the *Sandlance* both heard a long depth-charging attack in which at least forty charges were dropped. The *Gudgeon* never reappeared and it was determined later that she must have fallen victim to a Japanese antisubmarine patrol.

In spite of the renewed vigilance the American toll of Japanese shipping continued to rise, and this year (1944) the sinkings by the submarines were augmented by hundreds of thousands of tons of ships sunk by carrier planes and land-based aircraft of the U.S. Navy, the Marine Corps, and the Army Air Force. The production of aircraft in America had reached a rate whereby industry could supply all the needs of the European Theater of Operations and the Pacific; and a new emphasis was being added to the Pacific war by the Combined Chiefs of Staff.

As MacArthur moved into the South Pacific the Japanese tried to stop him at New Guinea. The reinforcement of the area got a high priority because MacArthur was coming too close to the Japanese-controlled Java-Sumatra oil supply. The Imperial General Staff siphoned off two Japanese divisions from China. They were loaded aboard nine transports at Shanghai and sailed on April 17 for western New Guinea by way of Manila. This convoy was regarded as so important that it was led by a rear admiral, Sadamichi Kajioka. His protective force consisted of a number of escort vessels, plus an effective air screen. The real weakness of the convoy was the flagship, a coal-burning mine-layer that made so much smoke the convoy was easily spotted by the *Jack* as it neared Luzon Island on April 25. Skipper Dykers was on the bridge at the time, having just run away from a periscope and a patrol bomber that dropped a depth bomb that missed by a wide margin. Dykers trailed the convoy all day and waited until after dark when the moon set before making an attack approach. The ships of the convoy knew he was out there but relied on the radar of the escort vessels to keep them informed. Once in a while an escort would peel off and make a run toward the *Jack*, whereupon Dykers would back off and try to probe at another spot. But the escorts were all around the convoy and they were alert. Finally Skipper Dykers decided to make an unusual sort of attack. He fired nineteen torpedoes set to run deep, to take them beneath the hulls of the escorts and then hopefully to hit the transports. There were so many transports that the plan worked, at least a little. The torpedoes did run beneath the escorts, but most of the ships managed to evade them. One did not. She was the *Yoshida Maru No. 1*, carrying an entire Japanese regiment. She sank fast, and the whole regiment, its equipment, and the crew of the vessel went down.

At Manila the Grand Escort Force turned the convoy over to the Combined Fleet since it was going directly into a war zone. That meant the *kaibokans* and small patrol craft that had brought the convoy down went back north, while Admiral Kajioka continued with his flagship, but with a new escort force of three destroyers, a minesweeper, and two submarine chasers.

On May 6, the convoy ran into the patrol zone of Lieutenant Commander Charles H. Andrews's *Gurnard,* that had been sent from Pearl Harbor to join the Fremantle submarine force and to patrol the Celebes Sea on the way. Andrews got his first sight of the convoy when the flagship's heavy smoke appeared nineteen miles from the submarine. He began to approach and soon saw one of the largest aggregations of ships ever put to sea by the Japanese other than in a full scale invasion: eight transports in three columns, surrounded by escorts on all sides.

Andrews was lucky. He fired three torpedoes each at the two big ships closest to him. Two torpedoes struck the lead ship, and the third passed behind and hit a ship in the second column. The second trio of torpedoes struck the second target. Andrews heard the impacts but did not see them because a destroyer was barreling down on him; he quickly dived. The escorts kept him down for two hours, and in that period the Japanese rescued most of the troops and some of the equipment from the sinking ships. The convoy went on but Imperial General Headquarters stopped it at Halmahera rather than let it go into waters that were heavily patrolled by Admiral Christie's submarines.

The *Gurnard* surfaced that night and ran through the flotsam left by the attack. The one damaged transport was still afloat but abandoned; Andrews put another torpedo into it and it sank.

By April 1944 the Japanese Imperial General Staff had come to the conclusion that the American advance in the Central Pacific could be stopped only by one big battle. Since the beginning of the war, the Japanese navy had been given responsibility for protecting the Pacific island empire. Their army occupied eastern China, the landmass of Southeast Asia, the Philippine Islands, the Dutch East Indies, and part of New Guinea. Army troops were stationed on the larger islands.

But the perimeter was still the navy's and the navy was responsible for air operations throughout the Pacific islands. Even after the Guadalcanal campaign, the Japanese army general staff knew very little about the Americans; they had been the navy's problem ever since the army forces captured the Philippines. Even at Guadalcanal, with twenty thousand Japanese troops ashore, the army command at Rabaul was unaware of American strength and its disposition.

The major thorn in the side of the Japanese navy was the shortage of oil in Japan, a direct result of the submarine operations against their tankers. In early 1944 the *Crevalle* sank the largest tanker of all, the seventeen-thousand-ton *Nisshin Maru*, off Borneo. The oil shortage created a serious problem in fleet disposition, and the decision was made to keep the major elements of the Combined Fleet in southern waters. Tawi Tawi, the western island of the Sulu Archipelago, south of the Philippines-proper, became the new fleet base. As soon as the ships arrived they were spotted by coast watchers and from that moment on the area was alive with American submarines.

In California the new frequency-modulation sonar system was coming along well, and the scientists gave Admiral Lockwood the welcome news that the device had neared the point where it could be used operationally. The Japanese were presenting Lockwood with a new problem: the extensive antisubmarine minefields planned by Admiral Oikawa. At that time the only way to learn of the existence of a new minefield was the hard way: to lose a submarine. Captured documents helped but they could not keep up with events. The Japanese were building new defenses all the time. The *Herring* was to be lost just because of that increased vigilance.

New Japanese defenses again evoked American concentration on wolf-pack techniques. These tactics were supposed to be ready when the time would come that wolf packs could enter areas then interdicted by mines, such as the Sea of Japan, that links Japan with Korea and Manchuria. Another reason for the stubborn experimentation was the contraction of the submarine operating areas caused by the American victories which were driving the Japanese forces ever nearer to their homeland.

The two admirals—Lockwood and Christie—were both trying out

247

the wolf-pack technique again. Improved short-range radio communications certainly helped. So did the decision not to have a supernumerary wolf-pack commander aboard but to give the responsibility to the senior skipper.

In May the *Herring* and the *Barb* were working as a small wolf pack and as they were moving west, Admiral Lockwood ordered them up to the Kuriles north of the main Japanese home islands. The Radio Intelligence interceptors had word of a three-ship convoy that was just leaving the port of Matsuwa Island. They arrived off the port in time, and the *Herring* moved in close, while the *Barb* stayed further out at sea. Skipper David Zabriskie, Jr. of the *Herring* sank an escort, then a freighter. The other ships ran out to sea to escape and the *Barb* was waiting for them there. Lieutenant Commander Eugene Fluckey, leader of the wolf pack had planned it just that way. He quickly sank one freighter, then chased the other one and sank it as well.

The *Herring* moved close inshore and sank two ships anchored in the Matsuwa Harbor. Either Zabriskie did not know about the Japanese shore batteries that guarded that harbor, or he was contemptuous of them. If so, it was a bad mistake; the gunners put a shell into the conning tower, sinking the boat with all hands.

The *Bang, Parche,* and *Tinosa* were also sent out from Pearl Harbor as a wolf pack to operate in Luzon Strait. Once again Lockwood was trying the supernumerary approach. The commander of the pack was Captain G. E. Peterson, who had spent most of the war in the Atlantic and had never before made a Pacific war patrol. The three boats found all sorts of targets but their sinking record didn't seem to be any better than it would have been had they been operating alone. The *Bang* was credited with three freighters, the *Parche* with two, and the *Tinosa* with two. Another wolf pack sent to the same area a little later performed very poorly. The *Picuda*, the *Peto*, and *Perch II* sank one river gunboat among them—that was all. The new *Perch* was almost lost in a spirited enemy counterattack.

Spirited was a good word for the Japanese antisubmarine activity as it developed in the middle of 1944. A real struggle developed between the submarines and the escorts, one that transcended the usual. The Japanese were constantly devoting more resources to the operation.

The number and size of Admiral Oikawa's minefields were increasing, and the Japanese were learning more about American submarines. One source of information, unsuspected by the Americans, was the talk-between-ships carried on by the wolf packs and by submarine skippers who happened to encounter a friendly boat at sea. The Japanese antisubmarine command scoured their universities and business firms and put together an intelligence team of experts in American vernacular speech; they also secured a good deal of information about submarine operations by monitoring voice broadcasts.

The American submarine skippers—or some of them—had been spurred by King and Nimitz's advice to go after escort vessels; one of them, Sam Dealey in the *Harder*, made the war against the escorts his personal vendetta. Early in June Dealey was on his way to pick up a group of coast watchers on Borneo and then reconnoiter the new Japanese base at Tawi Tawi. Near Tawi Tawi, Dealey came across a three-ship convoy guarded by a destroyer and another escort. He was chasing on the surface in heavy night clouds, when the moon suddenly appeared and silhouetted the submarine for the destroyer *Minazuki*. She came down fast on the track of the *Harder*. Dealey let her come, then submerged and turned hard left to bring his stern tubes training across the destroyer's track. When the *Minazuki* was just half a mile away Dealey fired four torpedoes; two of them hit the destroyer as she was plowing along at twenty-four knots—and she plowed her way right to the bottom. Three minutes later the *Harder* was on the surface again, chasing the convoy but without further luck.

The next day Sam Dealey encountered the new antisubmarine methods of the Japanese navy. A float plane spotted the *Harder* first and called for support. The destroyer *Hayanami* soon appeared. That suited Dealey just fine. He exposed a couple of yards of his periscope so the destroyer captain could get a good look and then waited. The destroyer began its run when it was about two and a half miles away, zigzagging as it came. Dealey waited, as he had the last time, until the *Hayanami* was about half a mile away and then fired three torpedoes in a spread. It didn't make any difference which way the destroyer captain turned—at that speed he was bound to drive into one of the torpedoes. The captain saw the torpedo wakes too late and turned.

249

Fifteen seconds after firing, the first torpedo hit the *Hayanami* in the bow; the turn swung the destroyer's stern around just in time to catch the second torpedo. In less than a minute the *Hayanami* sank with all hands aboard.

The Japanese recognized the deadly nature of this particular submarine; on that same day a squadron of six destroyers was sent out to search for and sink the offender. But Sam Dealey and the *Harder* were far away and down deep in the quiet of the sea and the destroyers never found them.

Dealey then took the *Harder* to British Borneo and picked up his six Australian coast watchers. The next morning the Japanese hunter-killer teams were out again; it was very early when a float plane caught the *Harder* on the surface. The pilot dropped a depth bomb just as Dealey took the boat down. The bomb exploded close by but did not do any serious damage. Again this pilot radioed his base and soon two destroyers came up to try to find the submarine. The sea was glassy, so Dealey didn't try to pick a fight but stayed below and when the destroyers finally left the area, so did Dealey. He moved toward Sibutu Passage near Tawi Tawi.

That night in the Sibutu Passage, Dealey encountered two more enemy warships. At least one of them was a destroyer; the other may have been one of the special anti-submarine vessels *(kaibokan)* or a converted minesweeper but whatever it was it was doing the job of a patrol vessel. Dealey tracked the enemy ships and when they overlapped he fired four torpedoes. Two struck the destroyer *Tanikaze* and she sank. At least one other struck the ship beyond; Dealey and his executive officer both looked through the periscope of the *Harder* to see if it sank like the first ship. No other destroyer was reported sunk that night but the Japanese did not keep the same sort of score on lesser patrol vessels, so it is probable that the second ship was not a destroyer but another sort of escort-patrol craft.

The next day Sam Dealey reconnoitered the Tawi Tawi anchorage and confirmed the presence there of a number of capital ships, including the battleship *Musashi*. That meant the anchorage was indeed a major Japanese base, a matter that was still in some doubt at Pearl Harbor until Dealey's radio report came in. Once again the new

250

alertness of the Japanese patrols showed: A patrol plane spotted the *Harder*'s periscope and what appeared to be another destroyer came charging at the submarine. Once more Dealey fired a down-the-throat shot, then took the submarine plunging down fast. The crew heard two explosions that sounded like torpedo hits and then rumblings and lesser explosions that sounded like a ship breaking up. But once again no Japanese destroyer was reported lost that day so if the torpedoes did sink the attacking ship, it was something other than a destroyer.

Sam Dealey took the *Harder* back to Fremantle at the end of his patrol. Admiral Christie was delighted to learn of all the attacks on the escort vessels and destroyers. He gave Dealey his nickname then— "The Destroyer Killer." The *Harder*'s record was made known in Australia and at Pearl Harbor for other skippers to emulate. The American's growing difficulty in countering the Japanese antisubmarine efforts made Christie and the other submarine base commands keep the pressure on their submarine captains.

21   UNSUNG

VICTORY

THE important victory in the Battle of the Philippine Sea in the summer of 1944 has always been painted as a triumph of the new American carrier forces. The fact is that of the three carriers sunk at the battle, two were destroyed by submarines. Without the submarine victory there is no telling what might have happened.

The battle was a direct result of the American invasion of Saipan in mid-June. For two months the Japanese had known that a new invasion was afoot although they were not quite sure of the target. The Imperial navy regarded the forthcoming invasion as an opportunity to fight the great battle that was supposed to decimate the American fleet and stop the drives of the Central Pacific and Southwest Pacific commands. The Japanese quite rightly attributed the success of their enemies' amphibious operations to the size of the American fleet and particularly to the air superiority that the American carriers had achieved. If the fleet were to be crippled the Americans would be unable to move. This reasoning was the basis of all Japanese naval planning after the American capture of the Marshall Islands in late 1944.

At one time Admiral Nimitz believed that Truk would have to become the target of an invasion but by April of 1944 plans had changed. The long-range *B-29* heavy bombers were in action against the Japanese but not very efficiently because the bases were located far off in western China which meant a long round trip and a small payload for the bombers. The Army Air Corps wanted bases closer to Japan. The logical area was the Marianas Islands. Besides, Truk had been virtually abandoned by the Japanese so it could be bypassed by the Americans.

The Japanese fully expected that the next American concentration to be in New Guinea. MacArthur had landed at Hollandia in April. On May 27 he landed at Biak an island off northwestern New Guinea, and put into jeopardy the Japanese hold on the southern Philippine Islands. The Imperial General Staff ordered the Biak threat eliminated and Admiral Soemu Toyoda, the new chief of the Combined Fleet, sent reinforcements down aboard destroyers and cruisers. That apparently wasteful effort was occasioned by the sad fate of *Bamboo Convoy No. 1*, which was not forgotten. The warships ran into trouble with American aircraft, and turned back, while the U.S. submarine *Hake* torpedoed and sank the Japanese destroyer *Kazagumo* at the entrance to Davao Gulf. The Japanese made another attempt at the end of the first week of June, this time sending six destroyers loaded with troops in the fashion of the old Tokyo Express to Guadalcanal. But this time the Fifth Air Force of the U.S. Army Air Corps plastered the destroyers with bombs and sank the destroyer *Harusame*. An Allied cruiser force came up and drove the Japanese back to the Philippines. Once more they had failed to reinforce Biak.

Admiral Toyoda then planned a major naval attack, hoping to draw the American carrier fleet into action in the south. That was one reason for the concentration at Tawi Tawi. But one day at the height of the Biak troubles, an intrepid Japanese search pilot flew around the Marshalls and discovered a large concentration of warships and attack transports in the harbors at Kwajalein and Eniwetok. At the same time other planes reported a buildup in the Solomons. The Americans had turned Guadalcanal into a major base.

Toyoda hoped to lure the American war fleet out to fight somewhere between Palau and New Guinea. Instead, he learned on June 11 that the American ships had left the Marshalls. Where were they bound? Soon enough air attacks on the Marianas told the story. The Japanese fleet began to move from three locations: Tawi Tawi, Batjan, and Davao. They would all assemble in the Philippine Sea under Admiral Jisaburo Ozawa, the new commander of the attack force, and would take on the Americans. The Japanese had planned their attack

carefully. They were short of carrier planes and skilled pilots following the long battle of attrition in the Solomons, Rabaul, and Truk.
They had lost their numerical carrier superiority because of the sinkings at Midway and the rapid American shipbuilding effort. But to
compensate for this they had many island bases that could be used to
support the carrier operations. When it was clear to Toyoda on June
13 that the Americans would strike at Saipan, the A-Go Operation
was put into effect. The nine Japanese carriers would find the American fleet and the planes would attack; meanwhile other planes from
Guam, Saipan, and Tinian would also attack the carriers and battleships. The carrier planes would land on the islands to refuel and
rearm and the land-based planes would land on the carriers. This
shuttle attack would, in effect, double the Japanese carrier strength
and was expected to defeat the Americans.

But the Japanese reckoned without considering the American
submarine force. This failure to plan for submarine activity was not
unreasonable. The American submarines had never before figured in
a fleet operation. But this time it was different.

Admiral Christie had half a dozen submarines around Tawi Tawi,
watching for the Japanese fleet to come out. When Sam Dealey was
stalking destroyers off Tawi Tawi he also saw the battleships *Yamato*
and *Musashi*. On June 13 Skipper Marshall Austin in the *Redfin*
watched the carriers, battleships, cruisers, and destroyers move out on
their way to the Marianas. That night he reported that the enemy fleet
was heading north. They soon passed into the area of Lockwood's
submarines, that were looking for them as they continued to stalk
merchant ships.

To reach the Marianas, Admiral Ozawa's fleet had to get by the
Philippine Islands. They could pass around the south, or the north,
or take the shortcut through San Bernardino Strait that connects the
Sulu Sea with the Pacific Ocean. That is how they went, and they were
seen there by Lieutenant Commander Robert Risser in the *Flying
Fish* who was patrolling at periscope depth in San Bernardino Strait.
A few hours later Lieutenant Commander Slade Cutter in the *Sea-
horse* sighted the Batjan contingent (led by *Yamato* and *Musashi*) in
Surigao Strait. The two reports reached Admiral Spruance just after

255

the American troops had landed on Saipan. What worried him more than anything else was the possibility that the Japanese would split their force and attack his Fifth Fleet with one section. While the main fighting force was thus occupied, the second Japanese force might sneak up and annihilate the ships standing off Saipan to support and supply the American invasion. If that were to happen the invasion might fail. With those two submarine reports in mind Admiral Spruance postponed the landings on Guam and insisted that Admiral Marc Mitscher, the carrier force commander, stick close to Saipan in support.

On June 15, Admiral Lockwood ordered the new submarine *Cavalla* to take a position about three hundred and fifty miles due east of San Bernardino Strait. Lieutenant Commander Herman Kossler, the skipper, had originally been given orders to go to San Bernardino Strait and replace the *Flying Fish,* whose patrol time was nearly ended. But Lockwood changed all that. Before beginning the new patrol Kossler was to be in touch with Lieutenant Commander William Deragon in the *Pipefish.* They met on June 16 and decided that the *Cavalla* would patrol just north of the straight line from San Bernardino Strait to Saipan and the *Pipefish* would patrol just south of it.

Just three hours later the *Cavalla* made radar contact with four ships. Kossler brought the boat to the surface and traveled at high-speed to get around on the other side of the ships and intercept their course.

The swing around end took four hours; at 3:00 in the morning Kossler saw the convoy and dived. Two of the ships were tankers, escorted by destroyers. He came back to periscope depth and soon was in position to attack. But as he got ready to fire his torpedoes, lookouts on one of the Japanese destroyers spied the periscope and that escort turned to attack. Kossler was forced to submerge and was kept there by an alert destroyer captain until the convoy had gone over the horizon. When he surfaced there was nothing but an empty sea. He had only the course and speed to go by.

Since Kossler knew the Japanese fleet was out and he was waiting for capital ships to come by, he radioed Pearl Harbor that he was letting the tankers go because to chase them would take too long and would move him out of the patrol zone. When Admiral Lockwood got that message Kossler was already on course back toward San Bernardino Strait. Lockwood knew that these tankers must belong to the Japanese fleet and would at some time come up with the fleet. He ordered Kossler to get back on the track of the tankers and stay there. The admiral sent the same message to the *Seahorse, Muskellunge,* and *Pipefish,* which were all in the general area. The *Albacore, Stingray, Finback,* and *Bang* were also given the word since their patrol areas were not far from the Marianas.

Not only was the Japanese fleet out but Admiral Ozawa's antisubmarine patrol planes were unusually active. The *Cavalla* couldn't make much speed because she was forever having to dive to avoid Japanese planes. Kossler fell far behind but from Pearl Harbor Lockwood encouraged him to keep on the track, and he did.

All day long Kossler kept going. Just before dusk he dove again to avoid a twin-engined bomber. The task seemed hopeless but Kossler didn't know that Admiral Lockwood's intuitive decision had put him on a collision course with Ozawa's main fleet. He learned about it around eight o'clock that night when the radar screen lighted up with pips, indicating the presence of many ships.

American naval doctrine called for a submarine captain who sighted the enemy fleet on the eve of a battle to report on the enemy disposition, course and speed, before doing anything else. Kossler saw at least one carrier in the force he was tracking and was sure that he could get a shot at it. Instead he followed doctrine and tracked the Japanese ships until his submarine was spotted; two destroyers were left behind to put the submarine down and keep it down until the fleet was long gone.

It was 10:45 on the night of June 18 before Kossler could surface and send a message to Pearl Harbor announcing the passage of fifteen or more large ships. He had, in fact, made the wrong decision. Lockwood came back with a message to continue tracking the ships and to attack when possible. It was a gentle way of saying he should have followed Lord Nelson's doctrine and laid his ship alongside the enemy without regard to procedure.

257

But if Kossler made a wrong decision, he was not the only one that day. Admiral Spruance joined in. When Kossler's message was intercepted and read by the admiral while he was off Saipan, Spruance worried more than ever. Kossler had reported only fifteen ships. Where was the rest of the Japanese fleet? Why was Admiral Ozawa loafing along instead of steaming in fast to do battle? Spruance reasoned that Ozawa had indeed split his force and was going to make a two-pronged attack on the Americans.

When the Kossler report was given to Admiral Marc Mitscher he saw that the Americans were close enough to Ozawa that if they steamed at full speed all night they would be able to launch a dawn air attack. But Spruance was not really seeking a fleet engagement; his primary task was to conduct the Saipan landings and protect them. Had Admiral Halsey been in charge, Mitscher would undoubtedly have been able to make his dawn attack, and he would have caught Ozawa flat-footed. The reason for the Japanese admiral's leisurely pace was that he was waiting for planes from Palau and other areas to ferry themselves to the Marianas. From that point they would be able to carry out the shuttle attack with the carrier but this couldn't be accomplished for twenty-four hours.

While Spruance was agonizing over his attempts to outguess Ozawa, Lieutenant Commander Sam Loomis sent a message to Pearl Harbor. He was the skipper of the *Stingray*, one of the boats that had been assigned to watch for the Japanese force. His message concerned a minor accident aboard the *Stingray* but in the transmission it was garbled; no one could read it. Spruance jumped to the conclusion that it was bad news about Ozawa and with great relief told Admiral Mitscher that he could not attack, but must retreat toward Saipan to protect the invasion force.

Thus the great American carrier fleet—15 carriers—lost its first chance to hit the enemy and perhaps determine the outcome of the battle.

Later that night, Admiral Ozawa did the unthinkable: He broke radio silence for a brief transmission to Guam to remind Admiral Kakuji Kakuta, commander of the First Air Fleet, of the latter's obligation. Altogether, Kakuta was supposed to have two thousand planes at his disposal throughout the Central Pacific and South Pacific regions. He was also supposedly able to put at least five hundred into the air at the Marianas for the great sea battle.

At Pearl Harbor and other radio installations, the Ozawa transmission was detected, and Admiral Nimitz was able to give Admiral Spruance something he had vainly been looking for: an accurate fix on the Japanese force. Spruance got it but he did not believe it. He preferred to rely on his suspicions of the garbled *Stingray* transmission. The U.S. Fleet continued to steam away from the enemy.

Very early in the morning Admiral Spruance suggested that Admiral Mitscher send a powerful force to strike at the islands. He was still thinking about his mission, to further the invasion. Luckily, Admiral Mitscher balked at this move, which would have left the carrier force defended only by a combat air patrol. He sloughed Spruance off with vague words, and thus saved his force from possible disaster.

By the morning of June 19 many of the carrier men were nearly gritting their teeth at the timidity of their leader. As they expected, Spruance's failure to take the initiative had given it to Ozawa. At dawn the Japanese admiral launched his search planes and at 6:30 in the morning the first strike against the American fleet got off. From that point on, four waves of Japanese planes took off from the carriers to attack; and because Spruance had failed to follow up the fixes on the position of the Japanese fleet, he did not even know where Ozawa was.

Admiral Lockwood's submarines had been searching diligently all night long. The *Stingray* and the *Bang* were to the east of the Japanese force, and found nothing. The *Finback* got a sight of the Japanese that night but, by the time its transmission came in, it didn't affect the battle.

About a hundred miles south of the *Finback* was Lieutenant Commander James Blanchard in the *Albacore*. All day on June 18, the *Albacore* had been tuning in to the various transmissions and was following the course of the activity. Blanchard could sense that something important was afoot if only from his own situation. The *Albacore* had never seen so many aircraft in such a short time. Again and again she was forced underwater by Japanese planes. The air activity stopped after dark on June 18th but in the morning, after the *Albacore* had made her trim dive and returned to the surface, she was forced down again at 7:15 A.M. by another plane.

Half an hour later the *Albacore* came up to periscope depth, and Blanchard looked around. He had come up on the edge of the Japanese fleet. He saw a carrier, a cruiser, and several other ships on the far side of these two. They were a little more than seven miles away. A few minutes later he saw another carrier with a cruiser and destroyers. There were many planes in the sky but they were not searching for submarines; they were heading out on their attack against the American force.

Skipper Blanchard decided to attack the second carrier, and although his torpedo data computer failed him in mid-attack, he managed to get six torpedoes off. He was never quite certain of what happened to them because, as the tracks became visible, all hell broke loose on the surface around the *Albacore*. Planes suddenly swarmed around the submarine and only the fact that she was below the surface saved her from a thorough strafing. As she submerged, a destroyer was approaching fast. Inside the *Albacore* the men in the control room counted as the submarine dove deep. The first torpedo's time ran out; a miss. So was the second, the third, and fourth, and fifth; but the sixth torpedo exploded. Blanchard would report to Admiral Lockwood that he had secured a hit on one carrier—no more. But it would be hours before he reported, because the Japanese were after him. The first depth charges were very close and knocked cork off the bulkheads. The submarine went deeper and got under a sonar-reflecting density layer. The Japanese lost the track; but every time the *Albacore* came up to two hundred feet the destroyers found her again and continued dropping depth charges. For the next three hours Blanchard played hide and seek with death.

The carrier Blanchard had hit was the thirty-two thousand-ton *Taiho*, the newest and biggest in the Japanese fleet, and the flagship of Admiral Ozawa. At the time of Blanchard's attack she was launching planes for the strike. It is odd that the men of the *Albacore* heard only one explosion because there were two. Warrant Officer Sakio Komatsu had just taken off from the carrier in his stub-winged Zero fighter (called a Hamp) when he saw the torpedo wakes racing toward the *Taiho*. With no hesitation he dived the fighter into the torpedo closest to the carrier; it blew the Hamp and Warrant Officer Komatsu into a thousand pieces. From the bridge of the carrier, Admiral Ozawa saw the act of bravery. It was what he had come to expect from his intrepid fliers.

The torpedo that struck the *Taiho* caused no concern at all on the admiral's bridge. The carrier had been built to take punishment. A single torpedo should not even decrease her basic speed, once adjustments had been made to prevent list. The problem belonged to the damage-control officer, who was directly responsible to the captain of the carrier. Admiral Ozawa felt no need to concern himself with it.

Initially the torpedo damage did not even stop flight operations. But there was one bit of damage that was bothersome. The torpedo explosion had distorted the operating mechanism of the forward flight elevator, which meant it could not be used to raise and lower planes from the hangar deck to the flight deck. The damage-control crews set out to fix the elevator but when they got down into the pit they discovered that they were ankle deep in aviation gasoline because the torpedo explosion had also ruptured one of the gasoline storage tanks. This too could be handled. Men with pumps were brought down to clear out the shaft, and then pump the gasoline out of the ruptured tank so it would cause no more trouble. That was done; all that remained was to rid the air of the intoxicating gasoline fumes that made it hard to work in the hangar deck.

At about noon the work was nearly finished. The damage-control officer, who was new at his job on this new carrier, decided that the best way to clear the fumes quickly was to open all the ventilation ducts throughout the ship, and then turn on the blowers to whisk the fumes away. It was not long before Admiral Ozawa began to smell gasoline fumes, for they were blown from the hangar deck to every nook and cranny of the ship. But the *Taiho* was still operating without difficulty. The admiral was far more concerned about other matters: First, the initial attack wave was a long time in returning. Second, another carrier was in serious trouble. It seemed almost impossible to believe, standing there on the bridge of the *Taiho*. The

261

attack had been going so well in theory. As far as Admiral Ozawa knew, the planes from his carriers had attacked the American ships. Admiral Kakuta's land-based airplanes were supposedly doing the same. Since the Japanese search planes had a radius of one hundred and fifty miles more than the American planes, Ozawa was not spotted because he had stayed beyond the American capability. But already one American submarine had created difficulty of a sort Ozawa could not remember having occurred during the war—and now came a second spoiler.

She was Lieutenant Commander Kossler's *Cavalla.*

After making his reports on the Japanese fleet, Kossler had carried out his orders and chased the tankers. All day on the eighteenth he had hurried along, up to the surface and down deep in response to Japanese patrol planes. He hadn't seen one sign of the tankers. Coming across the Pacific the *Cavalla* had run into a typhoon that battered her for several days, and more important, caused her to use up an inordinate amount of fuel. This long chase at as high a speed as could be managed had used up still more fuel. Kossler was becoming concerned about his ability to complete his patrol and get home. At about midnight on June 18 he decided the chase was fruitless and turned back toward San Bernardino Strait.

Even before dawn on June 19 the Japanese patrol planes were out, and they sent the *Cavalla* down several times. Actually the planes weren't looking for submarines that morning but for the American fleet; that was the reason for all the activity.

At 7:20 A.M. Kossler radioed Pearl Harbor about the unusual activity. It continued. At 10 o'clock more planes appeared and forced the *Cavalla* to submerge again. At periscope depth he sighted four planes circling around and the sound man reported screw noises. Heading toward the planes Kossler soon saw the masts of a ship. The next time he came up for a look, he saw a carrier, two cruisers, and a destroyer. He identified the carrier as being in the *Shokaku* class, then realized it was the *Shokaku* herself. He plotted an attack on the carrier and fired six torpedoes. Three of them struck and exploded; the other three missed.

By the time the torpedoes exploded the destroyer *Urakaze* was already moving against the source of those wakes. As the destroyer approached, the *Cavalla* dove underwater and just barely made it out of range of the destroyer's first run. Four depth charges came down, so close that they knocked out three sound sets and fouled up the piping of the hull ventilation system.

The destroyer kept the *Cavalla* down for hours. Kossler knew nothing of what was going on above him.

On the surface, the Japanese crew of the *Shokaku* were trying desperately to save their ship; black smoke streamed from her and flames kept rising above the flight deck. After noon, the planes from the early strikes began coming home but they could not land on the *Shokaku*. The *Taiho* and the *Zuikaku* took them instead. There was plenty of room on the decks of the two carriers; the number of planes returning was far smaller than anyone had expected. The only possible reason for it, the admiral's staff said, was that some of the planes must have landed at Guam or Tinian airfield as was suggested in the operational orders.

But then some of the handful of pilots came to the admiral's bridge to tell the story of being set upon, before they ever reached the carriers, by swarms of Grumman Hellcats. After some questioning, Admiral Ozawa began to suspect that what had looked so much like victory was becoming a dreadful defeat.

Hardly had the last plane landed when a series of alarming explosions shook the *Shokaku*. Her torpedoes and bombs were bursting forth. They ignited gasoline and spread flames throughout the ship, and the fires raged so madly that it was apparent that she could not be saved. She sank at three o'clock in the afternoon.

By that time Admiral Ozawa's concern had switched. The survivors of the second and third raids on the American ships came back, and the stories they told of the American defenses were alarming. The survivors of the fourth raid were not expected back; they had been told to attack and then land on Guam. It was just as well because after the *Shokaku* blew up, it became apparent that there was something dreadfully wrong aboard the *Taiho*. The new damage-control officer's unorthodox move in blowing the gasoline fumes away had gone awry. Instead of blowing out, the fumes had circulated through every

263

corner of the ship and stayed, hanging in the air. Suddenly, about half an hour after the *Shokaku* sank, an enormous, rolling explosion shook the flagship; an electric motor spark had ignited the fumes in one compartment and the chain reaction began. The flight deck simply heaved up, broke its moorings, and collapsed. The sides of the carrier blew out, the water rushed in, and she began to settle. With great difficulty the staff persuaded Admiral Ozawa to leave his ship. He knew now that victory had been an illusion, that a great defeat was in process. And while the American carrier pilots around their ships far to the east and over Guam were shooting down hundreds of Japanese planes, they had not yet found Ozawa's force. Ozawa was persuaded to move to the cruiser *Haguro*, as an emergency measure. It was anything but satisfactory; the *Haguro* didn't have adequate communications facilities to command the entire operation, and Admiral Ozawa was out of the battle. The *Taiho* continued to burn and settle; finally, as darkness fell she sank. Two carriers were down and the American planes had not yet found the Japanese fleet.

Finally, late in the day the American planes did find the Japanese task force and attacked in force. They sank the light carrier *Hiyo* and damaged the *Zuikaku, Junyo, Ryuho,* and *Chiyoda*. Admiral Mitscher wanted to chase the damaged ships and finish the job, but Admiral Spruance decided to stick to guarding the Saipan invasion force. There was another reason: The Americans had a brand new fleet of fast battleships but they didn't know how to use them, and Admiral W. A. Lee wanted to avoid a night engagement with the Japanese force because he was afraid he would be defeated. The Japanese battleship commander was equally indecisive because of the carrier and plane losses they had sustained; he didn't want to be caught during the daylight hours by the American planes. So the two fleets retreated, the Japanese back to Okinawa and then Japan, and the Americans to Saipan.

For some reason the loss of the *Taiho* was not reported to the headquarters in Tokyo in a way that would be caught by the American code breakers. They soon enough learned that the *Shokaku* had sunk but for many months they didn't know that the *Cavalla* had sunk the *Taiho* and while Kossler was a hero at Pearl Harbor, Lieutenant Commander Blanchard was regarded as just another submarine skipper who had missed his big chance to sink an aircraft carrier.

Because the loss of the *Taiho* was not known neither was the true role played by the American submarines in this battle. The conventional history was framed in those next few months: It described the Battle of the Philippine Sea as an enormous victory for the American carriers. But the fact is that by the time the carrier planes arrived, Admiral Ozawa's force was already in disarray and the cause of it was a pair of submarines.

22

INCREASING
VIGILANCE

IN mid-1944 the American campaign against Japanese merchant
shipping emerged as a major factor in slowing the ability of the
Imperial forces to prosecute the war. So many ships were sunk in the
East China Sea and the waters of the East Indies that war production
was affected. Just before the Saipan landings, one of Lockwood's wolf
packs, Blair's Blasters, had sunk five of seven transports of *Convoy
No. 353*. The convoy was carrying seven thousand troops and all their
tanks, trucks, field guns, and equipment to reinforce Saipan. The four
escorts of this convoy rescued most of the troops but the equipment
was lost and units were confused when they arrived just before the
Americans. Thus by the beginning of the Marianas campaign the
Japanese could see that the movement of troops anywhere had
become so dangerous that it was not carried out except under the most
demanding circumstances.

To meet the threat the Japanese were constantly improving their
methods of antisubmarine warfare. The war between the submarines
and the escort vessels grew more fierce. In June the *Swordfish* sank the
destroyer *Matsukaze*. The *Archerfish* sank *Coastal Patrol Vessel No.
24*. But the U.S. submarine *Golet* went off on patrol in those mined
waters northeast of Honshu Island and was never heard from again.
She may have struck a mine; more probably she was the victim of the
increased antisubmarine patrols in the area. The coastal defense forces
reported attacking a submarine at the end of June in that area, and
seeing a large quantity of oil, cork, and a raft rise to the surface. The
oil could have been the result of a punctured tank and would not

necessarily mean disaster—but cork and a raft had to come from inside the pressure hull.

There were only a few areas in which the Japanese felt safe to move shipping: One was the Inland Sea. Another was the Sea of Japan that was protected by a mine barrier at both major entrances. The other two areas were the East China Sea and the Yellow Sea that had been mined by Admiral Oikawa following the depredations begun by Mush Morton. The Americans had stayed out of these last two areas after losing submarines there due to unknown causes.

The "mysterious" sinkings were almost always attributed to mines but there was another factor, unknown to the U.S. Navy until after the war was over. The American torpedoes were the culprits in some sinkings through a ridiculous error created by staff officers at Pearl Harbor. In the beginning all torpedoes were fitted with an anti-circular-run device. But in the last days before the war began, Pacific Fleet submarine officers became very much concerned about their potential enemy's development of sonar. They felt that a submarine once located by an escort vessel had a very slim chance of escape. To enhance the submarines' weaponry, someone had the bright idea of deactivating the anticircular-run devices. The torpedoes were fitted with clamps that could make them run in a circle. Thus the beleaguered submarine, sitting safely down below the surface, could fire torpedoes at a destroyer above and the attacking enemy would either be sunk or so harried by the circling torpedoes that he would go away and leave the submarine alone.

Had submarine doctrine of World War II followed the old path where submarines stayed deep and never attacked on the surface, the gimmick might not have created any trouble. But the doctrine changed almost from the beginning of the war. Learning from the Germans, Admiral Withers encouraged submarines to attack on the surface and by 1943 many of them were doing so whenever possible. Nobody in the Bureau of Ordnance, in the naval torpedo factories, or the submarine force staffs remembered what had been done to the torpedoes and why. Thus, in addition to all their other deficiencies, the American torpedoes throughout the war were subject to circular runs.

In several cases when the submarines were attacking on the surface, the results were disastrous. The *Tullibee* had been destroyed by her own torpedo. It is quite possible that Mush Morton's *Wahoo* was sunk in the same way. There would be more; the trouble was that in such disasters either there were no survivors or they were captured by the enemy. The worst of it was that the most aggressive skippers, attacking most often on the surface, ran the greatest danger of being destroyed. The Japanese developed a circular-run torpedo that was designed to be dropped from an airplane against a submarine on the surface; it ran in concentric circles. The Japanese device never achieved the success in sinking American submarines that the American submariner's own standard weapons did.

The month of June 1944 was an excellent one for the U.S. submarines. When it became apparent that the Marianas were lost, Imperial General Headquarters began reinforcing Iwo Jima and Okinawa against attacks that were expected within months. The submarines sank nearly fifty Japanese cargo ships. The Army Air Corps in the Southwest Pacific sank another thirty. Altogether, the Japanese lost a quarter of a million tons of shipping that month. At that rate the Allies would sink half of Japan's merchant shipping before the year was out.

The Japanese had to move shipping in three areas no matter what happened. A major section of Japanese industry was located in Manchuria and this area was also a part of the Japanese granary. Some supplies could be carried by train to Korea and further south but this was a slow process because the whole Japanese supply system had been based on shipping that passed through the Yellow Sea. The Pacific Ocean, south of Japan, had to be traversed to reach Okinawa, the Bonin Islands, and the Philippines, all of which were major Japanese holdings. The oil, tin, and foodstuffs from Southeast Asia and the East Indies had to come north through the East China Sea.

The compression of the empire was accompanied by a rapid growth in the American submarine force. In mid-1944 there were more than one hundred and twenty-five American submarines in the Pacific, plus two Dutch submarines operating out of Fremantle under Admiral Christie, and a squadron of British submarines on the way to his area. Additionally, the American shipyards were building submarines for the Pacific at the rate of six per month. The Americans could blanket all these areas if they could overcome the mine problem set for them by Admiral Oikawa. Just now the happy hunting grounds were the Luzon Strait and the Formosa Strait, where the shipping had to move through narrow passages. This area north and east of Luzon Island became known to the Japanese that summer as "the sea of the Devil." The Americans had a much less spectacular name for it: Convoy College.

Admiral Lockwood sent several wolf packs into the Luzon Strait during that July of 1944. They sank so many ships that they worried the Japanese into renewed antisubmarine efforts. The attack on the night of July 30 was the closest Allied approximation, in the Pacific, of those days earlier in the war when the German U-boats were wreaking havoc in the mid-Atlantic. That night the *Hammerhead, Steelhead,* and *Parche* encountered an eastbound convoy in Convoy College. The *Hammerhead* made the first contact but then lost touch. The *Steelhead* found the convoy and tracked all day on July 30. It was apparent to Skipper David Whelchel that this convoy was important because all day long it was protected by four planes as well as surface escorts. He was right; once again the Americans had found a convoy full of tankers, heading for the Philippines.

Whelchel attacked after dark, hitting a tanker and a cargo ship. The tanker burst into flame and lit up the area for miles around, making a beacon for the *Parche.* The half dozen escorts clustered around the unhurt ships as the *Parche* headed into the convoy on the surface. The convoy changed course suddenly and came directly at the *Parche,* so close that the first freighter missed a collision by only two hundred yards. Commander Lawson Ramage had to move away from the convoy so that his torpedoes would have time to arm themselves before striking. There were so many targets that he was firing torpedoes from both bow and stern tubes. Japanese machine guns, antiaircraft guns, and four- and five-inch deck guns were firing at the *Parche.* Several ships tried to ram the submarine. Tracers came screaming by the bridge, and splashes of near misses bracketed the *Parche* until

Ramage sent his deck crew below, keeping only one man on the bridge to man the target bearing transmitter that connected with the TDC (torpedo data computer) down below. For forty-five minutes he ran in and out of the convoy, the burning tanker, and other ships lighting up the sky, amid the tracers making a fireworks display plus the explosions of torpedoes and ships. Ramage fired nineteen torpedoes; he sank four ships and damaged another.

Until this point most Japanese antisubmarine warfare was in the hands of naval districts. These local commands employed elements of the Japanese navy that were not regarded as part of the proud fighting fleet. Submarine chasing had always been looked down upon by the navy except when it involved attacks on their warships. The attitude began to change after August 3 when Admiral Oikawa was promoted to be chief of the Imperial Navy General Staff. His knowledge of the realities of the submarine threat prompted the changes. He demanded that the Combined Fleet take an active role in the escort of convoys and antisubmarine activity beyond the needs considered normal by the fleet. He didn't win his way completely. Admiral Toyoda, commander of the Combined Fleet, insisted that he had to keep his best and newest destroyers available for the great battle that was still in his mind. The Combined Fleet was no longer a major force, but its commander was regarded in Japan as the navy's chief operating officer as had been the case when Admiral Yamamoto commanded the greatest fleet in the Pacific.

One major change was the gathering of the Grand Escort Force under the direct control of the Combined Fleet. Much of the strength of the escort force was located at the southern Formosa port of Takao, which gave access to the Formosa Strait and the Luzon Strait, the two greatest danger spots.

The Japanese used their aircraft to sweep an area thirty miles ahead of a convoy. If enemy submarines were encountered the planes sent word to the escorts or to one of the four auxiliary carriers assigned to the force. They made many attacks on U.S. submarines during the next few months and operated under the misapprehension that they were sinking submarines at the rate of several each month—but actually they were not. In fact the increased number of American

271

submarines in the area continued to score often in spite of the Japanese vigilance.

One example of the way the war against the convoys went was *Convoy HI-71*. It consisted of ten merchant ships, carrying reinforcements and supplies for the Philippines from the East Indies. Most of the ships were tankers. The escort consisted of the destroyer *Yunagi*, a subchaser, and four new *kaibokans*: the *Sado*, *Matsuwa*, *Hiburi*, and *Mikura*. Manifesting how important this convoy was to the Imperial General Staff, the fleet had sent the light carrier *Taiyo*. The convoy also had air cover during the daylight hours. The American submarines, however, didn't accommodate them by attacking during the day. Three U.S. boats were involved: the *Rasher*, the *Bluefish*, and the *Spadefish*. The *Rasher* found the convoy first, not far northwest of Luzon Island. Lieutenant Commander Henry Munson radioed the other submarines and they closed in. They found the convoy that night. The *Rasher* attacked first. Munson fired one of his torpedoes at a ship; it exploded with an enormous roar and broke up immediately. Munson thought he had sunk a tanker; actually the victim was the carrier *Taiyo*, that was carrying an extra large supply of aviation gasoline, bound for Manila. The other two submarines and the *Rasher* then knocked off the ships one by one, until seven of the ten transport vessels had been sunk or damaged.

But in one case the increased Japanese surveillance paid off. This was in the destruction of one of the most aggressive submarines in the American fleet: Commander Samuel Dealey's *Harder*.

By the end of July 1944 Dealey's reputation as an intrepid fighter had been broadcast across America. In August he went on patrol again, this time assuming command of a wolf pack out of Fremantle, that consisted of the *Ray*, the *Haddo*, and the *Harder*. The point of operation was a bay on the west coast of Mindoro Island and the quarry was a convoy that was headed for Manila. Following the disaster that befell *Convoy HI-71* this second convoy commander decided to "hole up" in the bay for the night and continue the journey again the next day. He radioed Manila for extra escort support.

At sunrise on August 19 the convoy resumed its journey toward Manila. As the ships came out of the bay Dealey raised his periscope and attracted the attention of the escorts. While the escorts and cargo ships were getting excited about the *Harder*'s presence, the *Ray* and the *Haddo* moved in for the kill. Five cargo ships were sunk before the convoy could get away. This convoy was accompanied by a number of *kaibokans* and they showed no hesitation in using plenty of depth charges against the submarines. Their attack was quick and sure but the submarines dove and found a sonar-reflecting density layer below in which they could hide, so the patrol vessels soon lost track of them. While the depth-charge attack was occurring, it was the most severe that any of the skippers could recall. It was so heavy that Chester Nimitz, Jr., skipper of the *Haddo,* said he had to shout to make himself heard in the *Haddo*'s conning tower.

The *Harder* and the *Haddo* then moved to the opening of Manila Bay, where they arrived on August 21. That night both submarines picked up three ships on their radar sets. The ships headed into the bay. Nimitz suggested that the targets were too small to concern them but Dealey disagreed. He knew that this was to be his last patrol; his executive officer had suggested that he was already so close to exhaustion that he should not go on any more patrols. But he insisted; didn't he have to maintain his reputation as the destroyer killer? It seems obvious that that was the reason for his insistence. He told a skeptical Admiral Christie that it was imperative that he make this patrol. Imperative to whom? Not to Christie or the U.S. Navy.

Dealey insisted on attacking the small vessels. Probably he knew that they were *kaibokans.* They were in fact the weary defenders of *Convoy HI-71.*

The *Harder* led the attack; Dealey sank the *Hiburi* and the *Matsuwa.* The *Haddo* sank the *Sado.* Dealey had added to his reputation.

The two submarines then moved along the west coast of Luzon Island. On August 22 Dealey discovered a tanker escorted by the destroyer *Asakaze*; he fired four torpedoes and blew off the destroyer's bow. Two trawlers and another destroyer came out to tow the ship into safety but she sank on the way. Dealey had again boosted that precious reputation but he did not know it. He figured that the Japanese would tow the *Asakaze* to Manila the next day and he wanted another crack at her. Nimitz had shot off all his torpedoes so

273

he went to the new base at Mios Woendi on the eastern end of Biak Island to pick up more fuel and reload. The *Harder* was joined by the *Hake.*

On the morning of August 24, Lieutenant Commander Frank Haylor in the *Hake* saw two ships emerge from Dasol Bay. He identified them as a minesweeper and the old Thai destroyer *Phra Ruong* but he was wrong. They were a *kaibokan* and the former American four-stack destroyer *Stewart,* that had been captured by the Japanese after it was damaged and put into dry dock in Java near the end of the Dutch East Indies campaign of 1942. The Japanese had rebuilt the *Stewart* and renamed her. In their fashion they did not give a foreign warship a Japanese name but a number. She became *Patrol Boat No. 102.*

Lieutenant Commander Haylor didn't like it when the two craft came out with one purposefully heading for him. He broke off his tracking and went down deep. At just about that time the two patrol vessels were joined by a plane that had been sent to assist in the search for the submarine that had sunk the *Asakaze* that day before. The plane diverted the *Harder* by dropping a depth bomb, and that forced Dealey to submerge. The skipper of the old *Stewart (Patrol Boat No. 102)* then moved in. The old destroyer had been made into an effective antisubmarine vessel. She had 72 depth charges aboard that day: 220-pound charges, effective to a radius of 150 feet. She began dropping them in patterns of six charges each time on her runs across the spot where the sonar told her captain the *Harder* was lurking. The first set of charges exploded at 150 feet. The second run was set to explode at 180 feet. The next blew up at 270 feet, the next at 360 feet, and the last group at 450 feet. After the fifth run, oil began coming to the surface, followed by wood splinters and large pieces of cork. *Patrol Boat No. 102* remained in the area and made a sounding. It seemed that the submarine had sunk in nine hundred feet of water. As they remained in the area other debris began to come to the surface and the crew knew they had killed a submarine this time for sure—that the pressure hull had collapsed at the final depth. So Sam Dealey and the *Harder* never got back to Fremantle, victims of a ship made in America.

Nor was the *Harder* the only submarine lost at that time. The

Robalo was off Palawan Island in the Philippines when she suddenly exploded and sank. It was the second tragedy for the navy's Kimmel family: Admiral Husband Kimmel had been made the goat for the Pearl Harbor attack and Lieutenant Commander Manning Kimmel now lost his ship. He and a number of others got out and swam ashore to the island. They were captured and imprisoned at Puerta Princessa; they didn't survive the Japanese prison camp. The reason for the sinking was never really singled out: It could have been a mine. It could have been a battery explosion in the boat (as one of the survivors told other prisoners). It even could have been a Japanese plane or escort as some submarine officers believed.

It was probably a mine. Kimmel was running through shallow water in Balabac Strait at the time. A few weeks later, the *Flier* was in the same area in forty fathoms of water when it, too, hit one of the Japanese mines that blew a hole in the pressure hull. Fifteen or twenty men managed to escape from the sinking boat in the minute or so that it remained afloat. They included Lieutenant Commander John Crowley, the commanding officer, and his executive officer, Lieutenant James Liddell. They swam for hours, heading for coral reefs that lay off to the northwest but not until the moon came up could they orient themselves. A number of the swimmers drifted away and drowned. Eight men survived and managed to swim to Manatangule Island where they made contact with some Australian commandos put ashore earlier by the *Redfin*. At the end of August they were rescued by that same submarine that took great care in arranging the rendezvous. Lieutenant Commander Marshall H. Austin was a careful man these days after a near disaster in May. On that occasion the *Redfin* had been assigned to pick up a half dozen Australians at Dent Haven on northeastern Borneo. Submarines had safely landed agents there before, although the *Haddo* had been surprised by a Japanese patrol boat at that spot and had abandoned the pickup of those same Australians because of it. The security signal was to be a white sheet hung out at the rendezvous point. Coming up offshore, Skipper Austin saw the white sheet through his periscope, and that night surfaced and signaled the beach. Back came the proper reply, the flashlight signal of the Morse letter "V." Austin wanted more infor-

275

mation and signaled for it in Morse code. But the party ashore apparently could not read the code. Neither did the party ashore have a boat, according to a message from headquarters. So Austin sent Ensign Helz ashore with four men in a rubber boat to find the party and begin the rescue. They carried a Browning automatic rifle (BAR), a .30 caliber rifle, two carbines, and four .45 caliber automatic pistols; they also had aboard Very signaling lights and a booklet telling them how to survive in the jungle.

Almost as soon as the rescuers set out, their rubber boat was caught by the current and a strong wind and blown north of the spot where the signals had been seen. As they came in close to shore, Ensign Helz saw several lights, and decided to go into the beach, land there, and survey the situation before making any contacts. Just before they landed he saw a fire on the beach. He challenged and received the agreed-on code word reply. Then he called his party to come out to the beach to meet the rescuers. He received a muffled reply to this request. Getting a little suspicious, Helz challenged again. This time he received two responses, both correct: One from the beach and one from another point southeast of him. He thought the second light was from the submarine. So he landed with crewman Carinder, of his boat, covering him with the rifle. He and Carinder moved up the beach. He called to the shore party to put out their light. Just then a tall man wearing horn-rimmed glasses and wearing a high-peaked cap stepped out of the brush. He was carrying a rifle with a bayonet and he jabbed at Carinder. The seaman parried the blow with his rifle but could not fire because the Japanese was in the line of fire to the boat. He shouted to the others who were now coming up in file. Among them was Seaman Harrington who had served a hitch with the marines in Nicaragua and knew something about brush fighting; he was carrying the BAR. Harrington shot the Japanese soldier in the legs, which brought him down and then he sprayed bullets at another Japanese who had begun firing at Ensign Helz. They were under fire from at least one more rifle. Seaman Kahler shot another Japanese soldier and that man stopped shooting at them. As Carinder's Japanese attacker fell with the wounds in his legs, Carinder knocked the man's rifle upwards and hit him in the chin with the butt of his rifle.

They both fell. The Japanese got up first and began limping away. Carinder picked up the Japanese soldier's rifle but couldn't fire it; he found his own weapon and fired but by this time the Japanese was moving out of sight. Harrington began firing the BAR and the tracers streamed out into the brush.

Helz ordered the party back to the beach and into the rubber boat. They took her out and were about a hundred yards off the beach when someone began shooting at them. No one was hit and just before dawn they were back aboard the submarine with one souvenir: the Japanese soldier's .25 caliber rifle. The rendezvous had been compromised and Skipper Austin had to abandon the pickup. The Australians must have been captured and probably were tortured, so that the Japanese could get details of the rendezvous and set their ambush.

This time, at Palawan, the *Redfin* stayed off the beach, and Filipinos took the Americans out to the rendezvous in small boats, skirting a Japanese ship at anchor near the place. They boarded the *Redfin* and a week later were in Brisbane.

The loss of two submarines in Balabac Strait brought about an official inquiry, resulting in Admiral Christie's closure of the strait to submarines until further notice.

The heavy attacks in Convoy College brought stronger Japanese countermeasures. The Japanese began using radar to mount night air searches, so the submarines were often subjected to air attack as they recharged their batteries on the surface. One night the *Barb* had nine airplane contacts between midnight and 7:00 A.M. But the Americans were able to put so many submarines into this area that some of them managed to evade the watchers and launch attacks. The sinking of cargo ships continued apace.

However, the submarines did not go unscathed. The *Tunny* was attacked in Convoy College during her August patrol there and damaged so badly that she had to abandon the patrol and return to base. The *Barb* was bombed by a plane, and narrowly escaped destruction. Next day when she surfaced, parts of the bomb were found on the submarine's deck.

The Japanese were often at least as callous toward human life as were such Americans as Mush Morton, and they justified it in the

277

same way: Anything goes in war. The Imperial policy toward prisoners of war was notoriously vile. During the early days of the conflict, thousands of British and Australian troops had been captured in Southeast Asia, and for the first three years they had been put to work on railroads in Burma and Malaya. Many thousands had died during this travail. In Malaya alone, twenty-two thousand British soldiers had died while building a railroad. When it was completed the survivors were put aboard ships and dispatched to Japan where they were to be sent into the copper mines. The ships joined a nine-ship convoy that was assaulted by three American submarines. One escort and several cargo ships were sunk, including the *Rakuyo Maru,* which carried about two thousand of the prisoners of war. The Japanese seamen and guards abandoned ship, leaving the prisoners to drown but many of them succeeded in getting off the ship. In the water, the escorts picked up the Japanese but clubbed off the prisoners.

Three days after the attack the U.S. submarine *Pampanito* picked up a raft full of prisoners and sent a message to Admiral Lockwood that there were more survivors at sea. The *Sealion* joined up and together the two boats rescued more than a hundred of them but a number died at sea or almost as soon as they reached shore at Saipan, the new forward Pacific Fleet submarine base. Lockwood also dispatched the *Queenfish* and the *Barb* to help. On the way to the scene, the *Barb* sank the carrier *Unyo* as well as a tanker; then the two boats rescued an additional thirty-two British survivors of the *Rakuyo Maru.*

Despite the reluctance of the submarine skippers and the lack of proof that the presence of a supercargo wolf pack leader generated any more ship sinkings than his absence, Lockwood continued to send out high-ranking officers in charge of wolf packs. The unavoidable suspicion is that at least part of the reason was to give those officers a shot at a war patrol, although they were too high in rank and many of them superannuated for combat submarine warfare. The trouble in 1944, as always, was communication. The presence of the senior commander always meant more talk on the radio which was dangerous. When the submarines were attacking he had no function whatsoever except to kibitz with the commander of the boat on which he was riding. Still, it is hard to quarrel with success: The American submarines were so successful by 1944 that the Japanese were virtually unable to supply the homeland with war materiel and the outlying points of their shrinking empire with reinforcements. The Army Air Forces were sinking ships. The American aircraft carrier planes were sinking ships. In the third quarter of 1944 American submarines sank twenty-seven Japanese navy ships and one hundred and sixty-five of their cargo vessels. Japan was really under an Allied blockade from this point on.

As Admiral Halsey's Third Fleet began softening up the Philippines for the October invasion, the role of the submarines for lifeguard work was increased. This did not make some of the captains very happy but in the overall war picture it was an important tonic and protection for the carrier-based pilots. As the war continued, they began to take for granted the fact that if they were forced down at sea and could stay afloat, a submarine would come by and pick them up. And in fact, the increasing number of submarines made such use possible without cutting into the undersea force's ability to sink Japanese ships.

With the growth of the carrier task force and the enormous increase in the number of ships of all sizes in the American fleet, a new danger faced the American submarines in the third quarter of 1944. They had to be as careful of their friends as they were of their enemies. Lockwood and Nimitz worked out safety lanes, recognition signals, and other devices to prevent submarines from attacking U.S. ships and vice versa. But on October 3, while traveling in one of the safety lanes, the *Seawolf* was attacked by a carrier plane, that dropped dye markers inside the lane. Thereupon the destroyer escort (DE) *Richard M. Rowell* came up. The skipper saw the dye markers that were supposed to indicate an enemy submarine and then paid no more attention to the existence of the "safety lane" than had the carrier pilot. The DE attacked with the new hedgehog depth-charge throwers (which let a ship fire ahead of its bow at the target). So far, the escort carrier plane which dropped the dye inside the safety lane and the destroyer escort had violated just about every applicable order and instruction. The attacks were occasioned by the excitement of the carrier pilot as well as the captain and crew of the escort *Richard M. Rowell,* who had just seen their sister ship *Shelton* torpedoed by a Japanese submarine. There was one last safety factor, the submarine recognition signal, that was sent out as sound waves that could be picked up by the ship's soundman. The *Seawolf* sent its recognition signal by oscillator time and again, and the sonar operator of the *Richard M. Rowell* ignored it. He thought it was an attempt by the enemy submarine to jam his signals. The destroyer escort attacked a second time, and this time sank the American submarine. She went down with all hands lost.

In the Battle of Leyte Gulf in October 1944, the submarines *Dace* and *Darter* played key roles. Before the Japanese could even come near their objective, the *Dace* and *Darter* sank the *Atago,* the flagship of Admiral Kurita. He was the leader of the main force that was supposed to hit the American ships off the Leyte beachhead and destroy them. They also sank the cruiser *Maya* and damaged the cruiser *Takao* severely. The *Darter* ran aground a few hours later in those shallow waters off Palawan and had to be abandoned but she had done more than her job in that one night. Then along came the *Bream* that torpedoed the heavy cruiser *Aoba.* Before the battle was really going, the American submarines had put four Japanese heavy cruisers out of action. Later in the battle the U.S. submarine *Jallao* sank the Japanese light cruiser *Tama* off Cape Engano.

The U.S. submarine losses continued. the *Escolar* was lost on her first patrol, apparently to a mine. The *Shark* was lost to a Japanese escort. The *Tang,* which had run up the most enviable record of sinkings in the submarine service in four patrols, was sunk as she fired her last torpedo in the Formosa Strait; she was attacking a freighter and Commander Richard O'Kane fired one torpedo and then a second. The second torpedo was the last she had aboard. The executive officer was just telling the crew that they were about to "head for the barn," which this time meant Mare Island in California and home leave, when the electric torpedo made a circular run and smashed into the *Tang,* blowing her pressure hull apart and putting her underwater. Commander O'Kane and eight others on the bridge were thrown into the water; thirteen men below managed to rise one hundred and eighty feet from the bottom, using Momsen lungs. But in the end only nine of the crew survived to go into a Japanese prison camp. They were confined at the secret naval intelligence prison camp at Ofuna, near Yokohama, where they were starved and beaten in efforts to make them reveal whatever secrets they possessed. In the spring of 1945, the prisoners began to die from beriberi. As the Japanese war effort continued to deteriorate, the officers in charge became alarmed, particularly after the collapse of Germany and the announcement that those responsible for war crimes would be held accountable. Suddenly the *Tang*'s survivors were moved to a regular prisoner-of-war camp on Omori Island off Yokohama. When Emperor Hirohito announced the surrender of Japan, the guards fled rather than face the incoming Americans. By this time the *Tang*'s survivors weighed about ninety pounds apiece but all who survived the sea also came through the horror of the Japanese prison treatment.

The vigorous struggle between the U.S. submarines and the Japanese antisubmarine service continued. So desperate was their need for oil that the Japanese began sending many escorts with single tankers from the oil fields all the way to Tokyo Bay. On October 30, south of Kyushu, the *Trigger* torpedoed a ten-thousand-ton tanker; it didn't sink. Later that day the *Salmon* caught up with the same tanker and attacked, although the ship was guarded by four new *kaibokans*. The *Salmon* sank the tanker and then the *kaibokans* all attacked the submarine. They damaged her so severely that she surfaced to avoid sinking from the leaks in the pressure hull. For some reason the single *kaibokan* they saw did not attack immediately, which gave the crew of the boat a chance to repair the leaks. This *kaibokan* was *Coastal Defense Vessel No. 22*. When she did attack, the skipper of the *Salmon* charged at her and opened up with shots from the deck gun, the antiaircraft guns, and all the machine guns available; and then ducked into a convenient rain squall and escaped. The *Salmon* was met a few hours later by the *Trigger, Silversides,* and *Sterlet*. They escorted the *Salmon* and American planes from the Marianas came out to fly cover for the boat. The crew got her back to Saipan, but she was so badly damaged that she never went on patrol again.

281

Toward the end of 1944, the sinkings continued unabated. The Japanese preserved the lifeline from Formosa to the Philippines only by devoting most of their antisubmarine defense to this area, which meant that American boats in other areas, such as the Yellow Sea and the South China Sea, were relatively unmolested. One by one the tankers were sunk, and this loss had a most debilitating effect on the Japanese ability to conduct aggressive warfare. Also, as the war zone contracted, nearly every Japanese warship that sailed was—at least— threatened by submarines. On November 2 Lieutenant Commander Bernard Clarey in the *Pintado* sank the destroyer *Akikaze*. He was actually shooting at the carrier *Unryu* but the destroyer got in the way. On November 15 Lieutenant Commander Elliott Loughlin's *Queenfish* sank the aircraft ferry *Akitsu Maru* as she was loaded with planes on the way to the Philippines. Two days later Lieutenant Commander Gordon Underwood's *Spadefish* sank the escort carrier *Jinyo*, from the same convoy. She was also loaded with planes for the forces opposing General MacArthur in the Philippines. Lieutenant Commander Evan T. Shepard's *Picuda* sank a transport carrying many of the troops of the Japanese 23rd Division. November was the month that two of Admiral Lockwood's wolf packs sank nineteen ships.

Even the major remaining elements of the Japanese fleet were harried everywhere. Late in November the battleships *Kongo* and *Haruna* were ordered back to Japan from Brunei Bay, the important oil port in northwestern Borneo, and given a destroyer escort. On November 21 in the Formosa Strait, they were attacked by Lieutenant Commander Eli Reich's *Sealion II*, named for the first submarine lost in the Pacific war. Reich's first attack damaged the *Kongo* seriously with three torpedo hits but the destroyer *Urakaze* took the torpedoes meant for the *Haruna*. The destroyer blew up and sank but the *Haruna* was unhurt, much to Reich's disgust. He was following the ships when suddenly the *Kongo* blew up and sank before his eyes. He was the first American submarine captain to sink a battleship. The reason why the battleships were going back to Japan was to escort convoys of troops to various positions in the new, smaller perimeter of the empire. It was ignoble work for the proud battleships but necessary because of the growing shortage of escorts and destroyers and the

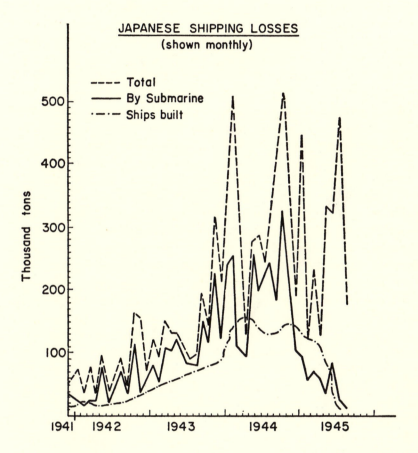

JAPANESE SHIPPING LOSSES
(shown monthly)

- - - - Total
——— By Submarine
·—·—· Ships built

Thousand tons

500
400
300
200
100

1941 1942 1943 1944 1945

continued buildup of the U.S. submarine force. The battleships *Ise* and *Hyuga* were spotted by the *Sealion II* a few days later but Reich didn't get a shot at either of them. However on November 28 Skipper Joseph Enright came across the supercarrier *Shinano* at the outer entrance to Tokyo Bay. The *Shinano* had been started as a battleship but during construction the Imperial General Staff had realized that the carrier was the most important seagoing weapon of the Pacific war—not the battleship. She had been converted to a sixty-thousand-ton aircraft carrier, the largest warship in the world.

The *Shinano*'s construction was really not complete. All of her firefighting equipment hadn't been connected; she was lacking some of her watertight doors and others had not been tested. The crew was new and unfamiliar with the ship. She was being moved only because of the intensification of air attack on the Tokyo Bay area. The Imperial Navy General Staff decided she would be better off in the Inland Sea, and she was carrying many of the workmen who were to complete her interior.

Enright fired six torpedoes at the *Shinano*, and four of them hit. Normally this large ship would have been able to continue on course but the watertight doors didn't work and the water poured from compartment to compartment inside the ship. When fires spread, the inexperienced crew could not stop them; the *Shinano* sank. When Enright returned to base and reported having sunk a carrier, Lockwood's staff didn't believe him because there had been no report of the sinking in the secret, coded Japanese messages. Eventually Enright was given credit for sinking a carrier but not enough credit to gain him a Navy Cross, that was invariably awarded for sinking a major warship. Lockwood's headquarters remained somewhat skeptical about the whole affair. The reason for their incredulity was that the *Shinano*'s construction was such a carefully-kept secret by the Japanese that the Americans didn't even know of her existence. After the war the truth was revealed and Skipper Enright was given his Navy Cross. By that time virtually nobody noticed.

On November 6 a four-boat wolf pack attacked the heavy cruiser *Kumano* off Manila Bay. She was coming out with a convoy and Admiral Halsey's planes had already damaged her in the bay. The

Ray, Raton, Bream, and *Guitarro* all attacked and blew the bow off the big ship but she was beached inside the bay and survived a little longer—until destroyed by Halsey's planes.

The targets were getting a little harder to come by. The Japanese escorts were more efficient and more determined. In the second week of November the *Growler, Hardhead,* and *Hake* formed a wolf pack and sank a tanker south of Mindoro. Immediately afterward, the *Hake* was beset by a *kaibokan* which dropped one hundred and fifty depth charges around the boat in a sixteen-hour period. At that same time the *Growler* was lost to an escort.

Lieutenant Commander James E. Stevens in the *Flounder* had the almost unique experience (shared by one of the Dutch boats) of sinking one of the flotilla of German U-boats sent into the Indian Ocean by Admiral Doenitz to give the Japanese a helping hand. Stevens sank the *U-537,* having learned of her course from a code breakers' message.

In the first week of December, Lieutenant Commander George Grider in the *Flasher* sank the destroyers *Kishinami* and *Iwanami* and a ten-thousand-ton tanker in one day; it really was in one sustained attack, punctuated by deep dives to avoid depth charges. This attrition of warships was not confined to the larger ones. Several submarines sank *kaibokans,* as well as the trawlers and even smaller patrol boats that the Japanese introduced to try to augment their shrinking force of warships.

On December 13 the *Bergall* damaged the cruiser *Myoko* which was on its way from Singapore to Camranh Bay. Inflicting damage on a ship at this stage of the war was often as good as sinking it, since the shortage of parts and materials often laid up a damaged vessel for months. This was brought home that month when the *Sea Devil* and the *Redfish* both torpedoed the carrier *Junyo.* She made it back into Nagasaki Harbor, but she never got back into the war.

The war went on. Commander Louis D. McGregor of the *Redfish* sank the new carrier *Unryu* on December 19 after having helped put the *Junyo* out of action. On December 30 the *Razorback* sank the old destroyer *Kuretake.*

Still, the American submarines were having trouble—with mines in particular. The *Albacore* and the *Scamp* were both lost to mines in the last few weeks of the year. The good news was that the frequency-modulation sonar system had finally been worked out and was ready to be installed on U.S. warships. In tests off the California coast in dummy minefields, the sonar system had been able to pick up the position of mines at a range of about a quarter of a mile. When a mine was detected an alarm system went off in the boat, a gonging, that the submariners christened Hell's Bells. The *Tinosa* was the first boat to be equipped with the new system and the crew did not like it. After she was fitted out in San Francisco Bay and made the voyage to Pearl Harbor, about half the crew asked for transfer off the boat and got it. The *Tinosa* then went off in December to Okinawa and found a minefield. When the skipper informed Admiral Lockwood, he (Lockwood) insisted on a complete survey of the waters around Okinawa, and it was made successfully although with a good deal of trepidation.

Thus 1944 came to a close, with a new device to combat the mines. The submarine war was really nearly over, for the American boats dominated the whole Pacific Ocean. Combined with the Army Air Corps bombers and the carrier planes, they had access to virtually every nook and cranny of the Japanese Empire. With ships being sunk in sight of houses on the Japanese homeland, with their cities laid waste by B-29s and carrier-based bombers, with the Inland Sea no longer safe because of mines dropped by B-29s, it seemed a whole generation had passed since Prime Minister Tojo promised the Japanese people at the start of the war that their cities would never be bombed and they would never feel the rigors of attack at home. By the end of 1944 they felt virtually nothing else.

The submarines had sunk nearly three million tons of shipping that year, more than half of the amount the Japanese possessed at the beginning of the war. The Japanese had lost two-thirds of their tankers, seven aircraft carriers, ten other heavy ships, and thirty destroyers. The U.S. submarine fleet had lost nineteen boats; the submarine force had the highest casualty rate of any service. The service was still dogged by the problem of finding enough aggressive skippers, and even in 1944 about one-third of the submarine captains

285

were relieved of duty after making unsatisfactory patrols. Three reserve officers had managed to crash the "company union" of Naval Academy graduates to become skippers, through the intervention of Admiral Nimitz. With the increase in carrier activity in the area around Japan and with major invasions of the Marshalls, Marianas, Palau, Biak, and Leyte the role of the submarines had changed. They had more chances to attack warships, and at the same time they spent more of their time in lifeguard duty. The torpedo shortage had been largely alleviated and all the old strictures about conserving torpedoes were gone. Skippers began to shoot at ships of under five hundred tons and no one complained. If they had not selected the smaller targets many patrols would have chalked up goose eggs, without any reflection on the abilities or aggressiveness of the skippers. The only submarine patrols that were truly effective in terms of tonnage sunk were those in the East China Sea and the Yellow Sea. The Sea of Japan still seemed to the Japanese to be relatively safe with its formidable triple minefields at both ends. With all this, however, there was still the problem of defective torpedoes and the unknown danger of circular runs. More boats would be lost in 1945.

23  Masters of the Pacific

BY the beginning of 1945 the Japanese economic and military machines were out of gear. Most of the Japanese submarine effort was devoted to supplying outlying garrisons. The *kaiten,* a desperation weapon, was added to the Japanese submarine fleet in an effort to do what should have been done from the outset of the war: sink Allied cargo vessels and tankers as well as warships. The *kaiten* was a small one-man submersible. It was to the submarine what the *ohka* or flying bomb was to the airplane. Like the *ohka,* the *kaiten* was carried by a mother ship, and launched within sight of the target. It too was a suicide craft. One difference was that a submarine could carry half a dozen *kaitens*; another was that the *kaitens* were extremely cranky and malfunctioned more often than not. Although they were deadly, they had no effect on the outcome of the war—certainly not nearly so much as the *kamikaze* aircraft. Japanese submarines did continue to sink warships but so few submarines were out that the Americans began to lull themselves into believing the naval war was ended. It took one or two major incidents (the Indianapolis) to shock the Pacific command back to reality.

More U.S. submarines were at sea beginning in January but they were sinking fewer ships and the vessels they attacked were much smaller. Lucky was the skipper who found a two- or three-thousand-ton freighter in his path. Most of them were already at the bottom. Once in a while the hunting was good as with one of the wolf packs early in January. The submarines were Lieutenant Commander Eliott Loughlin's *Queenfish,* Eugene Fluckey's *Barb,* and Even T. Shepard's *Picuda*. They formed into a wolf pack in the Formosa Strait to stop Japanese reinforcement of the Philippines as the Lingayen Gulf landings were under way. The pack was called Loughlin's Loopers.

The pack moved up from Guam toward the Bonin Islands and then turned west toward Formosa. On January 1 the *Queenfish* and the *Picuda* came across a patrol boat and attacked with their deck guns. When the boat was riddled with shells and all the crewmen were either dead or seemed to have gone over the side, Fluckey sent a boarding party to find code books and charts—and then gave orders to sink the boat. The deck guns opened up again and the fuel tanks were set afire. At that point a group of Japanese sailors who had been hiding below deck came rushing out and into the path of a four-inch shell that blew them to smithereens.

The wolf pack moved into the Formosa Strait and on the morning of January 7 picked up a seven-ship convoy. Fluckey saw it first; he went around the end and, when in position, prepared to attack a tanker but it changed course and got away from him. He surfaced and began running around end again. The *Picuda* had received his earlier report of the convoy and was in a good position as it came up to her. Skipper Shepard damaged the ten-thousand-ton tanker.

The next day the pack regrouped off the China coast and soon encountered another convoy, this one consisting of seven tankers and five freighters. They were bound from Japan to Singapore. The tankers were to go on to the oil fields to pick up cargo while the other ships were to go to the Philippines to deliver supplies and reinforcements. The *Barb* made another "end around" and then Fluckey fired three torpedoes at one freighter and three at a second. The first torpedoes hit and then Fluckey forgot about the second batch because he had hit an ammunition ship; it blew up with an explosion that completely disintegrated the ship, and sent the *Barb* down sideways. It took some time to get her back under control, and then Fluckey stayed down until after dark. Loughlin then fired at two ships and missed both. The *Picuda* attacked next and got hits on at least two ships. When darkness had fallen they were still trailing the convoy. Fluckey surfaced and shot again; his torpedoes blew up another ship. Loughlin attacked again and damaged a ship. Then they were through.

At the end of the day they were credited with sinking the *Anyo Maru,* the *Shinyo Maru,* the *Sanyo Maru,* and the *Hokoshima Maru;* the *Meiho Maru, Hisagawa Maru,* and *Manju Maru* were damaged. That was the end of their part of the action but not the end of the misadventures of the convoy. The eight escorts were still intact and they led the surviving ships into Takao to regroup. Here they were unlucky enough to arrive just as Halsey's carrier planes did: Two more tankers and two more freighters were destroyed. The next port of call was Hong Kong, where another air attack cost the convoy more ships and four escorts; the convoy was now reduced to two ships and four escorts. They moved on. Off the coast of Malaya one ship broke down, lagged behind, and was sunk by a submarine; so was one of the escorts. Finally a single tanker reached Singapore, with three escorts. None of the ships ever reached the Philippines. The *Indianapolis* was sunk by a Japanese submarine—the last U.S. warship so lost during the Pacific War.

A major change was made in the Southwest Pacific submarine command at the beginning of 1945. Admiral Christie had fallen afoul of Admiral Kinkaid, the new commander of General MacArthur's Seventh Fleet. The quarrel probably had its roots in personality differences as seems to have been the pattern in most difficulties among the American military leaders. Christie did not much care for Captain Fife, the commander of Brisbane submarines, and that created problems. Christie also had a strong yen for combat and made two unauthorized combat patrols of his own, one in the *Bowfin* with Skipper Walter Griffith and the other in the *Harder* with Sam Dealey. It was the latter that really got him into trouble. Christie was one of Dealey's admirers and before the last patrol he had sought a congressional Medal of Honor for him. Kinkaid had resisted, mostly to show his annoyance at Christie. Christie then went over Kinkaid's head and after Dealey was killed the congressional medal came through. This defiance had to be regarded by Admiral Kinkaid as personal disloyalty and at the end of 1944 he had his revenge: He persuaded Washington to promote Fife to rear admiral, give him command of the Southwest Pacific submarines, and to make Christie commander of the Puget

289

Sound Navy Yard in Bremerton, Washington. A navy yard command or a naval district command was the common way of getting rid of unwanted officers who were too competent to warrant destroying their careers.

In fact the change made little difference. Fife's questionable practice of moving submarines about like pawns on a chessboard was not a problem because there were so few Japanese planes and patrol craft to attack them. Even in Convoy College most of the escorts were now patrol boats. The last Japanese destroyer to be sunk by a submarine was the *Nokaze,* that was torpedoed by the *Pargo* on February 20, 1945. The last big tanker, the *Honan Maru,* was sunk by the *Bluegill* on March 28. By the standards of 1942 the *Honan Maru* was not even classed as a big tanker.

By the time General MacArthur invaded Luzon Island and began moving toward Manila the Japanese didn't have enough naval strength left to try to stop him on the sea. The only effective attack was being made by *kamikaze* aircraft.

In February, Subic Bay on Luzon Island was reoccupied by the Americans and became an advance submarine base. The entire submarine war had moved away from Pearl Harbor and Midway. The new rest camps were located at Guam and Saipan. The old problem of fuel conservation no longer bothered any of the skippers because they didn't have very far to travel to attack the enemy at his front door. In Japan, fuel became *the* problem. A good deal of nonsense has been written about the destructive effects of bombing Japan. In autumn 1944 when Commander Richard O'Kane was captured after the *Tang* was destroyed by its own torpedo, he and his surviving crewmen were landed at Kobe and taken by train across country to Yokohama.

After the war he reminisced: "The countryside may have been beautiful, but the fast, loaded trains, the hydroelectric lines coming down out of the mountains, and the buzzing industry were depressing to us indeed. This was particularly so at Nagoya, where we disembarked for a time. It was dark, but the factories were booming like Kaiser's shipyards, with the bluish light of arc-welding spread out through the city. Once before I had been discouraged, after Tarawa, when a stalemate in the Pacific seemed a real possibility. And here I knew that Japan, with her routes to China quite defensible, could be defeated only by invasion."

But fuel for the defense machine could not be supplied by hydro-electric plants. The routes to the East Indies oil fields were shut by the beginning of the year. There was no way the Imperial General Staff could count on fuel oil for its ships or on having aviation gasoline for its planes. The chemists were fermenting sweet potatoes to make alcohol to fly the planes and distilling pine tree roots to make oil for ships and tanks. There were still enough tankers left in Southeast Asia and in Japan to carry the oil from Sumatra, Java, and Borneo but in March the Grand Escort Force gave up the convoys as completely impossible and thereafter only a handful of tankers tried to run the American submarine blockade. The fuel blockade hurt Japan more than anything else the submarines accomplished.

The Japanese continued to lay mines to defend their home islands against submarines. The *Swordfish* was lost on a reconnaissance mission to Okinawa early in the year, probably to a new minefield off that island. The *Kete* was lost sometime late in March in the East China Sea, probably also to a mine. The *Trigger* was lost south of *Kyushu*, apparently to an escort vessel. The *Snook* was lost, probably off Luzon, and most likely to an escort; it was never determined. Toward the end of the war, so many Japanese vessels were sunk before they could make their reports, and so many records were lost that the number of mysteries increased. The *Barbel* was lost off Palawan to a patrolling plane. Suddenly in 1945 the Americans became aware of an enormous improvement in Japanese antisubmarine techniques. An improved radar was the answer, in systems used by planes and escort ships.

As the war ground to a close, with the attack on Iwo Jima and then Okinawa, some skippers began to run inordinate risks in order to sink ships. One such was Commander Frank Latta, the skipper of the *Lagarto*. He and Lieutenant Commander Ben Jarvis in the *Baya* decided to hunt in the shallow waters of the Gulf of Siam. They found a convoy but the escorts were equipped with radar and were alert. They drove the submarines off; the submarines tried again and were

291

driven off again. Latta must have made another attempt on his own and was sunk by one of the escorts, the converted minelayer *Hatsutaka*. Her attack on the submarine was an easy one. She had the new improved radar that found the submarine for her, and in the end the *Lagarto* was trapped in only thirty fathoms of water.

With so little to occupy them, the submarine commands became obsessed with matters that wouldn't have concerned them a few months earlier. Admiral Fife, who had moved his headquarters to Subic Bay (a million miles from anywhere, according to the submariners) wanted to sink the eight Japanese capital ships remaining in Singapore. He was particularly eager to "get" the *Ise* and the *Hyuga*, two battleships that had been converted to carriers. In February he learned that they were loading oil in drums in Singapore and preparing to race up through the Formosa Strait to Japan to deliver the precious oil. At that time there were twenty-six American and British submarines operating in the area. The Americans couldn't have asked for a better setup. The code breakers were "reading the enemy's mail." The Japanese were accommodating them to the nth degree by sending a stream of messages about the cargo of oil, sailing date, course, speed—everything a submarine commander could want. Right on schedule, the *Ise* and *Hyuga* left Singapore on February 11 and headed on the prescribed course north. They ran right through the gauntlet of twenty-six U.S. submarines; some of the boats got a chance to fire torpedoes but none of them did any damage. Fife blamed it on bad weather, the enemy's radar, and the high-speed at which they traveled. Lockwood blamed it on himself.

By summer, the American submarines went just about anywhere they wished. The *Tirante* was patrolling off Kyushu on June 11 and not finding much. Lieutenant Commander George Street saw a ship at the dock at Ha Shima, a little island eight miles from the entrance to Nagasaki Harbor. He decided to go in after it. He made a submerged approach threading through shoals and obstructions with the help of the sub's radar. Shortly after 11 A.M. on June 11 the submarine arrived at the position Street had chosen, half a mile off the dock. Looking over the ship, Street saw a Japanese deck-gun crew standing at a five-inch gun in their white uniforms. Street's first torpedo hit amid-

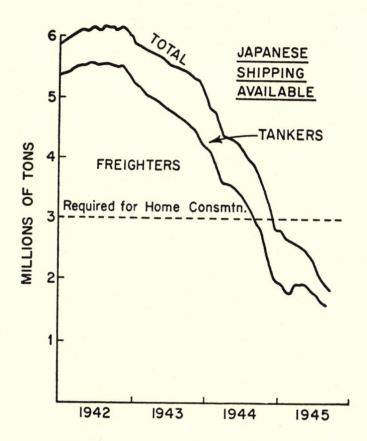

ship and exploded. The gun crew looked up, not out to sea, and began firing at the imaginary aircraft that had "bombed" them. Street fired another torpedo that missed. The gunners saw the wake then the submarine periscope, and began firing at it. But the third torpedo hit aft on the ship and blew up the deck gun and the gunners. Street took the *Tirante* to the surface and headed out of the channel at high-speed, while being fired on by Japanese guns of various sizes. None of the shells touched her. It was a remarkable performance showing great bravery and skill but it was all done for the sake of sinking a twenty-two-hundred-ton ship.

The new frequency-modulation sonar system with its mine-detection capacity came into play in this last year of the war. The *Bowfin* was one of the ships so equipped. Admiral Lockwood had sent her into a special training program so that Skipper Alexander Tyree and his crew would know how to operate the equipment. She patrolled that spring in the Honshu area where several submarines had been lost and had no difficulty, thanks to the FM sonar system. By late spring the blockade of Japan was nearly total. The B-29s laid mines in the Inland Sea, which caused the sinking of many ships. The only area that hadn't been touched for a long time was the Sea of Japan. The reason for this lack of action was the stout defense the Japanese had employed there. The three openings were all reported to be heavily mined.

La Perouse Strait, in the north of Japan, runs between Hokkaido Island and Sakhalin Island, and opens from the Sea of Japan into the Sea of Okhotsk, from which access is gained to the Pacific by threading through the Kuril Islands. The key area was the strait itself that was said to be heavily defended by the Japanese: They had laid minefields there; air bases ringed the area; patrol craft moved back and forth constantly on watch. All this was reported to Lockwood as he prepared.

The other possible entrance to the sea was through Tsushima Strait. This narrow body of water runs between Kyushu Island and the Korean peninsula and is bisected by several small islands in the middle. Like La Perouse Strait, Tsushima was said to be stoutly defended. A three-layered minefield was one of the major defenses.

The other entrance into the Sea of Japan was through Tsugaru Strait which was not considered because it was too narrow and was certain to be too heavily defended. That tortuous body of water runs between Hokkaido and the main Japanese island of Honshu.

In the spring the *Spadefish* and the *Seahorse* were sent with their new FM sonar systems to investigate the Tsushima Strait minefields. When they returned the planning was in its final stages. Nine submarines would penetrate the Sea of Japan. They would all be under the command of Commander E. T. Hydeman of the *Sea Dog*. The others were the *Crevalle, Spadefish, Tunny, Skate, Bonefish, Flying Fish, Tinosa,* and *Bowfin.* All were equipped with the new FM sonar sets. They left Lockwood's new base at Guam on May 27 and arrived in the Tsushima area on June 3.

That night the *Sea Dog, Crevalle,* and *Spadefish* ran through the strait. They didn't encounter any patrol boats. When they reached the minefield, they discovered that the Japanese had reinforced it in the previous few weeks. There were now four lines of mines, some of them designed to catch submarines at periscope depth and some to catch submarines going deep. It was an expert design and expertly carried out. The defenses included sonar systems, radar systems, and other electronic surveillance techniques unknown at that time to the Americans. Fortunately, armed with the FM sonar gear, the submarines were able to move through the minefields, skirting the mines. They went through in threes, over the course of three nights, so as not to arouse attention. The real danger was that a boat might catch a mine cable on a projecting metal surface of the submarine and drag the mine up against the boat. Luckily that didn't happen. The *Skate* did brush a mine cable, and it dragged along the entire length of the boat as she went past. Every man aboard heard it but it did no damage and the mine was not pulled loose.

Inside the Sea of Japan the submarines separated, each going to an assigned area for patrol. Action was not to start until June 9. They had a large area to work: The Sea of Japan stretches nine hundred miles from Tsushima Strait to La Perouse Strait. At its widest point, between Honshu Island and Vladivostok in Siberia, the sea is two hundred and fifty miles wide. The submarines steered clear of the whole north central and northeastern parts of the sea because this was really Soviet water; there was little Japanese activity there.

When the time to attack came, the submarines began searching for ships. In the next seventeen days they sank twenty-seven surface vessels and one submarine. It was one of the most successful and certainly the most spectacular submarine patrol of the Pacific war. One reason why the patrol was undertaken was to paralyze the Japanese with the knowledge that there was no place the Americans could not penetrate—and the results produced their psychological effect. There was only one unfortunate incident: The *Spadefish* sank an eleven-thousand-ton ship northwest of La Perouse Strait but it wasn't Japanese. It was Russian. It was the fourth Soviet ship sunk by an American submarine during the war.

The Japanese learned that there was intensive submarine activity in the sea very early in the mission but they did not react very quickly. They finally did react, however, when an antisubmarine patrol boat sank the *Bonefish* in the broad bay of north central Honshu called Toyoma Wan.

On June 24 all the surviving eight submarines assembled south of La Perouse Strait. U.S. Naval Intelligence teams had indicated that the Japanese had laid deep minefields to trap submarines and that they had some other electronic surveillance equipment at the narrow part of the strait. Commander Hydeman decided that if he took the boats out on the surface, the Japanese might be gulled into inactivity; they might, for example, believe that what was passing was a fishing fleet. It wasn't much of a hope but the submarines' radar would overlap if they were in formation and that would give them additional protection. The skippers were to be prepared to shoot it out on the surface with small vessels; they hoped they wouldn't encounter any large ones.

Lockwood arranged a diversionary action. The submarine *Trutta* shelled Hirado Shima, a little island to the east of Tsushima Strait, hoping to give the Japanese the idea that all the activity would be in the south.

The eight submarines went through La Perouse Strait on the night of June 24 at eighteen knots, on the surface. They saw a lighted ship that was probably Russian coming the other way. They saw a Japanese minelayer that either did not see them or didn't pay them any attention. They saw nothing else nor had any indication of the highly touted defense that was supposed to guard the strait. And then they were out and on their way back to safety. They never did discover why it had been so easy. By the time it was over they didn't really care.

24 THE NEW DIRECTION

THE great submarine wolf pack raid on the Sea of Japan was the high point of the war. After that raid all else was anticlimactical. There were more sinkings and a few more submarines were lost. The *Bullhead* was lost off the island of Bali on August 6 to a patrol plane that dropped two depth bombs. The *Spikefish* sank the submarine tanker *I-383* in the East China Sea on August 13. Then, suddenly the war was over.

When the war ended, and the Americans gained access to German and Japanese records and weapons designs, they learned that the enemy had been far ahead all through the war in matters relating to submarines. The Japanese torpedo was far better than anything the Americans had devised: It was faster, more powerful, and more reliable. The Germans had progressed a long way in submarine design, and had even turned some advanced materials over to the Japanese, who were beginning to fit their submarines out with snorkel breathing devices. That meant they would become more truly like submarines, not submersibles. The American boats still had to come to the surface every few hours to compress fresh air for the tanks and recharge the batteries for the electric motors by using the diesel generators.

In spite of the enemy's possession of more advanced weapons, the American submarines had accomplished something that the Germans had failed to do and the Japanese never tried: They had destroyed the enemy's ocean commerce and made prosecution of the war anywhere but in the homeland impossible. When the war ended there

297

were still plenty of tankers in Japan but no oil was coming up from Java, Sumatra, or Borneo. The last voyage of the *I-383* had been a desperate attempt to solve that problem by shipping oil under the sea since it could not safely travel on top of it. The sinking of the *I-383* was thus symbolic of the failure of even this gamble.

The secret of the American success was the opposite of the German story. The Nazis lost two hundred and fifty submarines to Allied action. The Japanese, who never tried the *guerre de course* (destruction of the enemy's merchant fleet), lost one hundred and seventy-six submarines. The Americans lost fifty-two submarines. The U.S. armed forces had won the Battle of the Pacific just as the Germans lost the Battle of the Atlantic. The reason for both was radar; British and American radar was the best in the world at the time of the Japanese surrender. The Japanese escorts were completely outclassed.

When the war ended Admiral Lockwood had some ideas about the future of submarines. He wanted to be appointed deputy chief of naval operations and given a new area: overall submarine command. But Admiral Nimitz and then Admiral Louis Denfield, the consecutive postwar chiefs of staff, did not like the idea. Lockwood was offered a promotion to full admiral and command of the Pacific Fleet or the Atlantic Fleet—whichever he wished. He refused the offer and retired to write books about submarines.

The submarines languished but that was no different from most of the rest of the military forces. When the war ended the American people wanted no more of the military. The armed services brought the troops home and Congress cut the military budgets so that most of the fleet had to be put into mothballs. The submarines began to line up in neat rows up the Thames River from the New London, Connecticut,submarine base and in the backwaters of San Francisco Bay. They, too, were put into mothballs.

The postwar concept of the naval defense strategy hinged totally on the aircraft carrier, platforms that could launch planes carrying atomic bombs. All other fleet units were designed and built to assist the carriers in this task. The *kamikaze* planes of the Battle of Okinawa had shown the vulnerability of picket destroyers which out in front of the fleet, gave radar warnings of coming attacks. Even before the war's end submarines had been tried in that role and it had worked well. That was one new concept: the submarines as pickets for the fleet. Another was the submarine as a launching platform for missiles to attack ports and even inland cities. The missile was the Regulus, similar to the V-1 missile the Germans had used in 1944 but carrying an atomic warhead. The attack system was crude: A submarine had to surface to launch the missiles that were carried in compartments on the deck. But even with this primitive atomic weaponry, the way was shown for the submarine to become one of the two most important types of warships in the postwar world.

Planning for use of weapons was seriously disrupted in 1950 with the outbreak of the Korean War. It was not the sort of war the navy was geared up to fight. In fact with most ships in mothballs, it was only by coincidence that the U.S. Navy was able to do anything to help stop the lightning drive of the North Koreans down the peninsula. What was left of the Pacific amphibious force was on maneuvers deep in the Pacific. A carrier and some assault ships were able to get into action. Later, by taking such venerable giants as the old battleship *Missouri* out of mothballs, the navy put together an amphibious force that was able to land troops at Inchon and change the course of the war. The carriers conducted actions against the North Koreans and the Chinese. Submarine actions, still largely veiled in secrecy even today, were confined more or less to the landing of agents, and intelligence and reconnaissance. The Korean War was a different sort of a war, limited by the Allied leaders, and against a nation that was not primarily supplied from the sea but from the mainland.

Like all other elements of the American defense forces, the submarine fleet was unprepared for the North Korean attack on South Korea. At that time the advance submarine force, stationed at Yokosuka naval base, consisted of one small submarine divisional command and four fleet-class submarines. The real difference between these boats and those of World War II was that they were equipped with the snorkel systems developed by the Germans and modified by the Americans.

During the Korean War there was virtually no submarine activity of the sort so common in the Pacific war. The closest to it came on

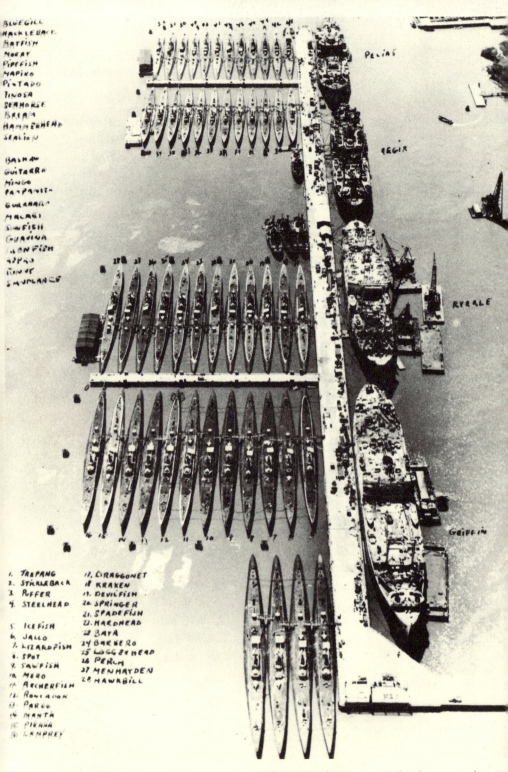

Here is much of the might of the U.S. Pacific Submarine Fleet at Mare Island Navy Yard in 19- ready for decommissioning.

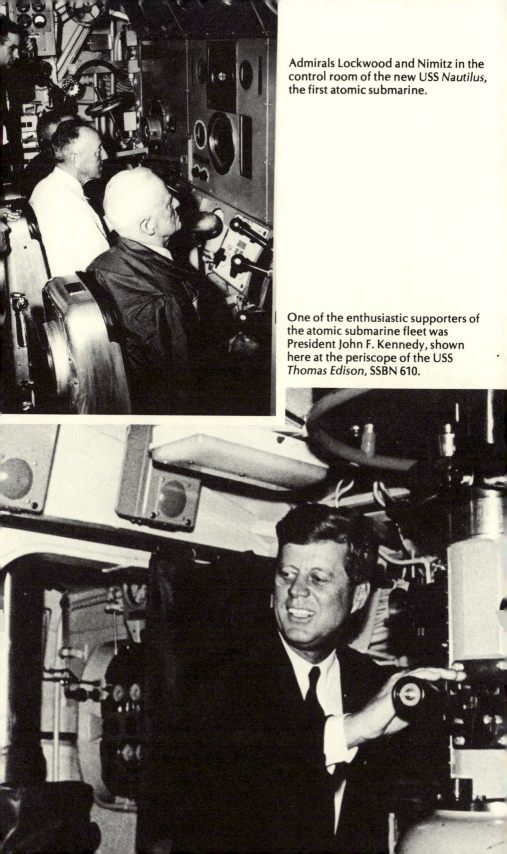

Admirals Lockwood and Nimitz in the control room of the new USS *Nautilus,* the first atomic submarine.

One of the enthusiastic supporters of the atomic submarine fleet was President John F. Kennedy, shown here at the periscope of the USS *Thomas Edison*, SSBN 610.

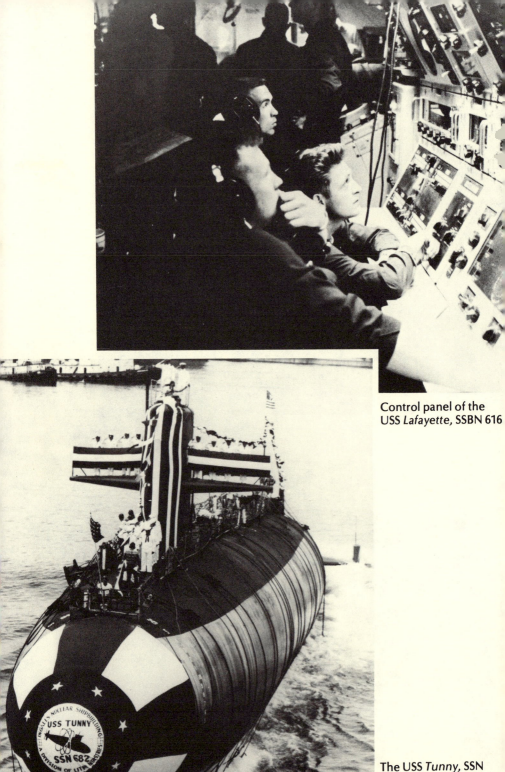

Control panel of the
USS *Lafayette*, SSBN 616

The USS *Tunny*, SSN
682, of the submarine
attack force

The USS George Washington, SSBN 598

The new Trident
submarine USS Ohio,
SSN BN 726

aris missile
ges from the
the Atlantic
le Test Range at
Canaveral,
da. These
les became
ational in the
in late 1960.

October 1, 1950, when the *Perch* was involved in a special mission on the shore of North Korea.

The *Perch* had been sent to Mare Island Navy Yard in 1948 for conversion to a troop-carrying submarine. Two of her four diesel engines were taken out and all ten of her torpedo tubes were removed to make way for more bunk space. All armament except the two .50 caliber machine guns and the two 40 mm antiaircraft guns were also taken off. She was fitted with a snorkel. When the work was completed she could carry one hundred and ten fully-equipped soldiers in addition to her usual crew of thirty-five to fifty men. (Her crew was cut back since no men were needed to man torpedoes or the big deck gun, and fewer men were needed to operate the engines.)

The *Perch* then went into training with troops of the First Marine Division. When the Korean War broke out she was sent off to Yokohama carrying a load of spare submarine parts for the small submarine base. Then began a series of training exercises with a view to using the *Perch* to mount a series of raids on the North Korean bases. Her skipper was Lieutenant Commander Robert D. Quinn.

Several sets of troops, army and marine, were taken aboard and trained in landing operations from the submarine. Taking lessons from the nearly fatal difficulties of the two submarines that had carried Carlson's Raiders to Makin Island, the submarine command equipped the *Perch* with a powerful motorboat called "the skimmer." It was employed to tow the rubber rafts filled with troops to the shore and to pick them up at the end of the exercise and return them to the submarine. The troops rode in seven rubber boats, and the skimmer took them to within five hundred yards of the beach. It also carried explosives that were landed after the troops got safely ashore.

But while American troops trained, the first mission involved sixty-three Royal Marines of the 41st Independent Commando, under Lieutenant-Colonel Douglas E. Drysdale, MBE, R.M. The British marines showed up near the end of September at the submarine base and began to familiarize themselves with the submarine and American procedures. They also began to eat their heads off. They had only recently left Britain, where eggs and meat were still rationed.

On September 25, 1950, the marines were loaded aboard the *Perch* and that evening she got under way heading toward Korean waters. On the twenty-seventh she moved through Tsuguru Strait. It was a dark night and the submarine went through on the surface at fifteen knots. From that point on greater watchfulness began. On September 29 she dived to avoid enemy aircraft and then stayed underwater most of the day at snorkel depth because of the heavy seas that buffeted the surface.

At five o'clock on the morning of September 30, the *Perch* reached a point ten miles off the North Korean coast and made her trim dive, and then carried out a periscope depth reconnaissance of the target area, at 40° 15′ N. This was a place where the north-south railroad came very near the shore, and the commandos were to blow a bridge and damage several culverts in order to tie up North Korean transportation.

For fourteen hours the boat stayed down as Skipper Quinn looked over the coast. The air grew foul from the exhalations of one hundred and forty-five men, but the air systems held out and the job was finished. That night at 7:30, Skipper Quinn surfaced and launched the skimmer; or tried to. The long submersion had admitted water into its engine system and the skimmer would not start. As it turned out this was good luck rather than bad, for as they lay on the surface and the mechanics worked over the engine of the skimmer, Quinn saw two sets of lights move into the target area. He deduced that these were trucks loaded with North Korean troops. How many more vehicles were in the convoy no one knew.

By this time all the British commandos were on deck and most of them were in their rubber boats waiting for the motorboat to get started. But Quinn saw that they had been "spooked," so he called them back. Finally the marines were taken back aboard the submarine and the boats stowed. As this was being done, a plane came over and circled—no more. The submarine moved out toward the sea and Quinn began a battery recharge. The *Perch* stayed on the surface all night without incident, and then at 5:45 on the morning of October 1, Quinn took her down.

Later that morning the *Perch* made a rendezvous with the American destroyers *Maddox* and *H. J. Thomas*. Some new planning had to

301

be done in view of the enemy's discovery of their plans. The skipper and Drysdale went aboard the *Maddox* for consultations. The enemy radar was more effective than they had expected since it had picked them up; and enemy intelligence was better than expected because the North Koreans had deduced what their mission was. What to do? In the end the British and American officers decided to carry out the mission anyhow but to stage a diversion that would give them a better chance of success.

That day several patrol boats were seen in the area selected for the attack, so it was obvious that the North Koreans were alert to just such a move. But the *Maddox* and the *H. J. Thomas* steamed in different directions, and by 7:30 that night Lieutenant Commander Quinn saw no pips on his screen that would indicate patrol craft were nearby. He decided to try the mission one more time. The submarine surfaced and the skimmer's engine was started. The rubber boats were put over the side, the British commandos boarded them, the skimmer towed them in very close to the shore—then stood off and waited. Another helpful diversion was staged that night by a bombing raid a few miles to the north; it was a diversion to draw the attention of the defenders.

The *Perch* lay close offshore as the hours passed. Inland, the marines were accomplishing their mission although without the total surprise they had hoped to achieve. They did manage to blow one culvert, then to mine a tunnel and destroy a train but they ran into enemy troops and got involved in a firefight. British Marine P. A. Jones was killed.

Lieutenant-Colonel Drysdale's men recovered Jones's body, then made their way back to the shore where they gave the recognition signals, and the skimmer returned to tow the boats back out to the submarine. At 2:39 on the morning of October 2 they were moving away from the scene of their raid and soon met the two destroyers that accompanied them back toward the submarine base in Japan.

At noon on October 2 the marines and the men of the *Perch* buried Jones at sea. The United Nations flag was run up on the submarine, and the Union Jack was laid over the shroud. Lieutenant-Colonel Drysdale conducted the service, eight Royal Marine riflemen fired three volleys above the body, and it was consigned to the sea as the two destroyers gave twenty-one-gun salutes. Thus Marine Jones became one of the most highly honored enlisted men in history.

Back in Japan, Lieutenant Commander Quinn had expected to see more such action but the word was that there would be no more raids. The enemy radar was too effective. The risk and value of the raids didn't match up. And so the *Perch* did not go raiding again.

American submarine operations during the rest of the Korean War were limited in scope and consisted largely of shadowing various Soviet and other freighters as they moved through waters near the peninsula. Operations were difficult all the time, and particularly so in winter. In fact the water became so cold and the sea so unpredictable in December 1950 that submarine patrols were abandoned because the snorkels froze up and endangered those vessels. The patrols were not resumed until April 1951. In the interim the weather around Korea was so bad that other ship operations were also curtailed. On the night of February 15 the submarine *Bugara* lost an anchor and went aground on the south edge of Tateyama Bay, 15 miles south of Yokosuka.

When the patrols were resumed, a dozen submarines remained on station in the waters off Korea, patrolling and watching but not engaging in any action against enemy ships. They did carry out a number of photo-reconnaissance missions. Some agents were landed or picked up behind the enemy lines. But when the war ended in 1953 the submarines had still to sink their first ship; nor had they suffered any battle damage. The Korean War, like the Vietnam War to come, was simply not a submarine war.

In the Vietnam War North Vietnam got its supplies through China as well as through the major port of Haiphong. But Haiphong was for political reasons left pretty much alone. American submarines that could have sunk many Russian and Chinese ships delivering supplies were forbidden to do so. Once again, the submarine role was limited by political action. There are no comparable stories from these conflicts to add to the tales of submarines at war as told in the days of the struggle against Japan.

As the submarine's role changed, so did the submarines. The Germans' Walther submarine, for which they had such great hope toward the end of World War II, did not become the wave of the future. Instead, the refinement of atomic power brought a new approach.

From the beginning the practical undersea craft had not followed the pattern set forth by Jules Verne in *Twenty Thousand Leagues under the Sea*. A submarine like the *Nautilus* had never existed. What did exist were still really only submersibles; the new models could travel for more extended periods under water than could their predecessors but they couldn't remain underwater for long periods of time. The atom changed all that. Enthusiasts said a submarine powered by atomic energy would be able to circumnavigate the globe underwater.

Chief among these enthusiasts was an obscure naval captain named Hyman Rickover. In 1947 Rickover was assigned to the U.S. Navy's Bureau of Ships which is responsible for all ship construction done for the navy. On a visit to the Los Alamos Atomic Energy Laboratory he became so enthusiastic about the new energy source that he took a course in nuclear physics at the Oak Ridge atomic energy establishment. He came away a firm believer in the atomic submarine as the superweapon of the future.

That belief was not shared by many in the navy; most high-ranking officers followed the historic tradition of preparing to fight the next war with the weapons of the last. But that attitude had to change because the world had never been in the state it was after 1945, a condition characterized by Winston Churchill as "the cold war." The United States and the Soviet Union were not fighting one another; their antagonism took the form of participation in various "brush wars" around the world, but both sides prepared more or less for a Third World War that would be fought with atomic weapons. That fact, plus his own enormous energy, enabled Captain Rickover to overcome the inertia of duly constituted authority and get his atomic submarine program underway. In 1948 Rickover organized the Nuclear Power Division of the Bureau of Ships. He also was appointed chief of the Naval Reactors Branch of the Atomic Energy Commission. He began planning the form of the first nuclear-powered submarine. In 1950 the plans were made for the U.S.S. *Nautilus*, and two years later the keel was laid.

The traditionalists in the navy did everything they could to stop the atomic submarine program. They were bent on the construction of a supercarrier, the *Forrestal,* and they wanted no part of Rickover or his plans. In a typical spiteful gesture the Naval Selection Board passed him over for promotion to rear admiral. If all had gone as they hoped he would have been forced to retire a few months later, and the nuclear program could then have been put on the shelf, where the admirals wanted it, and would no longer interfere with their plans to build more and bigger aircraft carriers.

But what the admirals didn't count on was a public memory better than their own. In the 1920s an army general named Billy Mitchell was hounded from the service because he insisted that air power must be developed as a major line of military preparedness. The American admirals and generals had not accepted this argument until the Germans showed in Spain just what air power could do; even then the American reaction was lukewarm. The United States went into World War II without a single plane that could stand up to the Japanese Zero fighter or the German Messerschmidt. The American admirals failed to draw the parallel but the American people could—and did. The result was a bitter quarrel within the naval establishment that still was not resolved in the 1980s. In 1982 Admiral Rickover was finally forced out of the navy when President Reagan refused to renew the special congressional appointment that had kept him in charge long after he should have retired by virtue of his age.

Late in the 1950s the atomic submarine began to come into its own. The *Nautilus* was launched and several other atomic submarines were built and placed in service. Admiral Rickover finally got his promotion but was rather ostracized within the naval establishment. Because of this continuing antipathy, Rickover created his own little atomic navy and personally selected the officers chosen for the atomic program. This unhealthy development had been brought about by the pigheadedness of the naval brass. It made Rickover almost a dictator in his own realm and that, too, was unhealthy. Rickover had his own publicity machine and used his prestige to cement his position. Fortunately the atomic program of the navy survived in spite of the pettiness that crept into it.

305

In 1959 during fleet exercises, the admirals were confronted with the unhappy truth that the atomic submarine *Skipjack* "sank" all the highly touted aircraft carriers. So much for aircraft carriers in a future war against the Soviet Union which was building its own atomic submarine fleet. The case could be made for conventional weapons, of course. They were needed in brush fire wars or such improbable conflicts as the Vietnam War where all the conventional rules of warfare (capture territory, destroy the enemy's war industry, interdict his supplies) were at least partially discarded. Atomic submarines were of no use in that sort of conflict. But for a worldwide war, an atomic submarine traveling silently beneath the sea for indefinite periods and firing atomic missiles from below the surface was the sort of weapon that had to be produced.

The year 1960 brought one dream to fruition. The nuclear-powered submarine *Triton* circumnavigated the globe underwater. The atomic submarine had proved to be a real submarine at last. The new submarines were much larger and much faster than the old ones. They displaced three thousand tons. They could achieve speeds underwater of more than 25 knots—in other words, they were far faster underwater than the old fleet-class submarines had been on the surface. They could remain underwater for months if necessary; as long as the crew could stand it. The atomic-power plant needed constant attention but refueling was measured in months, not miles.

The development of atomic missiles proceeded right along with the development of the submarine. On July 20, 1960, the nuclear submarine *George Washington* fired a Polaris missile from an underwater position. At the same time the United States and the Soviet Union began improving their tracking devices so that submarines were no longer as safe as they were at the beginning of the atomic age. Killer submarines were built by both sides; they can find and destroy the attack submarines of the enemy. The first American submarine of this sort, the *Thresher,* was lost in tests in the spring of 1963. Something had gone wrong at a great depth and the pressure hull caved in. The inquiry that followed never cleared up the mystery, nor did several books written about the disaster. The navy maintained a tight security about the matter and it has never been breached. Whether the security is essential for purposes of national defense or a cover-up of military ineptitude is a matter that also remains unknown. It comes down to the old problem that the public must either believe its military leaders—or not—and act accordingly.

The difficulty was repeated in 1968 with the loss of the *Scorpion*, that was found crushed on the bottom of the sea at ten thousand feet off the Azores. Once again the inquiry failed to provide the reasons for the disaster. Those who distrusted the navy talked about cover-up; those who believed in the navy claimed that more could not be said because of national security.

In the development of the nuclear-powered submarines, all the old patterns of struggle for ascendancy among nations have emerged, although in the 1980s the competition was limited to the United States and Soviet power blocs. Every development had its counter-development. In 1976 military expert Drew Middleton wrote that the *Trident* submarine of the U.S. Navy was "the ultimate in undersea weaponry." One thing is certain: That statement would not be true by the end of the 1980s. All sorts of technical changes occur every year. The *Trident* submarines, so-called because they were developed to carry the Trident missiles, took much less time to refit than the early atomic submarines, and that development could be expected to continue. They could patrol for two or three months without any real difficulty—except the boredom of the officers and crew.

It was also true that the principles of the new warfare had been proved and everything that happened from this point on would be improvements of application, just as the World War II U-boat was the ultimate in design of the submersibles that John Holland and Simon Lake had developed half a century before.

BIBLIOGRAPHICAL NOTES

I am much indebted to Ray de Yarmin, curator of the Pacific Submarine Museum at Pearl Harbor for the use of research materials and photographs for this book. Vice Admiral Ralph W. Christie, USN (Ret.) provided me with much information about his activities during World War II, and also about the *Harder, Bowfin,* and other submarines. Some years ago Lhad a long interview with Rear Admiral James Fife. I also used the diaries of Vice Admiral Charles Lockwood, located in the Navy Department's history division at the Washington Navy Yard.

Some of the stories of operations of American submarines, particularly in World War II, come from the patrol reports each skipper had to prepare at the end of a war patrol. I used the reports of the *Bowfin*'s nine patrols, as well as those of the *Harder*'s first five patrols, and individual patrol reports of the *Tang* and several other submarines. Mr. de Yarmin provided me with the unpublished compilations *Special Missions* and *Outstanding Patrols and Missions,* in the submarine museum. These were drawn from various patrol reports and the endorsements of higher commands. That material came from the Submarine Museum and from the Operational Archives of the Naval History Division in Washington. As always, I am indebted to Dr. Dean W. Allard, the chief of that division, and his staff for advice and guidance, as well as their cheerful provision of needed materials. For materials about the early American submarines I used Carroll Storrs Alden's study of American submarine operations in World War I, as it appeared in the United States Naval Institute Proceedings, in June

309

and July 1920. I also made use of W. J. Homes's *Undersea Victory,* and his *Double-Edged Secrets,* Clay W. Blair Jr.'s *Silent Victory,* and Theodore Roscoe's *United States Submarine Operations in World War II,* for the stories of individual boats.

After his retirement from active service, Admiral Lockwood wrote a number of books about submarine operations in World War II and his memoirs, which went back to his days at the Naval Academy and in the navy that was just beginning to make use of the submarine in the years before World War I. I used his memoirs, *Down to the Sea in Subs,* and the other books that are listed in the bibliography.

For a general history of the Pacific war I used Samuel Eliot Morison's many volumes relative to action in the Pacific in his *History of United States Naval Operations in World War II.* I also used research materials gathered for several of my own books on Guadalcanal, Carlson's Raiders at Makin, the invasions of the Gilberts, Marshalls, Marianas, and Leyte, and the last days of the Pacific war. For observations about the two top admirals—King and Nimitz—and members of their staffs and subordinate commands, I called on my own *How They Won the War in the Pacific.*

The story of the sinking of the *Harder* by the old American destroyer *Stewart* came from a Japanese magazine article. In 1942 the *Stewart* was damaged and put into dry dock in Java. She was abandoned there when the Allies were driven out by the Japanese. After the Japanese capture of Surabaya, the *Stewart* was rebuilt and renamed *Patrol Boat No. 102,* and enjoyed a distinguished career in the Japanese navy. The article about the adventures of the *Stewart* was written by Tomoyoshi Yoshima in the September 1981 issue of *Rekishi to Jinbutsu* (History and People) published in Tokyo by Chuokoron-sha, Inc. Mr. Yoshima was a junior officer aboard *Patrol Boat No. 102* during the war. I am indebted to Yukio Shinanaka of Chuokoron-sha for providing me with a copy of the magazine; the translation is my own. I am also indebted to various members of the Japanese Self-Defense Agency's military history section for searching the Japanese naval records and for steering me to sources, and to my wife, Olga Gruhzit Hoyt, for editing and typing.

BIBLIOGRAPHY

Adamson, Hans Christian, and Dissette, Edward. *Guerrilla Subma-rines.* New York: Bantam, 1972.

Anderson, William R., Cdr. USN, with Blair, Clay, Jr. *Nautilus 90 North.* Cleveland: World, 1959.

Barnes, Robert Hatfield. *United States Submarines.* New Haven: H. F. Morse Assoc., 1944.

Beach, Edward L., Capt. USN. *Around the World Submerged.* New York: Holt, Rinehart, & Winston, 1962.

Beach, Edward L., Cdr. USN. *Submarine!* New York: Henry Holt & Co., 1946.

Blair, Clay, Jr. *The Atomic Submarine and Admiral Rickover.* New York: Henry Holt & Co., 1954.

Blair, Clay, Jr. *Silent Victory.* Philadelphia: J. B. Lippincott, 1975.

Cope, Harley and Karig, Walter. *Battle Submerged.* New York: W. W. Norton, 1951.

Corey, Herbert. *The Autobiography of Simon Lake.* New York: D. Appleton-Century, 1938.

Cross, Wilbur. *Challengers of the Deep.* New York: William Sloane, Assoc., 1959.

DiCerto, J. J. *The Story of Polaris.* New York: St. Martin's Press, 1967.

Grider, George, as told to Lydel Sims. *War Fish.* Boston: Little, Brown, 1958.

Hara, Tameichi, with Fred Saito and Roger Pineau. *Japanese De-stroyer Captain.* New York: Ballantine, 1961.

311

Hezlet, Vice Admiral Sir Arthur. *The Submarine and Sea Power.* New York: Stein and Day, 1967.

Holmes, W. J. *Undersea Victory.* Garden City, N.Y.: Doubleday, 1966.

Holmes W. J. *Double-Edged Secrets.* Annapolis, Md.: Naval Institute Press, 1979.

Ingham, Travis. *Rendezvous by Submarine.* Garden City, N.Y.: Doubleday, Doran, 1945.

Ito, Masanori. *The End of the Imperial Japanese Navy.* New York: W. W. Norton, 1965.

Lockwood, Charles A., Vice Admiral USN (Ret.). *Sink 'Em All.* New York: E. P. Dutton, 1951.

Lockwood, Charles A., Vice Admiral USN (Ret.), and Adamson, Hans Christian, Col. USAF (Ret.). *Hellcats of the Sea.* New York: Greenburg.

Lockwood, Charles A., Vice Admiral USN (Ret.). *Down to the Sea in Subs.* New York: W. W. Norton, 1967.

Maas, Peter. *The Rescuer* (the story of Swede Momsen). New York: Harper & Row, 1967.

Middleton, Drew. *Submarine.* Chicago: Playboy Press, 1976.

Morison, Samuel Eliot. *History of United States Naval Operations in World War II.* 15 volumes. Boston: Atlantic, Little, Brown, 1953-1965.

O'Kane, Richard, Rear Admiral USN (Ret.). *Clear the Bridge!* Chicago: Rand McNally, 1977.

Orita, Zenji, with Harrington, Joseph, D. *I-Boat Captain.* Canoga Park, Calif: Major Books, 1976.

Roscoe, Theodore. *United States Submarine Operations in World War II.* Annapolis, Md.: Naval Institute Press, 1949.

Silverstone, Paul. *U.S. Warships of World War I.* Garden City, N.Y.: Doubleday, 1970.

Stafford, Edward Peary, Cdr. USN. *The Far and the Deep.* New York: G. P. Putnam's Sons, 1966.

Steele, George P., Cdr. USN. *Seadragon.* New York: E. P. Dutton, 1962.

Sweeney, James B. *A Pictorial History of Oceanographic Submersibles.* New York: Crown Publishers, 1970.

Woodbury, David, O. *What You Should Know About Submarine Warfare.* New York: W. W. Norton, 1942.

Yokota, Yutaka, with Harrington, Joseph D. *Kanukaze Submarine.* New York: Leisure Books, Nordon Publications, 1961.

Unpublished Materials

The Submarine in the United States Navy. Washington, D.C.: Naval History Division, 1969.

Subroc Missile. Washington, D.C.: Department of the Navy, Sea Systems Command, undated.

United States Navy Harpoon. St. Louis: McDonnell Douglas Corp., undated.

Trident System. Washington, D.C.: Trident System Project Office, U.S. Navy Department, undated.

Special Missions. Compiled by the Submarine Force, U.S. Pacific Fleet, undated.

Outstanding Patrols and Incidents. Compiled by the Submarine Force, U.S. Pacific Fleet, undated.

INDEX

Abemama Islands, 225-26
Aboukir, 36
Adak, 205
Adder, 22-23, 29-30
Admiralty Islands, 244
A-Go operation, 255
Air embolism, 33
Akagi, 108
Akikaze, 282
Aki Maru, 240-41
Akitsu Maru, 282
Alanthus, 63-64
Alaska, 57, 135, 137, 141-42, 150, 205
Albacore, 166, 257, 259-60, 285
Albany submarine base, 123, 126
Aleutians, 135-36, 142-46, 150, 166,
    205-06, 208
Alexander the Great of Macedon, 5
Alexandria Torpedo Factory, 68, 90
Allied Submarine Detection
    Investigation Committee (ASDIC),
    56, 67
Althena, 163
Amatsukaze, 113
Amberjack, 166, 172-74, 197-98, 227
Amchitka Island, 143
America Maru, 241
American Revolution, 5-8
Andrews, Charles H., 87, 246
Antisubmarine techniques, 37, 40-41,
    56

Antisubmarine warfare, Japanese, 112,
    135, 183, 192-93, 197, 207, 216, 221,
    229, 241, 243, 248-49, 251, 257, 267,
    271, 274, 281-82, 291, 294-95
Antisubmarine efforts, U.S., 217-18, 226
Anyo Maru, 289
Aoba, 280
Arare, 144
Archerfish, 267
Argentia, Newfoundland, 85, 87
Argonaut, 92, 160, 167, 181-82, 227
Argonaut II, 19
Aristotle, 5
Asakaze, 273-74
Asia, 7
Astor, Vincent, Lt. Cde., 51
Atago, 280
Athenia, 83
Atomic missiles, 306-07
Atomic submarines, 5, 304-07
Atrocities, 190-92
Atsuta Maru, 135
Atsutasan Maru, 96
Attu, 142, 205-06
Austin, Marshall, H., Lt. Cdr., 255,
    275-77
Australia Submarine command, 126
Aylward, Theodore, Lt. Cdr., 119
Azores, 40-41, 44-45, 307

B-17 bombers, 99, 138

B-29 bombers, 285, 293
Badders, William CM/M, 81-82
Balabec Strait, 275, 277
Bali, 297
Bang, 248, 257, 259
Bantry Bay, Ireland, 41-43
Barb, 248, 277-78, 287-88
Barbel, 291
Barber's Point, 30, 32, 34
Barchet, Stephen G., Lt. Cdr., 92-93
Barracuda, 24
Bataan Peninsula, 98, 109, 122
Bathysphere, 5
Batjan, 254-55
Battle of the Atlantic, 85
Battle of the Coral Sea, 123, 130-31, 135-36
Battle of the Java Sea, 112
Battle of Leyte Gulf, 280
Battle of Midway, 140
Battle of Okinawa, 298
Battle of the Philippine Sea, 253, 265
Baya, 291
"Bends," the, 33
Bennett, A.C., Lt., 42
Benson, Roy, Lt. Cdr., 208, 211
Bergall, 284
Biak, 254, 274, 286
Biddle, 65
Birmingham, 35, 125
Bismarck Islands, 154, 157
Bituitu Island, 225
Blackett Strait, 228
Blackfish, 234
Blair, Jr., Clay, 99
Blanchard, James, Lt. Cdr., 259-60, 265
Blandy, W.H.P., Adm., 208-09
Bluefish, 272
Bluegill, 290
Bole, J.A., Lt. Cdr., 172-74, 197-98
Bonefish, 294-95
Bonin Islands, 269, 288
Bonita, 24-26, 176
Borneo, 235, 247, 249-50, 275, 282, 291

Bougainville, 154, 228
Bowfin, 242, 289-90, 294
Brazil Maru, 165
Bream, 280, 284
Brindupke, Charles, Cdr., 221
Brinker, Robert M., Lt., Cdr., 231
Brisbane, 125, 154, 158-59, 163-65, 174-76, 181-83, 186, 188, 191, 195-98, 202, 207, 227-28, 244, 277, 289
British Royal Marines, 300-02
British Royal Navy, 15, 37-38
Brockman, William, Skipper, 139-40, 160-61
Brooklyn Navy Yard, 14, 30-31, 64, 73
Brown, F.E., Lt., 158-59
Brown, Francis, Lt. Cdr., 233
Brown, Jr., G.E., Lt., 3
Brunei Bay, 282
Bruton, Chester, Lt. Cdr., 132
Bruton, Henry C., Lt. Cdr., 165
Bugara, 303
Buin, 154
Buka, 197, 228
Bullhead, 297
Bureau of Ordnance, Navy, 68, 70-71, 102, 105, 124, 127, 146, 148-49, 176, 187-88, 192, 208-09, 212, 268
Bureau of Ships, 304
Burma, 130, 278
Burrough, Edmund W., Ens., 47-48
Bushnell, 41, 51
Bushnell, David, 6-7

Cable, Frank T., 16-17, 21, 23
Cachalot, 92
Calcutta Maru, 134
Camden, 53
Camranh Bay, 284
Canopus, 100
Capelin, 234
Carinder, Crewman, 276-77
Carlson, Evans Lt. Col., 159-62, 181, 300
Caroline Islands, 106, 108, 215

Carp, 24
Carpender, Arthur S., Adm., 151-52, 163-64, 175, 179, 182, 198
Casablanca Conference, 206
Cassedy, Hiram, Lt., 122
Castine, 26-28
Cavalla, 256-57, 262-64
Cavite, Naval Base, 47, 98
Celebes Sea, 246
Ceram Island, 196, 234
Cero, 218
Chalcedony, 211
Chappell, Lucius, Lt. Cde., 119, 126
Chapple, Lt. Cdr., 120-21, 123
Chester, 172
Chifuku Maru, 183
Chinnampo, 200
Chiyoda, 264
Chokai, 157
Christie, Ralph Waldo, V/Adm., 68-72, 86-87, 90, 125, 154-55, 158-59, 164, 166, 175, 178-79, 182, 198-99, 204, 209, 217, 219, 229, 242, 246-47, 251, 255, 269, 273, 277, 289
Christmas Island, 119, 126, 199
Churchill, Winston, 37, 84, 87, 217, 304
Chuwa Maru, 109
Chuyo, 4
Cisco, 231
City of Rome, 72
Civil War, 10-14
Clarey, Bernard, Lt., Cdr., 282
Clark, Alber, Skipper, 240
Clark Field, 99
Coastal Defense Vessel No. 22, 281
Coastal Patrol Vessel No. 24, 267
Coath, 16
Code-breaking, U.S., 1, 118, 120-21, 123, 131, 136, 142, 165, 206, 208, 232-33, 241, 264, 284, 292
Coe, James, Lt. Cdr., 119, 126, 177
Colclough, Oswald S., Capt., 142
Cole, C.W., R/Adm., 78
Columbia, 52

Combined Chief of Staff, allied, 245
Command and strategy problems, 150
Commerce raiding, 35-37, 56, 91
Connaway, Fred, Cdr., 1-3
Convoy HI-71, 272-73
Convoy No. 353, 267
Cooke, Jr., Charles M., 58, 60-65
Corregidor, 98, 100, 109-11, 120-22, 167
Corvina, 233-34
Craig, John, Lt. Cdr., 227
Cressy, 36
Crevalle, 247, 294
Crilley, Frank, Chief Gunner's mate, 31-34
Cromwell, John P., Capt., 1, 3, 5, 232
Crosby, M.J.K., 13
Crowley, John, Lt. Cdr., 275
Cutter, Slade, Lt. Cdr., 255
Cuttlefish, 23, 132, 137-38, 166

Dace, 244, 280
Darien, 199, 201
Darter, 280
Darwin, 100, 109, 153, 231, 234
Dasol Bay, 274
Daspit, Lawrence, R., Lt. Cde., 210
Daubin, Freeman A., 51, 123-24
Davao, Gulf of, 178, 254
David, 10-13, 19, 30
Davidson, J.F., Lt. Cdr., 86
Dealey, Samuel, Cdr., 219, 243, 249-51, 255, 272-74, 289
Deep-sea diving, 31-32
Delhi Maru, 238-39
Dempsey, James, Lt. Cdr., 111, 122
Denfield, Louis, Adm., 298
Deragon, William, Lt. Cdr., 256
De Tar, John, Skipper, 106, 134
Deutschland, 39
Diesel engines, 16, 19, 24, 51, 58, 87
Diesel, Rudolph, Dr., 16
Diving bells, 5, 10
Diver's gear, 5, 9, 31-32
Dixon, Lt., 12-13

Dobson, Rodney H., Lt., 72
Doenitz, Karl, Adm., 218-19, 284
Dolphin, 92, 118, 166
Dorsey, Herbert Grove, 67
Doyle, Lt., 81
Drake, Waldo, Cdr., 169
Drebbel, Cornelis Jacobszoon, 5
Drellishak, S.J., Chief Gunner's mate,
    31
Drum, 132, 134, 164, 234
Drysdale, Douglas, E., Lt. Col., 311,
    302
Du Pont, Adm., 14
Dutch East Indies, 98, 100-02, 106, 110,
    112, 117, 130, 134, 147-48, 153, 181,
    193, 235, 246, 267, 269, 272, 274,
    291
Dutch Harbor, 141, 147
Dykers, Skipper, 245

Eadie, Thomas, Chief Gunner's mate,
    76
Eagle, 7-8
Ede, Alfred L., Lt. (j.g.), 30
Edwards, Richard S., Adm., 28, 84-86,
    126, 149
Electric Boat Company, 15-17, 22-24, 57
Ellsberg, Edward, Cdr., 75
Emden, 36-37
English, Robert H., 124, 135, 138-40,
    146, 148-50, 160-61, 169, 178, 181-82
England, 218
Eniwetok, 254
Enright, Joseph, Skipper, 283
Escolar, 280
Espiritu Santo, 172-73
Exmouth Gulf, 153

Falaba, 36
Falcon, 74, 80-81
Fenno, Frank Welsey, Lt. Cdr., 109-10,
    123
Ferrall, William E., Skipper, 110, 126
Fertig, Wendell, Col., 195-96

Fielder, W.M., Ens., 2-3
Fife, James, Adm., 100, 123, 126, 147,
    152, 163, 179, 181-83, 188, 197-98,
    228, 233, 244, 289-90, 292
Fiji Islands, 156
Finback, 144, 257, 259
Fitch, Aubrey C., Adm., 99
Fitch, Graham, Lt. (j.g.), 73-75
Fitzgerald, John, Lt. Cdr., 230-31
Flasher, 284
Fletcher, Frank Jack, Adm., 140
Flier, 275
Flounder, 284
Fluckey, Eugene, Lt. Cdr., 248, 287-88
Flying Fish, 165-66, 255-56, 294
Formosa Strait, 110, 218, 271, 280, 282,
    288, 292
Forrestal, 305
Fox, Chief Gunner's mate, 59
Freeman, Charles L., Cdr., 96, 119, 123
Fremantle, 118-19, 123, 131, 151, 153-54,
    164, 175-78, 182, 187, 198-99, 204,
    207, 209, 231, 242, 246, 251, 269,
    272, 274
French, George R.W., Ass't Surgeon, 31
French-English War, 9
French Frigate Shoals, 136
Fuji Maru, 219
Fulton, Robert, 9
Fulton, 20, 181

Gainor, Lawrence, CE/M, 78
Gar, 131, 176-77
Garrison, Malcolm, Lt. Cdr., 241-42
Gasoline engine, 47-48
Gato, 134
Gavin, Stephen, S/1C, 62
George Washington, 306
George W. Goethals, 64-65
German naval radio system, 221
Ghormley, Robert, V/Adm., 155-56
Gibraltar, 38
Gilbert Islands, 1, 3, 106, 160, 162, 215,
    223-25, 232-33

Gilmore, Howard, Cdr., 144, 183-86
Glassell, Lt., 10-11
Goethals, General, 28
Golet, 267
Goyo Maru, 133
Grampus, 22, 227-28
Grant, A.W. R/Adm., 53
Grant, James D., Lt., 85
Grayback, 218-19
Grayling, 24, 108, 164-65, 231
Greater East Asia Co-Prosperity
    Sphere, 227
Great White Fleet, 27
Greenling, 132, 196
Grenadier, 132, 134, 229-30
Grenfell, Joseph, Cdr., 94
Gresham, Lt., 62
Grider, George, Lt. Cdr., 284
Griffith, Walter, Cdr., 242, 289
Grouper, 139, 196
Growler, 144, 183-86, 284
Grumman Hellcats, 263
Grunion, 146-47
Guadalcanal, 145, 154-57, 159-60, 162-
    63, 165-66, 172-74, 179-81, 183, 192-
    93, 224, 231, 243, 254
Guam, 137, 255-56, 258, 263-64, 288,
    290, 294
Guardfish, 167-71, 191
Gudgeon, 93-94, 105, 195-96, 199, 244
Guerillas, 109, 195-96
Guitarro, 284
Gulflight, 36
Gunnel, 87
Gurnard, 87, 246
Gygax, Felix Y., Lt., 52

Haddo, 242, 272-73, 275
Haddock, 221-22
Haguro, 264
Hainan Strait, 176
Haines, Capt., 160, 244
Haiphong, 313
Hake, 254, 274, 284

Halibut, 221-22
Halifax, N.S., 40
Halley, Sir Edmund, 5
Halmahera, 246
Halsey, William F., Adm., 99, 107, 118,
    175, 228, 258, 279, 283-84, 289
Halstead, O.S., 14
Hammann, 140
Hammerhead, 270
Hancock, J. Lewis, Lt. Cdr., 42, 44
Harbin Maru, 102
Harder, 243, 249-51, 272-74, 289
Hardhead, 284
Harding, Warren, 55
Harrington, Seaman, 276-77
Hart, Thomas C., Adm., 40-41, 69, 82,
    87, 90, 95, 98, 101-03, 105, 111, 125,
    176
Haruna, 282
Harusame, 189, 254
Hatsutaka, 292
Hawaii, 135-136, 138, 146, 160, 191, 222
Hayanami, 249-50
Haylor, Frank, Lt. Cdr., 274
Hayo Maru, 97
Hazeltine, Ens., 13
Hela, 35
Helz, Ens., 276-77
Henderson Field, 162, 173-74
Hendrix, C.N.G., Lt., 159
Hensel, K.G., Capt., 237-39
Herring, 247-48
Hersing, Otto, Lt. Cdr., 35
Hiburi, 272-73
Hirado Shima, 295
Hirohito, Emperor, 281
Hisagawa Maru, 289
Hitler, Adolf, 83-84, 240
Hiyo, 202-03, 208, 212, 264
Hiyodori, 198
H.J. Thomas, 301-02
Hobson, Frank, 76
Hogue, 36
Hokkaido, 166, 293-94

Hokoshima Maru, 289
Holland, 15, 21, 111, 123, 154
Holland IX, 20
Holland, John, 15, 16, 19-25, 307
Holland Torpedo Boat Company, 15
Hollandia, 254
Holmes, W.J., 138
Honan Maru, 290
Hongkong, 130, 186, 289
Honolulu, 30-32, 151
Honshu, 166-167, 169-70, 229, 231-32, 235, 267, 293-95
H.O.R. engine, 87-89
Hornet, 163
Hosho, 108
Housatonic, 12-13
Houston, 111
Howe, Lord Richard, Adm., 7
Howe, Sir William, 7
Hunley, 19, 30
Hunley, Horace, 11
Hunter-killer teams, Japanese, 228, 231-32, 243-44, 250
Hurt, David, Lt. Cdr., 113-16, 126
Hydeman, E.T., 294-95
Hydrophones, 37, 43, 54-56, 112, 192
Hyuga, 283, 292

I-Boats, 89, 117-18, 136
    I-1, 172; *I--4,* 163; *I-6,* 117; *I-9,* 117; *I-15,* 163; *I-16,* 172; *I-19,* 163; *I-20,* 172; *I-28,* 133; *I-63,* 76; *I-64,* 133; *I-76,* 172, 234; *I-124,* 172; *I-168,* 137, 140-41; *I-173,* 94; *I-222,* 172; *I-383,* 297-98
Ikazuchi, 243
Inchon, 299
Indian Ocean, 36-37, 117, 119, 129, 284
Indianapolis, 71, 287, 289
Indo-China, 117, 125, 153, 186
Inland Sea, 132-133, 137, 268, 283, 285, 293
Intelligence, Japanese, 137, 140, 249
Intelligence, U.S., 138, 154-55, 165, 202-03, 206, 218, 221, 248

Intelligent Whale, 14
Irvin, W.D., Cdr., 225-26, 241
Ise, 283, 292
Iwanami, 284
Iwo Jima, 4, 269, 291

Jack, 240, 245
Jacob, Tyrell D., Cdr., 96
Jacobs, Lt. Cdr., 102-04
Jacobs, Ted, SM/1C, 81
Jallao, 280
James, William, 9
Japanese High Commands
    Combined Fleet, 129-30, 135, 141, 203, 206-07, 246, 254, 271; Imperial Army, 156, 240; Imperial General Staff, 136, 144-45, 156, 180, 205-06, 215, 229, 245-46, 254, 269, 272, 283, 291; Imperial Navy, 239, 253, 271, 283; Navy Ministry, 129, 235
Japanese Units
    23rd Division, 282; 29th Division, Imperial Army, 240; 901 Naval Air Flotilla, 234; Carrier Division Two, 107; Carrier Division Six, 157; Fifth Squadron, 117; First Air Fleet, 258; Fourth Squadron, 117; Grand Escort Forces, Grand Escort Force, 234-35, 237, 246, 271, 291; Sixth Fleet, 206, 215; Sixth Squadron, 117
Jarvis, Ben, Lt. Cdr., 291
Java, 98, 101, 111-13, 147-48, 183, 291
Jikitanchiki (magnetic detector), 192
Jinyo, 282
Jones, P.A., British Marine, 302-03
Jones, Roy K., Lt. Cdr., 74-75
Juneau, 172
Junyo, 142, 202-03, 264, 284

Kaga, 108, 140
Kahler, Seaman, 276
Kahoolawe (Hi.), 210
Kaibokans, 193, 216, 234, 237, 230-40, 246, 250, 272-74, 281, 284

Kajioka, Sadamichi, 245-46
Kaimei Maru, 169
Kaiser Wilhelm, 15
Kaiten, 287
Kako, 158
Kakuta, Kakuji, Adm., 258-59, 262
Kalienewski, Edward, 76
Kamikaze, 287, 290, 298
Kamogawa Maru, 112
Kanko Maru, 102
Kasumi, 144
Katoomba, 158-59
Kazagumo, 254
Kearney, 85
Kefauver, Russell, Skipper, 240
Kelley, W.F., Fireman, 185
Kennedy, Marvin, Lt., Cdr., 166
Keokuk, 13-14
Kete, 291
Keyport (Wash.) Torpedo Factory, 90
Kimmel, Husband, Adm., 99, 275
Kimmel, Manning, Lt. Cdr., 275
King, Ernest J., Adm., 73-74, 87, 99,
    110, 118, 121, 125-26, 138, 146, 149-
    50, 155-56, 163, 175, 179, 198, 218,
    243, 249
Kinjosan Maru, 132
Kinkaid, Thomas, Adm., 242, 289
Kirkpatrick, Charles, Lt. Cdr., 133-34
Kishinami, 284
Kiska, 142-43, 146-47, 205-07
Klakring, Thomas B., Lt. Cdr., 167-72
Kobe, 132, 290
Kodiak, 141
Komandorski Islands, 206
Komatsu Sakio, Warrant Officer,
    260-61
Kongo, 282
Korean War, 299-303
Kossler, Herman, Lt. Cdr., 256-58,
    262-64
Kovieng, 154, 157
Kretschmer, Otto, Cdr., 93
Krupp armaments company, 16

Kumano, 283
Kure, 132
Kuretake, 284
Kuriles, 233, 241, 248
Kuril Islands, 206, 293
Kurita, Takeo, Adm., 280
Kwajalein, 107, 118, 133, 150, 162, 254
Kwantung Army, 240
Kyushu, 132, 292-93

Lae, 154
Lagarto, 291-92
Lake, 21
Lake, Simon, 15-16, 19-21, 25, 53-55,
    307
Lambert, Alexandre, 10
Langley, 98
Laotigashan Point, 200
La Perouse Strait, 212, 294-95
Latta, Frank, Cdr., 291-92
League of Nations, 106
Lee, Ezra, Sgt., 7-8
Lee, W.A., Adm., 264
Lend-lease, 85
Lent, Willis Ashford, Lt. Cdr., 93, 108,
    134
Leonardo da Vinci, 5
Lexington, 118, 130
Leyte, 280, 286
Liddell, James, Lt., 275
Life Magazine, 169
Lifeguard technique, 223-24, 279, 286
Lingayen Gulf, 97, 110, 122, 231, 288
L'Envincible, 9
Liscombe Bay, 215
Lockwood, Charles A., Adm., 1, 22, 29-
    30, 49-51, 87, 89-90, 125-27, 147-54,
    163-64, 175-77, 179, 182-83, 186-88,
    191, 199, 202-04, 207-12, 216, 218-
    22, 224, 231-33, 235, 237-39, 243,
    247-48, 255-57, 259-60, 267, 270,
    278-79, 282-83, 285, 292-93, 298
Logan, Edgar A., Lt., 42-43
Loomis, Sam, Lt. Cdr., 258

Los Alamos Atomic Energy
    Laboratory, 304
Loughlin, Eliott, Lt. Cdr., 282, 287-88
Loughman, W.F., Chief Gunner's
    mate, 31-33
Lunga Point, 155, 159, 173-74
Lunga Roads, 173
Lusitania, 37, 83
Luzon Island, 95-96, 245, 248, 270-73,
    290-91

MacArthur, Douglas, Gen., 98, 100,
    109, 120, 123, 145, 154-56, 159,
    164, 167, 175, 179, 182-83, 188, 195-
    96, 240, 245, 254, 282, 289-90
"MacArthur's Navy" (U.S. Seventh
    Fleet), 163, 175, 198
MacGregor, Edgar J., 218
MacKenzie, George K., Lt. Cdr., 228
Mackerel, 84-86
Mackie, Thomas, 123
Maddox, 301-02
Majaba, 172
Makassar Strait, 101, 104, 177, 234
Makin Island, 160-62, 167, 181, 225,
    233, 300
Malacca Strait, 229
Malay Peninsula, 101, 130, 229-30,
    278, 289
Manchuria, 27, 199, 240, 269
Maness, Lloyd, E/M 1C, 77-78
Manila, 109, 111, 118, 145, 195, 231,
    245, 272-73, 290
Manila Bay, 25, 47-48, 82, 95-100, 120,
    122, 283
Manju Maru, 289
Marcus, Arnold, Lt. (j.g.), 47
Marcus Island, 222
Mare Island Navy Yard, 34, 186, 208,
    280, 300
Marianas Islands, 105, 132, 215, 221-22,
    240-42, 244, 253-55, 257-59, 267,
    269, 281, 286
Marinduqu Island, 121
Markland, Capt., 71

Marlin, 84
Mars, 27-28
Marshall, Elliott, Lt. Cdr., 234
Marshall Islands, 1, 106, 131, 134, 150,
    215, 253-54, 286
Maryland, 34
Matsu (Pine) convoys, 240-41
Matsukaze, 267
Maui (Hi.), 210
Mazon, W.E., Lt., 223-24
Maya, 280
McCann, Allan, Cdr., 92
McGregor, Donald, Lt. Cdr., 131
McGregor, Louis D., Cdr., 284
McKinney, Eugene B., Lt. Cdr., 223-24
McKnight, John, Lt. Cdr., 103
McNair, Jr., F.V., Lt., 26
Meiho Maru, 289
Messerschmidts, 305
Michels, Fred, 76
Middleton, Drew, 307
Midget submarines, 172
Midway Island, 92, 135-139, 142, 145,
    172, 199, 201, 205, 218, 224, 228,
    238, 240, 255, 290
Mihalowski, John, TM 1/C, 81-82
Mikura, 272
Millican, W.J., Lt. Cdr., 150-51, 177,
    199
Minazuki, 249
Mindanao, 25, 101, 111, 178, 195-96, 244
Mindoro Island, 272, 284
Minegumo, 228
Mines, 8, 176-77, 193, 229, 232, 235, 239,
    247, 267-68, 270, 275, 280, 284-86,
    293-94
Mines, Mark XII, 176
Mios Woendi, 274
Missouri, 299
Mitchell, Billy, 305
Mitscher, Marc, Adm., 256, 258-59, 264
Miyodono Maru, 183
Mizuho, 134
Moccasin, 22

Molotov cocktails, 201
Molucca Passage, 101, 102, 234
Momsen, C.B., 76, 210-211, 218-220
Momsen lung, 76, 80, 210, 281
Moore, J.R., Lt. Cdr., 157
Morale, Japanese, 136
Morale, U.S., 126, 152-53, 156, 167, 213, 222
Morality against use of submarines in warfare, 8-9
Morton, Dudley W., Lt. Cdr., 85, 188-92, 199-202, 207, 212, 232-33, 268-69, 277
Moseley Stanley, Lt. Cdr., 94, 133, 137
Mumma, Jr., Morton C., Cdr., 97
Munson, Henry, Lt. Cdr., 272
Murasame, 228
Musashi, 242, 250, 255
Muskellunge, 211, 257
Muzzy, Capt.'s Clerk, 13

Nachi, 232
Nagasaki Harbor, 292
Nagoya, 290
Nagumo, Chuichi, Adm., 139, 141
Nansei Shoto, 170, 172, 199
Napoleon Bonaparte, Emperor, 9
Naquin, Oliver F., Lt., 76-77, 79-81
Narwhal, 24, 91, 166-67, 206
Natushio, 111
Nautilus, 139-40, 145, 160-61, 167, 196, 206, 224-25, 241
Nautilus (atomic submarine), 304-05
Nautilus (early), 9
Naval Appropriations Act, 39
Naval Reactors Branch of the Atomic Energy Commission, 304
Negroes, 195
Neilson, F.C.L., Chief Gunner's mate, 31
Nenohi, 144
New Britain Island, 154, 181, 196
New Georgia Island, 180, 183
New Guinea, 123, 130, 188, 190, 192, 215, 240, 245-46, 254

New Ireland, 154, 157
New Ironsides, 10-11
Newport Torpedo Factory, 44, 68-70, 90, 124, 178, 182, 209, 212
Nichols, John, Lt., 80
Nimitz, Chester, Adm., 106-08, 118, 121, 136-38, 140, 142, 144, 155-56, 160, 164-67, 169, 182-83, 202-03, 205-06, 208-11, 228, 242, 249, 253, 259, 279, 286, 298
Nimitz, Jr., Chester W., Lt. Cdr., 242, 273
Nisshin Maru, 247
Nokaze, 290
Nordenfeldt, Thorsten, 14-15
Nordenfeld II, 15
Norfolk Navy Base, 64
North Carolina, 163
North German Lloyd Line, 39
North Pass, 132
Northeast Pass, 132

Oak Ridge, 304
O'Brien, 163
Octopus, 21, 24
O'Hara, Raymond, PH/M 1/C, 77, 79
Ohio, 64-65
Oikawa, Koshiro, Adm., 235, 238-41, 243, 247, 249, 268, 270-71
O'Kane, Richard H., Lt., 188-90, 212, 232, 280, 290
Okinawa, 133, 218, 264, 269, 285, 291
Ohinoshima, 154
Olsen, Eliot, Skipper, 108
Operation Galvanic, 1, 224
Ordnance Island, Bermuda, 85
Ortolan, 57
Osaka, 132
Otta Pass, 131-32
Ozark, 28
Ozawa, Jisaburo, Adm., 254-55, 257-65

Paine, Lt., 11-12
Palau Islands, 96, 108, 178, 188-89, 193, 222, 242, 254, 258, 286

323

Palawan Island, 275, 277, 280, 291
Pampanito, 278
Panama Canal, 27-29, 58, 84, 86
Panay, 120, 231
Paramushiro, 233
Parche, 248, 270
Pargo, 219-20, 290
Paris, 218
Parker, Timothy A., Ens., 30
Parks, Lewis, Lt. Cdr., 134-35
Parsons, Charles, 195-96
Pathfinder, 35
Patrol Boat No. 102, 274
Paulding, 73-74
Pearl Harbor, 1, 4, 30, 34, 40, 56, 85, 91-
    95, 98-99, 101, 105-12, 117-18, 123-
    25, 129-32, 135-36, 138-40, 144, 146,
    148-49, 151, 155-57, 160-61, 164-69,
    173, 175, 178, 181, 186-87, 191-92,
    199, 201-03, 207-12, 219, 223-24,
    226, 229, 231, 233, 239, 244, 246,
    248, 250-51, 256-59, 262, 264, 268,
    275, 285
Penang, 230
Perch, 97, 111-15, 300-03
Perch II, 248
Periscopes, development of, 67-68
Permit, 120
Perth, 126, 151-54, 164, 175
Peterson, G.E., Capt., 248
Peto, 248
Phenix, 76
Philadelphia Navy Yard, 40, 49
Philippines, 25, 47, 56, 95-96, 98-99,
    101-02, 109-11, 123, 153, 178, 195,
    246-47, 254-55, 269-71, 275, 279,
    282, 288-89
Phillips, Lodner, 9
Phra Ruong, 274
Piaanu Pass, 131-32
Pickerel, 24, 96, 102, 228-29
Picuda, 248, 282, 288
Pierce, J.R., Cdr., 160, 181
Pigboats, 22, 50, 52

Pike, 22, 203
Pintado, 282
Pioneers (Japanese Seabees), 155
Pipefish, 256-57
Plan Orange, 106, 160
Plunger, 22, 94, 105, 112, 225
Pollack, 94, 105, 132-33, 137
Pompano, 134-35, 166, 232
Porpoise, 22-23, 25
Port Moresby, 123, 130, 133, 164
Portsmouth Navy Yard, 76, 78, 135
Post, Lt. Cdr., 199
Post, Jr., William Schuyler, 92-93
Prien, Alfred, M/M 2/C, 76
Prisoners, 4, 116, 230-31, 242, 275, 278,
    281
Puget Sound Navy Yard, 289-90
Pye, W.S., Adm., 99

Q-Ship, 131, 238-39
Queenfish, 278, 282, 287-88
Quezon, Manuel, 111
Quinn, Robert D., Lt. Cdr., 300-03

Rabaul, 107, 130, 154, 157, 163, 172,
    183-84, 186, 192, 197-98, 203, 215,
    228, 247, 255
Radar, 112, 168, 180, 183-84, 186, 192,
    277, 291-92, 294-95, 298, 302-03
Radio-detection, Japanese, 220
Rainbow, 25
Rakuyo Maru, 278
Ramage, Lawson Paterson, Lt. Cdr.,
    165, 199, 270-71
Rangoon, 230
Rasher, 272
Raton, 284
Ray, 272-73, 284
Razorback, 284
Reagan, Ronald, 305
"Recompression chamber," 32
Redfin, 255, 275, 277, 284
Reich, Eli, Lt. Cdr., 282
Rendova Island, 196

Rengi Island, 196
Reuben James, 85
Richard M. Rowell, 279-80
Rickover, Hyman, Capt., 304-05
Ringgold, 225-26
Eisser, Robert, Lt. Cdr., 255
Robalo, 275
Rooney, Roderick S., Lt. Cdr., 233
Roosevelt, Franklin D., 84-85, 87, 110
Roosevelt, James, Maj., 161
Roosevelt, Theodore, 27
Roseneath, Scotland, 87
Round Island, 201
Royal George, 9
Runner, 231
Russo-Japanese war, 21, 27
Ryuho, 264
Ryujo, 142

Sado, 272-73
Sailfish (former *Squalus*), 4, 76-82, 96-
    97, 111, 164
Saipan, 137, 221, 241, 253, 255-56, 258,
    264, 267, 278, 281, 290
Sakhalin Island, 293
Sakito Maru, 240
Salamana, 154
Salmon, 24, 26, 281
San Bernardino Strait, 255-57, 262
San Cristobal, 172
San Diego Naval Laboratory, 216
Sandlance, 241-42, 244
San Francisco Bay, 298
Sanyo Maru, 289
Saratoga, 118, 145
Sargo, 104, 111
Savannah, 44
Savo Island, 157
Scamp, 244, 285
Schacht, Kenneth, 1st Lt., 116
Schaefer, J.C., Chief. Elec., 48
Schoenrock, W.L., Chief, 159
Scorpion (atomic), 207
Scorpion, 239

Scott, John A., Lt. Cdr., 186-87, 202-03,
    211
Sculpin, 1-4, 78, 80-81, 119, 232
Sea Devil, 284
Sea Dog, 294
Seadragon, 110, 121, 150
Seahorse, 255, 257
Seal, 25
Sealion, 95, 100, 278, 283
Sealion II, 282
Sea of Japan, 247, 268, 286, 293-94, 297
Sea of Okhotsk, 292
Searaven, 119, 122, 196, 225
Seawolf, 95, 100, 109, 119, 178, 279
Seeadler Harbor, 244
Seminole, "Semisubmersibles," 13
Senkai Maru, 173
Severn (former Chesapeake), 29
Shad, 218-19
Shanghai, 245
Shark, 22, 98, 102, 280
Shelton, 280
Shephard, Evan T., 282, 287-288
Shinano, 283
Shinyo Maru, 289
Shiranuhi, 144
Shirogane Maru, 172-73
Shoho, 131
Shokaku, 130-33, 262-64
Shortland Islands, 172, 197
Siam, Gulf of, 29, 176-77
Siberote, 104
Sibitsky, Martin, 81
Sibutu Passage, 250
Silversides, 281
Singapore, 56, 101, 104, 193, 284, 288-
    89, 292
Skate, 24, 30-35, 49, 222-23, 294
Skipjack (atomic), 306
Skipjack, 24, 96, 118-19, 125-26
Slot, the, 166, 174
Smith, Lt. Cdr., 111
Smith, Charles, Capt., 195
Smith, Chester C., Cdr., 96

Snapper, 24, 121
Snook, 219, 221, 223, 291
Snorkel systems, 299-300, 303
Solomon Islands, 155, 160, 162-63, 181,
   183, 193, 196-97, 215, 228, 254-55
Sonar, 67, 92, 95-96, 112, 119, 192, 235,
   243, 247, 268, 274, 280, 285, 293-94
South Pass, 132
Soviet ships, 295
Spadefish, 272, 282, 294-95
Spear, Lawrence Y., 22-23
Spearfish, 122
Special missions, submarine, 108-10,
   119-23, 150, 172-74, 176, 179, 181,
   188, 195-97, 223, 225-26, 237, 279,
   286
Spikefish, 297
Spruance, Raymond A., Adm., 84, 226,
   255-56, 258-59, 264
Squalus see also *Sailfish,* 76-79, 81-82
Stark, Harold, Adm., 99
Staten Island, 7
Steelhead, 223, 270
Steel Seafarer, 84
Sterett, 41-42
Sterlet, 281
Stevens, James, Lt. Cdr., 284
Stewart, see Patrol Boat No. 102, 274
Stillson, George D., Chief Gunner, 31
Stingray, 24, 97, 102, 257-59
Stone, Hamilton, Lt. Cdr., 121, 126
Stovall, W.S., Lt. Cdr., 195
Street, George, Lt. Cdr., 292-93
Sturgeon, 24, 30, 35, 150
Styer, Charles W., Capt., 91
Subic Bay, 292
Submarine Chaser No. 13, 229
Submarine Patrol Boat No. 18, 198
Submarines, British
   A-Class, 16; *A-1,* 16; *A-5,* 16; *A-8,* 16;
   A-9, 16; *E-9,* 35
Submarines, U.S.
   Classes: A-class, 21-26, 29-30; *A-2,* 47;
   A-7, 47; B-class, 23, 25-26, 29-30;

C-class, 24, 28, 84; *C-5,* 52; D-class,
   24; *D-2,* 48; E-class, 24, 72; *E-1,* 41;
   F-class, 24; *F-1,* 48-49; *F-2,* 48; *F-3,*
   48; Fleet-class, 30, 35, 76, 79, 87, 90,
   98, 106, 146, 168, 176, 207, 306;
   G-class, 25; *G-2,* 52; H-class, 25;
   H-1, 53; *H-3,* 48; K-class, 25, 40-41,
   47; *K-1,* 40-41; *K-2,* 40-41; *K-5,* 40-
   41; *K-6,* 40-41; L-class, 25, 42-43,
   47; *L-1,* 41; *L-2,* 41-43; *L-3,* 41; *L-4,*
   41-42, 44; *L-8,* 70; *L-9,* 41; *L-10,* 41;
   M-class, 35, 172; *N-5,* 49; O-class,
   29, 41, 51; *O-5,* 58; *O-6,* 41; *Q-19,*
   38; R-class, 51; *R-1,* 85; *R-4,* 85;
   R-5, 85; *R-6,* 53; *R-7,* 85-86; S-class,
   53, 57, 84, 87, 102, 125, 135, 141-43,
   154, 163, 208, 233; *S-4,* 73-76, 78;
   S-5, 58-65; *S-17,* 86; *S-18,* 141; *S-23,*
   141; *S-36,* 103; *S-37,* 111; *S-38,*
   57-58, 97; *S-39,* 112, 119, 158-59;
   S-42, 154; *S-43,* 154, 159; *S-44,* 157,
   233; *S-48,* 53-55; *S-49,* 57; *S-51,* 72-
   73; *Salmon*-class, 91; T-class, 29;
   U-1 (early submarine sold to
   Austro-Hungary) 15; V-class, 57, 67,
   72, 92, 167, 176-77, 181
Divisions: Division 13, 89; Division 43,
   1, 232; Division 101, 237; early sub-
   marines, 14-15, 20-21; future role of,
   298-99; losses, World War II, 298;
   put in mothballs, 298-99, safety de-
   vices, 75-79, 81; squadrons: Squadron
   Two, 152, 163, 176, 210; Squadron
   Five, 85; Squadron Six, 92; Squadron
   Sixteen, 231, 234
Submersibles, 5
Sulu Archipelago, 247, 290
Sulu Sea, 255
Sumatra, 101, 229, 240, 291
Surabaya, Java, 98, 100
Surigao Strait, 255
Swordfish, 96, 100, 111, 237-39, 267, 291

Taei Maru, 134

Taigen Maru, 134
Taiho, 260-61, 263-65
Taiyo, 165
Taiyo Maru, 134, 203, 272
Takao, 271, 289
Takao, 280
Take (Bamboo) convoys, 240, 254
Tama, 280
Tamagawa Maru, 110
Tambor, 240
Tanabe, Yahachi, Lt. Cdr., 140
Tang, 233, 280-81, 290
Tanikaze, 250
Tarawa, 162, 233, 290
Tarantula, 23
Tarpon, 24, 95, 111
Task Force Three, 102
Task Force, 71, 198
Task Force, 72, 198
Tautog, 92, 131, 133
Tawi Tawi, 247, 249-50, 254-255
Tenaru River, 174
Tenryu Maru, 169
Theobald, Robert, R/Adm., 137, 142
Thetis, 76
Thrasher, 25
Thresher, 92-93, 150-51, 177, 199, 224
Thresher (atomic), 306
Tibbals, C.I., Chief Gunner, 76
Timidity of leadership, 123-24, 126, 134, 152, 154, 164, 180
Timor, 122, 153, 196
Tinian, 221, 255, 263
Tinosa, 210, 248, 285, 294
Tirante, 292-93
Toagel Mlungui Passage, 178
Tojo, Hideki, 180, 285
Tokyo Bay, 94, 105, 145, 207, 238, 281, 283
"Tokyo Express," 166, 254
Tokyo Rose, 154
torpedoes, early, 8-10, 13-14, 68
Torpedoes Mark V exploder, 71

Torpedoes Mark VI exploder, 70-71, 90-91, 93, 97, 103, 107, 110, 123, 127, 146-47, 150, 164, 175, 187-88, 190-92, 199, 202-03, 208-10, 217, 242
Torpedoes Mark IX, 178
Torpedoes Mark X, 68, 86, 103, 135, 157
Torpedoes Mark XI, 69
Torpedoes Mark XIII, 69
Torpedoes Mark XIV, 69-71, 93, 97, 103, 123-24, 126-27, 146-47, 149, 175, 210-12
Torpedoes Mark XV, 69
Mark XVIII torpedo, electric, 192, 209-10, 212
Torpedo problems, 86, 93, 95-97, 103, 105, 111, 123-27, 131, 133-34, 145-50, 153, 164-65, 170-71, 175-79, 186-87, 192, 199, 202-03, 207-09, 212-13, 216-17, 222, 242, 268, 286
Torpedoes, World War I, 42
Toyoda, Soemu, Adm., 254-55, 271
Trigger, 208, 212, 228, 281, 291
Trident, 307
Trincomalee, 129-30
Triton, 93, 108, 133-34, 143-44, 228
Triton (nuclear powered), 306
Trout, 92, 109-10, 165, 199, 240-41
Truk, 1, 4, 106, 108, 129, 131-32, 151, 164-66, 215, 222, 233, 242, 253, 255
Trutta, 295
Tsugaru Strait, 294, 301
Tsushima Strait, 293-95
Tulagi, 130, 145, 156, 173-74, 197
Tullibee, 221-22, 242, 269
Tuna, 25, 107, 134
Tunny, 186-87, 202-04, 208, 211, 244, 277, 294
Turbot, 25
Turner, Richmond Kelly, Adm., 156
Turtle, 7-8
Tyree, Alexander, Skipper, 293
U-Boats, German, World War I, 16, 23, 35, 38-39, 42-43, 67, 83

U-Boats, German, World War II, 50-51, 83-86, 118, 121, 146, 165, 179, 217, 222, 270, 284, 307

U-9, 35-36

U-15, 35

U-20, 37

U-21, 35

U-65, 43

U-111, 50

U-117, 50

U-140, 50

U-537, 284

UB-88, 50

UC-97, 50

Ultra, 1, 3, 4

Umstead, Scott, Lt., 43

Underwood, Gordon, Lt. Cdr., 282

United States Army, 111, 147, 156

United States Army Air Forces (until 1943 U.S. Army Air Corps), 98, 138, 181, 205, 245, 253-54, 269, 279, 285

United States Asiatic Fleet, 48, 82, 87, 95-102, 105, 107-08, 112, 127, 131, 152

United States Atlantic Fleet, 52, 84, 87-88, 298

United States Caribbean Naval District, 84

United States Fifth Air Force, 254

United States Fifth Fleet, 256

United States Joint Chiefs of Staff, 120, 155-56, 183

United States Marine Corps, 138, 156, 159, 173, 245, 300

United States Marine Corps Second Raider Battalion, 159-62

United States Naval Academy, 22, 29, 52, 152, 286

United States Navy, 15, 20-22, 24, 27-29, 56-58, 67, 72, 83-84, 90, 99, 106, 109, 125, 138, 153, 156-57, 160, 167, 169, 178, 195, 209, 245, 268, 273, 299, 304, 307

United States Navy General Board, 67, 69-70, 90, 125

United States Navy Submarine School, 39, 52, 72, 146

United States Navy Submarine Base, New London, Conn., 17, 26, 57, 146, 237, 298

United States Neutrality Patrol, 84-85, 87

United States Northern Pacific Force, 137, 141-42, 205

United States Pacific Fleet, 90, 99, 107-08, 121, 135, 138, 140-41, 149-50, 155, 164, 167, 188, 204, 208, 225, 244, 298

United States Seventh Fleet, 198, 289

United States South Pacific Force (Third Fleet), 173, 175, 198

United States Southwest Pacific Force, 124-26, 131, 148, 150, 152-55, 175, 204, 209, 216, 233, 244, 253, 289

United States Third Fleet, 198, 279

Unryu, 282, 284

Unyo, 4, 222, 278

Urakaze, 262-63, 282

Vandercarr, James C., Lt., 41

Vella Lavella, 197

Versailles Treaty, 50, 106

Vickers arms company, 15

Victorious, 187

Vietnam War, 303, 306

Villamor, Jesus, Maj., 195

Viper, 23

Vladivostok, 294

Voge, Richard, Lt. Cdr., 112, 164, 202, 220, 241

Von Tirpitz, Adm., 15-16, 36

Wahoo, 166, 188-93, 199-201, 212, 232, 269

Wainwright, Jonathan M., Gen., 109

Wake Island, 202, 223-24

Wallace, Lewis, Lt. Cdr., 95

Walther submarine, 304
Washington, George, 7
Washington Naval Conference, 1921,
    55-57, 68, 70, 72, 91
Wasp, 163
Warder, Frederick B., Lt. Cdr., 95, 109,
    119, 126, 177-78, 219-220
War of 1812, 9
Weddigen, Otto, Lt. Cdr., 35
Wewak, 188-89, 191, 193, 201
Whelchel, David, Skipper, 270
White, David, Lt. Cdr., 94
Widgeon, 211
Wilhelmshaven, 218
Wilkes, Capt., 97-98, 100, 102-05, 111-
    13, 118, 121, 125, 127
Wilkin, Warren D., Capt., 80-81
Williams, William W., Ens., 185
Willingham, Joseph, Cdr., 131-33, 177
Withers, Jr., Thomas, R/Adm., 90-95,
    107-08, 110-11, 113, 123-24, 131-32,
    135, 151, 268
Wolf pack, 1, 216, 218-22, 232, 247-49,
    267, 270, 272-73, 278, 282-84, 287-
    88, 297
Wolf, 36

World War I, 23, 25, 29, 35-45, 51-52,
    55, 68, 76, 83-84, 105, 176
World War II, 1-5, 69, 83, 299, 304-05,
    307
Wright, Jr., C.Q., Lt., 41

Yamaguchi, Kosaburo, Lt. Cdr., 234
Yamagumo, 1, 4
Yamakaze, 145
Yamakuni Maru, 238
Yamamoto, Isoroku, Adm., 118, 129-30,
    135-37, 144, 155-57, 192-93, 197,
    207, 227, 271
Yamato, 135, 255
Yellow Sea, 199-201, 239, 268-69, 282,
    286
Yokohama, 281, 290, 300
Yokosuka Naval Yard, 21, 299, 303
Yorktown, 140, 145
Yoshida Maru No. 1, 245
Youker, Joseph S/1C, 63
Yunagi, 272

Zabriskie, Jr., David, Skipper, 248
Zero fighters, 162, 260-61, 305
Zuiho, 144
Zuikaku, 130-33, 144, 166, 263-64